Global Austria

Austria's Place in Europe and the World

Günter Bischof, Fritz Plasser (Eds.)
Anton Pelinka, Alexander Smith, Guest Editors

CONTEMPORARY AUSTRIAN STUDIES | Volume 20

UNO PRESS

innsbruck university press

Book design: Lindsay Maples
Cover cartoon by Ironimus (1992) provided by the archives of *Die Presse* in Vienna and permission to publish granted by Gustav Peichl.

Published in North America by
University of New Orleans Press
ISBN 978-1-60801-062-2

UNO PRESS

Published in Europe by
Innsbruck University Press
ISBN 978-3-9028112-0-2

iup

Contemporary Austrian Studies

**Sponsored by the University of New Orleans
and Universität Innsbruck**

Publication of this volume has been made possible through generous grants from the Austrian Ministry of European and International Affairs through the Austrian Cultural Forum in New York as well as the Federal Ministry of Science and Research. The Austrian Marshall Plan Anniversary Foundation in Vienna has been very generous in supporting CenterAustria at the University of New Orleans and its publications series. The College of Liberal Arts at the University of New Orleans and the Auslandsamt of the University of Innsbruck provided additional financial support as did the Cultural Office of the City of Innsbruck.

PREFACE

The Twentieth Anniversary Issue

Günter Bischof

The publication of the twentieth volume of *Contemporary Austrian Studies* (CAS) represents a minor triumph for the dedicated commitment of CenterAustria at the University of New Orleans (UNO) to the serious scholarly study of twentieth/twenty-first century Austria. We share this triumph with the Department of Political Science at the University of Innsbruck. This publication series has become a mainstay of a transatlantic university partnership that has been growing for almost forty years and is quite unique in its intensity of both faculty and student exchanges and a rich cross-fertilization of ideas.

The continued publication of CAS is all the more remarkable since the crisis in the public higher education arena in Louisiana has not been kind to university budgets, including the steady production of scholarly work and publications on a regular basis. These pressures to cut the financing of higher education budgets have afflicted the State of Louisiana for the past three years. To a lesser degree the same is true for Austrian university budgets, where massive cuts are also announced for the year 2012. This is the actual environment in which this publication series is carried on against all odds on both sides of the Atlantic.

Looking at this publication series quantitatively, over the course of the past twenty years we have moved 408 manuscripts through the editing process—190 were published in the first ten volumes and another 218 in volumes XI to XX. Along the lines of Francis Bacon's *bonmot* that "histories make men wise [...] logic and rhetoric, able to contend," about two-thirds of the manuscripts dealt with historical subjects and one-third with political science. In history we had a fairly even distribution of manuscripts over the principal periods of Austrian *Zeitgeschichte* since 1919 (post-World War I, World War II, post-World War II to the advent of what might be called the "populist turn" in 1986, 1986-2000, and finally the past ten years). Political science manuscripts have dealt more with the most recent past than those dealing with history. While in history the post-World War II period to the end of the Cold War has been addressed most prominently, in political science the past decade has had pride of place.

In the past ten volumes, we have caught up with the immediate post-World War I period with the *Postwar* volume (XIX), following the issue on the 1930s *The Dollfuss/Schuschnigg Era* (XI). We have also addressed a separate volume on World War II (XVII), following previous essays and roundtables on Austrian memories of World War II and post-World War II restitution of property apprehended by the Nazis. Volumes on the *The Changing Austrian Voter* (XVI) and *The Schüssel Era* (XVIII) reflect the interest of political scientists in the immediate past, while *Austrian Foreign Policy in Historical Perspective* (XIV) contained essays that spanned the entire twentieth century diachronically. We have also addressed separate volumes to larger societal issues such as *Religion* (XIII) and *Sexuality* (XV). A special interest in larger themes of the Austrian-American relationship have been addressed in *The Marshall Plan* (VIII), followed by *The Americanization/Westernization of Austria* (XII). The current volume on *Global Austria* (XX) continues and broadens this theme of vast outside influences changing Austrian society in the twentieth century. We would like to warmly thank Alexander Lassner, Hermann Denz, Michael Gehler, Dagmar Herzog, Barbara Stelzl-Marx, Peter Berger, Anton Pelinka, and Alexander Smith for serving as guest editors of volumes during the past decade.

Political/social, diplomatic/international, and economic history have been most prominent in our pages through the entire twenty-year run. More recently cultural history and issues of identity have also been covered. Domestic politics and political culture have been most prominent in the political science category, but Austria's relationship with the European Union has been a topic regularly addressed, too. We have carried on with our annual review of Austrian politics over the past ten years for those readers who like a quick overview of Austrian elections and basic economic data.

We have taken great pride over the years in the reviewing culture of

	CAS 1-10				CAS 11-20					
	1918-1938	1938-1945	1945-1983	1984-2000	pre-1914	1918-1938	1938-1945	1945-1983	1984-2000	2000-2010
HISTORY										
Political/Social	2	5	5		2	11	8	8		2
Diplomatic/International			11	2	1	5		8	2	2
Economic			11	2		8	1	4		4
Intellectual	1				1	2		1		2
Memory			12	1		2		2		1
Culture/Identity		2	1			2		6		
Religion								3		5
Gender	1	3	3		1	1		7		2
Intelligence		2	3							
POLITIAL SCIENCE										
Domestic/ Political Culture			11	17				3	3	10
Foreign Relations/ International		2		9						3
European Union				6						2
ROUNDTABLES/ FORUMS				3			3	2		3
REVIEW ESSAYS				12						15
BOOK REVIEWS				51						51
ANNUAL REVIEW				10						10
INTRODUCTIONS				21						9
TOTAL				190						218

CAS. One hundred and two book reviews and twenty-seven review essays in these twenty volumes attest to that. We have regularly tried to get top experts on both sides of the Atlantic to pen critical book reviews of some of the most important books published on Austrian affairs. Whether these reviews are read by anyone else but the authors and editors we do not know.

Needless to say, the editors would like to think that these volumes measure up to a high standard of scholarship, and their peers have the last word on the quality of *Contemporary Austrian Studies* as a serious and engaging scholarly forum. Unfortunately, we have never had the time nor the means to do a serious study or survey of the *reception* of these volumes in the scholarly community, let alone in the broader public. Circumstantial evidence seems to suggest that the Anglo-American scholarly community peruse and cite the essays in these volumes more regularly than colleagues in Austria. As someone who tries to read much of the literature on twentieth-century Austria appearing on both sides of the Atlantic, my sense is that few Austrian colleagues and students are familiar with this publication series. Whether that is due to an unwillingness to read English or a rugged determination to ignore foreign and foreign-language scholarship will never be known. While most major American research universities have subscriptions to the CAS series, that does not seem to be the case in Austria. CAS has been regularly reviewed in the *German Studies Review* but few other scholarly journals have bothered to review CAS volumes, probably reflecting the fact that while individual CAS volumes are monographic in the nature of their topical essays, it is still a serial publication with book reviews. Austrian newspapers now and then take short notice of CAS; Austrian scholarly journals seem to ignore it.

Within the UNO-University of Innsbruck partnership, many people have helped to keep CAS going over a period of twenty years and make it a success. At Innsbruck's Department of Political Science, Anton Pelinka was my co-editor for the first fifteen volumes, and Fritz Plasser has shared those duties for the past five years. It is hard to imagine more reliable partners than Anton and Fritz. For most of that time Ellen Palli, Anton's and Fritz's hard-working office manager, was involved in the everyday business of the production of volumes, and she also type-set most of the volumes. Franz Mathis was delegated by the Senate of the University of Innsbruck to coordinate the UNO partnership. I cannot think of a more congenial counterpart than Franz—he was always a pleasure to work with. More recently, Klaus Frantz had taken on that job. *Rektors* Manfried Gantner and Karlheinz Töchterle have blessed this project as well. Erich Thöni, the University of Innsbruck's "foreign minister" has been productively involved in the partnership with UNO from the beginning. Matthias Schennach from the *Auslandsamt* of the University of Innsbruck has been generous over the years in giving us financial support. Margaret Davidson, who has been serving as CenterAustria representative in Innsbruck for many years, has jumped into the fray when needed. Christina Sturn, who started out as a CenterAustria fellow at UNO and has been coordinating the UNO office at the University of Innsbruck for a couple of years, has been helpful, too. The fantastic thing about our deep university partnership is that all these people have become dear friends over the years and enriched our life here at UNO.

At UNO, the superior and fun staff of CenterAustria has contributed as much as anyone to the completion of CAS year after year. Robert L. Dupont has been "present at the creation" as the Dean of Metropolitan College (and later Vice Chancellor). From the beginning he has been the most vigorous supporter of CAS and all the activities of CenterAustria in UNO administrations over the past twenty years. After his retirement from administrative work, he joined the History Department and has joined CenterAustria as a senior fellow. He still is giving us vital support. More recently Dean Susan Krantz of the College of Liberal Arts has "inherited" CenterAustria and helped us and CAS to keep going. Gordon "Nick" Mueller, the founder of the UNO-University of Innsbruck partnership (in 1983) and the founding director of CenterAustria (1997) has also supported CAS with great excitement from the very beginning.

Gertraud Griessner has managed the office staff since the inception of CenterAustria. Without her incredible efficiency and good cheer the Center's work (including CAS) simply could not be done. She never hesitates to take on more work and new jobs with a ready smile. I have never heard her complain. She has embraced every project readily and helped give it direction. CenterAustria simply would not be the success it is without her. Other than Gertraud and myself, CenterAustria never had any regular staff. Or rather, we have new staffers here every year with the appointment of CenterAustria fellows and "Ministry fellows." We get a University of Innsbruck student every year that works some hours at CenterAustria. The Austrian Federal Ministry of Science and Research finances an Austrian dissertation student every year to come to UNO and work on his/her dissertation, next to contributing a number of hours to CenterAustria. These "Ministry fellows" have been the regular "staff" that helped produce CAS volumes. They correspond with authors, track manuscripts, and try their hand at some copy editing; they also help the co-editors maintain their sanity during production time in the preparation of photo-ready copy. The Ministry fellows Tanja Stampfl, Martin David, Sonja Niederacher, Josef Köstlbauer (for two years), Sigrid Harrer, Marion Wieser, Michael Maier, and Alexander Smith (for two years) have been indispensable to the success of the project. Alexander Smith's contribution to this volume has been so substantial as editorial adviser and author that he has been promoted to the status of guest editor in this volume. I would like to think that all the fellows have learned some valuable tools for life in the course of their CAS work, next to making some excellent contacts in the community of Austrianists.

Even scholarly publications need their "sugar daddies" in this day and age of budgets evaporating at public universities in the U.S. The financial support of the Austrian Ministry of European and International Affairs (formerly Foreign Ministry), the Ministry of Science and Research, as well as the Austrian Marshall Plan Foundation all have been critical for the publication of this journal. At Foreign Affairs, Ambassador Emil Brix as director of cultural affairs has continued the tradition started twenty years ago by his predecessor Wolfgang Marboe to support the publication of CAS with an annual grant administered through the Austrian Cultural Forum (ACF) in New York. At ACF, Directors Christoph Thun-Hohenstein and Andreas Stadler, as well as Ernst Aichinger and Martin Rauchbauer, have been extremely generous with their support. At Science and Research, Josef Leidenfrost, Barbara Weitgruber, Christoph Ramoser, Ulrike Csura, Florian Gerhardus, and Alois Söhn have given us regular support and encouragement. CenterAustria has benefitted from the generous financial support of the Marshall Plan Foundation in Vienna; its directors Eugen Stark and Wolfgang Stoiber are genuine friends of CenterAustria and its activities and make our lives easier every day. At the Picture Archives of the Austrian National Library, Hans Petschar and Michaela Pfunder have been very generous in providing illustrations for our past two volumes.

Our publishers have been essential in making this publication series viable. Volumes I through XVII were printed and marketed by Transaction Publishers of New Brunswick, New Jersey. Irving Louis Horowitz, Mary Curtis, Anne Schneider, and Cheryl Orson have ably shepherded CAS through the Transaction publication process through these years. Were it not for financial and administrative pressures on campus, we would never have left Transaction. In another of the many joint ventures proliferating in our partnership with Innsbruck, volumes XVIII through XX have been published jointly by UNO Press and Innsbruck University Press (iup). The director of UNO Press, Bill Lavender, has taken us under his wing with his usual debonair ways and made launching our project with UNO Press easy, pleasant, and efficient. Lindsay Maples has done wonderful work as coordinator and copy editor. At iup Birgit Holzner has spirited us into a productive relationship, and Vice Rector for Research Tilmann Märk has given this project his blessing, too.

Last but not least, our international scholarly advisory board has guided us to maintain the scholarly integrity of CAS. Among them only Peter Pulzer (Oxford) has served on the board for all twenty volumes. We would like to thank all of them, especially Professor Pulzer, who also contributed to this volume. These are the board members that served over the years:

AUSTRIA

University of Innsbruck
Günther Pallaver (Political Science)
Max Preglau (Sociology)
Alan Scott (Sociology)
Rolf Steininger (History)

University of Salzburg
Ingrid Bauer (History)
Ernst Hanisch (History)
Reinhard Heinisch (Political Science)
Sonja Puntscher Riekmann (Political Science)
Reinhold Wagnleitner (History)

University of Graz
Siegfried Beer (History)
Konrad Ginther (Law)
Helmut Konrad (History)
Manfred Prisching (Sociology)

University of Vienna
Felix Butschek (Economics)
Peter Gerlich (Political Science)
Hanspeter Neuhold (Law)
Helga Nowotny (Social Sciences)
Oliver Rathkolb (History)
Sieglinde Rosenberger (Political Science)
Dieter Stiefel (History)
Gerald Stourzh (History)

Vienna University of Economics and Business
Peter Berger (History)

Austrian Academy of Sciences
Heidemarie Uhl (History)

CANADA

Hans-Georg Betz (Toronto — Political Science)
Robert Keyserlingk (Ottawa — History)
Franz Szabo (Edmonton — History)

FRANCE

Jacques Le Rider (Paris — History)
Michael Pollak (Paris — History)

GERMANY

Oscar Gabriel (Stuttgart — Political Science)
Dietmut Majer (Karlsruhe — Law)
Margareta Mommsen (Munich — Political Science)
Wilhelm Kohler (Tübingen — Economics)

HUNGARY

Sándor Kurtán (Budapest — Political Science)

ITALY

Mario Caciagli (Florence — Political Science)

UNITED KINGDOM

Tim Kirk (Newcastle — History)
Kurt Richard Luther (Keele — Political Science)
Peter Pulzer (Oxford — Political Science)
Ruth Wodak (Lancaster — Linguistics)

UNITED STATES

John Boyer (Chicago — History)
Evan Burr Bukey (Arkansas — History)
Gary Cohen (Minnesota — History)
Wolfgang Danspeckgruber (Princeton — Political Science)
Christine Day (UNO — Political Science)
David Good (Minnesota — History)
Malachi Hacohen (Duke — History)
Michael Huelshoff (UNO — Political Science)
Robert Jordan (UNO — Political Science)
Pieter Judson (Swarthmore — History)
Radomir Luza (Tulane — History)

Ad multos annos!

New Orleans, March 2011

Table of Contents

FORUM: The Globalization of Austrian Studies

BOOK REVIEWS

Introduction

Anton Pelinka

1

Contemporary Austria's global role has been overshadowed by its past for a long time. As the Habsburg Empire's successor state with the most visible—especially cultural—links to this empire, Austria had (and perhaps still has) an advantage as well as a disadvantage in the global arena: The small republic is measured by the grand and not so grand accomplishments of one of the largest empires of "Old Europe." Contemporary Austria also had (and still has) to fight to overcome the shadows of a past—shadows which identify Austria with Nazism and the Holocaust.

With Austria's European Union membership, a process of normalization could have been expected: Austria became a rather mainstreamed smaller European democracy, following the example of "Western democracy," and closely linked to its neighbors which—with the exception of Switzerland (and Liechtenstein)—have been EU members from the beginning of the integration process or have become members of the same Union Austria had joined in 1995 in the meantime. Austria's democracy may be considered still more "consociational" than "competitive"; Austria's still domestically cherished neutrality status may be seen as a deviant case in Central Europe; Austria's culture may be still measured more by the cultural giants of an imperial past—from *Haydn* and *Mozart* to *Mahler*, to *Klimt* and *Schiele*, to *Hofmannsthal* and *Schnitzler*. But there are not too many arguments left to claim an "Austrian exceptionalism."

Nevertheless: The perception of contemporary Austria is still strongly influenced by the imprint of the past. In the second half of the twentieth century, the academic discourse on contemporary Austria was the discourse about the past—and its post-1945 consequences. *Carl Schorske* and *William Johnston* revived the picture of an Austria which had a remarkable impact on the twentieth century intellectual and scientific history. *Peter Pulzer* reminded the sometimes all too forgetful Austrian academia to which extent Austria had been the hotbed of political anti-Semitism. *William Bluhm* concentrated on the process of reshaping an Austrian identity which was neither imperial nor pan-German. And it had been the academic work of Austrian exiles like *Kurt Steiner* and *Frederick Engelmann* who were among the first to describe and analyze how the Second Republic was able to overcome the burden of the past.

2

Volume XX of *Contemporary Austrian Studies* intends to locate Austria in the global arena of the twentieth century. What impact did Austria—its culture and politics, its economics and intellectual atmosphere—have on the world? And: How did, how does Austria respond to the challenges of globalization—a phenomenon which has risen perhaps not to a new meaning but to a new intensity during the last century? Austria—defined by history and geopolitics, by its different and often competing narratives—is of course not an island and especially not an "island of the blessed." It had and has to respond to the variety of factors coming from the world outside Austria: Economic and political, cultural and military influences do not permit to see Austria as an isolated entity. But at the same time, Austria is influencing its global environment also. Austria is part of a global give and take.

The authors of this volume are reflecting the complexity of this give and take. In his essay, *Andreas Exenberger* links the present globalization discourse with the beginning of the twentieth century: Between *Stefan Zweig*'s *Die Welt von Gestern*, the perspective of an Austrian witness to the catastrophe of summer 1914, and the globalized communication as expressed in the perception of the "Arab Spring" in 2011—between the second decade of the twentieth and the second decade of the twenty-first century, globalization played a permanent and decisive role. As part of the process of redefining its identity beginning in 1945, Austria opened its doors: for trade and tourism, for academic exchange and political networking. There may not have been a real alternative to this opening, but how it was done and to which result is the general topic of the whole volume.

The following articles are dealing with specific aspects of Austrian contributions to different global sectors: *Steven Beller* concentrates on the long-term effects of Vienna's fin de siècle. Austria's intellectual and cultural impact, shaped by the multinational empire, survived the end of this empire—at least for a certain period. *Tim Kirk* confronts the phenomenon that even after 1918 Austria's political development was responsible for a wide range of international interest—in Austro-Marxism and Austrofascism. "Red Vienna," the showcase of Austrian Social Democracy, and the (not so holy experiment) of an authoritarian state, based on Political Catholicism, still influence the academic discourse. *Hansjoerg Klausinger* describes the reasons for the politically polarizing global attraction of the Austrian School of Economics. "Reaganomics" and "Thatcherism" had been—rightly or wrongly—identified with a way of systematic thinking born in Austria around 1900. *Andreas Resch* and *Dieter Stiefel* remind us of the history Vienna has played as a financial center for Central, Eastern, and South-Eastern Europe for a long period. The Danube Basin's economic and financial center has been Vienna—and since 1989, we can observe a kind of revival of Vienna's central position in this part of Europe. *Eric Frey* underlines the recent successes Vienna had as an international conference site: The tradition of the Viennese Congress, 1814-15, is not only an aspect of the past—it lives on. *Alexander Smith* brings the Austrian oil and gas company OMV and its success story as a case study into the general topic of globalization. The OMV is one example that Austria's impact is not only to be seen in the world of music and literature.

3

The more historically oriented articles are followed by the analyses of current developments: *Rainer Münz*'s essay explains the explosiveness of demography and migration for Austria today. An increasing interest in immigration to but also in emigration from Austria is to be seen in the context of an aging population. *Fritz Plasser* and *Gilg Seeber* focus on the most recent trends of Austrian politics and the Austrian party system. Austrian exceptionalism, after 1945 defined by "consociational democracy," may not exist anymore in the traditional form, but there is still a lot to be seen exceptional in Austrian politics. *Emil Brix* concentrates on a topic which got a new meaning as well as a new importance due to the political transformation in former communist Europe—Central Europe and Austria's role. Austria, for decades rather isolated as a Western outpost almost surrounded by communist countries, has become part of an area of new openness defined by open borders, free trade, and cultural exchange. *Sonja Puntscher Riekmann* explains the changes and challenges the EU membership implies—the consequences of membership in an elitist club which redefines the politics of all member states. The long-term impact of joining a supranational community is perhaps the most significant aspect for Austria in the twenty-first century.

The "Forum" discusses the possibilities and limitations of Austrian Studies—between Habsburg and European Studies. Academics' experiences from different disciplines and different countries—from the United States, the United Kingdom, France, Australia, China, and Japan—allow a resume about the present "state of the art" Austrian Studies have reached. Austria, as a German-speaking country, has to deal with the "big brother-small brother" dilemma (not so different from Canada vis-à-vis the U.S.); a dilemma exemplified by the (necessary) insistence that *Wolfgang Amadeus Mozart* as well as *Ingeborg Bachmann* have been Austrian. The review of events during 2010 and several book reviews give the whole volume its usual character: an interdisciplinary, broad view on a specific, Austria-related topic—in this volume the meaning and the impact of globalization for and on Austria; and the information about Austria's current affairs as it is to be expected from this series.

When the first volume of *Contemporary Austrian Studies* was published in 1993, *Günter Bischof* and I—we two representing our two universities—were co-editors. Following my retirement from the University of Innsbruck in 2006, *Fritz Plasser* took over my function. I am happy to say that what had started as an adventure two decades ago became a well-established series. And I am especially grateful for the excellent cooperation between *Günter Bischof*, *Fritz Plasser*, *Alexander Smith*—the other "guest editor"—and myself concerning volume XX. Our task was to design and to implement a book which should stress the necessity for Austria to look beyond its borders; and to focus on the degree of globalization which had characterized the Austrian society, politics, economics, and culture already in the past.

4

Contemporary Austrian Studies was founded to provide insights into the complexities of post-Habsburg Austria. This volume concentrates on the different levels of Austria's interactions with the world at large—with Austria's immediate neighborhood and beyond. There may be an "Austrian way" in different spheres—from social policy to the promotion of high culture ("*Hochkultur*"). But any Austrian way is confronted with an ever changing world.

Bibliography

Bluhm, William T. *Building an Austrian Nation: The Political Integration of a Western State.* New Haven: Yale University Press, 1973.

Engelmann, Frederick. *Government by Diplomacy: The Austrian Coalition 1945-1966.* Vienna: Braumüller, 2001.

Johnston, William M. *The Austrian Mind: An Intellectual and Social History, 1848-1938.* Berkeley: University of California Press, 1983.

Pulzer, Peter. *The Rise of Political Anti-Semitism in Germany and Austria.* rev. ed. London: Peter Halban, 1988.

Schorske, Carl E. *Fin-de-Siècle Vienna: Politics and Culture.* London: Weidenfeld and Nicholson, 1980.

Steiner, Kurt. *Politics in Austria.* Boston: Little, Brown, 1972.

Globalization and Austria: Past and Present

Andreas Exenberger

Introduction

Early in 2011, the intensity of global media connections was dramatically evident. At first, uprisings in the Arab world were widely recognized (even as "Facebook revolutions" and hence as only enabled by a certain aspect of globalization) and raised concerns in several parts of the world that people may become all too inspired by the events they watched on TV. Later, the disastrous events in Japan, followed by billions, also influenced public opinion in politically relevant ways. In these days of catastrophe, even weather forecasts from a place thousands of kilometers away become common in the evening news all around the world. Obviously related to globalization, news spreads, sometimes even in real time, and also to areas remote with respect to free press. While this is not a new phenomenon at all historically, the scope and also the speed of interconnectedness have indeed grown considerably. Communication became "mass," and it became extremely cheap during the twentieth century. Hence, today the impact of events is not only global, but—at least potentially—total (in the sense of decisive and far-reaching at the same time).

However, it is often stated that the world a hundred years ago was more globalized than today's world—an assessment with quite some truth to it. Austria and Austrians did play their part in this process of shaping, promoting, and also depressing globalization. Thus, when introducing an issue about "Global Austria," it is more than appropriate to refer to one of these great Austrians who helped to shape globalization in the course of the twentieth century. A passage from the memorable *Die Welt von Gestern* (*The World of Yesterday*) by Stefan Zweig (1881-1942) documents the experience of the outbreak of the so-called "Great War," which took place in the middle of an already widely globalized world. Zweig writes,

> The summer of 1914 would have been memorable for us even without the doom which it spread over the European earth. I had rarely experienced one more luxuriant, more beautiful and, I am tempted to say, more summery. Throughout the days and nights the heavens were silky blue, the air soft yet not sultry, the meadows fragrant and warm, the forests dark and profuse in their tender green; even today, when I use the word summer, I think involuntarily of those radiant July days.[1]

In this very same summer, the most industrialized production of death until then was unleashed. It took place in a cosmopolitan Europe, already shaped by decades of cultural and economic, as well as political and technical globalization, which Stefan Zweig described. At least for the intellectual elites, but partly also for the working class, crossing borders and passing oceans had become normal—and increasingly so. Goods from all corners of the world—not only luxuries, but also bulk commodities—were traded, and deep-ocean cables connected all continents. Europeans with money invested it in Bolivia and China and in reaction to news that spread within hours, no longer days or months. But violence had already spread worldwide, particularly as colonial warfare, long before tensions within Europe grew and finally exploded in 1914 to destroy this "world of yesterday."

Zweig, who after having fled the Nazis committed suicide in Brazilian exile in 1942 (precisely out of despair about that destruction), could not have imagined that a century later a comparable world would exist again, connected—not always for the good—not only by communication, travel, and trade, but also by media coverage, investment, and international organizations. However, though a comparable world, it was not the same, as not the least Austria exemplifies: in 1914, the Austro-Hungarian Empire was still a world power (albeit of medium rank) and a multiethnic state (albeit hierarchical). Today the Republic of Austria is a rather small and open country, but neither fully aware of the level of its integration into an emerging "Europe" (not to speak of the world), nor of the level of already achieved internal cultural diversity fostered by migration.

What follows in this text, unfolds in five steps: First, a brief description of how globalization is measured today and how Austria performs in that context is provided; secondly, we will take a brief look at how globalization is treated in scholarly literature; thirdly, we will discuss what globalization is today and what it was yesterday; in the fourth and most important step we will focus on the elements of that process which are of particular relevance for Austria; and finally there will be a brief summarizing outlook, which particularly presents data about the opinions of Austrians relevant to the subject. By that, we aim at providing a general framework in which the other contributions to this volume can be contextualized. Consequently, its form is a mixture of a conceptual general survey about globalization and of an exemplar description of some of its significant elements in the Austrian context—many of them to be further elaborated later in the volume.

Measuring Globalization?

As a first step to conceptualize globalization, the question of measurement will be discussed. While this is not the place to discuss the appropriateness of several attempts of quantification, they give a good impression how globalization is usually treated and allow a first look at the significance of Austria in it. However, different indices measure slightly different things.[2] In the Maastricht Globalization Index (MGI),[3] published for 2000, 2004, and 2008, eleven variables in five "domains" are considered: the number of embassies, membership in international organizations, arms trade (political domain), the relative level of trade, FDI, and private capital flows (economic domain), the relative number of migrants and tourists (socio-cultural domain), relative intensity of phone traffic and internet use (technological domain), and the ecological footprint deficit (ecological domain). The CSGR Index of Warwick University,[4] published for the years between 1982 and 2004, roughly contains the same variables—separated into three "sub indices" of economic, social, and political globalization—, but also includes income transfers, worker remittances, international mail traffic, trade in films, books, and newspapers, and participation in UN peacekeeping missions. Finally, the possibly most refined index, the KOF Index of Globalization from Zurich University (KIG),[5] published for 2002 and annually since 2005, contains twenty-four variables in three statistically weighted spheres (thirty-six percent for the economic, thirty-eight percent for the social, and twenty-five percent for the political sphere). The KIG additionally contains the number of McDonald's restaurants and of Ikea outlets, the relative number of radios and cable televisions, and variables measuring restrictions of international flows, i.e. hidden import barriers, tariffs, trade taxes, and capital account restrictions (interestingly, restrictions on the movement of people are missing).

Overall, these indices point to an extraordinary degree of globalization taking place in Austria. In the latest KIG of 2011, Austria ranks second among 156 countries (twelfth in economic, second in social, and fourth in political). Overall, only Belgium outperforms Austria, while Singapore, Switzerland, and France are heading the dimension-specific lists. Austria is followed by the Netherlands, Sweden, Switzerland, and Denmark, while Germany is sixteenth, the United Kingdom twenty-first, the United States twenty-seventh, Japan forty-fourth, and China ninety-second. In the MGI 2008, Austria ranks sixth among 117 countries, surpassed by Ireland, Belgium, Switzerland, the Netherlands, and France. Here it is particularly worth noting that Austria is also unfavorably connected: While providing a "biocapacity" well above average to the world, Austrians use even more, resulting in a "footprint deficit" of more than fifty percent in the aggregate, which leads to local consumption based on the biocapacity of others (not only future generations, but particularly people in exporting countries around the world). Finally, in the CSGR of 2004, Austria was also sixth, surpassed by Singapore, Belgium, Canada, the United Kingdom, and the United States.

Hence, according to these indices Austria is extraordinarily globalized. But this holds not only for the country, but also for the capital city of Vienna. For example, it is eighteenth in the Global City Index of Foreign Policy/A.T. Kearney in 2010,[6] and even seventh among the cities ranked in the Global Power City Index,[7] both led by New York. However, the most relevant of these indices—because it explicitly relies on relational data and thus measures connectivity—is published by the Globalization and World Cities (GaWC) Research Network.[8] In the last of these analyses in 2008, Vienna is categorized only in the group "alpha minus" (together with Zurich, Frankfurt, and Budapest, among twenty-one others), which is described as "very important world cities that link major economic regions and states into the world economy." Nineteen cities are ranked higher, with London and New York constituting the highest category. In all of these indices, other Austrian cities are insignificant.

In the end, these measuring exercises are interesting for their ability to condense an awful lot of data into a single number, with sometimes surprising results. However, they are certainly subject to normative preoccupations, they are omitting elements and they are necessarily reductionist. Consequently, they actually do not provide an answer to the question of how global a country (or a city) really is, but more to the question of how internationally connected a country (or a city) is with respect to those channels of connection about which data is collected.

A More Detailed View into the Globalization Discourse

Globalization is a catchword, albeit a much used one.[9] This becomes clearer and clearer the deeper one digs into the abundance of texts about globalization and different aspects of this phenomenon. As Jürgen Osterhammel and Niels Petersson phrased it in the introduction to their small book about the history of globalization, one already needs "pathfinder literature" to master this intellectual cornucopia.[10] Those who talk or write about globalization often do not talk or write about what it is—and then categories become confused, concepts are mixed, a general meaning is presumed or a very specific one applied. Sometimes the usage of the term is similar to the relabeling of perishables, when "globalization" is simply affixed to something already known and actually named differently.[11] While this does not hold for the above-mentioned indices, which are all clearly defined and sometimes also well-based on theoretical literature, it generally holds for scientific treatments of the subject.[12]

However, "globalization" is still a useful concept of analysis, for two reasons: It is a "macro concept" (comparable to "industrialization" or "modernization"), and it is procedural, thus refocusing the analysis to developments and change. While the first approach refers to Osterhammel and Petersson, it is also consistent, for example, with the concepts of David Held (and others).[13] When referring to these views it is crucial to preserve analytical sensitivity for globalization's multidimensional character. The second approach points to the specific character of globalization as a process.[14] Sociologist Ulrich Beck, one of the founding fathers of German globalization research, has described it as a process by which transnational actors have connected nation states by their actions, at the same time undermining the sovereignty of these states.[15] However, while it is important to stress the concept of *agency* in this context, this understanding is still too narrow, because it neglects the degree of simple (i.e. unintended and not easily controllable) "occurance," even if it owes its very existence to human actions (or omissions).

The historical concepts of trend and cycle, both actually results of collective human action, can further clarify this.[16] They are useful tools for globalization research, especially when globalization is understood as a trend or a dispositive, shaping humankind's history, while at the same time acknowledging the disruptions and slowdowns in the meta-narrative. These contribute to a "thickening" of the understanding of globalization as a process much more cyclical than linear, in which it starts and unfolds, often in an asynchronous manner in time and space, collapses and restarts again. In this view, historical processes are seen as shaped by the conflict between different trajectories related to trend(s) and cycle(s) leading to growing imbalances in the "system," which enable (or at least facilitate) change.[17]

Also, the picture of a globalization "wave" or "waves" of globalization is much used.[18] While economic research still focuses on the most recent wave, often dazzled by the astonishing speed of a process also personally witnessed, and the scientific establishment of the term only in the 1980s, historical research has shown that comparable processes had already existed long before. These analyses of course referred to and connected with earlier research on the world economy, colonialism, and imperialism and particularly stressed the parallels between globalization waves at the end of the twentieth and at the end of the nineteenth century.[19] Shortly after that new parallels were drawn to early colonialism in the aftermath of the so-called voyages of discovery, and a new, even earlier "first" wave was born. Finally, scholars with even more courage for generalization and thinking in long terms—partially departing from the concept of Kondratieff's business cycles—inscribed the idea of globalization in even longer time periods.[20] Also connections to the emerging field of global (or world) history came quite naturally.[21]

The lively and sometimes fierce debates about the question of when globalization actually "began" indeed are often strongly influenced by different answers to the question of what globalization essentially is. It is generally accepted that the process is not restricted to the contemporary world and is non-linear in unfolding. However, in the light of the tremendous and multifaceted literature about the issue, coming from different disciplines, it seems to be almost impossible to achieve something like a general meaning, or at least understanding, of globalization, not to speak of operationalizable indicators. Whoever strives for measuring is rapidly to be found in environments like the world of price convergence (the decreasing difference between the prices of the same good at different places), of variables measuring different kinds of connections (like in the indices mentioned above), or the question how many languages are spoken worldwide. A rather open but workable general meaning is developed by David Held and others, who have proposed in the introductory chapter of their *Globalization Reader* to view globalization as a multidimensional combination of the extensity of global networks, the intensity of global links, the velocity of global flows, and the impact propensity of global interconnectedness.

What is Globalization Today and What was it in the Course of the Twentieth Century?

Consequently, globalization is not easy to grasp, and for the purpose of an introductory essay like this, at best on an exemplary basis. Some of its elements have already shaped the process for long periods, like long-distance trade, migration, the transfer of capital, or world empires, world religions, and world voyages; and some for shorter periods, like actual world markets, mass migration, or worldwide communication. But only a few allow viewing globalization as a recent phenomenon: the Internet as a manifestation of the increase in speed and intensity of various kinds of "communications" and "transfers"; the closely connected phenomenon of a strong increase in the absolute volume of trade and even more of capital transfers between countries and continents; the spread of democracy within and between countries and the increased institutionalization of international relations (governmental as well as non-governmental); and the emergence of a truly "global" consciousness (referring to global problems and challenges, but also to geopolitics).

None of these phenomena is completely new, nor unique, to human history, which is at odds with the hype during the 1990s, when everything seemed to be globalization. They are more continuations of earlier, often long-run processes than novelties. This maybe holds the least for the impact potential of processes in one place on the course of life in increasingly distant other places and in an increasingly encompassing way. But it also holds for this, as well as for the acceleration of globalization, its degree of integration (which have both clearly increased recently), and even for its degree of expansion (which was more prominent in earlier "waves").

Thus, while it is easily possible to place the last three decades, but also the whole twentieth century into a long-run history of globalization, some serious changes took place during this century, which altered the character of the whole process. This is insufficiently understood so far for the "interruption" between the two waves, the "crisis" of globalization in the period from 1914 to 1945—which for Austria in particular was a real watershed. Anyway, not only did global institutionalization clearly intensify in this period (not just in the form of the League of Nations), but this view also neglects the degree of integration and connection between countries and people by violence and crisis. Certainly, we see a complete restructuring of the European political scene and a transformation of the global economy, but we also see a global epidemic, first steps of institutionalization, revolutions in communication technology, a global economic crisis as well as two "world" wars (of which the first, as a matter of fact, was not particularly "global"). Hence, people remained and became more and more connected, although more often in an unfavorable and sometimes even in a murderous way. Also "ideas" spread over the whole course of the century, which is regarded as a distinguishing feature of globalization in the twentieth century, especially in the political sphere.[22] Over the course of the century, communism, authoritarianism and fascism, liberalism, and finally also democracy blossomed all over the world.

Several dimensions of globalization are of particular relevance for the description of the twentieth century. The first concerns economics: We clearly see that an increasing number of countries and share of people owe their wealth or their livelihood to international exchange and global connections. The intensity of this trend is a little obscured by the fact that trade strongly reemerged after the Second World War (and capital transfers even stronger from the 1970s on, when controls were relaxed) and experienced a steep downward trend in the above-mentioned "interruption" period. The second dimension concerns politics: We see equally clearly that after expansion and integration organized by patterns of "colonization," which had shaped nineteenth-century and earlier globalizations, inter- and intra-state democratization and institutionalization shaped it in the second half of the twentieth. This is also somewhat obscured by the global trend toward authoritarianism in the interwar period and by the separation of the world into a Western and an Eastern hemisphere during the Cold War, but it is still a major trend. The third dimension concerns communication: While the big time-space compression in humankind's history took place in the nineteenth century, when communication times between continents were reduced from weeks and months to minutes (by the telegraph) and when the transport of goods was dramatically eased, particularly over land (by the steam engine), communication continued shaping the process in the twentieth century, when newspapers, radio, television, and finally the Internet created real mass media and mass channels of multilateral communication, which became a cheap mass phenomenon. The fourth dimension concerns the movement of people: While migration is certainly anything but new in history and had already become "mass" in the nineteenth century (when larger numbers—occasionally even in absolute terms—immigrated into certain "new worlds"), it is still a powerful force of change for societies. In the twentieth century, particularly the speed of movement changed (by air traffic) and a totally new phenomenon emerged in that context: mass tourism. Starting only in the postwar period (as a mass phenomenon), today almost a billion people travel abroad year by year, which is in absolute and relative terms far from anything experienced historically. Finally, the fifth dimension concerns global consciousness: Hardly ever before was the world so "connected" as a global community of fate, as *one* world facing certain challenges (like resource depletion, global warming, or the danger of a nuclear apocalypse), including a consciousness of shared responsibilities and of common solutions. In that context, one should finally add environmentalism (strongly emerging in the 1970s), changing humankind's relationship to nature as shaped by industrialization, and a new quality of global self-perception facilitated by technical progress through space voyages.

Austria's and Austrians' Role in Globalization

What then is Austria's—and the Austrians'—role in the process? A summarizing introductory answer to that question is necessarily anecdotal, but Austria is also an interesting case study of globalization and globalization history, especially if the focus of analysis is on the question what globalization means in a second-order center. However, as we have seen, Austria performs extraordinarily in several indices of globalization, which also holds for its capital city Vienna, having its own place in that history.

A century ago Vienna was an international center, strongly connected to other centers—at least in Europe—on economic, political, cultural, and intellectual grounds. The world Stefan Zweig referred to was much more about Vienna (and thus a network of metropolises) than about Austria (and thus interwoven countries). Influential artists and scientists were active from Vienna, which was an international and multiethnic city in those days (and hence neither fully "global" nor fully "cosmopolitan"). Other articles in this volume refer in greater detail to the culture of modernism, economics (the "Austrian School"), and politics (Austro-Marxism and -fascism). There could also be an article on architecture, painting, music, or film. In the latter area Austrians had a remarkable impact on the emerging film industry in Hollywood, especially as directors like Fred Zinneman (Oscar winner for *From Here to Eternity* and *A Man for all Seasons*, but also director of *High Noon*), Billy Wilder (Oscar winner for *The Last Weekend* and *The Apartment*, but also director of comedies like *Some Like it Hot*), or Otto Preminger.[23]

In all these respects Vienna is a good example of how a metropolis keeps its central role in culture or finance (also discussed later in this volume in far more detail) for some time after having lost its political or economic function—a process for example still in place in London. Vienna lost most of its functions in 1918, but it kept many characteristics of a center until—as Zweig called it—it was reduced to a "German provincial town" by the Nazis. This connection is very direct: It is needless to mention that a large part of the intellectual and artistic capacity still located in Vienna after 1918 (including the above-mentioned filmmakers) was in one way or the other "Jewish." This capacity was so brutally expelled from the city during the 1930s and the war years that it never recovered again. This holds not only because a lot of the people carrying that capacity were murdered or remained in exile but also because the intellectual climate had considerably and sustainably changed after 1945, not least because a lot of pressure on intellectuals not fitting the Austrofascist ideology was already imposed in the 1930s. An example of that may be the case of the social scientists conducting the famous Marienthal study in 1932: Paul Lazarsfeld "voluntarily" left Austria in 1933 for the United States (as a Rockefeller Fellow), Marie Jahoda after imprisonment (for her political activities) in 1936 for the United Kingdom, and Hans Zeisel (after marriage) in 1938 also for the United States. But, "Exile was an opportunity of a lifetime for only a small minority. Those in the shadows are not seen."[24] Certainly, Vienna remained a culturally significant place, especially in the performing arts (music and drama), but it definitively lost its rank in science.

What Vienna gained after 1945 was that it turned into an international meeting place. Already popularized by the famous movie *The Third Man* by Carol Reed (1949), Vienna became a center of East-West espionage, increasingly so after Austrian independence and the declaration of neutrality in 1955. But more importantly, it also became a place for high diplomacy and conferences (also elaborated in greater detail later in this volume). In 1961, John F. Kennedy and Nikita Khrushchev met for the Vienna summit, the first direct meeting of the heads of the two new superpowers.[25] In 1979, the SALT II Treaty on arms control was also signed in Vienna by Jimmy Carter and Leonid Breshnev. This also reflected the growing international significance of Vienna during the Kreisky era, when an active foreign policy also ranked high on the domestic political agenda. Consequently, in the 1970s Vienna also became the third office of the United Nations (after New York and Geneva). The Vienna International Center ("UNO-City") was built between 1973 and 1979 and hosts several UN sub organizations, among them UNIDO (UN Industrial Development Organization), IAEA (International Atomic Energy Agency), and UNHCR (UN High Commissioner for Refugees). Finally, since 1965 the OPEC (Organization of the Petroleum Exporting Countries) headquarters has been located in Vienna, which made the city also a location of international terrorism (OPEC ministers hostage-taking incident in 1975).

Regarding economics, Austria (and Vienna) has shown a comparably slow transition toward industrialization. Particularly large parts of the rural areas remained dominated by agriculture until the middle of the twentieth century. But as a relatively small and landlocked country, Austria also relied on international exchange for economic growth. The structure of the Austrian economy, which is based on small and medium-sized enterprises (SMEs), also shaped the way of integration into the globalized economy. Today, some of these Austrian SMEs regularly are world leaders in market segments or niche markets (especially a considerable number of components of sophisticated machinery in various branches are developed and produced in Austria). However, there are also some classical "global players" (i.e. multinational companies and big corporations) that have originated in Austria or have their headquarters here (like OMV, referred to later in this volume). But they are comparably smaller than, for example, in neighboring Switzerland, which is a heritage of a rescaling process after the loss of the Austro-Hungarian Empire, when the domestic market as the economic base of these companies had shrunk dramatically.[26] This particularly holds for financial institutions and the remaining international engagement of these banks contributed to the deepening of the Great Depression in Austria, as the case of the Creditanstalt in 1931 shows, which heavily affected neighboring countries and the whole financial system. Further, the rare examples of really big Austrian companies often originated in public enterprises (or still are), which is a heritage of corporatist economic policy after World War II, which was also serving a full employment policy (among those are OMV, voestalpine, ÖBB, Telekom Austria, and Verbund). However, while big companies in Austria are not really big by international standards and while they rarely are significant players on the world market, they usually have to be globally oriented to sustain their size (at least when they are in production).

In the economic sphere, tourism is a sector of particular importance in Austria. It "has contributed more than any other area of the tertiary sector to furthering the modernization process in those Austrian regions in which industrialization alone might not have been sufficient."[27] What is even more significant, Austria has become one of the most important locations of mass tourism worldwide, at least on a per capita basis. In 2009, on average fifteen overnight stays were counted per inhabitant, which translates into an average excess population of more than 300,000 persons, or almost four percent (in certain tourist regions, these values are larger by multitudes and may exceed 500 overnight stays per inhabitant and 300 percent excess population). In the context of globalization, two aspects are especially worth noting: First, the numbers of tourists arriving in Austria increased dramatically in the 1960s and 1970s, while they have more or less stagnated since; second, in this stagnation phase the composition of these tourists changed continuously and became more diversified and hence global in origin, although only gradually.

Table 1: Tourism Indicators, 1960-2000[28]

Year	Overnight Stays			Top 3 Concentration Ratio
	Total (in millions)	Foreigners (in millions)	Share (in percent)	
1960	44.8	27.8	62.1	...
1965	67.5	46.6	69.0	...
1970	86.3	63.6	73.7	0.385
1975	105.4	79.9	75.8	0.419
1980	118.7	90.2	76.0	0.370
1985	112.6	85.1	75.6	0.308
1990	123.6	94.8	76.7	0.260
1995	117.1	87.0	74.3	0.304
2000	113.4	83.5	73.6	0.265
2005	119.2	87.7	73.6	0.258
2009	124.3	89.9	72.3	0.237

From the beginning of mass tourism, the major source country has been Germany, followed by Austria. Form 1970 until today these countries had shares of forty-four to sixty percent of all arrivals and twenty-two to twenty-seven percent, respectively. Usually the Netherlands have ranked third, continuously since 1971 with four to 8.5 percent. The concentration ratio mentioned in Table 1 mainly decreased due to a shrinking share of Germany, while especially the shares of other neighboring European regions (Italy, Switzerland, Central Europe) have increased. In the same period, only a share of four to eight percent came from outside Europe, but this share has steadily increased after all.

Austria is also becoming more and more global with respect to its resident population (another issue addressed in more detail in another study in this volume). While before the 1960s, number and share of foreign-born population rather decreased (besides short-term refugee movements in the aftermath of the Hungarian Crisis in 1956) to only 100,000 people and less than 1.5 percent of the population, it rose due to the invitation of so-called "guest workers," mainly from Yugoslavia, to more than 300,000 (and about five percent of the workforce) until the early 1970s. Afterwards it remained rather stable, not least because of economic problems, which resulted in political action discouraging further immigration (the foreign-born workforce decreased by a third in the decade following the first oil crisis). This situation turned dramatically in the years between 1988 and 1993, when the number of foreign-born people almost doubled and stabilized—with a slight upward trend—at that level afterwards. Generally, the composition of this population became more and more multifaceted over time. But while diversity in the migrant population grew quite naturally with its quantity, this increase was not especially biased in favor of migrants from more distant parts of the world, but—after Austrian accession—toward immigration from the European Union and recently especially from Germany. On the other hand, migration (and asylum) policy has become more and more rigid with respect to migrants (and refugees) from outside the European Union and the OECD.

Hence, the Austrian population has become more global over time, particularly from about 1990 on, but mainly due to Europeanization. However, given a migrant share of more than ten percent, Austria today clearly is an immigration country. Further, 17.8 percent of the Austrian population had so-called "migration background" in 2009, which is 1.47 million of 8.26 million inhabitants (390,000 are regarded as "second generation").[29] With immigration also religious diversity in Austria grew. Traditionally being a Catholic country (with a significant tradition of official tolerance, at least in the twentieth century), it is increasingly faced with Muslim, orthodox, and recently even protestant immigration.

Austria participates in most international governmental organizations and has a rather active diplomatic service, which places it well in the political dimension of globalization in the twentieth century. Austria also increasingly participates in mass communication, although it does not host any globally significant newspapers, radio or television stations, and telecom or Internet enterprises. But due to its integration into global information networks, the media landscape has become more and more German-influenced, and the political and entertainment culture became more and more U.S.-influenced. Finally, Austria is also rather global related to a side arena of the social sphere—sports. Austrians are well integrated in international sports and are continuously present at Summer as well as Winter Olympics. Moreover, the country itself hosted several international sports events. However, they usually are of limited significance: The European Soccer Championship in 2008 (co-hosted together with Switzerland) was certainly globally recognized, but "European" by definition; several skiing events (among those Alpine as well as Nordic World Championships), where Austria holds special expertise, are of partial relevance at best; only two Olympic Winter Games (hosted by Innsbruck in 1964 and 1976, particularly the first of which also contributed to a more widespread presentation of the country to the world) can be regarded as truly global events, but they are also related to winter sports only and took place before broadcasting really became global.

Conclusion: How Global is Austria?

Austria is well integrated into globalization in all its dimensions, but not particularly active in it. It is prominently placed in several indices of globalization, it ranks high in several indicators, and there are considerable connections in place. However, what is missing in all of these indices are indicators about the issue to what extent Austrians regard themselves as "global" or at least as part of a greater community.

The general spin of the Austrian political discourse is pointing to rather disturbing conclusions in that respect. While there is an official policy of humanitarianism and international engagement, also with respect to an established historical tradition, and an increasing (but rather small) share in the population actively engaging in solidarity issues, particularly everyday policy and practice in the migration/integration/asylum complex, the recurring significance of xenophobic elements in election campaigns, and endemic scapegoating of foreign institutions (particularly those in "Brussels") for developments regarded as harmful, are hardly encouraging. However, there are some scattered pieces of information on that issue.[30] For example, referring to a large-scale poll conducted in Austria in 1994, 1996, 1999, and 2002, a stable relationship between micro-, meso-, and macro-solidarity is revealed: While about ninety-five percent of the sample agree to the sentence "to help is easy for me" with regard to family members (micro level), only about seventy percent agree on it with respect to more distant people from the same community (meso level), and only about fifty percent agree to it with respect to strangers and foreigners (macro level). However, this is time-series and not cross-country data and hence does not tell too much about Austrians in a comparative perspective. This problem is overcome if we look at budgetary figures, where we find a clear hierarchy: In the Austrian case, roughly a third of public expenditures (about eighteen percent relative to GDP) is spent on social transfers (national/local level), only a small fraction (less than one percent relative to GDP) on transfers within the European Union (international level), and even less (less than 0.5 percent relative to GDP) on official development assistance (global level). However, this is a numerical relationship, which is fully in line with international averages within the OECD or the EU. Finally, there is also data available about the question of identity, based on Eurobarometer surveys. In this context, Austrians do not differ too much from the European average, with a notable exception: Austrians do regard themselves even less as world citizens than Europeans on average do. Further, Austrians (as most other Europeans) regard themselves overwhelmingly as citizens of their nation state and their home region, and much less as Europeans.

Table 2: Percentage of "Senses of Belonging," 2008[31]

	Valid Answers	To a Great Extent	Somewhat	Not Really	Not at All	Balance
Extent of Feeling European						
Austria	998	25.5	47.5	20.7	6.3	32.6
EU-27	26,282	29.6	44.3	17.7	8.4	34.5
Extent of Feeling "National"						
Austria	1,000	76.8	18.1	4.0	1.1	82.8
EU-27	26,462	79.6	15.7	3.3	1.4	84.4
Extent of Feeling "Regional"						
Austria	997	73.0	20.4	5.8	0.8	79.5
EU-27	26,329	69.4	23.4	5.6	1.6	76.7
Extent of Feeling "Citizen of the World"						
Austria	990	10.6	33.2	35.9	20.3	−11.1
EU-27	26,027	24.5	35.9	25.3	14.3	15.5

All in all, there is a poorly researched discrepancy between the official image (also reflected in equally official numbers) of Austrian openness and connectedness, and a much more differentiated picture if we look at actual distributional issues, opinions (be it declared or omitted), and practical actions. This could even lead to a specific Austrian globalization discourse,[32] i.e. the analysis of specific actions and events related to globalization which results in a stronger emphasis on local (even subnational) cultures, networks of exchange, or social formations, which has not been raised so far. However, it is clearly documented—by data about regional identity mentioned above and also by certain political discourses and reactions to continuous contact with "foreigners" as especially experienced in tourist regions—that Austria would be a good place for such an analysis.

The aforementioned "scapegoating" fits in here very well, and even more so in a broader historical context. Interestingly, a deeply rooted political discourse was at least partly reinvented in the context of globalization in Austria. It was the "victim discourse," which historically helped to come to terms with Austrian involvement in the Holocaust by portraying Austria and the Austrians as Hitler's "first victim" (meanwhile it is the accepted narrative to recognize a clearly positive Austrian attitude towards the Anschluss in 1938). In this discourse, overlapping with the European integration discourse, there is little space for positive consequences and chances related to globalization, but large space for dangers and negative consequences: Economic competition from overseas (including outsourcing), people all too easily crossing borders (including criminals), and harmful political decisions made elsewhere (most prominently in "Brussels," which has become a proverbial phrase in Austria ever since EU accession in 1995, but also at international conferences) figure prominently. While it is easy to describe this as political strategy by elites to mask their own responsibility (and sometimes failure), it is also confirmed by data. In the already mentioned Eurobarometer survey in 2008, questions about attitudes towards the European Union ("Brussels") and globalization also were included. In that context, for example, sixty-two percent agree that the EU imposes its view on Austria, while twenty-six percent disagree.[33] Consequently (and contrary to the pan-European picture), a majority of Austrians view EU membership as disadvantageous (forty-seven to thirty-six percent, compared to thirty-one to fifty-four percent EU-wide). Further, this balance is negative in only two other countries: Hungary and the United Kingdom.[34] The same holds for globalization, where Austrians—but comparable to Europeans—predominantly stress negative consequences, especially the relocation of companies (culminating in the statement that globalization is only profitable for large companies, not for citizens), and an aggravation of social imbalances.

In sum, Austria is a rather "globalized" place with respect to the usual indicators, which points to a large degree of international connection. On the other hand, perception in Austria is quite different, and people are generally skeptical about it. However, as a second look at the sketchy picture presented above shows (and as will be shown in much more detail later in this volume), Austria is economically (tourism, SMEs, etc.), politically (international meeting place, etc.), socially (migration, etc.), but also technologically (although more at the user than the provider level), and environmentally (footprint deficit) related and well connected to the world. Additionally, Austria also has a history of active formation of and passive impact on the process and of participation in it. Especially Vienna as an international metropolis figured as an important center for the arts and science, but also for the economy and particularly finance, at least until the 1930s. Also the (forced) Austrian exodus in the interwar period was globally significant and influential. Overall, Austria provides an interesting and multifaceted example of what globalization looks like "on the ground." Therefore, a volume dedicated to this question is long overdue.

Notes

1. Stefan Zweig, *Die Welt von Gestern: Erinnerungen eines Europäers*, 32nd ed. (Frankfurt: Fischer, 2000; orig. 1944), 246. The quote is from the English translation *The World of Yesterday* (Lincoln: University of Nebraska Press, 1964), 214.

2. For a comparison of different approaches, see for example Axel Dreher, Noel Gaston, and Pim Martens, *Measuring Globalization: Understanding its Causes and Consequences* (New York: Springer, 2008); or, for a short version available online, Axel Dreher et al., "Measuring Globalization—Opening the Black Box: A Critical Analysis of Globalization Indices," Bond University Messages 32, September 2009, <epublications.bond.edu.au/cgi/viewcontent.cgi?article=1031&context=gdc&sei-redir=1#search=%22Measuring+Globalization:+Opening+the+Black+Box:%22> (23 March 2011).

3. See <www.globalisationindex.info/MGI/MGI.html> (20 March 2011).

4. See <www2.warwick.ac.uk/fac/soc/csgr/index/> (20 March 2011).

5. See <globalization.kof.ethz.ch/> (20 March 2011).

6. See <www.foreignpolicy.com/articles/2010/08/16/metropolis_now> (20 March 2011).

7. See <www.mori-m-foundation.or.jp/english/research/project/6/pdf/GPCI2009_English.pdf> (20 March 2011). The reason for the rather high score is mainly the recognition of livability and environmental factors in this ranking.

8. See <www.lboro.ac.uk/gawc/world2008t.html>. For more on the methodology of measurement see the regular research bulletins of the network at <www.lboro.ac.uk/gawc/publicat.html>, particularly no. 2, also published as J.V. Beaverstock et al., "Globalization and World Cities: Some Measurement Methodologies," *Applied Geography* 20, no. 1 (2000): 43-63.

9. The word as such originated in the mid-twentieth century. It first appeared in English dictionaries in the early 1960s, but did not become academically popular before the 1980s, when it was applied in business research, and generally in the 1990s, when it became the catchword it has been until today. Its first use in academic research is ascribed to Theodore Levitt, "The Globalization of Markets," *Harvard Business Review* 61, no. 3 (1983): 92-102. It was further popularized in Kenichi Ohmae, *The Borderless World: Power and Strategy in the Interlinked Economy* (New York: Harper Perennial, 1991).

10. This book—interestingly enough—is one of the rare examples of a text originally published in German as *Geschichte der Globalisierung* (Munich: C.H. Beck, 2003) and later translated into English as *Globalization* (Princeton: Princeton University Press, 2005).

11. The most prominent example of this strategy is the mixup of "globalization" with free trade, liberalization, or even progress.

12. For more on that see Andreas Exenberger, "Poverty and Globalization: Problem and Solution, or Two Sides of the Same Medal?" *International Trade and Finance Association Working Papers* 14 (2006), 4-7, <services.bepress.com/itfa/16th/art14>.

13. See prominently David Held and Anthony McGrew, eds., *The Global Transformations Reader: An Introduction to the Globalization Debate*, 2nd ed. (Cambridge: Polity Press, 2003).

14. Consequently, the term "globalization process" is needlessly doubling. It is not possible to live in a "globalized world," because the end of the process is only a theoretical construct. See on that, for example, Malcolm Waters, *Globalization* (London: Routledge, 1995).

15. For further details, also on the distinction of "globalization" to "globality" and "globalism," see Ulrich Beck, *What is Globalization?* (Cambridge: Polity Press, 2008). This book, originally published as *Was ist Globalisierung? Irrtümer des Globalismus—Antworten auf Globalisierung* (Frankfurt: Suhrkamp, 1997), is another of the rare examples of German books translated into English recently.

16. See for example Fernand Braudel, *Civilization and Capitalism, 15th-18th Centuries*, Vol. 3, *The Perspective of the World* (London: Collins, 1984); or Immanuel Wallerstein, *World System Analysis: An Introduction* (Durham: Duke University Press, 2004).

17. For more details on the related concept of a "transitional TimeSpace," see Immanuel Wallerstein, *Unthinking Social Science: The Limits of Nineteenth-Century Paradigms* (Cambridge: Polity Press, 1991).

18. See for example Richard E. Baldwin and Philippe Martin, "Two Waves of Globalization: Superficial Similarities, Fundamental Differences," in *Globalization and Labour*, ed. Horst Siebert (Tübingen: Mohr Siebeck, 1999), 3-58; Kevin O'Rourke and Jeffrey G. Williamson, *Globalization and History: The Evolution of a Nineteenth-Century Atlantic Economy* (Cambridge, MA: The MIT Press, 1999); and Robert T. Robertson, *The Three Waves of Globalization: A History of a Developing Global Consciousness* (London: Zed Books, 2003).

19. See very elaborate on that Harold James, *The End of Globalization: Lessons from the Great Depression* (Cambridge, MA: Harvard University Press, 2001). For contrary opinions, particularly on the embryonic stage of international institutionalization, see for example Alexander Nützenadel, "'A World without Famine?' Internationale Ernährungspolitik im Zeitalter der Weltkriege," *Comparativ* 3 (2007): 12-27. Essentially, even Adolf Hitler, another—in a diabolic way—historically "great" Austrian, connected people, albeit in the most hideous and disastrous way of world war and genocidal mass violence.

20. See for example Andre G. Frank and Barry K. Gills, *The World System: Five Hundred Years or Five Thousand?* (London: Routledge, 1999); George Modelski, Tessaleno Devezas, and William R. Thompson, eds., *Globalization as Evolutionary Process: Modeling Global Change* (London: Routledge, 2008); and Robertson, *The Three Waves of Globalization*; but also Ronald Findlay and Kevin H. O'Rourke, *Power and Plenty: Trade, War, and the World Economy in the Second Millennium* (Princeton: Princeton University Press, 2007); and Michael D. Bordo, Alan M. Taylor, and Jeffrey G. Williamson, *Globalization in Historical Perspective* (Chicago: University of Chicago Press, 2003).

21. See for example Barry K. Gills and William R. Thompson, eds., *Globalization and Global History* (London: Routledge, 2006); Anthony G. Hopkins, ed., *Globalization in World History* (London: Pimlico, 2002); Patrick Manning, *Navigating World History: Historians Create a Global Past* (New York: Palgrave Macmillan, 2005); John R. McNeill and William H. McNeill, *The Human Web: A Bird's Eye View of World History* (New York: Norton, 2003); Margarete Grandner, Dietmar Rothermund, and Wolfgang Schwentker, eds., *Globalisierung und Globalgeschichte* (Vienna: Mandelbaum, 2005); and Peter Feldbauer, Gerald Hödl, and Jean-Paul Lehners, eds., *Rhythmen der Globalisierung: Expansion und Kontraktion zwischen dem 13. und 20. Jahrhundert*

(Vienna: Mandelbaum, 2009).

22. Richard Baldwin and Philippe Martin regard this as decisive difference between the nineteenth and twentieth century waves, which is closely connected to the predominance of transport technology for the nineteenth, but communication technology for the twentieth century. See Baldwin and Martin, "Two Waves of Globalization."

23. This changed considerably, because the Austrian film industry was seriously influenced by these losses and turned rather provincial after the war and almost inexistent later. With respect to more contemporary "exports," particularly well-rewarded action star Arnold Schwarzenegger and Oscar-winning Christoph Waltz could be mentioned (besides—maybe—Michael Haneke and Christian Berger as internationally recognized and rewarded director and cinematographer, respectively).

24. Friedrich Stadler, "The Emigration and Exile of Austrian Intellectuals," in *Austria in the Twentieth Century*, ed. Rolf Steininger, Günter Bischof, and Michael Gehler (New Brunswick: Transaction, 2002), 134.

25. See Stefan Karner et al., eds., *Der Wiener Gipfel 1961: Kennedy—Chruschtschow* (Innsbruck: Studienverlag, 2011).

26. Between 1913 and 1937, the number of firms with more than 1,000 employees declined from seventy-four to only forty-nine, and overall employment dropped by almost half. Franz Mathis, "The Austrian Economy: Basic Features and Trends," in *Austria in the Twentieth Century*, ed. Steininger, Bischof, and Gehler, 226.

27. Ibid., 233. These mountainous regions (especially Tyrol, Carinthia, and Salzburg) experienced considerable growth effects from tourism, including, as Mathis mentions, "the stimulating effect guests' purchasing power had on other sectors of the economy."

28. Data until 2000 taken from Sylvia Leodolter and Rudolf Kaske, eds., *Tourismus in Österreich: Zukunftsbranche oder Einstieg in die Arbeitslosigkeit* (Vienna: Kammer für Arbeiter und Angestellte, 2001), 141, 143 (originally from the WIFO database of the Austrian Institute of Economic Research). Data for 2005 and 2009 taken from Statistik Austria, see <www.statistik.at/web_de/statistiken/tourismus/beherbergung/ankuenfte_naechtigungen/030028.html> (9 March 2011). Top 3 Concentration is calculated as sum of the squares of the respective shares of arrivals of those three countries with the highest share.

29. Data is taken from the online documentation of Statistik Austria, see <www.statistik.at/web_de/statistiken/bevoelkerung/bevoelkerungsstruktur/bevoelkerung_nach_staatsangehoerigkeit_geburtsland/022498.html> (9 March 2011).

30. The following data is presented in more detail in Andreas Exenberger, "Globale Solidarität? Über die Reichweite von Solidargemeinschaften," in *Solidarität: Vom Wert der Gemeinschaft*, ed. Clemens Sedmak (Darmstadt: Wissenschaftliche Buchgesellschaft, 2009), 204-09. The data is based on Hermann Denz, "Solidarität in Österreich: Strukturen und Trends," *SWS-Rundschau* 43, no. 3 (2003): 321-36, and Paul M. Zulehner et al., *Solidarität—Option für die Modernisierungsverlierer* (Innsbruck: Tyrolia, 1996).

31. Data based on the Eurobarometer survey 69.2 in 2008 (<zacat.gesis.org>). Balance refers to a weighted balance of answers: Balance = [% Answer 1 + (½ * % Answer 2) – (½ * % Answer 3) – % Answer 4].

32. On "glocalization," see Roland Robertson, "Glocalization: Time-Space and Homogeneity-Heterogeneity," in *Global Modernities*, ed. Mike Featherstone, Scott Lash, and Roland Robertson (London: Sage, 1995), 25-44; and Zygmunt Bauman, "On Glocalization: Or Globalization for Some, Localization for some Others," *Thesis Eleven* 54, no. 1 (1998): 37-49.

33. Additionally, forty-three percent agree that Austria's voice counts in the EU, while forty-six percent disagree, and twenty-two percent agree that the Austrians' voice counts in the EU, while sixty-five percent disagree.

34. Further, Austrians do regard EU membership as beneficial well below the EU average: thirty-six percent regard it as good, twenty-six percent as bad, and thirty-six percent as neither-nor, while the EU-wide values are fifty-two, fourteen, and twenty-nine percent, respectively. Comparable is the picture only in Hungary; worse only in the United Kingdom and Latvia.

Fin de Fin-de-Siècle Vienna?
A Letter of Remembrance

Steven Beller

Fin-de-siècle Vienna as a topic in cultural and intellectual history had a good, if relatively short, life and provided inspiration and purpose for many (to say nothing of employment and income for quite a few academics and writers). As someone who was involved in the latter stages of fin-de-siècle Vienna's career, I was greatly saddened to recognize that it had recently passed away.

It might seem odd to talk of a historical topic passing away. While they refer to real events, topics are not animate and therefore neither actually live nor die. There is a sense, however, in which they can succeed or fail, be attractive and cogent or non-descript and unconvincing, innovative or old-hat, "live" or "die." They are concepts, constructs of our reason and imagination, hermeneutic devices for understanding, grasping the world of our experience. The German word for concept, *Begriff*, with its sense of gaining a hold on something, sums this up well. The viability or vitality of a concept is a product of its usefulness in allowing us to grasp the meaning of some thing or event. An elaborated and articulated concept that explains a multiplicity of connected things and events is what Thomas Kuhn called a paradigm. A historical topic such as fin-de-siècle Vienna purports on one level to be simply an area of research, for instance the historical events happening in and around turn-of-the-century Vienna, but is on another level always informed with intellectual assumptions and assertions, a set of hypotheses and its own logic through which the raw data of the area of research are processed.

Sometimes a topic can catch fire with the academic community and even the educated public, occasionally the uneducated public, because it speaks, both in its subject matter and its approach, to the wishes and needs of a certain context and time. It can come alive in the imagination of thousands and millions, and this not only has to do with the "facts" of the topic, but even more with the implicit, specific approach with which the topic handles those "facts." The flame can go out, however: The broader interest in the topic can be diverted, or withdraw, if the topic is not strong enough, cogent enough, intellectually impressive enough, or simply relevant enough for the inevitably changing intellectual, cultural, and also socio-political context in which it must operate. Once that flame goes out, being an intellectual construct, the topic can always—in theory—be revived, resurrected, or transformed into a more attractive, updated one, revamped to suit new times, with even a new rationale. It is never completely "dead"—unlike for living beings, reanimation is always a possibility, however remote. Yet most topics that lose their relevance and cogency are, in effect, left for dead. As historical topics go, I am sad to say, fin-de-siècle Vienna is at best rapidly becoming, at worst has already become, an *ex*-topic (to paraphrase Monty Python).

To realize the extent of fin-de-siècle Vienna's demise, we just need to think back to its heyday in the 1980s. I got to know fin-de-siècle Vienna in 1980, at a dramatic stage in its career. Carl E. Schorske's lavishly produced book, *Fin-de-Siècle Vienna: Politics and Culture*, was published that year and to me at the time it appeared to burst upon the scene to fanfare and accolades. Any appearance of sudden triumph was deceptive, however, for this was not by any means an overnight success. Schorske's book did not mark the beginning of fin-de-siècle Vienna's brilliant career, but rather the culmination of its ascent.

The origins of fin-de-siècle Vienna as a topic stretch back at least to the early 1960s. It was then, in a series of occasional historical articles related to the culture of turn-of-the-century Vienna, that Schorske had begun to roll out the elaborated conceptual construct that became fin-de-siècle Vienna. There had been much written on Vienna before then, and the former Habsburg capital had already had a fairly prominent profile, as the home of the waltz, schnitzel, strudel, Freud—and Hitler. As a cultural and intellectual center of modernism, however, its general reputation was very much as a second-ranker, behind such powerhouses as Paris, New York, Weimar Berlin, or even London. There were many Viennese émigrés around after the Second World War who knew better, most brilliantly Hermann Broch, but they either kept quiet or were ignored by the larger public. Most in that public, and the academy, would have scoffed in the 1960s at the notion that it was Vienna that was the real "capital of the twentieth century." Schorske's invention of fin-de-siècle Vienna as a coherent, well-grounded parable of the origins of early modernism slowly but surely changed this perception until by the early 1970s Vienna was promoted in the league of cultural centers to the first division.

The irony was that Schorske's model for fin-de-siècle Vienna was not primarily obtained from study of Vienna itself (even if there are strong traces of Broch's work in it), but rather from what Schorske had perceived to be the relationship of politics and culture in America in the 1950s. Immersed in the Freudian psychologizing of the time, Schorske's success was based on his ability to show how cultural modernism was as much based on a retreat from the political, into the psychological realm, as it was an all-conquering norm for modern society. Cultural modernism was thus tied to the *failure* of political modernism, of the progressive, liberal (quasi-socialist) kind advocated by American academics and intellectuals in the 1950s and 1960s, not to its success. Looking for past examples of the same phenomenon, Schorske could have chosen various milieux, but what place else would be so perfectly suited to uncover the original sin of cultural modernism than the birthplace of that cultural modernism's theoretical basis, psychoanalysis? Hence Freud's Vienna was Schorske's felicitous choice as the site in which to demonstrate his theories. Thus was born fin-de-siècle Vienna—a topic whose main subject was not Viennese, but rather American academic and cultural elites, who were also the main audience.

This was a very happy combination. A theoretical explanation of the relationship between political and cultural modernism was wedded to the exploration of the origins of the Freudian father-figure, and was boosted by the fact that Vienna at the turn of the century was both a fecund center of cultural and intellectual innovation, but also still possessed a common culture among the educated elite that lent coherence to any explication of the development of that culture. (Vienna 1900 would, indeed, have been strong enough to stand on its own, without the crutch of the fin-de-siècle Vienna moniker.) This all made Schorske's gambit of composing a comprehensive intellectual history of fin-de-siècle Vienna a winner. Members of the educated elites in America and the West could see themselves explained while apparently reading about Vienna. They could see their assumptions about the efficacy of psychoanalysis and of Marxian sociology, à la Frankfurt School, affirmed, with the slight twist that it was the failure of old-style political modernism, rational liberalism, that had led to the modernist culture that they practiced. (But then, from their perspective, liberalism had deserved to be replaced by even more modern and rational socialism in any case.) Schorske's disclaimer that he was only writing essays of internal analysis of cultural artefacts, and making no absolute claims about the larger world, only added an intellectually fashionable modesty to burnish the project, and was largely ignored by those who were attracted to the intellectual power and richness of the topic he had apparently unearthed.

Soon enough fin-de-siècle Vienna was taken up as a topic by other historians, philosophers, and writers who each saw their own part of the landscape made available through the Schorskean lens of fin-de-siècle Vienna. As with all effective concepts, fin-de-siècle Vienna worked to provide a firmer grasp on the confusing reality of what had happened in Vienna around 1900, and perhaps no more effective use of its central theses was made than in Allan Janik and Stephen Toulmin's *Wittgenstein's Vienna*, published in 1973, which took Schorske's concept, explicated in his articles, and applied it to one particular question in the history of ideas, the origins and real meaning of Wittgenstein's *Tractatus Logico-Philosophicus*. Herbert Marcuse once claimed, probably correctly, that the publishing success of that book introduced the main outlines of fin-de-siècle Vienna to a broader audience several years before Schorske's own blockbuster was published. Nicolas Powell's *Sacred Spring* (1974) and Peter Vergo's *Art in Vienna* (1975) served a similar function as regards the arts. Other historians, not so convinced by the Schorskean model, explored different paths into the subject of Austrian intellectual history. Most notable here was William M. Johnston's *The Austrian Mind*, with quite different methodologies. Yet these too were brought willy-nilly into fin-de-siècle Vienna's orbit, and both profited from, and fed into, its increasing popularity.

Then there was the long list of Schorske's own pupils, including Gary Cohen, Peter Jelavich, and David Luft, who spread the topic's themes and methodology within American academia, through their own teaching courses and, in time, the products of their own research projects. One of the most brilliant contributions to the topic of fin-de-siècle Vienna had already appeared in 1974, William J. McGrath's *Dionysian Art and Populist Politics in Austria*. By the time Schorske published his own collection of essays in 1980, with some new work, admittedly, but mostly reprints of those seminal essays stretching back to the 1960s, fin-de-siècle Vienna was already a hot topic, the pump having already been primed for years. The very fact that the book was so lavishly produced, with such care taken over the illustrations and format, was itself a sign that the success of the publication was seen to be assured, as it was as much an affirmation as an assertion of fin-de-siècle Vienna's cultural and intellectual significance. Even so, the success of the book, and of the topic, was probably greater than even Schorske's most ardent admirers had thought it would be. Fin-de-siècle Vienna simply took off in Gerschenkronian dimensions.

As an eyewitness, it seemed to me as though fin-de-siècle Vienna simply chimed with the times. If Schorske and his allies had prepared the ground well, it was very friendly ground. This was not only a phenomenon of the narrow academic community. Posters of Klimt paintings adorned student rooms; Mahler was becoming almost popular. Visconti's 1971 film of *Death in Venice*, ostensibly about a German musician in Venice, had been in truth a Mahlerfest. Nicolas Roeg, famous for another film set in Venice, *Don't Look Now*, in 1980 released *Bad Timing*, set in none other than Vienna, albeit contemporary Vienna, but decorated with Klimts and exuding the sort of Freudian psychologizing associated with fin-de-siècle Vienna. There was even a song by Ultravox, *Vienna*, which sat at the top of the British pop charts for a few weeks in 1980. Even the politics of the time seemed to affirm the significance of fin-de-siècle Vienna. The 1970s had been a period in which the optimism of the apparently straightforward success of early sixties modernity and cultural modernism had, especially after 1968, given way to a more crisis-prone and ambivalent age—with the victory of Nixon in the United States and Heath in Britain, and then the Oil Crisis from 1973 and the economic problems that ensued. 1979 saw the flailing Labour Party in Britain turfed out by Margaret Thatcher's Tories; in the United States Reagan beat Carter in 1980. Just as in fin-de-siècle Vienna, it seemed that progressives and liberalism were on the run from reactionary mass politics. Culturally and intellectually too, the modernist project itself looked in jeopardy, challenged by various versions of "postmodernism." Perhaps it was worth looking away from the perceived centers of that culture, Paris and New York, toward alternative sites where modernism had not had such a clear path for it, such as fin-de-siècle Vienna. Whether coming or going, fin-de-siècle Vienna seemed to be the center of attention.

If 1980 appeared the "annus mirabilis" of fin-de-siècle Vienna, it turned out only to be the beginning of its ascendancy. By the mid-1980s fin-de-siècle Vienna had become more than *one* of the capitals of twentieth-century modernism in contemporary eyes, it was being seen as *the* "birthplace of the modern world." The new status of fin-de-siècle Vienna was reflected in, and partly caused by, a series of blockbuster exhibitions and associated conferences that spread the word about the Habsburg capital's hitherto unrecognized greatness as a center of modernity. The first in the series was at the Edinburgh Festival of 1983, which its director, John Drummond, devoted to the theme of Vienna at the turn of the century, with not only the exhibition, *Vienna 1900*, curated by Peter Vergo, but also much Mahler, and even a production of Karl Kraus's supposedly unproducible *Last Days of Mankind*, among much else in an already established fin-de-siècle Vienna oeuvre. Then came the lavish exhibition, *The Arts in Vienna*, at the Palazzo Grassi during the Venice Biennale in 1984. Fin-de-siècle Vienna came home in 1985 to an Austrian capital beginning to bask in its new fame, if slightly puzzled by it, in the exhibition *Traum und Wirklichkeit*; then in 1986 the circus moved on yet again and fin-de-siècle Vienna was

Exhibition Poster, 1985

© Austrian National Library

the subject of not one but two major exhibitions: the fabulously over-the-top *L'Apocalypse Joyeuse* in Paris, and then the somewhat more subdued, but still fine, *Vienna 1900: Art and Design* in New York. It seemed only fitting that the two cities formerly held to be the capitals of modernism should pay homage to the newly regnant fin-de-siècle Vienna. Most of these exhibitions were surrounded by conferences, and even old London, not itself up to an exhibition (unless one counts Edinburgh during the festival as a London suburb) roused itself to hold a conference on fin-de-siècle Vienna with the evocative title *Decadence and Innovation* in late 1986. Vienna, and specifically fin-de-siècle Vienna, was on top of the world.

It had in fact all become a bit much, the fashion for all things Viennese. By the late 1980s, there were shades of the Sorcerer's Apprentice in the way in which fin-de-siècle Vienna had gone from being an intriguing idea to being a compelling topic in cultural and intellectual history, and then had grown to being a major alternative center to mainstream modernism, and then the "capital of the twentieth century." Schorske had never actually meant this claim to be made, and I am fairly sure he has never made it, but as the leading spirit of fin-de-siècle Vienna's ascent, and the acknowledged intellectual father of the string of exhibitions, he remained mute while others made ever more outlandish claims for Vienna's importance in the constellation of modern cultural capitals.

One group that remained a little perplexed by fin-de-siècle Vienna's immense new fame was, ironically enough, Austrians. During the prosperity and progressive reform of the 1970s under Bruno Kreisky, Austria had had little need to understand the failure of liberalism or look back to fin-de-siècle Vienna. The Austria that had counted then had been that of the "Austrian model" and Austro-Keynesianism. It was one thing to have fancy coffee tins from Meinl with Klimtian women on them, or Bernstein conduct Mahler, but quite another to concentrate on a Viennese past that seemed irrelevant to the new, socialized future. By the 1980s, admittedly, the hegemony of the Socialist Party was beginning to wear thin, and in 1983 disappeared, prompting Kreisky's resignation and a coalition with the Freedom Party (FPÖ)—the self-proclaimed heirs to the very liberalism that Schorske had seen failing in fin-de-siècle Vienna. In this environment, embracing the world's acclaim for your capital city as the birthplace of modernism had its compensations, both in a boost in national (and civic) self-confidence, and in ever larger numbers of culture tourists and their expenditures.

The vision of fin-de-siècle Vienna offered by Schorske was actually very sympathetic to the Kreiskian world view: What had upset modernity was the emergence of irrational mass politics, in the form of Schönerer's

German nationalism, Karl Lueger's Christian socialism—and Theodor Herzl's Zionism. Not mentioned in the same breath by Schorske was Victor Adler's Social Democrats (Kreisky's forerunners), even though Adler had been an ally of Schönerer at one stage and very much a part of this swing to mass politics, as William McGrath had outlined. Schorske's explanation had been that Adler had gone over to the working class and so had ceased to be in the same category as the "bourgeois" trio he had written about. This made little historical sense, but it would have been music to the ears of someone such as Kreisky, who no doubt would also have reveled in the—for many explosive—idea of Herzl's Zionism being associated with German nationalism and Christian social anti-Semitism.

There were also more geopolitical reasons for some Austrians to take to fin-de-siècle Vienna, or at least the importance it purveyed to Vienna 1900. The 1980s were also the era when "Central Europe" emerged as a serious concept in the public diplomacy of the West, and its sympathizers in the eastern, Soviet bloc. Emphasizing the significance of Vienna as a center of global modern culture could shift the locus of interest eastward to the center of the continent, and shine a light on those other former centers of (Western) modernism that were now in the communist East, such as Budapest, Prague, Cracow, and even, at a stretch, Warsaw. This was the strategy of Kundera's notion of Central Europe, infused ideas of "anti-politics," and was the basis of *Projekt Mitteleuropa*, the Austrian contribution to the genre written by Erhard Busek and Emil Brix, published in 1986, but thought out significantly before that (see Brix's essay in this volume).

Whatever the reasons, Austrians by 1985 were prepared to accept fin-de-siècle Vienna's place in the modern cultural firmament, and the exhibition *Traum und Wirklichkeit* was an immense success, both internationally and nationally. Fin-de-siècle Vienna was employed to boost the self-image of Austria as a giant not only in music and the arts, but now also more intellectual fields. Freud was acknowledged in ways he had rarely been before, as were the many others on the long list of Viennese luminaries. Even so, there were lingering doubts in Austria and Vienna about whether fin-de-siècle Vienna had been quite as important as it was now being made to appear, and there would also have been some anxiety, suppressed though it might be, about how relevant this was to contemporary Austria, how appropriate it was to claim fin-de-siècle Vienna's legacy for modern-day Austria, because, as everyone knew at the time, even if they had persuaded themselves otherwise, there were serious problems in establishing the connection between the people who had created the culture of fin-de-siècle Vienna and the current population of the Austrian capital. As if scripted, the Waldheim Affair of 1986 reopened a different narrative, not only about Austrian involvement in the Second World War, but also about what Austria had lost during that war, or rather *which* Austrians had been "lost" during it. Inevitably, I think, this had a critical impact also on the reception of fin-de-siècle Vienna, in Austria but almost more significantly in America and Western Europe, because the group of people who had done most to create fin-de-siècle Vienna had also been the greatest victims of Austria's time as part of the Third Reich: Vienna's Jews.

There was nothing particularly novel about seeing Viennese Jewry as central to the city's modern cultural and intellectual life at the turn of the century. This claim had, admittedly, often been seen in a negative light, as an anti-Semitic accusation against the perpetrators of Vienna's "decadence" or the destruction of Austria's traditional Catholic values, or indeed *German* values, but it had also been seen in a very positive light, by such as Friedrich Torberg. Whether positive or negative, the central role of Jews in Viennese modern culture went back a long way, to the fin de siècle itself. One could well argue that one of the major innovations in the topic of fin-de-siècle Vienna was that the Jewish aspect had *not* been as central as in other explanations of Viennese modernism, and that this was one thing that had made it attractive to both its Western audience in New York, London, and elsewhere, as well as its advocates in the more progressive parts of Austria's educated class, precisely because it put social class in the stead of religious or ethnic categories in its explanation of the relationship between politics and culture. Talking of "liberals" and the "bourgeoisie" and their problems in the era of mass politics as the source of modernism's inspiration was much more universalist in its form, and hence much more acceptable to the progressively educated, than explaining Vienna's intellectual and cultural achievements through the "outdated" categories of religion, ethnicity, or, worse, the taboo category of "race," by saying, in so many words, that it had all been the work of "the Jews." Some such line of thought had clearly been considered by Schorske, because he is quite explicit at certain points in stressing that there was nothing particular about Jews in Vienna, that they "merely shared" the liberal values of the other members of the Viennese haute bourgeoisie and were alienated as members of a class (not an ethnic group). When it came to Freud this distinction became rather difficult to make, but at least Schorske's effort to make it endeared him to the liberal Western elites and the Kreiskians in Vienna itself.

The problem was that, when the cultural and intellectual achievement of Vienna 1900 was looked at more closely, it really took a great deal of energy *not* to notice that a truly remarkable number of the people involved, especially in the more intellectual and literary fields, were indeed Jewish or of Jewish descent. Moreover, it had not simply been the irrationalism of "mass politics" that had threatened the educated elite in Vienna, but, explicitly, anti-Semitism. All this pointed to a more ethnicized dichotomy, between Jews and their non-Jewish opponents, as the central driving force of what had happened in Vienna at the turn of the century. It was hard to escape the suspicion that this, and not abstract notions such as fin-de-siècle Vienna's alienation of the bourgeoisie, had been what had driven Vienna's modernism.

Even as Schorske and fin-de-siècle Vienna were taking their plaudits in Paris, figures such as George Steiner were in effect giving an alternative reading of Viennese modernity along ethnic lines. What was involved here was more (or less) than simply an interpretation of Viennese modernism: Many of the critics of Schorske and fin-de-siècle Vienna, and there were increasingly many the higher the Viennese wave ascended, felt challenged or even threatened in their own worldviews and academic fiefdoms, as they saw the fin-de-siècle Vienna empire and its particular methodology expand to other centers and even other fields—and they responded accordingly by trying to put breakers in its way. To take Steiner as an example: If Viennese modernity was about the transformation from *homo economicus* to *homo psychologicus* and was driven by political alienation of a class and its retreat into the cultural realm, then the "language turn" that was the centerpiece of Steiner's version of modernity (going back to *Language and Silence* from 1967) was not the centerpiece that he thought, or wanted, it to be. Hence, for Steiner there were both personal and much larger impersonal, historical-cultural stakes at play in the success or failure of fin-de-siècle Vienna as a topic and paradigm. And the high-stakes nature of the debate over fin-de-siècle Vienna that occurred in the 1980s and beyond was similar for many others, such as Dominick La Capra, Peter Gay, and indeed Stephen Toulmin (and Allan Janik). But Steiner's was a particularly salient voice, because he linked his "language turn" challenge to the fin-de-siècle Vienna paradigm with the old, almost traditional, even reactionary, claim of there being something "Jewish" about Viennese and Central European modern culture. And a major problem for Schorske and fin-de-siècle Vienna was that the ground on which Steiner stood was ultimately more solid than that of fin-de-siècle Vienna, because the factual record did show an extraordinary participation of Jews in creating and sustaining the culture that had made fin-de-siècle Vienna so famous.

As is often the case in such matters, the research that showed that the old stereotypes about Viennese modern culture being largely "Jewish" were true had already been mostly completed before Steiner's claims in 1985, and certainly long before the Waldheim Affair indirectly brought it (back) to center stage in 1986. The thought did not suddenly arise with the revelations about Waldheim's (and Austria's) wartime past; but the affair did shift attention away from the more neutral, class-based explanations for fin-de-siècle Vienna's prominence, toward a more ethnicized one, that stressed the fact that this modern culture had been largely a product of a *Jewish* liberal bourgeoisie, and that it could not be fully understood without taking this Jewish dimension into account. Nor could the immensely prestigious legacy of this culture of fin-de-siècle Vienna, of which Austrians had recently come to be so proud, be honestly claimed without acknowledging that the *ethnic* group at its center had been, in effect, wiped out (forced out or killed), with the help of Austrians, between March 1938 and April 1945. By the end of the 1980s, the second wave of interest in fin-de-siècle Vienna concentrated much more on its Jewish dimension, in such books as Robert Wistrich's *The Jews of Vienna in the Age of Franz Joseph*, or my own *Vienna and the Jews*.

This ethnicization of the debate over Vienna 1900 and its legacy to modern Austria did not destroy fin-de-siècle Vienna as such, but it did considerably muddy the waters, relativizing and complicating what had been a rather pristine, universalizable explanatory model. It also strongly politicized it, because it became part of the internal Austrian battles over the meaning of modern Austria, and who and what was "Austrian," and who did and did not "belong" in the historical narrative of the contemporary Austrian nation. Abroad, especially in New York and environs, fin-de-siècle Vienna became entangled in questions in the media, albeit the more refined parts, about whether Austria was really part of the liberal West, or had dealt adequately with its Nazi past, and how much, despite its appearance as a responsible world citizen, it still needed monitoring and indeed educating from the West, specifically the Western elites, in New York and elsewhere, who had once fully accepted Schorske's version of what fin-de-siècle Vienna stood for. What had been an ethnically neutral discourse about culture as a refuge from politics was now faced with political battles over the ethnic identity of the very artefacts at the center of the fin-de-siècle Vienna pantheon. In terms of "belonging," it was significant that the debate now started to shift to questions of possession: whose culture this really was. Was it that of modern-day Austrians, or of the group that had provided many of the culture's creative figures, and even more of the social and financial support: Vienna's Jews—and their heirs living in the lands of emigration? This was meant not only in abstract terms, but also very concrete ones.

The beautiful "golden" portrait by Klimt of Adele Bloch-Bauer was a striking case in point. Painted by Klimt in the 1900s, this icon of fin-de-siècle Vienna had remained in the possession of Bloch-Bauer's husband, the industrialist Ferdinand Bloch-Bauer, until stolen by the Nazis in 1938. It was then displayed in the massive Klimt retrospective of 1943, under Baldur von Schirach's patronage, with the title "Portrait of a Golden Lady." Under this "Aryanized" (or at least de-Semiticized) title, the painting continued to be exhibited at the Belvedere and catalogued in collections for many years after 1945. It was only relatively recently, in the 1970s I believe, that it regained its old title, with the name of its Jewish subject. Even then, when discussed by Schorske, the ethnicity of Adele Bloch-Bauer and the fate of the picture in 1938 was hardly mentioned or regarded as significant. But by the mid-1980s, this picture along with many other Klimt portraits of society ladies, mostly Jewish, were being used as Exhibit A in the claims to the significance of the Jewish side of Vienna 1900, in terms of patronage of the artists, if not, in this instance, of the artists themselves. The story then took a further turn when the painting then became Exhibit A in one of the most prominent battles over the question of, literally, to whom the culture of Vienna 1900 belonged. Maria Altmann, Bloch-Bauer's heir, sued the Austrian government for ownership of the painting, and, after many years of legal battling, manfully led by Randol Schoenberg, Arnold Schoenberg's grandson, eventually forced the Austrian government to cede ownership. Negotiations for the painting to be bought by the Austrian government having fallen through, the painting was then sold by Altmann to Ronald Lauder, and the painting now graces the Neue Galerie in what some might well regard as its *spiritual* home, New York's Upper East Side.

An important stage in this drama had been the Austrian government's own coming-to-terms with the injustices of the period after March 1938, especially as concerns Aryanization of property, with the Restitution Law of 1998. Yet this itself had been a response to increasing calls from many in the West, both academics and émigrés, as well as Austrian academics, journalists, and politicians, to do something to settle what was by now regarded as this gaping wound of injustice and guilt associated with Austrian conniving at dispossessing its Jewish citizens, not only in 1938 but also *after* 1945. It was no coincidence whatsoever that the Austrian journalist who was absolutely central to the campaign to restitute the Klimt paintings to Altmann was the same individual who had been at the center of the attempts to delve into Waldheim's real war record: the late and much missed Hubertus Czernin. The fact that he himself had been of Jewish descent (as well as a scion of an illustrious Austrian aristocratic dynasty) only added poignancy to his achievement at making Austrians face up to their past.

In some respects this turn in events to an actual cataloguing and balancing the books, as it were, of the Jewish part to the heritage of fin-de-siècle Vienna, has had its own problems. The concentration on the quotidian research into provenance and restitution, of calculation of damages, and negotiations over monetary compensation for past damages (and mass murder), has somewhat taken the edge off, and diverted from, the moral and spiritual questions which still ought to dominate discussions of the relationship between modern-day Austrians and the Jewish part to Viennese and Austrian culture (and hence identity). The sense that Austrians either have paid off the Jews, or at least are on the way to settling past wrongs by restitution, and hence are freeing themselves of that burden of history, has allowed far too many to ignore the implications of that history for current political questions in Austria, such as that over immigration and integrating people of "non-Western" cultures. Reading what some Austrian politicians and commentators say about Turks in Austria today, one wonders whether the lessons about just how much Austria owes to those who were "outsiders" in terms of its cultural and intellectual richness have really been absorbed to any significant degree at all. That said, the fact that there has been this sea change on the question of ownership of Austrian culture, and who was responsible for what, seen in ethnic terms, and in terms of inheritance, and hence, ironically, of descent, has taken discussions over the socio-political basis for turn-of-the-century Viennese art a long way away from the paradigm of fin-de-siècle Vienna, as it was understood before Waldheim.

The Waldheim Affair was a largely internal Austrian matter, but the mid-1980s saw another global event, the beginning of the end of the Cold War, that also had a significant impact on the career of fin-de-siècle Vienna. The thawing of East-West relations brought on by Gorbachev's arrival in the Kremlin led to no less than revolutionary change in communist Eastern Europe, that is to say all the countries on Austria's northern and eastern borders, and quite a few beyond that which had once been part of the empire of which Vienna had been the capital. What had seemed mere pipe dreams of the authors of *Projekt Mitteleuropa* now came true in ways they could barely have imagined even in 1986. Things had begun to change rapidly several years before 1989, in the realities of "East Central European" politics and economics, and also in the conceptualizations of Central Europe mentioned above, but the events in that remarkable year and the next couple completely changed the map of Europe, and, for a time at least, made a concept such as Central Europe meaningful in ways it had not been for decades. To put it in simple terms relevant to fin-de-siècle Vienna, all those signposts in Vienna to various Czech, Slovak, and Hungarian cities, that had once seemed charmingly archaic and virtually irrelevant before the 1980s, now pointed to actual destinations. It was as though Austria, and particularly easterly-lying Vienna, had had its Cold War straitjacket removed.

This change in contemporary Vienna's situation was bound to have an effect on how the historical Vienna, including fin-de-siècle Vienna, was perceived. Fin-de-siècle Vienna as a topic, with its emphasis on how political alienation led to a liberal retreat to culture and the psyche, had been a product of Cold War America, and the Cold War's death knell can also be seen as the beginning of the end for fin-de-siècle Vienna. The fall of the Wall and the rediscovery of a Central European area did, it is true, vastly expand the reach of fin-de-siècle Vienna. Historiographically it was almost as though Vienna had been given back its imperial hinterland as research into other Habsburg cities, most notably Budapest, Prague, and Cracow, was conducted along the same methodological lines as for fin-de-siècle Vienna, these other cultural centers, as it were, seen in fin-de-siècle Vienna's light, and almost as its suburbs. Soon enough, however, research projects into these other centers took on a life of their own and began to divert attention away from the center, competing with the imperial capital, just as they had during the times of the monarchy. In terms of academic attention, the really big winner of the disappearance of the Wall and the reuniting not only of Central Europe but indeed of Europe, was not in the Habsburg realm at all but was Vienna's old nemesis, Berlin. It was true that together Berlin and Vienna could headline a "Central Europe 1900" topic (which also included Prague, Budapest, and so forth) that did indeed provide the sort of cultural and intellectual predominance around the turn of the century that some had claimed for fin-de-siècle Vienna, but this still meant fin-de-siècle Vienna now was only part of a larger phenomenon and had to share the spotlight, if it was still directly in the spotlight at all.

The broadening of regional perspectives made possible by the end of the Cold War changed the geographical context of fin-de-siècle Vienna—and the historiographical one. It meant an expansion from fin-de-siècle Vienna to Central Europe 1900, but also a change from a socially based approach (alienated liberal bourgeoisies) that put national issues at the margin and stressed the supranational nature of the monarchy and its cultural world, towards a much more nationally based model. Away from the imperial capital, the dominance of national, and nationalist, concerns became much more evident, also within cultural modernism. Indeed the cultural worlds of the main provincial centers of the monarchy now liberated from communist rule, Prague, Budapest, and Cracow, all illustrated in their own way that nationalism had not been seen as the opponent of modernism, as implicit in the fin-de-siècle Vienna model, but in many ways its main ally. Far from being a threat, the nation, whether Czech, Magyar, or Polish, had been seen by many of the leading cultural figures as both the means to modernity, and indeed its goal. Bartók, for instance, was intent on composing music that was both a great advance in modern classical music, and authentically Hungarian. It is true that in each of these centers there had also existed variations of the supranational, or non-national, modernism that had been at the center of fin-de-siècle Vienna, and there was indeed a common urban culture in the region that had been the very embodiment of "Central Europe," most evocatively conjured up in Claudio Magris's magisterial *Danube*, but in all the cities outside of the imperial capital there had been a tension, even a competition, between these national and non-national sorts of modernism; when the national forms of modernism had looked beyond their borders, they had looked toward international links, with Germany, France, Italy, Russia, or even Britain, for inspiration rather than to imperial Vienna. Moreover, Vienna herself, research began to show, had not been as immune to this nationalist modernist trend as the fin-de-siècle Vienna paradigm had suggested, and "modern" liberalism had not so much been defeated by nationalism, as had transformed into it—it was just that the nationalist politics, and cultural modernism, in Vienna was German, not Austrian.

The non-national, "Central European" modernism, which was centered on fin-de-siècle Vienna, had provided the matrix to some of the most significant contributions of the region to modern culture generally, but the network on which that matrix was based was only part of the modernist world in the monarchy, and it was a network that had as its nodes of attraction in each city the various coffeehouses, academic circles, journals and literary groups whose personnel were in very large part comprised of Jews. In other words, to the extent that "Central Europe 1900" adhered to the non-national modernist model of fin-de-siècle Vienna, it was largely the world of the monarchy's urban, assimilated Jewish bourgeoisie. To the extent that the narrative of Central European modernism was not nationalized, it was still increasingly seen as ethnicized.

There were countervailing pressures on the historiographical perspective from the developments within the new dispensation of post-Cold War Central Europe in the 1980s and 1990s. Whereas new-found national pride, and a return to national-cultural categories, after the purely sociological (socialist) approaches of the communist era, put renewed emphasis on seeking national cultural uniqueness, as outlined above, in the modern culture of Prague, Budapest, or Cracow 1900, the almost simultaneous next step, after gaining real national sovereignty was, perhaps ironically, to surrender this in a race to become part of "Europe" (the European Community and then the European Union). Ethnicization and nationalization were thus followed by Europeanization as processes affecting the once apparently unimpeachable status of fin-de-siècle Vienna.

The first country in the region successfully to make what seemed the inevitable transition to being a full member of the EU was Austria herself. Once freed from the restrictions of the Cold War, it appeared to most Austrians obvious that she should join with the rest of "Europe," and after negotiations and a probationary period this occurred in 1995. Most of her formerly "East European" neighbors followed in 2004, after many years of negotiation and preparation. The integration of Austria and her now Central European neighbors into Europe might have had positive results for fin-de-siècle Vienna, one would think, bringing Vienna once more fully into the network of European cities and *primus inter pares* within *its* Central European region, but the consequences were almost all detrimental for fin-de-siècle Vienna (though astoundingly positive for actual modern-day Vienna). As a member of the EU, Austria, and its capital, lost its special status between East and West, and some of this loss of uniqueness rubbed off on fin-de-siècle Vienna, too. One might have supposed that the accession of the other Central European countries would establish a Višegradian (neo-Habsburgian) regional group within the EU, but this has not, by most accounts, occurred. Instead, countries tend to operate according to *ad hoc* coalitions of interests within the Union, with regional blocs not being that significant. In any case, the Central European members had only really been prepared to see any Central European status as a step to full European status, becoming members of "the West" was the main goal, not languishing in the middle of the continent. And this was Austria's main purpose in joining the Union as well—a defensive measure, prompted out of fear of being left out, along with all those other former successor states. In this dynamic there was little if any sentiment for emphasizing either fin-de-siècle Vienna or even Central Europe 1900. One wanted to be European, not part of old Habsburg Central Europe.

Moreover, in the EU that emerged after 2004 it was clear that reunited Germany, with its new capital of Berlin, was the main player. Austria might be a major investor in the region, retracing commercial and financial networks from imperial days, but the major action was, as it had been also in 1900, to the north, with Berlin and Warsaw (a non-Habsburg center) the main political and economic connection, and Prague, and even Budapest, looking in Berlin's direction. And if they were not looking to the regional powerhouse of Berlin, then they were looking even further west, to Brussels. Brussels had also been a Habsburg city, at one time, and it is true that there were many ways in which the Habsburg Monarchy's experience and history—as a "neo-medieval" quasi-pluralist, multinational and polyglot, supranational, quasi-federal empire-monarchy—had important parallels with, and lessons for, the newly forming European polity based in Brussels. This was, or at least should have been, a boon to study of the monarchy, and in certain respects, Vienna 1900, but this sort of understanding of the monarchy had little if anything to do with the Schorskean model, so the new European prominence of "Habsburg" Brussels did nothing for fin-de-siècle Vienna. Republic Austria, along with its capital, behaved in a manner appropriate to what it had become, just another small nation in the Union's membership—small fry, very prosperous and secure small fry, but still small fry, while the major action occurred elsewhere. Fin-de-siècle Vienna receded from the spotlight accordingly.

What finally led to fin-de-siècle Vienna's demise was not the consequences of the Waldheim Affair, the end of the Cold War, or the enlargement of Europe, but the profound changes that have taken place in our understandings of the modern world—of the very meaning of what it is to be modern—and the projection of these changed understandings back into the past. The reorientation that culminated in the 1980s of a turn to *post*-modernism appeared at the time to be a major reason for the popularity of fin-de-siècle Vienna; there was even talk in the celebratory mood of the mid-1980s that fin-de-siècle Vienna, as the site of a modernism that challenged Parisian orthodoxy and was based on the failure of (political) modernity rather than its success, had in fact presaged the rise of postmodernism. In the longer run, however, the idea of postmodernism proved rather a Trojan horse for the advocates of fin-de-siècle Vienna, because it fundamentally challenged the validity of the modernist culture on which the significance of fin-de-siècle Vienna was, ultimately, based. The very circumstance that it was at times impossible to distinguish between fin-de-siècle Vienna's modernism and postmodernism also pointed to major flaws in the whole conceptual basis of fin-de-siècle Vienna—and postmodernism.

In any case, the postmodern mood did not, in the end, last all that long, at least as a distinct movement. By the 1990s, with economic growth and the optimism of a post-Cold War world and the promise of a non-ideological "third way" in Western politics, Bill Clinton in the White House, Tony Blair in Downing Street, postmodernism was not so much cast aside as swept up in the emergence of what one might term "neomodernism." This meant that, instead of the end of the century being greeted with gloom and trepidation, it was seen positively as the birth of a new era. This was not good for a topic such as fin-de-siècle Vienna that had the sense of decline and ending in its very title. Hence, in the 1990s a renewed emphasis on the *positive* aspects of *Vienna 1900* appeared in the historiography of turn-of-the century Vienna (and Central Europe), challenging the image of decadence and retreat popularized by fin-de-siècle Vienna.

Contemporary developments and historiography conjoined in intriguing ways to undercut the fin-de-siècle Vienna model. The Freudian predominance over Western culture, and the model of *homo psychologicus* that underlay Schorske's definition of the modernist mentality in his fin-de-siècle Vienna paradigm, were increasingly compromised as Freud's psychoanalytic theory came under broad attack within the disciplines of psychology and psychiatry, and as economics, neoliberal economics, once again recaptured the high ground for a *homo economicus* that Schorske and his supporters had once regarded as long deceased. "It's the economy, stupid" was many things, and one of them was a rebuttal of the core tenets of fin-de-siècle Vienna. If Austria was important intellectually in the 1990s it was because of the political thought of Karl Popper with his concepts of open society and culture clash, and the economic theories of the Austrian School of von Mises and his disciple, Friedrich von Hayek (see Klausinger's essay in this volume). Hence, it was the *progressive* world of politically committed left-liberalism in Vienna 1900, which had produced Popper, not the world of aesthetic retreat, that now attracted attention, notably in the work of Malachi Hacohen. The fact that Popper had been fiercely anti-Freudian further compromised the reputation of what was basically a Freudian paradigm in fin-de-siècle Vienna.

Economic neoliberalism and its associated political neoliberalism (in Europe, neoconservatism in America) supplanted old-fashioned liberal and socialist economic models in the 1980s, and this success continued in many respects into the supposedly "third way" 1990s (which only moderately adjusted a neoliberal economics now accepted even by the leadership of the moderate left). Neoliberalism(neoconservatism)'s success brought into a different perspective another basic assumption of fin-de-siècle Vienna: the failure of liberalism, with subsidiary questions of the nature of liberalism's rationality, and the supposed "irrationalism" of its mass-political adversaries. The inconsistencies of Schorske's interpretation of rational liberalism's demise at the hands of irrational mass politics, especially Karl Lueger's Christian Social (anti-Semitic) Party, had received a thorough airing in

John Boyer's work, *Political Radicalism in Late Imperial Vienna*, as early as 1981. James Shedel, in his work *Art and Society*, also from 1981, had also pointed out that the Viennese bourgeoisie, especially the numerous element in the Habsburg bureaucracy, could not really be said to have been alienated from power in the way Schorske had suggested. He subsequently developed a cogent critique of this supposed crisis of Austrian liberalism by applying David Blackbourn and Geoff Eley's very influential criticisms of the analogous German concept of the *Sonderweg* to the Austrian case. As with Blackbourn and Eley, Shedel came to a much more positive conclusion about the political health of the bourgeoisie in Austria, and the success of the bourgeoisification of Austrian society, and, along with an increasing number of revisionist historians, began to see the Habsburg state before 1900, and indeed up to 1914, as a positive, progressive entity, reversing the received wisdom of the monarchy as decadent and doomed.

It was only in the *1990*s, however, that the full extent of the misinterpretation inherent in talk of a failure of liberalism in the *1890*s became evident. The work of Pieter Judson showed that political liberalism had not so much failed as shifted its bases of power and transformed into what had once been seen as its opposite, a form of mass politics: German nationalism. Liberal politicians might have lost their Viennese bastion to Lueger's Christian Socials, but in other centers, such as Graz and the industrial heartland of northern Bohemia, they remained a significant, even predominant factor. They did so, however, by developing the nationalist side of the logic of liberalism; according to Judson, liberals simply changed the criterion of their exclusionary logic from who is or is not rational, to who is or is not German. Interest in the nexus between liberalism and nationalism was greatly enhanced within Austria and among scholars of Austria by the rise of Jörg Haider's Freedom Party in Austria's domestic politics from the mid-1980s onward, until it achieved the status of second-largest party in the parliament in 1999's elections, and (junior) partner in the Schüssel coalition government of 2000. Judson's interpretation of the direct connection between the two put in a new light the apparently irrational transformation of a moderately progressive coalition partner of the Socialist Party in 1983-85 into a xenophobic, populist anti-establishment, charisma-fuelled politically far-right juggernaut, and made it seem almost a logical outcome of the particular tradition of Austrian liberalism.

The crisis that the black-blue coalition represented for the progressive left in Austria should have renewed interest in the topic, and explanatory framework, of fin-de-siècle Vienna. Here, after all, was the rational side of Austrian politics overcome by a bout of what appeared as completely irrationalist mass politics from the far right, with its enabler on the moderate (Catholic) right. The parallels with fin-de-siècle Vienna on one level were evident. The problem for fin-de-siècle Vienna was that it was now the heirs of Austrian political liberalism who were identified as being the main force of irrationalist mass politics in the country, and it was Austrian liberalism that had been identified, by respectable scholars, as the source of the German/Austrian nationalism now driving the FPÖ. Clearly, there was something about this that struck outside observers, and not a few Austrian intellectuals and politicians, as a bit odd: it all depended on a certain definition of "liberalism" that in other contexts was quite inappropriate. What about the cultural liberals, for instance, who had remained true to the first, rationalist, anationalist version of liberalism, both in 1895 and 1995? Was there not a difference between liberal forms of nationalism, and the more radical forms of nationalism that led to, among other things, anti-Semitism? How did, to go back to another critique of fin-de-siècle Vienna, the liberalism of Viennese Jews fit into this revisionist schema? Whatever one's view of this debate about the legacy of liberalism to Austria in the early twenty-first century, however, it seemed clear that the ideological and political waters had been more than sufficiently muddied to make the schema of fin-de-siècle Vienna no longer operative as an explanation of contemporary Austrian developments, and hence either suspect historiographically, or worse irrelevant.

By the mid-1990s, fin-de-siècle Vienna as a dominant paradigm in the study of Vienna 1900 was already looking in real trouble. The conference *Beyond Vienna 1900*, held in 1995 at the Center for Austrian Studies in Minneapolis (of which I was one of the organizers), showed both the centrality of the fin-de-siècle Vienna paradigm to the subject of Vienna (and Central Europe) 1900, and also the many ways in which the various components of that paradigm had come under criticism, and indeed refutation. Most of the problems with the topic outlined above were on display at the conference: the lack of adequate acknowledgement of the Jewish dimension to the cultural achievement; the ways in which the Central European context contradicted as much as confirmed the fin-de-siècle Vienna model; the way in which the topic of fin-de-siècle Vienna had ignored the positive aspects to both the political development and cultural production of Vienna around 1900; and the questioning of the assumptions underlying the "failure of liberalism" thesis. Fin-de-siècle Vienna as an explanatory model looked fairly ragged by the conference's conclusion; however, there remained a consensus that fin-de-siècle Vienna was the starting point of research into Vienna 1900, the foundation on which other research, critical though it may be, could support itself. By the time the proceedings of the conference were published, 2000, the ground had shifted yet further from under fin-de-siècle Vienna, so that its centrality in terms of research was no longer as generally accepted, and this process has only continued since.

The development of greater integration of the European Union, now including Austria and from 2004 (most of) the monarchy's successor states, was accompanied by a renewed appreciation for polyglot and multinational polities such as the monarchy, and the general trend in historical research into Austria-Hungary was to see the political, economic, and social developments there in ever more positive terms. Even the apparently illogical and functionally redundant aspects of the monarchy's dualist structure (to say nothing of the intricacies of governmental and political structures within the Austrian half) could be seen in a fresh light, given the Union's own "neo-medievalist" structures and her own continuing success despite (or because of?) these. The continuing process of restitution of cultural artefacts, which is still under way, led to an ever greater emphasis on research into the Jewish aspect to Viennese modern culture, even if it verged on the administrative.

One of the most interesting recent developments in research into Vienna 1900 has been an increased emphasis on the natural sciences. Fin-de-siècle Vienna had stressed the aesthetic and psychological character of Vienna 1900's achievement, and the expressionist backlash, but had, almost by definition, discounted the achievements of Viennese science. Austrians, whose postwar national self-image had emphasized Austria as a center of aesthetic culture, had been more than happy to go along with fin-de-siècle Vienna's confirmation of their national myth, but the fact of the matter was that Vienna, and Austrian universities and cities more generally, had also been a major participant in the scientific advances of the late nineteenth and early twentieth century, with many Nobel Prize winners and major scientific figures such as Ernst Mach and Ludwig Boltzmann. Before 1914, Vienna had been a pioneer in radiology and nuclear physics, for instance. This had long been known in theory, and a few dedicated researchers worked away, but the scientific world of Vienna 1900 had been left in the shadow of fin-de-siècle Vienna and it was only in the last ten years that a renewed effort to reclaim that heritage has been made, for instance in the restoration and commemoration of the Lieben Prize, and that major research on scientific topics, such as Deborah Coen's *Vienna in the Age of Uncertainty*, has appeared. Coen, too, framed her book as a refutation of yet more aspects of Schorske's fin-de-siècle Vienna, but there was a sense by now that this was flogging a dead horse, for most of what was valuable in Coen's account of the Exner family and its scientific achievements had not needed any reference to Schorske or fin-de-siècle Vienna at all, and her whole concept of probability as the underlying principle of Vienna 1900 was something quite divorced from fin-de-siècle Vienna. In such a context, with such a topic, fin-de-siècle Vienna was, if truth be told, no longer relevant.

The world had moved on. Just as the rise of China and India and the threat of Islamicist terrorism post-9/11 has in the last decade completely changed our perspective on world events, away from an Eurocentric, to a broader (and more balanced) view of global developments, so, historiographically, the once buzzing research community of and around fin-de-siècle Vienna grew ever less buzzing, ever quieter—fin-de-siècle Vienna found itself ever more in a byway rather than on the grand avenue it once had graced. Part of this had been the result of fin-de-siècle Vienna's own success—so much had been researched into and written about fin-de-siècle Vienna that there was little more to say, with even the middle-ranking research subjects "done." Even the extensive criticism of fin-de-siècle Vienna was, in its own way, a great compliment to the power of the original vision. It can still be said that, had not fin-de-siècle Vienna been constructed, then Vienna 1900 and Central Europe 1900 would not have received as much attention as they did, nor would research have had anything like the intellectual coherence that it ended up having, thanks to Schorske's paradigm. Some time in the last couple of years, however, things have become so quiet around the topic that it is time to recognize that all good things, even fin-de-siècle Vienna, come to an end—that it is, as a living topic, moribund.

This would not be reason for excessive mourning, if fin-de-siècle Vienna had left its relatives, the fields of Vienna 1900 and Central Europe 1900, with a rich and powerful legacy and in a strong and promising (intellectual and cultural-political) position. My fear is, however, that it has not. I am not sure that fin-de-siècle Vienna can itself be blamed for this. Some might claim that the very success of fin-de-siècle Vienna took attention away from other aspects of Vienna 1900, other explanatory models that, in the end, have proven more accurate and more cogent, and more relevant to what are now twenty-first century concerns. Disciples of the fin-de-siècle Vienna approach took the lead in exploring many aspects of Vienna and Central Europe 1900, but critics might object that the research tools they used and their methodology were not the best practices available, nor did they leave their fields in a sustainable condition once they had left. Fin-de-siècle Vienna, according to this view, has led to the mother lode of Vienna 1900 being mined out in ways that have left subsequent explorers with, as it were, conceptual hazards and methodologically fractured and damaged research faces. Fin-de-siècle Vienna's flaws as a paradigm have made rescuing the research agenda of Vienna 1900 almost impossible, while spoiling the quality of the vast research resources that it superficially discovered, and then only under false assumptions.

There is, I think, some truth to this. Had the Schorskean model been more accommodating to ethnic and national concerns, had its model of liberalism been more sophisticated, and its chosen explanatory mechanism of political alienation leading to cultural achievement been more supple, then it would not have broken down so relatively quickly, theoretically. On the other hand, it was the relatively pristine simplicity of fin-de-siècle Vienna's model that was one of its most attractive features, and its ideological suitability to its original context, in the late 1950s and early 1960s, that gave it its initial intellectual cogency, which was sustained and greatly developed in the next couple of decades, partly because the ideological context of the Cold War did not really change that much ("1968" notwithstanding). Had fin-de-siècle Vienna been what many *now* would have wanted it to be, as a historical topic, then it would probably never have achieved the popularity that it did *then*, and as such it would never have conveyed to Vienna 1900 the great significance that the "capital of the twentieth century" had achieved by the mid-1980s. One can be critical of where fin-de-siècle Vienna led research into Vienna 1900, but the fact remains that without fin-de-siècle Vienna, Vienna 1900 might never have become the academic research and cultural-intellectual magnet that it became.

Fin-de-siècle Vienna brought to Vienna 1900 an attention that is, for reasons inherent in Vienna 1900 rather than fin-de-siècle Vienna, difficult to sustain. Chief among Vienna 1900's problems as a self-sustaining focus of research and intellectual attention is that it was at the center of an empire, and a cultural network, that is no more. Instead, Vienna and Austria tend to be at the margins of attention, despite the end of the Cold War that divided Europe in two, or even because of it. As far as the related field of Central Europe 1900 goes, the end of the Cold War actually led to a *decrease* in American government funding of research by American scholars in the field, because the defeat of communism had ended the foreign-policy rationale for that funding. Just at the time when archives were opening up, and when all sorts of opportunities arose for increasing mutual understanding, funding was cut off. One might think that, in compensation, there might have been an increase in interest in Central Europe as a regained field of area studies and hence of historical studies as well, and there was some of this in the 1980s and 1990s, the founding of the Central

European University being a major beneficial factor here. Yet this was still not enough to make Central Europe a solid citizen, as it were, among the categories of American academia, and even when the "Central European" aspect was recognized, this was really only a relabeling of the region once called "Eastern Europe," or at best "East Central Europe"—in other words the former communist bloc—in which Vienna was not included.

Without the nimbus of fin-de-siècle Vienna, Vienna 1900 has suffered the fate of all centers of *former* empires, polities and networks generally, which is to be on the margin, or at best between other more compelling entities. Vienna 1900 might still be in the middle, between west and east, south and north, but it is no longer at the center of a significant region or network. It does not have the heft of Berlin, a center of German history and culture, or of Paris, still the center of French history and culture. French and German history are major recognized categories, whereas Austrian history remains a minor interest, and even Habsburg Austrian history remains undervalued, and has to compete against the national histories of all the other successor states—and their capitals. Ironically, the decline of the fin-de-siècle Vienna paradigm, partly due to the effects of the end of the Cold War, has led Vienna 1900 once more to the margin, even as contemporary Vienna has ceased to be on the margin of the West on the Iron Curtain and is now firmly embedded in Europe's middle.

Two other aspects of Vienna 1900, related to its supranational and imperial context, also militate against its academic attraction and popularity among the wider general public. As the imperial capital, and the center of an "Austrian," Central European culture that had competed with the national cultures of the various regional components of the empire, Vienna 1900 has remained a stepchild of the rest of the Central European area, which is more concerned, still, in focusing on the various national histories, and national cultures, or looking at those cultures' European or international connections, not those to the former imperial center. There have been over the last couple of decades various exceptions to this, with Cracovians, for instance, intent on strengthening ties to Vienna (partially as a counterweight to Warsaw), but generally these efforts to recall the ties to Vienna have not been all that much in evidence—outside of the various Austrian Cultural Forums in the region. As far as post-Cold War cultural connection goes, Europe has tended to out-trump (Viennocentric) Central Europe.

The other supranational characteristic of Vienna 1900, or Central Europe 1900 for that matter, which has, on balance, not worked in favor of its general popularity, has been the fact that so much of it was the product of the region's Jewish bourgeoisie. I have discussed above some of the reasons for the anxiety invoked when emphasizing the Jewish aspect of Vienna 1900, and the particular controversy surrounding this in connection with the Waldheim Affair. Beyond these considerations, however, lie more problems, to do with, yet again, definitions, this time of Austrian and Jewish identity. Even if Jews created or enabled most of the modern culture of Vienna 1900, it remains very problematic to say in any straightforward way what was actually "Jewish" about their participation (and hence the resulting culture). It is even problematic to talk about this in terms of being a supranational aspect of Vienna 1900, for, after all, were Jews not an ethnicity, and hence the Jewishness, far from being supranational might be regarded rather as *below* the national level, as a subculture? Jews actually, as a diasporic group, both spanned and were part of the national culture, were both within and beyond, their Jewish aspect acting both above and below the national level; and it is perhaps not happenstance that they were particularly influential in a supranational, multinational polity such as the Austro-Hungarian Monarchy.

Then again, many if not most of the Jews or individuals of Jewish descent who participated in modern culture in Vienna 1900 did not think of themselves as contributing to a *Jewish* culture but rather to a general, cosmopolitan modern culture, or, some of them, to German (Hungarian, Czech, Polish, etc.) national culture, or even to "Austrian" culture, however defined. Many of the survivors of this assimilationist group and their heirs, therefore, did not want this to be seen as a Jewish issue; many of those Jews who did accept the idea of there being a Jewish *national* culture rejected much of the Jewish side to Viennese modern culture precisely because of its cosmopolitan, non-national aspect. From a Zionist perspective, the modern culture of Vienna 1900 was not *really* Jewish, and hence not to be acknowledged positively. Even from the perspective of American and other diasporic Jews sympathetic to a secular Jewish culture, the modern culture of Vienna 1900 did not fit at all easily into prescribed canons of what was "Jewish culture." There were nevertheless many who did recognize the Jewishness of much of Vienna 1900, but they were mainly concentrated among the émigré generation, and that generation is, inevitably, passing on. In Vienna itself some in the small Jewish community have adopted the modern culture of Vienna 1900, quite intelligently, as their *Jewish* identity, but this group does not have the numbers to really make its voice heard on the larger stage. Squeezed between the ideological needs of assimilationism and Zionism, the embrace of the Jewish aspect to Vienna 1900 has been unable to find a large constituency, and this has worked to the detriment of the popularity of Vienna 1900 without its fin-de-siècle Vienna gloss. Vienna 1900, when seen as largely a product of Viennese and Habsburg Jewry, returns to the status of being, in Gustav Mahler's inimitable phrase, "*unerwünscht.*"

Had the nation state of which Vienna became the capital in 1955 (sic!) been willing to embrace the complex supranational, both cosmopolitan and multiethnic heritage of the modern culture of Vienna 1900, then these problems of "in-betweenness," imperial heritage and Jewishness might not have been problems but rather badges of honor, and points in favor of Vienna 1900's popularity and importance. But the Austrian Second Republic has generally not operated as heir to this grand tradition of the "Austrian idea" (or thereabouts), but rather as a small nation, either on the neutral edge between West and East, or within the European Union. There have been notable and honorable exceptions to this approach, most saliently in Kreisky's grand concept of Austrian foreign policy—perhaps the exception that proves the rule—and in advocates, such as Erhard Busek, of a special Central European role for Austria in the new Europe (as in the old Europe), but overall the "small-nationers" have tended to win out.

Concepts of a Central European role for Austria tend to have been confined to financial networks in the succession/accession states, or turning Vienna into a major transport hub, whether through Vienna's ritzy new airport or the new rail station currently under construction to provide Vienna, really for the first time, a *central* station rather than just a "*Wien Mitte.*" These are in themselves not to be scoffed at (and the sheer financial investment of Austrian banks in the former lands of the monarchy is indeed remarkable), but the small-nation mentality remains, I fear, dominant. There have been attempts to rekindle pride in Vienna 1900's scientific heritage, which almost by necessity was cosmopolitan, but ironically much of the initiative and funding for such efforts, such as the restoration of the Lieben Prize, came from Austrian Jews and wealthy Jewish émigrés, and have still to achieve major resonance among the Austrian public. The indications for even those aspects of research into the more "acceptable" aspects of the heritage of Vienna 1900 and Central Europe 1900, in the humanities, are not encouraging when the Austrian government decides, as it did recently, to zero out state financial assistance to all extra-university research institutes, such as the International Research Institute for Cultural Studies (IFK) that specialized in encouraging just this sort of research, or the Institute for the Human Sciences (IWM) that embraced a similar, more Central European, agenda. There will probably be some sort of Austrian fudge of this funding issue, but it is yet another sign that modern-day

Austria does not tend to "think big" enough about subjects such as "Vienna 1900," with the result that the latter is left in effect as a cultural-historical orphan, at best an unregarded, Cinderella-like stepchild, without the fin-de-siècle Vienna allure that could make pumpkins into carriages, and mice into dashing steeds.

The irony of this is that, whether within the realm of the history of ideas, or cultural history, or intellectual history, or transnational history, total history, modern European history, or whatever relevant academic discipline, the field of Vienna 1900 is ultimately of much greater significance than the topic of fin-de-siècle Vienna. Much like Cinderella, it really deserves a coach and horses, a beautiful ball gown, and glass slippers for that matter, but it has been kept from full recognition by the attention paid to the brilliance of fin-de-siècle Vienna, and the marginal/mediate character of Vienna 1900's situation described above.

Quite aside from fin-de-siècle Vienna, the culture and experience of Vienna 1900 remains remarkably relevant to contemporary affairs. In American politics alone, it is hard to understand anything going on in the current labyrinth of Internet myths, political lies, media gullibility, spin, and suggestibility of the uninformed, misinformed, confoxed, electorate, without reference to at least two major figures from Vienna: Karl Kraus, the Jon Stewart of Vienna 1900, and the "father of spin," Edward Louis Bernays, who, incidentally, was Freud's nephew twice over. Moreover, without the continued recognition of Vienna 1900 and its Central European partners as *at least* an alternative focus of the movements and developments that came together to give us our modern world, the old, monolithic, highly deceptive, and frankly rather boring narrative depicting Paris (and its American epigones) as the capital of twentieth-century modernism gets to be brought out again in such programs as *Paris: The Luminous Years*, with barely any irony, or acknowledgement that, in fact, Paris was only one of many centers, and, next to Vienna, in many aspects, not the most important.

The fact is that Vienna 1900 really was a very powerful center of modern culture and thought, partly because of the real crises in the political and social realm against which many members of its cultural and intellectual elite really were reacting (primarily as Jewish individuals threatened by the incipient totalitarianism of anti-Semitism), and partly because of the other side of this same coin: the very fact of Vienna's being such a center of marginality *and* mediation, paradoxical though that might seem. Against the relative simplicity of the almost Cartesian account that is the Parisian version of modernity and modernism, the Vienna-based version relies on, and demonstrates, the plural sources of modernism, and the fact that it was the role of connection between traditions, and between worldviews, between networks, that was Vienna's greatest asset, and its greatest achievement. Vienna 1900's apparent weaknesses as a subject of historical interest were actually the sources of its immense vivacity and strength as a center of intellectual and cultural innovation at the turn of the century. It was because it was a conduit between east and west, south and north that it attracted so many people from such disparate backgrounds who engaged in one of the greatest "culture clashes" the world had seen to that point, or certainly one of the most fruitful in modern times (if also one of the most fatal, as this was also Hitler's Vienna). Vienna 1900 also served as a supremely ambivalent capital to an empire and region dominated by questions of national and ethnic difference, and this transnational, multinational, supranational, and meta-national experience provided material for approaches to the problem of nationalism and pluralism in the modern world that we are still grappling with, not least in the spiritual successor to this Habsburg transnational model, which is, after all, the European Union. And finally, the group that did most to create this complex and diverse, pluralist and critical version of modern culture, was precisely the Viennese Jewry (and Central European Jewry) which is now, so tragically, largely missing from the scene. But the other side of the evil pursuit of purity that led to their genocide at German (and Austrian) hands, was the fact that they were at the heart of the pluralist and critical culture, which the monolithic, nationalist, and totalitarian versions of modernity could not tolerate. But it was precisely this critical-pluralist version of modernity that won out in the end, and, despite appearances, still dominates our modern world. We are, to that extent, still all children of Vienna 1900, whether we like it, or recognize it, or not.

The question, therefore, is not whether Vienna 1900 has lost its importance as a field—from the above it clearly has not. Instead, what we must pursue, in the wake of fin-de-siècle Vienna's demise, is the search for another "topic" or paradigm that can represent Vienna 1900 as effectively as fin-de-siècle Vienna once did. This is not a novel idea. Allan Janik was calling for a "new paradigm" for the study of Vienna 1900 back in 1995 (published in *Rethinking Vienna 1900* in 2000); nor is there a lack of models out there with which to work. Janik himself (with Stephen Toulmin) developed in *Wittgenstein's Vienna* a methodological model that, with all its reliance on the outdated assumptions of fin-de-siècle Vienna, is still extremely cogent and attractive. This is because it took Vienna only as part of its context, and traced out a whole web of connections and influences on Wittgenstein that went well beyond Vienna's or even the monarchy's

Sigmund Freud, around 1926 ©Austrian National Library

boundaries, concentrating instead on connections with the rest of the intellectual and cultural world. With appropriate adjustments to the socio-political context in which Wittgenstein was seen to operate, *Wittgenstein's Vienna* is as sound an introduction to the central intellectual achievements of Vienna 1900 now as it was in 1973.

Magris's model of a plural, diverse Danubian cultural world, the world of the other Europe that did not go the normal, Rhenish way to the western sea, and was suspended in a pre-national, quasi-feudal condition that encouraged insight into the complexities and irrationalities, the paradoxes and inconsistencies of life, also modern life, provides an attractive way into the subject at hand. Perhaps the most cogent conceptualization of this role of Vienna and its region as a meeting place of contrasting value systems, a site of both difference *and* mediation, is provided in Alfred Pfabigan's essay "Freud's 'Vienna Middle,'" a title that plays on the current, commuter railway station in central Vienna, *Wien Mitte*. It is the way in which Vienna 1900 was not so much central as mediatory that Pfabigan stresses, using the example of Freud's negotiation between Nietzschean irrationalism and the very rationalist, scientific method that Freud used in psychoanalysis to regulate and make consistent the grand but wild, untamed insights that Nietzsche and his followers had made concerning the unconscious, animalistic urges that drove human nature. Pfabigan's treatment of the case of Freud is intriguing and, I think, convincing, but even more intriguing is the concept of the "middle" that he has picked up on, because, with its sense of mediation, connection, but also, ironically, of lacking the certainty of centrality, missing a (national) norm against which all else is judged, and hence providing a space for relative and synthetic thinking, it echoes other recent (and subsequent) approaches to Vienna 1900, which emphasize it as the capital of the "age of uncertainty" (Deborah Coen), or of a "golden age of cultural exchange" (William M. Johnston), or as the site, with Budapest, of a "transnational, transterritorial, transethnic" "third culture" (Peter Weibel). Somewhere in this conglomeration of connection, mediation, uncertainty, and exchange a powerful new paradigm for Vienna 1900, a new topic, is waiting to be developed and presented to the world.

It will take someone with greater entrepreneurial flair than I in the world of the academic market of ideas to come up with the exact formula, but I think the way forward lies in seeing Vienna as the focal point of what might best be described, in the spirit of Magris's *Danube*, as the other Europe, or even the other modernity, where the normal, decisive, and certain logic of modernity, the "either/or" logic of the law of the excluded middle, never held sway, or at least not for long. Things were just too complex, too confused and conflated, appearance and reality too interdependent, loyalties and identities too divided and cross-cutting, for the normal, straightforward logic of being "one thing or the other" to operate effectively. Hence, Vienna became the focus of a world where the logic of the law of the included middle, of "not only... but also," "both... and" was the norm—a norm abnormal for modernity, but suited much better to human experience. This was a world in which the emphasis had to be on connections and relations, hence on language and its crisis, and on the diverse realities that lay behind the façade of holistic totality. This world consisted of the high ratiocinations of the Vienna Circle, and of the Schoenberg circle, but also the ready wit of the coffeehouse, and even the (convention-breaking) frivolity of the operetta world. Somewhere between the anti-metaphysical, pluralist empiricism of Otto Neurath and the acid, exposing satire of Karl Kraus, there lay a world of unflinching intellectual and cultural pursuit, a *critical* modernism, that challenged and upended the certain verities and unities both of tradition and of an overconfident and absolutizing modernity. That was why the world and culture of Vienna 1900 (1930) was felt to be so threatening by others that it had to be destroyed; but that is also why it had such a profound impact on the way we, in the pluralist, diverse and inclusive modern world, think—or at least should do if we were true to our values.

If this concept could be attractively packaged and presented, I think Vienna 1900's future would be bright, despite what I have said above. There is even evidence that many are already thinking along these lines, and perhaps my pessimism concerning Vienna 1900's post-fin-de-siècle Vienna career is misplaced. There have been at least two major exhibits (with conferences) on topics associated with Vienna 1900 in London alone in the last couple of years, on "Madness and Modernity" (2009) and "Vienna Café 1900" (2008). Perhaps Vienna 1900 is due for a comeback? A major art exhibition is set to open in Melbourne, Australia (with Christian Witt-Dörring and William M. Johnston as its guiding lights), and Vienna 1900's future is set to be the subject of a panel at the German Studies Association conference this year, as I noticed in the latter stages of completing this essay. The Chinese are even evincing new interest in Freud, as well as in the Vienna Circle. So perhaps all this is far too dark an account of fin-de-siècle Vienna's career, with far too negative a prediction as to Vienna 1900's future. I would like to think so, but I suspect that, from all the factors outlined above, a more positive outcome remains most unlikely. Whether there is yet life left in the research field of Vienna 1900, I am very unsure that it will ever be quite as viable, as vibrant as it was when represented by fin-de-siècle Vienna—but perhaps some new, post-postmodernist scholar can come up with a form of representing Vienna 1900 that at least does justice to its subject, and gives it the audience it deserves? Fin-de-siècle Vienna might have passed on, but let us at least hope that future historiography of Vienna 1900 will record that there was still life beyond fin-de-siècle Vienna.

Select Bibliography

Barea, Ilsa. *Vienna*. New York: Knopf, 1966.

Bassett, Richard. *Waldheim and Austria*. London: Penguin, 1988.

Beller, Steven. *Vienna and the Jews, 1867-1938: A Cultural History*. Cambridge: Cambridge University Press, 1989.

Beller, Steven, ed. *Rethinking Vienna 1900*. Oxford: Berghahn, 2001.

Beller, Steven. "The Tragic Carnival: Austrian Culture in the First World War." In *European Culture in the Great War: The Arts, Entertainment, and Propaganda, 1914-1918*, edited by Aviel Roshwald and Richard Stites, 127-61. Cambridge: Cambridge University Press, 1999.

Beller, Steven, and Frank Trommler, eds. *New German Critique* 93 (Fall 2004): Austrian Writers Confront the Past.

Boyer, John W. *Political Radicalism in Late Imperial Vienna, 1848-1897*. Chicago: University of Chicago Press, 1981.

Boyer, John W. *Culture and Political Crisis in Vienna, 1897-1918*. Chicago: University of Chicago Press, 1995.

Broch, Hermann. *Hugo von Hofmannsthal and his Times*, trans. Michael S. Steinberg. Chicago: University of Chicago Press, 1984.

Bukey, Evan Burr. *Hitler's Austria: Popular Sentiment in the Nazi Era, 1938-1945*. Chapel Hill: University of North Carolina Press, 2000.

Bunzl, Matti. *Symptoms of Modernity: Jews and Queers in Late Twentieth-Century Vienna*. Berkeley: University of California Press, 2004.

Busek, Erhard, and Emil Brix. *Projekt Mitteleuropa*. Vienna: Ueberreuter, 1986.

Clair, Jean, ed. *Vienne 1880-1938: L'Apocalypse Joyeuse*. Paris: Centre Pompidou, 1986.

Clare, George. *Last Waltz in Vienna*. London: Macmillan, 1981.

Coen, Deborah R. *Vienna in the Age of Uncertainty: Science, Liberalism, and Private Life*. Chicago: University of Chicago Press, 2007.

Cohen, Gary B. *Education and Middle-Class Society in Imperial Austria, 1848-1918*. West Lafayette: Purdue University Press, 1996.

Cohen, Gary B. "Nationalist Politics and the Dynamics of State and Civil Society in the Habsburg Monarchy, 1867-1914." In *Central European History* 40, no. 2 (2007): 241-78.

Cornwall, Mark, ed. *The Last Years of Austria-Hungary: A Multi-National Experiment in Early Twentieth-Century Europe*. Exeter: University of Exeter Press, 2002.

Czernin, Hubertus. *Die Fälschung*, 2 vols. Vienna: Czernin, 1999.

Deák, István. *Beyond Nationalism: A Social and Political History of the Habsburg Officer Corps, 1848-1918*. Oxford: Oxford University Press, 1990.

Edinburgh International Festival 1983: Complete Programme Guide. Edinburgh, 1983.

Field, Frank. *The Last Days of Mankind: Karl Kraus and his Vienna*. London: Macmillan, 1967.

Good, David F. *The Economic Rise of the Habsburg Empire, 1750-1914*. Berkeley: University of California Press, 1984.

Gubser, Mike. *Time's Visible Surface: Alois Riegl and the Discourse on History and Temporality in Fin-de-Siècle Vienna*. Detroit: Wayne State University Press, 2006.

Hacohen, Malachi Haim. *Karl Popper: The Formative Years, 1902-1945*. Cambridge: Cambridge University Press, 2000.

Hamann, Brigitte. *Hitler's Vienna: A Dictator's Apprenticeship*. Oxford: Oxford University Press, 1999.

Höbelt, Lothar. *Defiant Populist: Jörg Haider and the Politics of Austria*. West Lafayette: Purdue University Press, 2003.

Ingrao, Charles W., ed. *Austrian History Yearbook* 28 (1997): Forum: New Views of Fin-de-Siècle Vienna, 273-92.

Ingrao, Charles W., ed. *Austrian History Yearbook* 33 (2002): Forum: The Other Modernisms, 141-238.

Janik, Allan, and Stephen E. Toulmin, *Wittgenstein's Vienna*. New York: Simon & Schuster, 1973.

Jászi, Oscar. *The Dissolution of the Habsburg Monarchy*. Chicago: University of Chicago Press, 1929.

Johnson, Lonnie. *Central Europe: Enemies, Neighbors, Friends*. Oxford: Oxford University Press, 1996.

Johnston, William M. *The Austrian Mind: An Intellectual and Social History, 1848-1938*. Berkeley: University of California Press, 1972.

Judson, Pieter M. *Exclusive Revolutionaries: Liberal Politics, Social Experience, and National Identity in the Austrian Empire, 1848-1914*. Ann Arbor: University of Michigan Press, 1996.

King, Jeremy. *Budweisers into Czechs and Germans: A Local History of Bohemian Politics, 1848-1948*. Princeton: Princeton University Press, 2002.

Le Rider, Jacques. *Modernity and Crises of Identity: Culture and Society in Fin-de-Siècle Vienna*. New York: Continuum, 1993.

Luft, David S. *Eros and Inwardness in Vienna: Weininger, Musil, Doderer*. Chicago: University of Chicago Press, 2003.

Luft, David S. *Robert Musil and the Crisis of European Culture, 1880-1942*. Berkeley: University of California Press, 1980.

Magris, Claudio. *Danube*, trans. Patrick Creagh. London: Collins Harvill, 1989.

Marchetti, Maria, ed. *Le Arti a Vienna*. Milan: Mazzotta, 1984 [Catalogue to Venice Biennale].

McCagg, William O. *A History of Habsburg Jews, 1670-1918*. Bloomington: Indiana University Press, 1989.

McGrath, William J. *Dionysian Art and Populist Politics in Austria*. New Haven: Yale University Press, 1974.

McGrath, William J. *Freud's Discovery of Psychoanalysis: The Politics of Hysteria*. Ithaca: Cornell University Press, 1986.

Mitten, Richard. *The Politics of Antisemitic Prejudice: The Waldheim Phenomenon in Austria*. Boulder: Westview Press, 1992.

Okey, Robin. *The Habsburg Monarchy: From Enlightenment to Eclipse*. New York: St. Martin's Press, 2001.

Oxaal, Ivaar, Michael Pollak, and Gerhard Botz, eds. *Jews, Antisemitism and Culture in Vienna*. London: Routledge & Kegan Paul, 1987.

Pauley, Bruce F. *From Prejudice to Persecution: A History of Austrian Anti-Semitism*. Chapel Hill: University of North Carolina Press, 1992.

Pelinka, Anton. *Austria: Out of the Shadow of the Past*. Boulder: Westview Press, 1998.

Pick, Hella. *Guilty Victim: Austria from the Holocaust to Haider*. London: I.B. Tauris, 2000.

Pollak, Michael. *Vienne 1900: Une Identité Blessée*. Paris: Gallimard, 1984.

Powell, Nicholas. *The Sacred Spring: Arts in Vienna, 1898-1918*. London: Studio Vista, 1974.

Pulzer, Peter. *The Rise of Political Anti-Semitism in Germany and Austria*, rev. ed. London: Peter Halban, 1988.

Pynsent, Robert, ed. *Decadence and Innovation: Austria-Hungary in the Fin-de-Siècle*. London: Weidenfeld & Nicolson, 1989.

Reifowitz, Ian. *Imagining an Austrian Nation: Joseph Samuel Bloch and the Search for a Supraethnic Austrian Identity, 1846-1918*. Boulder: East European Monographs, 2003.

Robertson, Ritchie, and Edward Timms, eds. *The Habsburg Legacy: National Identity in Historical Perspective*. Edinburgh: Edinburgh University Press, 1994.

Schnitzler, Arthur. *The Road to the Open*. Evanston: Northwestern University Press, 1991.

Schorske, Carl E. *Fin-de-Siècle Vienna: Politics and Culture*. London: Weidenfeld & Nicolson, 1980.

Schorske, Carl E. "A Life of Learning." In *Recasting America: Culture and Politics in the Age of Cold War*, edited by Lary May, 93-103. Chicago: University of Chicago Press, 1989.

Schorske, Carl E. *Thinking with History: Explorations in the Passage to Modernism*. Princeton: Princeton University Press, 1998.

Shedel, James. *Art and Society: The New Art Movement in Vienna, 1897-1914*. Palo Alto: SPOSS, 1981.

Singer, Peter. *Pushing Time Away: My Grandfather and the Tragedy of Jewish Vienna*. New York: Harper Collins, 2003.

Sked, Alan. *The Decline and Fall of the Habsburg Empire, 1815-1918*. London: Longman, 1989.

Snowman, Daniel. *The Hitler Emigrés: The Cultural Impact on Britain of Refugees from Nazism*. London: Chatto & Windus, 2002.

Spiel, Hilde. *Vienna's Golden Autumn, 1866-1938*. London: Weidenfeld & Nicolson, 1987.

Stadler, Friedrich. *The Vienna Circle: Studies in the Origins, Development, and Influence of Logical Empiricism*. Vienna: Springer, 2001.

Steinberg, Michael P. "Fin-de-Siècle Vienna" Ten Years Later: "Viel Traum, Wenig Wirklichkeit." In *Austrian History Yearbook* 22 (1991): 151-62.

Steiner, George. *Language and Silence: Essays on Language, Literature, and the Inhuman*. London: Macmillan, 1967.

Steiner, George. "Le Langage et l'Inhumain." In *Revue d'esthétique* 9 (1985): 65-70.

Stone, Norman. *Europe Transformed, 1878-1919*. Glasgow: Fontana, 1983.

Timms, Edward. *Karl Kraus: Apocalyptic Satirist*, 2 vols. New Haven: Yale University Press, 1986, 2005.

Varnedoe, Kirk. *Vienna 1900: Art, Architecture, and Design*. New York: Museum of Modern Art, 1986.

Vergo, Peter. *Art in Vienna, 1898-1918*. Oxford: Phaidon, 1981.

Vergo, Peter, ed. *Vienna 1900: Vienna, Scotland, and the European Avant-Garde*. Edinburgh: National Museum of Antiquaries of Scotland, 1983.

Waissenberger, Robert, ed. *Wien 1870-1930: Traum und Wirklichkeit*. Vienna: Residenz, 1985.

Weibel, Peter, ed. *Beyond Art: A Third Culture*. Vienna: Springer, 2005.

Wistrich, Robert S. *The Jews of Vienna in the Age of Franz Joseph*. Oxford: Oxford University Press, 1989.

Ideology and Politics in the State that Nobody Wanted: Austro-Marxism, Austrofascism, and the First Austrian Republic

Tim Kirk

> By the beginning of the next week it was all over, except for the Government's vengeance on its prisoners. The workers were made to fly the white flag. The Engels Hof was renamed the Dollfuss Hof. Every man over eighteen from the Schlinger Hof was in prison, including the sick and the cripples. Terrorism became economical, since a new law stopped the unemployment pay of those who had been arrested. Meanwhile Frau Dollfuss went among the workers' families, distributing cakes. [...]
>
> One evening, while we were having supper in a restaurant a man named Patterson came to our table. He was a journalist, who did a movie gossip-column for one of the daily papers [...] a breezy stupid thick-skinned person, whose curiosity knew no inhibitions: in fact he was very well suited to his job.
>
> "Well Mr Bergmann," he began heartily, with the fatal instinct of the very tactless, "what do you think of Austria?"
>
> Christopher Isherwood, *Prater Violet*

Christopher Isherwood's short book about an Austrian film director in England who follows with increasing fury the depressing news from

Vienna during the coup d'état of 1934 is less well known than his books about Berlin—just as the political upheavals in Austria are less well known than those that brought down the Weimar Republic. Although Austria-Hungary was a great European power, whose political affairs and cultural achievements were reported across the world, the defeat and dismemberment of the empire had reduced Austria to a country scarcely larger than Scotland, just one among many successor states in Central Europe demanding the attention of the diplomats, politicians, and the international press. Nevertheless, the world's interest in Austria did not stop abruptly in 1918. The collapse of the monarchy itself was described by a contemporary "without fear of exaggeration as the biggest purely *political* event of its kind in the whole history of modern Europe."[1] The mass strikes and revolutions that accompanied the collapse of the empire were extensively reported, as were the successive economic and political crises that afflicted Austria in the 1920s and 1930s. Despite the loss of its imperial hinterland, Vienna remained one of the largest and most cosmopolitan cities in Europe, and many of the intellectuals and artists of "fin-de-siècle" Vienna who have attracted so much attention from cultural historians continued to live and work there in the 1920s. The city itself, much admired abroad before the war for its achievements in urban planning, continued to attract attention as "red Vienna," a model of municipal socialism that brought social justice to its citizens in the face of formidable opposition—and also balanced the books.[2]

In Austria itself the history of the First Republic has frequently been reduced to the story of a brief and doomed democratic interlude between the moribund authoritarianism of the Habsburg Empire and the destruction of parliamentary democracy at the hands of fascist movements domestic and foreign. In short, it has been a negative yardstick against which to measure the relative economic success and political stability of the more fortunate Second Republic, and in this respect it echoes in many ways the kind of fatalistic historiography associated with the Weimar Germany. Yet despite the undeniable problems it faced, the achievements of the First Republic were considerable, and its creative potential was enormous, as more recent approaches to its history have shown.[3] Outside Austria there have been relatively few serious general studies either of the history of the First Republic itself or of the competing ideologies that shaped its political landscape.[4] This essay is concerned both with the origins and nature of Austro-Marxism and "Austrofascism" and their role in the political development and demise of the republic, and with the place of both as political movements in the broader political history of Europe from the emergence of popular politics in the late nineteenth century to the Second World War.

The Origins of Austro-Marxism

The roots of Austro-Marxism are both long and broad. It developed as an identifiable school of political thought during the last decades of the empire, and its origins are associated with the intellectual fecundity of late imperial Vienna although it has rarely featured much in the many cultural histories of the Viennese fin de siècle. Its essence was famously summed up by Otto Bauer in an article in the *Arbeiter-Zeitung* in 1927. The essay was written in response to attempts by the right to distinguish Austrian social democracy as a "particularly malign form of socialism," more radical and dangerous than the Social Democratic parties of Western Europe. But it provided the opportunity for a potted history and an explanation. The term was first used, Bauer wrote, by an American socialist (albeit one from a Russian-Jewish background), Louis Boudin, in 1907. It was used in the years before the First World War—its real heyday—to describe "a group of young Austrian comrades active in scholarly research [...] the best known among them being Max Adler, Karl Renner, Rudolf Hilferding, Gustav Eckstein, Otto Bauer, and Friedrich Adler."[5] Renner, Hilferding, and Max Adler had been friends at Vienna University, where they had studied under Carl Grünberg, the later founder of the Frankfurt Institute for Social Research. They were at once the "chief theoreticians of Austrian social democracy," and its future political leaders; and they were also much like many another such "circles" in Vienna at the turn of the century: a small tightly knit group of like-minded friends with a range of interests in philosophy, political economy, social thought, and the law who met at the *Café Central*. They were particularly associated with the educational association "*Zukunft*" (founded in 1903) and engaged with contemporary issues in the *Marx-Studien* launched in 1904, and in the daily and periodical press of the Social Democratic Workers' Party (SDAP), notably *Arbeiter-Zeitung* and *Der Kampf*.[6]

Austro-Marxism took shape at a propitious time both in the development of Marxism and in the history of the Habsburg Empire. In a series of interventions during the 1890s Eduard Bernstein's revisionism had challenged many of the basic assumptions of orthodox Marxism, opening up divisions in the international labor movement which have never been fully healed. On the basis of his own observations of contemporary society, Bernstein had concluded that the working class was not becoming increasingly impoverished as Marx had expected; that the revolution was by no means inevitable; and that the German Social Democratic movement should therefore work as a party of progressive reform within existing political structures in order to ameliorate the working and living conditions of the working class. In many ways this was a welcome development to intellectuals in the party. They wanted to establish within Marxist thought a scholarly framework of ideas capable of engaging systematically with new intellectual developments, and this meant locating Marxism itself in a broader European intellectual tradition, accepting that it was a product of its time, and that its precepts needed to be revisited as circumstances changed. But it was also a problematic development for the Austrian SDAP, as it was for labor parties across Europe. The party, which had only recently emerged from years of political persecution, had achieved a fragile unity between moderates and radicals, which its leader, Victor Adler, was anxious to preserve. The result was a compromise of a kind that was to define the identity of Austrian social democracy: its program retained much that was orthodox, while its political practice presented the party with a number of practical reasons to work for reform within the existing political order.

The first was the opportunity in 1905 to work with the state for the introduction of universal manhood suffrage, and then for Social Democrats to enter parliament when the new legislation was applied in the election of 1907. Another was the problem of nationalism. The relationship between the nation and the state was the most pressing political issue in Europe during the last decades before the First World War, and nowhere more so than in Austria-Hungary, where the pressure from nationalism threatened to blow the state apart. In the age of the nation state the Habsburg Empire looked increasingly like an anachronism, despite the fact that other major powers such as Russia, the U.S., and imperial Britain and France scarcely matched up to the ideal type. Moreover, the increasingly authoritarian racism of many nationalists in Central and Eastern Europe was fueling pressure to think of the nation in terms of ethnic homogeneity, an impossibility within the existing structures of the empire. The problem here was less the need to depart from Marxist orthodoxy, than to address an issue that had been largely neglected by Marx and Engels. Elsewhere in Europe the national question was postponed until the advent of socialism; in Austria the issue was more pressing.

Karl Renner tackled the subject in early pamphlets at the turn of the century, and challenged the assumption that the achievement of national statehood was a necessary stage on the road to socialism.[7] Instead, he had suggested the principle of "non-territorial national autonomy," where national groups would organize as juridical entities independently of the specific territory they inhabited, like members of different religious confessions. This solution was—and is—a controversial one that challenges received ideas about the indivisible authority of the nation state and the requirement of sovereign territory for the fulfillment of national self-determination.[8] Renner's focus was on a workable constitutional and legal framework which would resolve the conflicts generated by the nationalist movements, and he argued that the empire should be democratically transformed into a "*Nationalitätenstaat*," a concept that was anathema to the nationalist right.[9] For many pragmatic and self-interested reasons social democracy was to become one of the "centripetal" forces working to hold the Habsburg state together during its final years, and was referred to facetiously by its enemies as "*K.K. Sozialdemokratie*."[10]

Otto Bauer's major work, arguably the most sophisticated Marxist treatment of the nationalities problem, was published in 1907, just as universal male suffrage was introduced in Cisleithania and the Social Democrats, the only genuinely supranational party in Austria, entered the Reichsrat as the largest party.[11] Bauer agreed with Renner, at least initially, that the national principle should not be based on territory. He set out to redefine what is meant by a nation debunking several existing theories, including the racist theories of the contemporary radical right. Although he used the term "national character" himself, he rejected ahistorical notions of a mysterious national soul that supposedly embodied the essence of nation and lasted endured forever. For Bauer, national character was a social construct, determined in part by the physical evolution of a population, and in part by the transmission and consolidation of a national culture, but above all changing over time in response to changing circumstances.[12]

Although Bauer's work was a response to the specific conditions of the Habsburg Empire and questions facing the Austrian Social Democratic Party, it also had implications beyond that immediate context. Lenin and Stalin were particularly critical, fearing the possibility of pressure from the nationalities in the Russian Empire for a federalization of the Russian Social Democratic Labor Party (RSDLP). Social Democratic support for national self-determination was correct, but they thought that the national-cultural autonomy for which Renner and Bauer argued would promote the fragmentation of the party along national lines (as had undeniably happened in the Austrian party during the early twentieth century). Lenin judged the concept of "cultural-national autonomy" to be akin with "ideals of the nationalist petty bourgeoisie."[13] Stalin visited Lenin in Krakow at the end of December 1912, and then went on to Vienna in January 1913, where he

Otto Bauer, around 1925 ©Austrian National Library

wrote most of his own work on *The National Question and Social Democracy*. He argued that it was no business of socialists to promote nationalism and, taking his (unacknowledged) cue from Kautsky, defined the nation in terms of language, territory, and economy. Although he criticized Bauer's "psychological" definition, he also added "national character" to the list of his own criteria for nationhood. After the Russian revolution the nationalities problem in the USSR was addressed through the creation of national republics and autonomous regions, which suffered from the same problem as the successor states of interwar East Central Europe in that they contained within them further national minorities requiring extra-territorial national-cultural autonomy.[14]

Austro-Marxism and the Austrian Revolution

For Austria, of course, the First World War changed everything. The strength of Slav nationalism prompted Bauer to part company with Renner on the national question and advocate political independence for the nationalities. Renner supported the idea of domestic truce (*Burgfrieden*) throughout the war and published his ideas in *Marxismus, Krieg und*

Internationale in 1917, which was badly received by those who had been seeking to reestablish international links between the labor movements of the belligerents. The party avoided the split experienced by the German SPD, but it was from this point that the left dominated.

Defeat, revolution, and the collapse of the state presented Austrian Social Democrats with new and urgent problems in a context where the only certainty seemed to be continual change. In November 1918, Karl Renner found himself presiding over the provisional government of a German-Austrian rump state, and had to confront a very practical aspect of the nationalities problem: a contested border. As he complained to his colleagues in the council of ministers, it was impossible to govern without even knowing where the frontiers of the state were, and with Czech policemen entering the German-speaking towns and villages of Bohemia and Moravia, ousting the German-speaking authorities and claiming the territory for the newly created *Nationalitätenstaat* of Czechoslovakia.[15] The question was now no longer about the position of minorities in a multinational empire, but about the right of Austria's Germans to national self-determination and union with the Reich.

The SDAP emerged as the dominant political force at the end of the war and continued to avoid the damaging rift of the kind suffered by organized labor in other parts of Europe. The Communist Party (KPÖ), founded in November 1918, attracted little support and the Social Democrats' participation in the grand coalition of 1918-20 ensured the passage of important constitutional and welfare legislation that effectively implemented long-standing party policies. The "incompleteness" of the revolution, however, which ushered in radical political and constitutional changes but left social and economic relations virtually unchanged, posed practical and theoretical problems, not least the question of what actually constituted democracy.[16] Plans to socialize the economy through state control of the means of production were stillborn in the face of Christian Social and German National opposition, and there was a great deal of communist agitation to resolve the issue by moving from parliamentary democracy to a councils system. In the context of widespread shortages of food and heating fuel, it was feared that this was a solution which might attract a following.

The decision of the party leadership to stay with "bourgeois democracy" was emphatic.[17] Russian peasants felt themselves to be proletarian, Bauer maintained in a speech to the party congress in 1918, but Austrian peasants considered themselves bourgeois; a councils system would have no support in the countryside, and attempting to impose it would probably lead to civil war.[18] So the commitment to working with "bourgeois democracy" was reinforced by an acute awareness of the possibility of a counter-revolution from the provinces. Party leaders were also mindful of the country's dependence on both Western capital and the goodwill of the Entente, and they were right to be concerned. Writing from Berne in April 1919, Lord Acton painted lurid portraits of the leading Social Democrats in Vienna, basing his views on memoranda from "persons who are well acquainted with the situation in Austria and Hungary." Bauer himself was presented as an extremist, whose early release from Russian captivity raised suspicions that he was "deliberately sent back to Austria on a Bolshcvistic mission." Similarly, Julius Deutsch was depicted as "a fanatical Social Democrat," and the *Volkswehr* as numerically weak and morally unsound, its power in Vienna a result only of its possession of the arsenal and all the ammunition and "made up of men who wish to live in luxury without having to work, and in consequence possesses no moral courage nor stamina." According to Acton, a thousand picked soldiers, preferably British, "would strike terror into the hearts of the Volkswehr and put an end to the present intolerable situation."[19] So, while affirming its solidarity with the "heroic Russian Proletariat," and condemning the white terror in Hungary (and the Entente machinations behind it), the party congress of 1919 noted that "German Austrian social democracy is not in a position to employ the same methods of struggle as the Russian Soviet Republic."[20] Nevertheless, Bauer complained in a letter to Karl Kautsky in January 1920 that the Christian Social Party was sabotaging all the coalition's work, and that the *Länder* simply refused to obey Vienna.[21] It came as something of a relief when the party was more or less compelled to bring to an end its uneasy collaboration with the bourgeoisie after the election of that year.

If the revolution presented the Social Democrats with unexpected opportunities and challenges, it also presented Austro-Marxism with new theoretical problems. Bauer wrote in 1927 that war and revolution had "dissolved the 'Austro-Marxist' school."[22] The new circumstances, and in particular the messy reality of an unanticipated and unfinished revolution, required an explanation. Bauer sought to explain the effective stalling of the revolution in terms of a political stalemate in which class forces were evenly balanced, and the state effectively a neutral agency.[23] Although the working class had demonstrated its strength and had been able to make political gains, he reasoned, its economic weakness prevented any further progress; and even if workers were to assert themselves against the Austrian bourgeoisie, the country's dependence on international capital was enough to prevent any decisive action. But, as Raimund Loew has argued, the Entente was not really in a position to act against the threat of Bolshevik revolution in Central Europe, despite the intervention in Hungary: Bauer and his colleagues had independently rejected the Bolshevik model as inappropriate for Austria and made a positive choice in favor of parliamentary democracy, a choice he ultimately ascribes to a "fatalistic" determinism in the Austro-Marxist interpretation of Marxism and history, and one which was to make resistance to fascism impossible.[24]

Counter-Revolution and Fascism

The emergence of fascism as a new and distinctive form of politics prompted a range of explanations and strategies from Marxists across Europe, from the variety of self-contradictory assessments made by Gramsci in 1921 to the rigidities of the official Stalinist line.[25] The prototype Italian movement had emerged from the gangs of thugs hired by local farmers and businessmen to protect their interests, and similar movements had sprung up across Central and Eastern Europe, including Austria, as part of a broader counter-revolutionary reaction to the events of 1918. The legitimacy of the republic and its constitution was by no means universally accepted, and among the dispossessed elites of the collapsing monarchy and right-wing intellectuals there was at least ambivalence and often outright hostility to democracy. Tensions were heightened by the installation of radical "Soviet" regimes in neighboring Hungary and Bavaria, and the expectation of a similar radicalization in Vienna. As the old Austrian army disintegrated in the aftermath of defeat, there was a real need for improvised self-defense against foreign incursions, particularly along the Yugoslav border with Styria and Carinthia, and a perceived need for defense against plunder by the retreating soldiers making their way through Austria to homes in the successor state. A law of 1918 permitted local armed formations to guard against looters, which were then "formed in most places under various names: Bürgerwehr, Stadtwehr, Ortswehr, Bauernwehr, Einwohnerwehr, Heimwehr, Volkswehr &c. These formations comprised citizens of all classes and opinions."[26] But in the conservative provinces there was also considerable hostility to the new republic's socialist-dominated army, the *Volkswehr*, combined with a determination to resist the anticipated depredations of the "socialist" state, which was trying to organize supplies from a reluctant countryside to feed the starving towns and cities.[27]

The memoirs of the future Heimwehr leader, Prince Ernst Rüdiger von Starhemberg, provide an insight into the way many on the right sized up the postwar situation: Both citizens and property were at risk from marauding gangs, which the disorganized republican state and its weak security forces were unable or unwilling to control:

> Discipline had broken down. Everyone was hungry, and the rations officially distributed from improvised food kitchens were all too meagre. Hence the frequent plundering of wayside farms. There were [...] looting expeditions by townsfolk, whom hunger and privation, the future Heimwehr leader whom hunger and privation made susceptible to the influence of anarchist agitators. The new republic's security police were barely organised, and were, anyhow, too few to protect village property. To that end peasants, farmers' sons and agricultural labourers banded themselves together into a local guard, called "Feld- und Flurwache" (rural defence force).[28]

Similar combat units formed throughout the Austrian provinces, the most radical being the *Frontkämpfervereinigung* (Veterans' Association) in Vienna and eastern Austria. Cross-frontier links were very quickly established to coordinate counter-revolutionary activity in what has been called a "transnational theater of paramilitary ultra-violence" in which, despite recruitment from the peasantry, activists often tended to constitute "a fairly homogenous transnational milieu of predominantly middle- and upper-class political radicals characterized by youth and war-induced militancy" (although not all were old enough to have seen active service).[29] Vienna was the haunt of Hungarian refugees from the "Soviet" regime of Béla Kun, and there were strong links between the *Heimwehren* and the radical right in Germany, especially with the Bavarians. The Escherich organization (*Orgesch*) supplied the Tyrolean and Upper Austrian units with arms, while refugees from the Kapp putsch and the Hitler putsch found shelter in Austria.[30]

The early Heimwehr was a sporadic and fragmented force for counter-revolution, counted by its socialist counterpart, the Republican Defense League, a formation under centralized authority created out of the workers' guards in 1923. The Heimwehr was transformed into a mass movement with its own ambitions for political power by the events of 1927 and the drawn-out political crisis they unleashed: the murder of civilians by *Frontkämpfer* in the village of Schattendorf in the Burgenland in January; the acquittal of the murderers in Vienna in July; and the subsequent riot by socialist workers which culminated in the burning down of the Palace of Justice and the government's security forces opening fire on unarmed civilians. At home the government increasingly came to see the Heimwehr as an ally against the socialists and saw to it that its organizational structure was tightened up and its links with the army and the police were strengthened. Abroad, it received support both from the Horthy regime in Hungary and, increasingly, from Mussolini's fascist regime in Italy.[31]

The ascendancy of the Heimwehr also needs to be seen in the context of a hardening of anti-democratic attitudes on the Austrian right during the 1920s, and particularly within the broad church of political Catholicism.[32] The Christian Social Party engaged directly in democratic politics while Catholic intellectuals promoted more authoritarian solutions, ranging from Othmar Spann's sustained critique of liberalism, published as *Der wahre Staat* (1921) and inculcated in generations of students at Vienna University, to the concept of "true democracy" espoused by Ignaz Seipel, the most influential and powerful Austrian politician of the period.[33] That such voices ultimately prevailed was, like many other ostensibly Austrian developments, the consequence of a broader European pattern of radicalization and susceptibility to authoritarianism in European Catholic politics.[34]

Pressure mounted for an authoritarian revision of the constitution, which was partly met by the constitutional reforms of 1929, but intensified during the economic crisis of the following years. The political conditions and sequence of events that prepared the way for the Dollfuss dictatorship are both well documented: the emergence of the Heimwehr as an independent electoral force encroaching on Christian Social constituencies in the provinces; the open espousal of fascist ideology by Heimwehr leaders at Korneuburg, followed by the failed "*Pfrimer-Putsch*" in Styria in 1931; the dismissal of parliament on a procedural pretext in 1933; and then, finally, the armed suppression of the labor movement by government security forces and the promulgation of a new, arguably fascist constitution a year later.[35]

It would be invidious to dwell again here on whether the Dollfuss-Schuschnigg regime per se constituted a fascist dictatorship or not, and it is clear that the controversy around naming it has as much to do with post-1945 political sensibilities as it does with the nature of the regime itself. Suffice it to say that it was at least a coalition of authoritarian conservative and fascist elements, and that it is by no means clear that all of the fascism in the mix was accounted for by the Heimwehr.[36] More importantly, for the purposes of this debate, is what the relationship of Austrofascism was to the wider world, and what impact it had. The term "clerical fascism" is useful in this context. It was used by contemporaries on the left and, although it has been a contentious term, has since been used sporadically by historians.[37] The tone was set for clerical fascisms across Europe by the papal encyclicals *Rerum novarum* (1891) and *Quadragesimo Anno*: the first a belated coming to terms, following years of denial during the pontificate of Pius IX with the realities of industrial modernity; the second a restatement forty years on of the essential principles from the politically assertive Vatican of the interwar years.[38] *Rerum novarum* and the Catholic social teaching that followed upon it was essentially a critique of capitalism and democracy that suggested corporatist alternatives to the inevitability of class conflict. It reflected an influential body of conservative social thought then current in Catholic Europe, including Austria, and its assumptions would have underpinned the moral and political education of many of the political leaders who established clerical dictatorships in the 1930s.

Corporatism was the political leitmotif of Austrofascism from the slogans at Korneuburg to the pious programmatic statements of the *Ständestaat*. "We reject western democratic parliamentarianism and the party state!" Steidle had proclaimed in 1931. He went on: "We are determined to put into its place the self-government of the Estates and a strong leadership which develops, not from the representatives of the parties, but from leading personalities of the large Estates. [...] We are fighting against the subversion of our nation by the Marxist class struggle and the shaping of the economy by liberal capitalism."[39] These points neatly encapsulate the importance of corporatism to radical right-wing regimes across Europe, whether they were expressed in the language of "*Volksgemeinschaft*" or of "corporations." They also explain the apparent contradiction of fascism's antipathy to both "Bolshevism" and "plutocracy": The concern was with the baneful effect of "class struggle" on the life of the national community, whether institutionalized in "bourgeois" parliamentary democracy or enshrined in workers' rights, trades unions, and social welfare. The ostensible "anti-conservatism" of the radical right was largely hostility to "business conservatism" (i.e. economic liberalism), and this was as prominent a part of the outlook of Austrofascism as of comparable regimes.[40]

Corporatism was prominent in the ideology, propaganda, and self-representation of the regime, but did the dictatorship of Dollfuss and Schuschnigg actually function as a "Christian corporate state"? The formal institutions of the state were comprehensively reformed and "estates" replaced parliament and local councils. Opposition parties were suppressed and the Fatherland Front was created as an organization that would transcend sectional interest and class conflict. In reality, however, these institutions were hollow, and it is significant that the majority of legislation passed between 1934 and 1938 was implemented by means of the same War Economy Enabling Act that had been used to circumvent parliamentary authority before the coup.[41] Similarly, the Fatherland Front could never be a convincing mass movement: The regime had swept to power on a surge of unpopularity; real political vitality was demonstrated only by the illegal Nazi movement; and Austria's political weather was being made increasingly in Berlin rather than Vienna. The regime's attempts to create a new sense of Austrian national identity, distinct from the people's ethnic and cultural German identity, had only very limited success, just as attempts to fashion a convincingly Austrian "style" in art found it difficult to escape from the pervasiveness of modernism.[42]

Austrian Ideologies and the Wider World

Austro-Marxism and Austrofascism, along with their organizations (the SDAP, the Heimwehr movement, and the Dollfuss-Schuschnigg regime), dominated the history of the First Austrian Republic to the extent that it became a battleground between them for political control, and the events of 1934 fictionalized by Isherwood mark the point at which the latter prevailed. This history and this relationship brings the two political phenomena together, but otherwise it is difficult to compare them.

Austro-Marxism, whether one refers to the body of theoretical work or its manifestation in the Austrian party and its associational life was an integral part of the broader international labor movement and of the intellectual history of Marxism. Much of its impact was felt in Austria itself, but Bauer's work on the nationalities problem, and perhaps even more Hilferding's treatise on imperialism, had far-reaching international significance, and both went on to occupy ministerial positions (Hilferding in Germany). Its attempt after the First World War to evolve an institutional home in an effort at conciliation between the Second and Third Internationals (the proposed *Arbeitsgemeinschaft sozialistischer Parteien*) earned it the sobriquet "two-and-a-half International." Although it was an experiment that soon petered out and the Austrians rejoined the mainstream as Social Democratic Party, it did give Austro-Marxism a distinctive international role and reputation.[43] It was the identity of Austro-Marxism as a third way between Stalinism and reformism that attracted attention after the war at a time of Cold War détente and "Eurocommunism." Collections of documents, monographs, and scholarly articles were published in English, French, German, and Italian, conferences were held and there were special issues of journals.[44] Most of the attention was positive, but not entirely uncritical either in Austria itself or abroad.[45]

Austrofascism, on the other hand, has been the ideology that dare not speak its name, and to that extent it has frequently (but not always) been used as an approximate cover term for a number of disparate phenomena, and as a result the controversies around its definition show no signs of abating. This is of course part of a more general problem with the definition of fascism, which veers between rigid "objective" typologies and subjective mentalities. However it is applied, whether to "Heimwehr fascism," the "corporate state," or the diffuse ideology uniting the two, it cannot be said to have had the same kind of impact either within or beyond Austria. The dictatorship itself achieved little that was positive or enduring, and has often seemed an interlude characterized by a loss of initiative on the part of Austria's ruling class that culminated in the Nazi takeover. While it was very much part of broader political developments in interwar Europe, it was subordinate to more powerful external influences rather than a generator of influential original thinking or action. Its gestation was assisted by material support and ideological influence from outside, above all Italy and Hungary, but also the Vatican, and in that respect it was not dissimilar to fascist movements and authoritarian regimes in other small European states of the interwar years. There was little specific interest in this particular Austrian experiment from the outside world, except for a flurry of interest from Catholic intellectuals—not least in Ireland, where parliamentary government continued, but the ideology of corporatism was not without resonance.[46] The "martyrdom" of Dollfuss at the hands of Nazi assassins has ensured a certain kind of sympathetic treatment abroad, but there was for a long time very little critical or scholarly literature outside Austria. Similarly, the demise of Austria's independence at the hands of the Nazis has prompted many to see the foregoing dictatorship as the lesser evil.[47] If there has been a revival of interest more recently in Austrofascism it has come only in Austria itself for the most part, and much later than for Austro-Marxism, not least because it was a taboo subject for many years.[48]

It is worth returning in conclusion to an earlier point. Isherwood's novella notwithstanding, attention was deflected away from Austria for much of the First Republic, and on the whole only the crises and conflicts were reported abroad. This has distorted our understanding of interwar Austria, both in the democratic period and under the dictatorship. The First Republic was a positive and progressive stage in Austria's political and cultural development, and although its potential was thwarted, its history deserves fuller attention.

Notes

1. R. W. Seton-Watson, "Austria and Her Neighbours," *Slavonic and East European Review* 13, no. 39 (1935): 549.

2. Helmut Gruber, *Red Vienna: Experiment in Working-Class Culture 1919-1934* (Oxford:

Oxford University Press, 1991); and Jill Lewis, "Red Vienna: Socialism in One City 1918-1927," *European Studies Review* 13 (1983): 335-55.

3. See, for example, Helmut Konrad and Wolfgang Maderthaner, eds., *Das Werden der Ersten Republik ...der Rest ist Österreich*, 2 vols. (Vienna: Carl Gerold's Sohn, 2008).

4. Charles Gulick, *Austria from Habsburg to Hitler*, 2 vols. (Berkeley: University of California Press, 1948) remains unmatched in terms of scale and range. F. L Carsten, *The First Austrian Republic 1918-1938: A Study Based on British and Austrian Documents* (Aldershot: Gower, 1986) is a manageable scholarly overview in English (and much of volume two comprises lengthy analyses of first Austro-Marxism and "clerical-fascism"). Tom Bottomore and Patrick Goode, eds., *Austro-Marxism* (Oxford: Oxford University Press, 1978) provides an anthology of excerpts from the work of leading Austrian Marxists. Günter Bischof, Anton Pelinka, and Alexander Lassner, eds., *The Dollfuss/Schuschnigg Era in Austria: A Reassessment*, Contemporary Austrian Studies 11 (New Brunswick: Transaction, 2003) in this series provides the most recent overview of "Austrofascism" in English. Norbert Leser, *Zwischen Reformismus und Bolschewismus: Der Austromarxismus als Theorie und Praxis* (Vienna: Europa Verlag, 1968) provides a wide-ranging account of Austro-Marxism in German; and the revised edition of Emmerich Tálos and Wolfgang Neugebauer, eds., *Austrofaschismus: Politik—Ökonomie—Kultur 1933-1938*, 5th ed. (Vienna: Lit, 2005) provides the most recent and wide-ranging collection of material on Austrofascism in German.

5. Otto Bauer, "What is Austro-Marxism," in Bottomore and Goode, eds., *Austro-Marxism*, (Oxford: Clarendon Press, 1978), 45. The term was rarely used after the war. See also Paul Pasteur, *Pratiques politiques et militants de la social-démocratie autrichienne 1888-1934* (Paris: Belin, 2003), 66.

6. See Leszek Kolakowski, *Main Currents of Marxism*, vol. 2, *The Golden Age* (Oxford: Clarendon Press, 1978), 240-43; Bottomore and Goode, eds., *Austro-Marxism*, 8-15.

7. Synopticus, *Staat und Nation* (Vienna, 1899) and Rudolf Springer, *Der Kampf der österreichischen Nationen um den Staat* (Vienna, 1902), cited in Norbert Leser, "Austro-Marxism: A Reappraisal," *Journal of Contemporary History* 11, nos. 2-3 (1976): 133-48. See also Günther Sandner, "Austromarxismus und Multikulturalismus: Karl Renner und Otto Bauer zur Nationalitätenfrage im Habsburgerstaat," published by Kakanien Revisited, <www.kakanien.ac.at/beitr/fallstudie/GSandner1.pdf>.

8. Ephraim Nimni, "Nationalist Multiculturalism in Late Imperial Austria as a Critique of Contemporary Liberalism: The Case of Bauer and Renner," *Journal of Political Ideologies* 4, no. 3 (1999): 297-99.

9. Bottomore and Goode, eds., *Austro-Marxism*, 31. Nationalist ideologues on the right disparaged the "*Nationalitätenstaaten*" that emerged in East Central Europe after 1918. See Herbert Scurla, *Die Dritte Front: Geistige Grundlagen des Propagandakrieges der Westmächte* (Berlin: Herbert Stubenrauch, 1940), cited in Tim Kirk, "Deutsche Kulturpolitik und öffentliche Meinung in Südosteuropa: Die Wiener Presse- und Kulturberichte Südosteuropas," in *"Mitteleuropa" und "Südosteuropa" als Planungsraum: Wirtschafts- und kulturpolitische Expertisen im Zeitalter der Weltkriege*, ed. Carola Sachse (Göttingen: Wallstein, 2010), 202.

10. See Oscar Jaszi, *The Dissolution of the Habsburg Monarchy* (Chicago: University of Chicago Press, 1961), 177-85. Jaszi's famous analysis of the problems of the last years of Austria-Hungary was first published in English in 1929. Gulick, *Austria from Habsburg to Hitler*, 1370.

11. Otto Bauer, *Die Nationalitätenfrage und die Sozialdemokratie* (Vienna, 1907); translated as Otto Bauer, *The Question of Nationalities and Social Democracy*, edited with an introduction by Ephraim J. Nimmi and translated by Joseph O'Donnell (Minneapolis: University of Minnesota Press, 2000).

12. The discussion of these points is lengthy and in some respects now seems very outdated:

Bauer, *The Question of Nationalities and Social Democracy*, 19-36. See also the very different summaries of Bauer's position in Kolakowski, *Main Currents of Marxism*, vol. 2, 285-90, where it is located in a history of Marxist thought; and Nimmi's introduction to the English translation, *The Question of Nationalities and Social Democracy*, xv-xlv, which explicitly avoids discussion of the book's position in Marxist ideology to concentrate on its contemporary applicability.

13. Raimund Loew, "The Politics of Austro-Marxism," *New Left Review* I/118 (1979): 22.

14. See Robert C. Tucker, *Stalin: A Revolutionary 1879-1929: A Study in History and Personality* (London: Chatto and Windus, 1974), 150-57; and Terry Martin, *The Affirmative Action Empire: Nations and Nationalism in the Soviet Union, 1923-1939* (Ithaca: Cornell University Press, 2001), 32. I am grateful to my colleague David Saunders for drawing these references to my attention.

15. Archiv der Republik, Ministerratsprotokolle, Nov. 1918.

16. See Andrew Arato, "Austromarxism and the Theory of Democracy," in *The Austrian Socialist Experiment: Social Democracy and Austromarxism, 1918-1934*, ed. Anson Rabinbach (Boulder: Westview Press, 1985), 135-40.

17. Leser, *Zwischen Reformismus und Bolschewismus*, 296-300.

18. *Stenographisches Protokoll des Parteitages der sozialdemokratischen Arbeiterpartei,* 31 Oct. to 1 Nov. 1918, 110-12, cited in F. L. Carsten, *Revolution in Central Europe 1918-1919* (Aldershot: Wildwood House, 1988), 31-32

19. Memorandum from Lord Acton to Earl Curzon, 12 Apr. 1919, BDFA II F 1 Doc 8, 8-9.

20. Resolutions passed at the Congress of the Social Democratic Party of German Austria. Inclosure in letter from Mr. Lindley to Lord Curzon, Vienna, 7 Nov. 1919. British Documents on Foreign Affairs, Part II, Series F, Vol. 1, Central Europe 1919-1922, Doc 21 [150809], 33-34.

21. Carsten, *Revolution in Central Europe*, 302.

22. Bauer, "What is Austro-Marxism," 46.

23. Otto Bauer, *Die österreichische Revolution* (Vienna: Wiener Volksbuchhandlung, 1923), translated as *The Austrian Revolution* (London: Leonard Parsons, 1925).

24. Loew, "The Politics of Austro-Marxism."

25. See David Beetham, *Marxists in the Face of Fascism* (Manchester: Manchester University Press, 1983).

26. Report by Colonel de Ligny, French officer of the Inter-Allied Control Commission. Inclosure in letter from Mr. Lindsay to Earl Curzon, 11 Jan. 1921. British Documents on Foreign Affairs, Part II, Series F, Vol. 1, Central Europe 1919-1922, Doc 146 [C 1168/716/3].

27. Ludwig Jedlicka, "The Austrian Heimwehr," *Journal of Contemporary History* 1, no. 1 (1966): 127-44; Bruce Pauley, *Hahnenschwanz und Hakenkreuz: Steirischer Heimatschutz und österreichischer Nationalsozialismus 1918-1934* (Vienna: Europa Verlag, 1972), 33-46.

28. Ernst Rüdiger Starhemberg, *Between Hitler and Mussolini: Memoirs of Ernst Rüdiger Prince Starhemberg: Former Vice Chancellor of Austria* (London: Hodder and Stoughton, 1942).

29. Robert Gerwarth, "The Central European Counter-Revolution: Paramilitary Violence in Germany, Austria and Hungary after the Great War," *Past & Present* 200, no. 1 (2008): 170-80. On the peasantry and the Heimwehr, see the review article by Franziska Schneeberger, "Heimwehr und Bauern—Ein Mythos," *Zeitgeschichte* 16, no. 4 (1989): 135-45.

30. Gerwarth, "The Central European Counter-Revolution," 183-84; Jedlicka, "The Austrian Heimwehr," 129-30; and Ludger Rape, *Die österreichischen Heimwehren und die bayerische Rechte 1920-1923* (Vienna: Europa Verlag, 1977).

31. See Lajos Kerekes, *Abenddämmerung einer Demokratie: Mussolini, Gömbös und die Heimwehr* (Vienna: Europa Verlag, 1966) on the role of Hungary and Italy in the destruction of Austrian democracy.

32. See Helmut Wohnout, *Regierungsdiktatur oder Ständeparlament: Gesetzgebung im autoritären Österreich* (Vienna: Böhlau, 1993), 20-23.

33. See John Haag, "Marginal Men and the Dream of the Reich: Eight Austrian National-Catholic Intellectuals," in *Who were the Fascists? Social Roots of European Fascism*, ed. Stein Ugelvik Larsen, Bernt Hagtvet, and Jan Petter Myklebust (Bergen: Universitetsforlaget, 1980), 239-48; Robert Stöger, "Der christliche Führer und die 'wahre Demokratie': Zu den Demokratiekonzeptionen von Ignaz Seipel," *Archiv* 2 (1988): 54-67; and Wohnout, *Regierungsdiktatur oder Ständeparlament*, 24-32.

34. Martin Conway, *Catholic Politics in Europe 1918-1945* (London: Routledge, 1997), 47-77 (esp. 48).

35. Emmerich Tálos and Walter Manoschek, "Zum Konstituierungsprozeß des Austrofaschismus," in *Austrofaschismus*, ed. Tálos and Neugebauer, 7-25; and Carsten, *The First Austrian Republic 1918-1938*, 151-78.

36. See the brief survey of then available assessments in Karl R. Stadler, *Austria* (London: Ernest Benn, 1971), 126. He reminds us that Nolte's *Faschismus in seiner Epoche* distinguished between "Heimwehr fascism" and the "Austrofascism of Dollfuss," and that Carsten, while hesitating to designate the "corporate state" fascist, used the term "clerico-fascist" to describe a number of regimes, from Portugal and Austria to Slovakia.

37. Gulick, *Austria from Habsburg to Hitler*, 1403-570; Klaus-Jörg Siegfried, *Klerikalfaschismus: Zur Entstehung und sozialen Funktion des Dollfußregimes in Österreich: Ein Beitrag zur Faschismusdiskussion* (Frankfurt: Peter Lang, 1979); more recently: Robert Pyrah, "Enacting Encyclicals? Cultural Politics and 'Clerical Fascism' in Austria, 1933-1938," in *Clerical Fascism in Interwar Europe*, ed. Matthew Feldmann and Marius Turda (London: Routledge, 2008), 158-70.

38. Wohnout, *Regierungsdiktatur oder Ständeparlament*, 44-56.

39. Cited in F. L. Carsten, *Fascist Movements in Austria from Schönerer to Hitler* (London: Sage, 1977), 172.

40. Diamant makes a telling point about the tendency of Western observers that expect an identification of conservatives with an anti-state intervention, business-friendly ideology, whereas continental European conservatism was often "étatiste." Alfred Diamant, "Austrian Catholics and the First Republic, 1918-1934: A Study in Anti-Democratic Thought," *Western Political Quarterly* 10, no. 3 (1957): 606.

41. Wohnout, *Regierungsdiktatur oder Ständeparlament*, 305-20.

42. See, for example, Margarethe Lasinger, "Wie modern war doch die Biedermeierzeit: 'die pause' und andere Kulturzeitschriften im Ständestaat," in *Kunst und Diktatur: Architektur, Bildhauerei und Malerei in Österreich, Deutschland, Italien und der Sowjetunion 1922-1956*, vol. 1, ed. Jan Tabor (Baden: Grasl, 1994), 260-74.

43. Adolf Sturmthal, "Austromarxism on the International Scene," in *The Austrian Socialist Experiment*, ed. Rabinbach, 177-85; Leser, "Austro-Marxism," 136-37.

44. For example Bottomore and Goode, eds., *Austro-Marxism*; Yvon Bourdet, *Otto Bauer et la révolution* (Paris, 1968); Hans-Jörg Sandkühler, *Austromarxismus: Texte zu Ideologie und Klassenkampf von Otto Bauer* (Frankfurt: Europäische Verlagsanstalt, 1970).

45. See, for example, Raimund Löw, Siegfried Mattl, and Alfred Pfabigan, *Der Austromarxismus: Eine Autopsie: Drei Studien* (Frankfurt: isp-Verlag, 1986); Loew, "The Politics of Austro-Marxism";

and Pasteur, *Pratiques politiques et militants de la social-démocratie autrichienne*, 66-70.

46. See, for example, the apologia for the dictatorship by Brendan Lawler, "Dollfuss and his work," *Studies: An Irish Quarterly Review* 26, no. 101 (1937): 78-88.

47. J. D. Gregory, *Dollfuss and his Times* (London: Hutchinson, 1935); and Gordon Brook Shepherd, *Dollfuss* (London: Macmillan, 1961). The theme of Dollfuss biographies is dealt with by Lucile Dreidemy, "Dollfuß-Biographien: Zwischen Mythos und Geschichte," unpublished paper presented at the German Studies Association, Washington, 2009.

48. Tálos and Neugebauer, eds., *Austrofaschismus* has reset the agenda in this respect. An earlier volume in the *Contemporary Austrian Studies* series has taken the issue outside Austria: Bischof, Pelinka, and Lassner, eds., *The Dollfuss/Schuschnigg Era in Austria* (see especially Tim Kirk, "Fascism and Austrofascism"). See also Florian Weininger, "Fascism or Authoritarian Rule? The Representation of the Dollfuss-Schuschnigg Regime in U.S. Historiography," unpublished paper presented at the German Studies Association, Washington, 2009. A version of this paper and that of Lucile Dreidemy will be published in Ilse Reiter-Zatloukal, Christiane Rothländer, and Pia Schölnberger, eds., *Österreich 1933-1938: Juristisch-historische Bestandsaufnahmen und Perspektiven* (forthcoming).

The Austrian School of Economics and its Global Impact

Hansjoerg Klausinger

In the twentieth century economic science has witnessed—in a truly Kuhnian manner—a series of scientific revolutions and correspondingly the ascent and decline of various paradigms. Heroes were proclaimed and as time went by exposed as villains. The era after World War II that once seemed certain to be remembered as "The Age of Keynes" turned, with the advent of stagflation and the specter of zero growth, into an "Age of Schumpeter," and with the eventual breakdown of the centrally planned economies into an "Age of Hayek"—leaving the present audience in speculation how the future post-crisis era will be called. In any case, two of the patrons of these ages were economists of Austrian origin, indicating the importance of the Austrian contribution to current economic thought, the topic to which the following shall turn.

Being an Austrian Economist

When speaking about the Austrian contribution to Western culture and civilization, it has been usual not to take too narrow a view by relying on the location of birth or on citizenship, but to count as "Austrians" those whose major works were produced or shaped by their specific experiences in Austria. In this vein, the species of being an "Austrian economist" will be broadly defined, too. Furthermore, taking account of the advantage of a longer-term perspective in judging the merit and influence of the work of individual economists, we will concentrate on the impact of the "old"

Austrian economists, most of them now defunct. Thus, at the danger of committing grave injustice towards the presently living and to those of the second half of the twentieth century this survey will focus on the cohort of Austrian economists born at the turn of the century and many of them living up almost to its end.

All this being said, it will come as no surprise that the main object of the following investigation will be the Austrian economics community of the interwar period, in the ambit of the Austrian School of Economics, and its contributions in shaping the evolving mainstream view of economics in the twentieth century.

To begin with we have to introduce the Austrian School and its representatives.[1] The school had been founded by Carl Menger (1840–1921) and its teachings spread by his two most famous disciples, Friedrich Wieser (1851–1926) and Eugen Böhm-Bawerk (1851–1914). The distinct characteristics of the Austrian School consisted in its subjectivist explanation of value, derived from the individuals' imputation of utility to quantities of goods, its view of the economy as guided via markets and prices by consumer sovereignty, and the foundation of capital theory on the time structure of production. In the interwar period the school was represented by its third and fourth generation. Among the older ones, Ludwig Mises (1881–1973) stood out as the leader. He extended the Austrian approach to a monetary economy, pointing to the intimate relation between money, inflation and crisis;[2] notably, over the years the type of liberalism that he advocated became ever more radical. Of the younger generation the most well-known today, due to Nobel Prize fame, is Friedrich August Hayek (1899–1992), besides his less glamorous colleagues, Gottfried Haberler (1900–1995) and Fritz Machlup (1902–1983), who also started their careers as eminent economists from interwar Vienna.

At some distance from the above-mentioned core members of the Austrian School, Vienna was also the home of economists who regarded themselves (and were regarded in turn) outside the school, although some were closely affiliated, personally and institutionally, to it. Preeminent among these, and of the same generation like Mises, was Joseph Schumpeter (1883–1950). Of the younger, the most important was Oskar Morgenstern (1902–1977), who despite his close ties to the core Austrians, having succeeded Hayek as the director of the Austrian Institute for Business Cycle Research, increasingly tried to differentiate his scientific position from that of the followers of Mises. In this regard, he associated himself with the positivist philosophers of the Schlick *Kreis* and, still more importantly, with the mathematicians that participated in the famous Menger *Kolloquium*.

Friedrich A. Hayek, around 1930 ©Austrian National Library

This loose group, led by Karl Menger (1902–1985), the son of the school's founder, which included also Abraham Wald (1902–1950) and, as a regular guest, the Hungarian John (Janos) von Neumann (1903–1957), proved pivotal in developing a new formalized approach to economic theory, which paved the way for the rise of general equilibrium theory and the theory of games.

To complete the picture, mention shall also be made of strands of thought within the Austrian economics community of the interwar period distinct from and opposed to the Austrian School. These ranged from Austro-Marxism, with its well-known representatives Otto Bauer and Karl Renner, over adherents to romanticism and Catholic Social Teaching that advocated the ideal of a "corporate state," to the universalism of Othmar Spann, the most radical critic of liberalism, socialism and democracy. None of them left permanent marks on the mainstream of economic thought and therefore they will be neglected in the following. Yet, besides, we should not forget that among the younger students at the University of Vienna and also among Morgenstern's collaborators at the Institute there were some that should make a name as profound economists or historians, like Josef Steindl, Kurt Rothschild and Alexander Gerschenkron.

Looking at the biographies of nearly all the eminent Austrian economists just mentioned, a striking common feature is their emigration during the 1930s so that the careers pursued and the successes accomplished by them belonged to an Austrian economics community in exile.[3] Specifically, Mises left Vienna in 1934 for Geneva, then immigrated to the United States in 1940. Hayek wrote his major works in Great Britain, as professor at the London School of Economics, 1931–1950, and then as a member of the University of Chicago. Machlup immigrated to the United States in 1935 and taught first at the University of Buffalo and later on at the renowned Princeton University. Haberler was in Geneva working for the League of Nations before he became professor at Harvard University 1936, where he remained for the rest of his life. Schumpeter had already left Vienna for Bonn in 1925, after his debacles both in Austrian politics and in the Vienna banking business, and in 1932 accepted the invitation to an economics chair from Harvard. Morgenstern persisted in his activities as the Institute's director and as a policy advisor to the Austrian government until he abandoned his efforts and accepted a visiting professorship of an American university shortly before the Anschluss. Karl Menger had left Austria in 1937 for the University of Notre Dame, whereas Wald, a stateless, Romanian-born Jew, escaped from Austria just at the last moment, and continued his work as a statistician at Columbia University. Thus, in some way, the immigration of these Austrian economists to Great Britain and the United States preceded (and certainly contributed to) the transformation of economics into a science dominated by the Anglo-Saxon countries, and in this sense emigration proved conducive to the global impact of the Austrian School.

Yet although we shall see that in the longer term the Austrian economists made a vital difference to the future evolution of economics, in the short term the Austrian School did not survive emigration, at least not as a homogeneous body of thought. Although the core members of the school remained true to their Austrian beliefs, some of them amalgamated their teachings with what was to become the neoclassical mainstream. In contrast, Mises proved uncompromising and assembled a small number of disciples, which for some time—before the neo-Austrian renaissance in the United States—experienced the dire existence of a kind of sect dispersed in the fringes of the mainstream. The members of the Austrian School were also all but purged from the academic scene in Austria after the Anschluss, and after the war it never recovered from the loss of intellectual capital drained away by emigration.[4]

The Controversies of the 1930s

In the 1930s and beyond, the fate of the Austrian School was determined by its involvement in a series of controversies, in all of which—as it appeared to contemporary observers—it was on the losing side, its old-fashioned opinions and prejudices being swept away by the progress of modern economics.[5] This section will focus on these controversies—on the nature of capital, on money and the cycle, and on economic calculation—before the next will show how the Austrian approach returned with a vengeance as a critique of the postwar mainstream.

The most arcane of these controversies centered on the nature of capital and the specifically Austrian approach derived from Böhm-Bawerk.[6] Put shortly, the dispute was on whether the capital structure of an economy, that is, the ensemble of capital goods in relation to the output produced, is to be represented by the time it takes to transform, say, the services of labor into a consumption good, or by a stock of capital in relation to output, where both can be reduced to a homogeneous fund, a sum of purchasing power. The insight inherent in the Austrian view is that even in a stationary setting, when the economic process is just replicating itself over time, inputs into the productive process must precede outputs in time, and therefore the maintenance of capital cannot be taken for granted. In effect, at any point of time a portion of output has to be spared to replace worn-out capital goods and thereby safeguard future production. Capital consumption, capital equipment shrinking due to excessive consumption, might thus arise from ill-guided actions of the economic subjects (or from economic policy). The Austrians accused their opponents, in contrast, to treat the capital stock as if it were permanent of itself.[7] However, in the whole debate the main deficiency of both approaches escaped the attention of the participants, namely the difficult and in some sense indeed insoluble problem to consistently reduce the diversity of the existing ensemble of capital goods to a single number, be it interpreted as a time period or as a fund. Presently, the narrow limits under which such a valid aggregation of capital can be performed are well-known, although often disregarded in the practice of research.[8]

The controversy on money and the cause of business cycles and crises was more of a sensation as it was topical—in the face of the Great Depression of the 1930s—as well as personalized as a clash between Hayek and the British economist John Maynard Keynes.[9] Drawing on Mises' business cycle theory, Hayek propagated the thesis of inflation as the origin of crisis and depression. Accordingly, the excessive creation of money and credit is responsible for generating an unsustainable capital structure of the economy in the upswing ("overinvestment" or "malinvestment") that must be scrapped in the crisis. Capital consumption and a lack of saving characterize the crisis and the depression, so that the crucial problem does not lie in a deficiency of purchasing power but in its distribution being incompatible with the capital structure created in the boom. The Keynesian diagnosis was much simpler: Depressions and unemployment are associated with a deficiency of effective demand in relation to the productive capacity corresponding to full employment. Typically, such effective demand failures indicate "underconsumption" or "oversaving," or put differently too low a level of investment activity (possibly due to a lack of "animal spirits" among entrepreneurs or to an excessive preference for holding wealth in liquid form). So, evidently, the conflicting approaches proposed contradictory diagnoses for the depression—"overconsumption" versus "underconsumption"—and also diametrically opposed therapies: Hayek advocated austerity and monetary restriction, whereas the Keynesian solution favored expansionist policies on all accounts. At the onset of the Great Depression both approaches were considered as on an equal footing, yet the experience of deflation and the stubborn rejection by Hayek and his followers of any anti-deflationist policies made the Austrian soon a minority position, with little support by public and educated opinion.

The most fundamental of the three controversies dealt with the issue of socialist economic calculation and thereby with the comparison of the economic systems of capitalism and socialism.[10] Mises first formulated the question—How is economic calculation, and thus the rational disposition over resources, possible in a socialist commonwealth, without money, markets and prices?—and answered it in the negative.[11] He argued that the lack of information and incentives that in a market system money prices do provide makes economic calculation impossible. The defenders of socialism and a planned economy countered Mises' impossibility thesis by pointing out that the most highly developed theoretical system for the explanation of the market economy—Walrasian general equilibrium theory[12]—demonstrated the formal similarity of capitalism and socialism. The state of general equilibrium, taken to be descriptive of a market economy, is determined by the solution of a system of equations, each one representing the balance between demand and supply in the market for a specific good or productive service. Then, given these equations (and the data of the individual consumers and producers from which demand and supply derive), the central planner could just find and implement this solution and thus overcome the problem of calculation (this has been called the "mathematical solution" to the calculation problem). Although such a solution was not considered feasible in these times, this might change in the future due to the advances in mathematics (and what was to become computer sciences), and anyway the argument established that rational disposition in socialism was not a logically contradictory notion. Another counter-argument was proposed by adherents to "market socialism." Accordingly, state-owned firms only need to be instructed to mimic the behavior of profit-maximizing producers, when confronted with prices set by a central planning board, and then by a process of trial and error—not dissimilar to that of "tatonnement" that Walras had imagined to be effective in a market economy—would arrive at a consistent (that is, general equilibrium) solution. Again, to most contributors to the controversy it was obvious, and in any case heavily emphasized by Hayek and others in supporting Mises, that the market as well as the mathematical solution were impracticable on several accounts.[13] However, the standard interpretation of the outcome of this debate, for many decades to come, was that from a theoretical point of view Mises' conjecture had been successfully refuted.

Thus, from the perspective of the postwar mainstream of economic theory, it appeared that the Austrian School in all these three controversies had suffered defeat. Consequently, it is small wonder that the reputation of the Austrian School, or of what still remained of it, reached a historical low in these times.

The Postwar Mainstream and the Austrian Critique

The postwar mainstream rested on two pillars, Keynesian (macro-) economics and neoclassical theory within a general equilibrium framework, linked by what became known as the "neoclassical synthesis."[14] Accordingly, the main fault of the capitalist system was seen in its proneness to widespread unemployment due to effective demand failures that could be dealt with by Keynesian remedies. Yet, as soon as full employment was thereby restored, the validity of neoclassical theory could be trusted again. With the monetarist counter-revolution of the 1970s, the quest for monetary stability replaced Keynesian policies as the required supplement to neoclassical theory, yet the general equilibrium framework remained largely unquestioned and was applied to an ever widening range of problems. As will be seen, in particular with regard to the idea of general equilibrium, Austrian economists contributed both to its evolution and to powerful strands of criticism.

The first important Austrian contribution refers to the formalization of general equilibrium theorizing that originated from Karl Menger's *Mathematisches Kolloquium*.[15] Up to then, a familiar simplification[16] represented the model of general equilibrium by demand and supply equations (making demand and supply depend on an array of prices) and by the requirement of market clearing that for the goods produced and the services used in production demand must equal supply. Given the "data" of the economy, that is, the properties of demand and supply functions resulting from tastes and technology as well as the endowment of services, the problem was to ascertain a solution of this system of equations. Earlier authors (and some still up to the 1950s) contented themselves with counting equations and unknowns (equilibrium prices and quantities). Yet, such a procedure was, of course, deficient: It did not work for non-linear equations, it did not even suffice for linear equations to guarantee reasonable solutions (that is, non-negative prices and quantities), and it could not take account of free goods (with zero prices) where demand and supply need not match. It was at the initiative of Menger (and the Hungarian-born banker Karl Schlesinger) that the problem of "proving the existence" of a meaningful solution to such a system was discussed among the mathematicians of the Menger *Kolloquium*, preeminently by Wald and von Neumann.[17] The preliminary results arrived at this occasion, although for some time beyond the grasp of most economic theorists, paved the way for modern general equilibrium theory in two regards: first, it marked the application of "higher mathematics"—going beyond simple calculus—to economics. Second, and most importantly, it was the beginning of the age of "formalization" in economics—one of the very first instances of an economic question treated as a problem of mathematics or logic, that is, of deriving conclusions from a set of axioms.[18] It is noteworthy that the participants of the Menger *Kolloquium* included von Neumann, who in the late 1920s had worked on the axiomatization of quantum mechanics, and Morgenstern, who in the 1930s—inspired by his participation in the Vienna circle of philosophers—had urged to introduce this type of "exact thinking" into economics.

The same protagonists, von Neumann and Morgenstern, opened up yet another novel avenue of research in analyzing social settings by the means of game theory.[19] The analogy derives from the practice of parlor games, like chess, where reasonable players will act strategically, that is, take into account their adversaries' reaction to their own choices and so on. Another aspect of game theory is that it can take account of cooperation among players, giving rise to the forming of coalitions and bargaining among (groups of) players. Indeed, Morgenstern emphasized game theory as a theoretical instrument to analyze the role of power in economics, and in social organization in general, an issue totally absent from standard general equilibrium theory. (Von Neumann in the 1950s was affiliated with the Manhattan Project and the RAND Corporation and used game theory for the analysis of strategies for the most frightening of power games, namely that of nuclear war.) Anyway, in this early view game theory constituted a strong challenge to the mainstream for its capacity to model an economy that departed from the conditions of perfect markets and tranquil competition characteristic of neoclassical theory. Yet, this was not how things eventually developed: Instead of such models of cooperative behavior, it was non-cooperative game theory, spurred by the pivotal work of John Nash, that attracted most of the specialists in the field and—after its renaissance in the 1970s—became a common and indispensable method in the economists' box of tools. In fact, in some fields the approaches of general equilibrium and non-cooperative game theory, with the concept of Nash equilibrium, appear as almost interchangeable, as alternative formulations of the same problem leading to the same results. Thus, what in the minds of its inventors had started as a powerful challenge to orthodoxy has become, and is nowadays conceived of as, a complement to it and thereby an important strand of the mainstream.

These were the contributions, and criticisms, of the Austrian "mathematical economists." Yet, the debate on the proper domain and role of equilibrium analysis had been early on the agenda, although expressed in non-mathematical form. A well-known productive criticism of this kind is at the core of the work of Schumpeter, who both admired and at the same time was out to destroy the Walrasian paradigm. His work is all about the contrast between the static and dynamic approach, each conceived in a specific way.[20] Statics refers to an economy of given, known and constant, external conditions such as tastes and technology, so that in such a tranquil environment it will eventually approach a state of rest—the type of equilibrium envisioned by Walras (and later on the object of formal general equilibrium analysis). This differs crucially from dynamics. Here these external conditions are not only subject to change, but this change is an endogenous characteristic of, it is built into, the economic system of capitalism. In a capitalist economy it is dynamic entrepreneurs who, by trial and error, are constantly putting forward innovations, e.g. new goods or new methods to produce goods, which in a process of "creative destruction" replace the products of traditional ("static") producers. In this view entrepreneurship and innovation prove to be the crucial driving forces of economic progress. Whereas the static economy only exhibits "adjustment" (towards equilibrium), the distinguishing feature of the dynamic economy is "development," the unceasing destruction of old equilibrium relationships for the sake of progress. Therefore, according to Schumpeter, the fatal deficiency of the methods of static analysis, and in particular of the equilibrium method, is that the vitally important phenomena of dynamics are not amenable to it. General equilibrium theory, although a major intellectual achievement, will thus not provide the key to the explanation of the actual processes exhibited by a capitalist economy.

Equally important in our review of the Austrian critique are Hayek's second thoughts on the equilibrium method. This was a crucial issue since the Austrians' apparent defeat in the calculation debate had derived from the similarity of the capitalist and the socialist solution of the economic problem when analyzed within an equilibrium framework: For, with the data of the problem given, the general equilibrium solution to which the market economy was supposed to tend could as well be executed by a central plan. Yet, in a famous article of 1937 Hayek challenged this view by questioning the "givenness" of the data: given to whom?[21] The key difference between the problem depicted by general equilibrium and the "real world" is that actually neither in a market economy nor in any conceivable planned economy is the wealth of economy-wide information given, that is, known to any single person. Indeed, much of this knowledge is dispersed among the economic agents: consumers are aware of their tastes, producers know or have an incentive to find out the best ways for producing their goods. The virtue of the market economy does not consist in its grinding out a state of general equilibrium. Rather, the "marvel" of the price system lies in bringing about coordination between disparate plans in a world of dispersed knowledge—prices signaling scarcities throughout the system without the need for consumers and producers to have full information on the system's data. Accordingly, the main accomplishment of markets and the price system is the capacity for adapting to new conditions, yet with parsimonious requirements for information processing at the level of the individual. Focusing on adaptation also means that the system's responses to changes, the market processes of adjustment, are considered more important than the eventual ("fictitious") end state of this process, the resting point of equilibrium. Furthermore, the actual process of competition goes beyond merely passive adjustment to external changes, it rather provides the incentives for discovery—in this sense the knowledge of technology is not even "given" to the individual producer, but must be found out as part of the process.

In the end, Hayek's novel approach highlighting the coordination problem in a world of dispersed knowledge pointed to a fundamental weakness both of the general equilibrium framework and the defense of socialism associated with it: In order to be able to solve the general equilibrium system the economist as the model builder must assume to have full knowledge of all the data, a knowledge that cannot be imputed to the individual agents the decisions of whom the system is intended to describe. In the same vein, a socialist central planner—deprived of the use of a price system—will never be able to avail oneself of the information needed for solving the calculation problem. Although starting from a totally different angle, Hayek ends up at a critique of equilibrium theorizing in some aspects similar to that of Schumpeter, namely that for all its logical rigor it leaves out phenomena that are crucially important in understanding—and evaluating—the working of a capitalist market system.

Finally, the Austrians played also a part in the demise of Keynesian economics. Although swamped by the Keynesian revolution, the Austrians, in particular Hayek and Mises, always stood firmly by their old convictions.[22] Their objections to Keynesian economics were twofold, theoretical and political. The theoretical criticism concerned the lack of subjectivist ("microeconomic") foundations, as the Keynesian system is largely based on relations between aggregates (like the volume of production, national income, or the price level). What was lacking was an explanation of the behavior of the individuals who in sum constitute these aggregates. This preoccupation with aggregates led to the neglect of structural changes within these aggregates (e.g. "overinvestment"), which according to the

Austrians made up for the true causes of cyclical fluctuations. Politically, Keynes and still more so his followers were thought guilty of being soft on inflation, if not even advocating inflation for the sake of full employment. This kind of inflationism was regarded a grave danger to the viability of the market economy because of its dysfunctional social effects and its being the ultimate cause of depression and unemployment. Admittedly, in the theoretical discourse among economists the influence of the Austrian criticism was at best minor, as the slow demise of Keynesianism resulted primarily from the success of the monetarist counter-revolution led by Milton Friedman.[23] Indeed, Hayek was almost as much opposed to monetarism as to Keynesianism, since the monetarist theses were alike based on mechanistic relationships between economic aggregates. Yet, in the realm of politics Hayek joined forces with Friedman, with whom he shared many of the ideals of classical liberalism, and he became well-known as one of the most outspoken defenders of the monetarist agenda embraced by the policies of Thatcher and Reagan.[24]

The Austrian Heritage and the Neoliberal Agenda

Looked at from the position of the twenty-first century, what will be the Austrian heritage to be preserved alive in a future mainstream of economic thought? In this regard, there are two aspects to be distinguished: the Austrian critique of the postwar mainstream of the neoclassical synthesis and its advocacy of the so-called neoliberal agenda.[25] These two have been, of course, interlinked.

The relationship between the postwar mainstream and neoliberalism is double-edged. On the one hand, general equilibrium theory, in its formalized version, depicted the reference norm of a fully coordinated market economy; it may be interpreted as a response to the criticism that the decentralization implicit in a market order must lead to chaos ("the anarchy of the market"). Moreover, it demonstrated that under idealized (static) conditions the general equilibrium solution will be efficient in a welfare sense, a property to be thus attributed to the market economy in general. On the other hand, the approach lent itself easily to the introduction of all sorts of market failures, ranging from externalities, public goods and asymmetric information to Keynesian unemployment, all of which call for policy interventions into the market process. Whereas leftish critics regarded the postwar mainstream as an apology of the market, disguised in the clothing of formal language, the Austrian critique as sketched above stressed the insufficient attention paid to the dynamic features of a market economy. According to them, the general equilibrium approach missed crucial aspects of the working of the market economy and thus provided a measuring rod that was vitally flawed.

In order to see how theoretical critique and political advocacy became intertwined, we shall shortly examine a few examples of this neoliberal "twist" of the Austrian critique.

Let's start with Hayek's idea of the market process and coordination in a setting of dispersed knowledge. Eschewing the rigid assumptions of general equilibrium modeling, Hayek turns to problems that appear more relevant and to a description of the economy by market processes more realistic than that of the equilibrium framework. Consequently, he bases his judgment on the market economy not on the achievement (or not) of static criteria of efficiency, but on the system's capacity for self-correction and for providing incentives to discover novel solutions to evolving scarcities. It is also from this perspective that Hayek argues against state intervention and regulations that inhibit the working of the market process. Schumpeter is a slightly different case. His theory of economic development emphasizes the necessity of innovation and entrepreneurship as a prerequisite for economic growth and progress and thereby for the survival of the capitalist system itself. However, he was aware of the irrational motives lying behind entrepreneurial action as well as of the danger of speculative excesses and ill-guided ventures. Those who have proclaimed, in the final quarter of the twentieth century, the "Age of Schumpeter" drew from this the conclusion that to create the required room for entrepreneurship and creative destruction, the prevalent obstacles and hindrances to a truly "free market system" had to be cleared away.

Moreover, with regard to Hayek and Schumpeter, a look beyond their writings in pure economics to those on social philosophy or sociology proves enlightening. Both have been the authors of very successful, yet in their conclusions diametrically opposed, treatises on the fate of capitalism: *The Road to Serfdom* and *Capitalism, Socialism, and Democracy*.[26] In *The Road to Serfdom,* Hayek comes close to putting forward an inevitability thesis, according to which any attempt to implement socialism or a planned economy, if consistently pursued, must end up in totalitarianism. Thus, Hayek's case for a society modeled on the features of classical liberalism, and in consequence for a pure market economy without epithets (in contrast to the "social market economy" of German origin), is more deeply rooted than just in the economic benefits it may generate. Rather, it follows from the primacy attached to the value of liberty and the serious perils thought imminent from any deviation from the right path of a hundred-percent liberalism. Schumpeter, in contrast, combined his admiration for the times of classical capitalism, as in nineteenth-century Britain, with a deeply-seated pessimism on the outlook for the survival of capitalism—with the erosion of the social background necessary to stabilize and protect the entrepreneurial class the "march into socialism" appeared to him nothing but inevitable. Latter-day Schumpeterians have thus put Schumpeter on his head, transforming his dystopia of the coming of socialism into a utopia of restoring capitalism.

From a methodological point of view it must be noted that in advocating the superior dynamic properties of market processes or of entrepreneurship, both Hayek and Schumpeter step outside the modeling strategies of mainstream economics. Yet, outside the strictures of equilibrium theorizing it is impossible to establish a logical proof for the coordination-enhancing nature of market processes, an alleged "tendency towards equilibrium," or the net benefits of "creative destruction." As is so often the case, there is simply a trade-off in analysis between "realism" and "logical stringency." Indeed, Hayek justifies his beliefs neither by the logics of model-building nor by the empirics of statistical investigations, but by recourse to historical experience, namely the observed resilience of market systems to adverse shocks. This may justify the heretical remark that even when accepting all the Austrian criticisms and sharing their skepticism of both general equilibrium theorizing and the practices of socialism, it is not compelling to unreservedly endorse their policy conclusions. So even if it seems difficult, the scientific accomplishments of the Austrian economists may be appreciated and treated separately from their political agenda.

Turning eventually to the sphere of politics, the agitation of Austrian economists has certainly contributed to the so-called neoliberal turn in economic policy: monetary stability, low inflation and budgetary discipline as the goals of macroeconomic management, deregulation, the easing of restrictions of all kinds, especially in the labor market, the rollback of corporatism and social policy, and the Washington consensus as the guideline in international relations—all these appear to be taken just out of an Austrian economist's policy blueprint. Indeed, at the turn of the millennium it seemed as if a new era of never-ending capitalist prosperity had been entered, market optimism dominated and ever more regulations were discarded as obstacles to the free sway of the market. Unfortunately, shortly after macroeconomists had coined the term the "Great Moderation" for the absence of cyclical disturbances in the past two decades,[27] the current financial and economic crisis intervened. Thereby, at least in the lay public, if not among economists and financial analysts, the belief in the irreversible triumph of capitalism, coming close to an end of history, appears to have been shaken.

Concluding Observations

Hayek once remarked that "a school has its greatest success when it ceases as such to exist because its leading ideals have become a part of the general dominant teaching."[28] Now has this happened to the Austrian teachings, and is there thus still a justification for the existence of a distinct Austrian school?

This question is difficult to answer due to the awkward state of present-day economic science. The consensus underlying the postwar neoclassical synthesis has been partly destroyed, not least due to the power of the Austrian critique. Accordingly, although the core of it has not drastically changed, there is now a much greater variety of approaches accepted within the current mainstream of economics. There are "consensus models" in specific fields of economic research, and it might even appear that the mainstream has been split up into many diverse currents of research that exist to some extent independently of each other. The already noted variety of approaches that make up the body of game theory may be mentioned as an example. Some historians of economic thought have gone so far as to distinguish between "mainstream" and "orthodoxy"/"heterodoxy" such that there is an "edge of economics" where some heterodox ideas become accepted and appreciated by the economics community (or, more precisely, its elite).[29] In this confusing state of affairs, many insights deriving from the contributions of Austrian economists have been incorporated (some in a form such that their Austrian origin is no longer easily recognizable) into specific fields of current research, for example into the economics of information and mechanism design. Yet, it would be an exaggeration to maintain that the Austrian critique of equilibrium theorizing had been fully accepted, still less that the adherence to equilibrium models had been discarded as a result. In this sense, although in many particular instances theses of Austrian origin have now become part of educated opinion within the economics community, economists are far away (and some would believe, for good reasons) from claiming that "We are all Austrians now."[30] For the Austrian true-believers, in particular for the hard core of radical libertarians, there is thus still good reason for labeling themselves members of a distinct (neo-)Austrian school.

Notes

1. On the following see, for example, Robert Leonard, *Von Neumann, Morgenstern and the Creation of Game Theory: From Chess to Social Science, 1900-1960* (Cambridge: Cambridge University Press, 2010); Hansjoerg Klausinger, "Volkswirtschaftliche Theorien: Joseph Schumpeter—Ludwig Mises—Othmar Spann," in *Das Werden der Ersten Republik … der Rest ist Österreich*, vol. 2, ed. Helmut Konrad and Wolfgang Maderthaner (Vienna: Carl Gerold's Sohn, 2008), 139-56; and as a primary source Friedrich A. Hayek, "The Austrian School of Economics" [1968], as reprinted in *The Fortunes of Liberalism: Essays on Austrian Economics and the Ideal of Freedom* (vol. 4 of *The Collected Works of F. A. Hayek*), ed. Peter G. Klein (Chicago: University of Chicago Press and London: Routledge, 1992), 42-60.

2. See his *Theorie des Geldes und der Umlaufsmittel*, 2nd rev. ed. (Munich and Leipzig: Duncker & Humblot, 1924); translated as *The Theory of Money and Credit* (London: Cape, 1934; reprinted, Indianapolis: Liberty *Classics*, 1981).

3. On the emigration of the Austrian School see Earlene Craver, "The Emigration of the Austrian Economists," *History of Political Economy* 18 (1986): 1-32; Earlene Craver and Axel Leijonhufvud, "Economics in America: The Continental Influence," *History of Political Economy* 19 (1987): 173-82; Hansjoerg Klausinger, "'In the Wilderness': Emigration and the Decline of the Austrian School," *History of Political Economy* 38 (2006): 617-64; and for biographical information Harald Hagemann and Claus-Dieter Krohn, eds., *Biographisches Handbuch der deutschsprachigen wirtschaftswissenschaftlichen Emigration nach 1933*, 2 vols. (Munich: Saur, 1999).

4. Of course, at the University of Vienna Erich Streissler must be mentioned as an intimate and appreciative adept of the Austrian tradition.

5. See Stephan Boehm, "Austrian Economics between the Wars: Some Historiographical Problems," and Mark Blaug, "Commentary," both in *Austrian Economics: Tensions and New Directions*, ed. Bruce J. Caldwell and Stephan Boehm (Boston: Kluwer, 1992), 1-30 and 31-34.

6. The most prominent and persistent adversary was the American economist Frank H. Knight; see Avi J. Cohen, "The Hayek/Knight Controversy: The Irrelevance of Roundaboutness, or Purging Processes in Time?" *History of Political Economy* 35 (2003): 469-90.

7. Joseph A. Schumpeter, *History of Economic Analysis* (London: Allen & Unwin, 1954; reprinted, Routledge, 1994), 565, contrasts these positions as "advance economics" versus "synchronization economics."

8. See Avi J. Cohen and Geoffrey C. Harcourt, "Whatever Happened to the Cambridge Capital Controversies?" *Journal of Economic Perspectives* 17 (2003): 199-214.

9. Hayek's most important piece on this topic is *Prices and Production* (London: Routledge, 1931; 2nd rev. ed., 1935); these and other contributions will be conveniently available in Hansjoerg Klausinger, ed., *Business Cycles I and II* (vols. 7 and 8 of *The Collected Works of F. A. Hayek*) (Chicago: University of Chicago Press and London: Routledge, forthcoming). The foundation of Keynesian economics is, of course, John Maynard Keynes, *The General Theory of Employment, Interest and Money* (London: Macmillan, 1936), reprinted as vol. 7 of *The Collected Writings of John Maynard Keynes*, ed. Austin Robinson and Donald Moggridge (London: Macmillan and Cambridge: Cambridge University Press, 1971).

10. See for a "revisionist" Austrian account Don Lavoie, *Rivalry and Central Planning: The Socialist Calculation Debate Reconsidered* (Cambridge: Cambridge University Press, 1985).

11. By the way, Mises' criticism was triggered by the propagation of a "natural economy" of war-type socialism by the Austrian philosopher Otto Neurath.

12. For an overview of Walrasian general equilibrium theory and its modern development see Bruna Ingrao and Giorgio Israel, *The Invisible Hand: Economic Equilibrium in the History of Science* (Cambridge, MA: The MIT Press, 1990).

13. For a summary of the contemporary debate see Friedrich A. Hayek, ed., *Collectivist Economic Planning: Critical Studies on the Possibilities of Socialism* (London: Routledge & Kegan Paul, 1935).

14. Neoclassical theory in this sense culminated in John R. Hicks, *Value and Capital* (Oxford: Clarendon Press, 1939, 2nd rev. ed. 1946), and Paul A. Samuelson, *Foundations of Economic Analysis* (Cambridge, MA: Harvard University Press, 1947, enlarged ed. 1983). The view of the neoclassical synthesis was popularized in the various editions of Samuelson's textbook, *Economics: An Introductory Analysis*, 1st ed. (New York: McGraw-Hill, 1948), now co-authored by William D. Nordhaus in its 19th edition (2010).

15. See E. Roy Weintraub, *General Equilibrium Analysis: Studies in Appraisal* (Cambridge: Cambridge University Press, 1985), ch. 6.

16. Due to Gustav Cassel, *Theoretische Sozialökonomie*, 4th ed. (Leipzig: Winter, 1927), translated as *The Theory of Social Economy*, new rev. ed. (London: Benn and New York: Harcourt, Brace and Co., 1932).

17. This resulted in a series of four papers by Wald, 1934-1936, and one by von Neumann 1937.

18. See E. Roy Weintraub, *How Economics Became a Mathematical Science* (Durham: Duke University Press, 2002); and Mark Blaug, "The Formalist Revolution of the 1950s," *Journal of the History of Economic Thought* 25 (2003): 145-56.

19. See their *Theory of Games and Economic Behavior* (Princeton: Princeton University Press, 1944). On the evolution of game theory see Leonard, *Von Neumann, Morgenstern and the Creation of Game Theory*, and Nicola Giocoli, *Modeling Rational Players: From Interwar Economics to Early Modern Game Theory* (Cheltenham: Edward Elgar, 2003).

20. See Joseph Schumpeter, *Theorie der wirtschaftlichen Entwicklung*, 2nd ed. (Munich: Duncker & Humblot, 1926), translated as *The Theory of Economic Development* (Cambridge, MA: Harvard University Press, 1934).

21. "Economics and Knowledge," *Economica*, N.S. 4 (1937): 39, reprinted in *Individualism and Economic Order* (Chicago: University of Chicago Press, 1948; and London: Routledge & Kegan Paul, 1949), 39. See also his "The Use of Knowledge in Society," *American Economic Review* 35 (1945): 519-30, reprinted as chapter 4 of *Individualism and Economic Order*, and "Competition as a Discovery Procedure," in *New Studies in Philosophy, Politics, Economics and the History of Ideas* (London: Routledge & Kegan Paul, 1978), 179-90.

22. See, for example, Friedrich A. Hayek, "The Campaign Against Keynesian Inflation," in *New Studies in Philosophy, Politics, Economics and the History of Ideas*, 191-231.

23. See Milton Friedman and Anna J. Schwartz, *A Monetary History of the United States, 1867–1960* (Princeton: Princeton University Press, 1963); and also Harry G. Johnson, "The Keynesian Revolution and the Monetarist Counter-Revolution," *American Economic Review* 61 (1971): 1-14.

24. During the Thatcher years Hayek apparently developed a taste for engaging in public controversy, in particular in the pages of *The Times* and with his favorite opponent, the post-Keynesian Nicholas Kaldor. This series of controversies ran from December 1976, on the alleged socialist character of the German economy, to September 1980, on recommendations for reflation.

25. I use the term "neoliberal" only with the utmost caution because in its meaning in everyday English it is more often than not used in a pejorative sense. Here it simply denotes a set of policy prescriptions conforming to liberal values (in the European sense).

26. Friedrich A. Hayek, *The Road to Serfdom* (Chicago: University of Chicago Press, 1944); see

also the reprinted "definitive edition" as vol. 2 of *The Collected Works of F. A. Hayek*, ed. Bruce Caldwell (2007); and Joseph A. Schumpeter, *Capitalism, Socialism, and Democracy* (New York: Harper, 1942).

27. See James H. Stock and Mark W. Watson, "Has the Business Cycle Changed and Why?" *Macroeconomics Annual* 17 (2002): 159-218; and also the speech on "The Great Moderation," at the meeting of the Eastern Economic Association, Washington, 20 Feb. 2004, by Ben S. Bernanke, then governor, presently the chairman of the United States Federal Reserve System.

28. Hayek, "The Austrian School of Economics," 52. He believed that the Austrian School "has to a great extent come to enjoy such a success" (ibid.).

29. See, for example, David Colander, "The Death of Neoclassical Economics," *Journal of the History of Economic Thought* 22 (2000): 127-43; and idem., Richard P. F. Holt, and J. Barkley Rosser, "The Changing Face of Mainstream Economics," *Review of Political Economy* 16 (2004): 485-99.

30. Not even in the highly hedged version attributed to Milton Friedman with regard to Keynesianism that, "In one sense, we are all Keynesians now; in another, nobody is any longer a Keynesian" (*Time*, 4 Feb. 1966).

Vienna: The Eventful History of a Financial Center

Andreas Resch and Dieter Stiefel

The last century and a half has been a time of radical change for Austria with marked disruptions in the political, economic, and social development of the nation. Vienna as a financial hub also experienced dramatic changes on several occasions. Phases of economic disintegration and integration, of crises and rapid growth, have alternated many times. In the nineteenth century, Vienna was a financial center for Central, Eastern, and South-Eastern Europe, and it is again today. Within this period, however, lies an eventful story.

The last Decades of the Habsburg Empire

The history of the development of Vienna as a financial center goes back to the eighteenth century.[1] In 1771, the Vienna Stock Exchange was the first to be founded in Central Europe.[2] It was created after those in Antwerp, London, and Paris, but a quarter of a century before Berlin.[3] Initially, the Stock Exchange served the exclusive purpose of trading in government securities. From the 1830s onwards, trading in railroads in particular was added. After 1848, a wave of liberal reforms ensued in neo-absolutist Austria that expanded and enlarged the scope of economic developments.[4] After the loss to Prussia in the 1866 war, the Austro-Hungarian compromise ("*Ausgleich*"), the bringing into force of the constitution of 1867, and, on an international level, the end of the American Civil War and the contribution payments by France after the Franco-Prussian War of 1870-71 constituted

Great Hall of the Vienna Stock Exchange in 1877 ©Austrian National Library

the background for the "*Gründerzeit*" until 1873. In Vienna, the 1873 World Exposition gave further impulses. In this context, the number of stocks listed on the Stock Exchange increased from eight (1848) to thirty-nine (1867), and finally up to 378 (1873). For a time, the Vienna Stock Exchange thus became the largest speculative market in Europe. There were peaks of 90,000 transactions a day, and the number of persons authorized to access the Stock Exchange increased from 870 in 1855 to 2,941 in 1873.

In 1816, the Privilegierte Oesterreichische National-Bank was founded, practically the state's banker, which also regulated the discount and lombard business (*Escompte- und Lombardgeschäft*), and created a department for agricultural credits from 1855 onwards. The Österreichische Nationalbank had quickly succeeded, after the paper money inflation during the Napoleonic Wars, in reestablishing a credible silver standard.[5] After the Austro-Hungarian compromise, from 1867 onwards it became the Austro-Hungarian Bank (Oesterreichisch-ungarische Bank) and until then had eighteen branches. In the decades up to World War I, the governments of both states of the Dual Monarchy implemented a very solid financial policy. As a consequence, the transition to the gold standard could ensue in 1892. From 1900 onwards, the *Krone* (crown) succeeded the *Gulden* (guilder) as the new currency. As a consequence, Austria-Hungary went from the "periphery to the centre" of Europe, with regard to its currency system.[6]

The first half of the nineteenth century was still the epoch of private bankers. In 1847, ninety-two private banks existed in Vienna, including well-known names such as Rothschild or Geymüller. Their business consisted mainly in government bonds and credit to the aristocracy. Only in a few cases did they participate in financing industry and the beginnings of railroad construction.[7] This banking structure did not, however, correspond at all to the requirements of incipient industrialization. Above all, the construction of railways needed capital to a hitherto unknown extent. This need was met by issuing shares which in Austria were often oversubscribed several times. However, the speculative nature of this was obvious, and when railway companies encountered their first problems, the shares were sold off again. Private banks were not willing or financially capable to apply supporting measures. Therefore, the state had to intervene until it ultimately became the majority shareholder and continued the construction of railways by itself. However, in 1854, owing to a budget crisis due to the Crimean War, the railways had to be privatized again. The requisite of an efficient banking system was thus on the table.

In the middle of the century, universal banks based on shares brought about decisive innovation in the financial sector. In 1855, the k.k. privilegierte Österreichische Credit-Anstalt für Handel und Gewerbe, modeled on the French Crédit Mobilier (1853), was founded at the state's initiative. It had the economic task to promote industry and the construction of railways. Its share capital of 100 million guilders was larger than that of the Nationalbank or of the French Crédit Mobilier, and, on the occasion of the foundation, was oversubscribed tenfold. The emergence of large-scale joint-stock banks marked the end of private bankers. They either receded into niches or understood the trends of the time and became major shareholders in the new banking system, as the House Rothschild did. In 1853, the Niederösterreichische Escompte-Gesellschaft, which mainly granted loans to the middle classes, was founded; in 1863, the k.k. privilegierte allgemeine Bodencredit-Anstalt and the Anglo-Österreichische Bank; in 1864 the k.k. Pfandleihgesellschaft (later called Verkehrsbank); and in 1880 the Länderbank.[8] In many foundations, foreign capital was also involved, particularly in the case of the Anglo-Österreichische Bank and the Länderbank (France).

The *Gründerzeit*, which achieved Austria's industrial breakthrough, was a very speculative phase that ended with the 1873 crisis. A concomitant phenomenon was a series of foundations of banks, many of which did not survive the crisis. The number of banks in the Austrian half of the empire decreased from 141 to forty-two between the years 1873 and 1885. The collapse of the Stock Exchange had extremely varied repercussions. Among the stocks there were numerous cases of total loss; industrial shares on average lost forty-nine percent of their value between March and October 1873, shares in construction companies lost seventy-four percent, and bank shares fifty-eight percent.[9] Fixed-interest securities fared better; government bonds lost only four percent of their value. The number of shares listed on the Stock Exchange decreased only by seventy percent to 114.

As a reaction to the 1873 crisis, Austrian banking policy became considerably more conservative. Many investors experienced substantial losses, which resulted in a fundamentally anti-capitalist attitude in the following years. In the 1880s, trade law became more restrictive and cost disadvantages for large-scale enterprises were stipulated. After the large tax reform of 1896, joint-stock companies were also disadvantaged compared to individual enterprises, and their foundation remained hindered. In the 1890s, a severe form of additional taxation was introduced for sales made on the Stock Exchange.

Whilst the number of joint-stock companies in the Netherlands increased between 1886 and 1912 from 653 to 3,566, and in Italy from 583 to 1,215, in Austria there was only an increase from 380 to 557. As a result, Austria lagged far behind Europe's development. Stock exchanges and joint-stock companies could only develop mildly and the market of capital shifted toward government bonds. Unlike the stagnating stock market, the face value of government bonds in Austria increased between 1873 and 1893 from 345 million to 2.45 billion crowns, and the value of Hungarian bonds increased within the same period from 986 to 4,380 million crowns, of which more than sixty percent were in the hands of Austrian investors. The restriction of the Austrian capital market after the 1873 crisis resulted in the flux of large means toward Hungary, whose government pursued an ambitious policy of modernization and industrialization.[10]

Not only did large-scale banks increase in importance during the nineteenth century, but also the sector of savings banks and credit cooperatives for the simple financial needs of trade, peasants, workers, and employees. The aforementioned banks and cooperatives managed to invest small savings to produce an interest, and they became important providers of mortgage loans. In 1819, the Erste Oesterreichische Sparkasse was the first savings bank to be founded in Vienna, after which a dynamic growth began in all crown lands. The number of savings banks in the Austrian half of the empire increased to 273 by the 1870s, and to 627 by the first decade of the twentieth century. This sector was not concentrated in Vienna and was almost untouched by the 1873 crisis. The value of the assets of savings banks increased from 3 million guilders of Austrian currency in the 1820s (6 million crowns) to 5.14 billion crowns after 1900. In addition to the savings banks, by 1912 there existed more than 10,000 credit corporations which administered deposits amounting to around 25 million crowns.[11]

A characteristic of Viennese banks was the foundation of industrial companies. The lucrative construction business was the result of the transformation of an enterprise into a joint-stock company; either as a consequence of failure, in which case loans were transformed into assets, or as a result of success, in which case the growing size of an enterprise shed favorable light onto the new corporate form. In either case, the bank issued the shares and retained a substantial portion in its own portfolio. As a result of this development, universal banks had before World War I extensive industrial companies with branches in all regions of the monarchy. The largest of them alone, the Creditanstalt, had before World War I about 130 industrial holdings. Of the assets of the Viennese bank, eleven percent were invested in effective ownership and shares in syndicates.[12] The share capital of Viennese banks increased over the course of this development from 1883 until 1912 from 183.5 million guilders (367 million crowns) to 881.5 million crowns. As a result, a tight personal network between banks and industry emerged. At that time, this company network was called "finance capitalism," in which the industry was dominated by the banks. More recent studies, however, interpret this rather as networks of interdependencies.[13]

Apart from in Vienna, by 1914 only a few banks of supraregional importance had emerged in Austria, above all the Banca Commerciale Triestina and the Živnostenská Banka in Prague. In the Hungarian half of the monarchy, the Budapest banking system experienced dynamic growth, often in conjunction with the Viennese banks. The biggest institution became the Hungarian General Creditbank (Magyar Általános Hitelbank), which had strong links with the Wiener Creditanstalt and the House Rothschild.[14] Despite the emergence of institutions in other parts of the empire, Viennese banks assumed a leading position within the Danube region. The equity of all Austrian banks amounted to 1.35 billion crowns before World War I, of which around two-thirds belonged to Viennese institutions.[15] The Viennese banks reinforced their strong position by opening numerous branches. In 1896, the ten largest Viennese banks had thirty-four branches, increasing by 1913 to 127 branches, twenty-five of which are in the territory of today's Austria. However, the center was in Cisleithania; in Hungary there were three branches, eight abroad, and basically no branches at all in the Balkans. Viennese banks had not penetrated the whole economic area of the monarchy; rather, they had focused on those regions which were the most developed in industrial terms. The centers were the Bohemian and Alpine industrial areas.

The Decline in the Interwar Years

From the point of view of banks, World War I was a disturbing factor for business. On the one hand, the relationships with the important Western European financial markets were interrupted, in particular to France and Great Britain. A banking system is by definition internationally oriented, and political constraints caused difficulties. On the other hand, the importance of banks decreased as a consequence of war finance. A significant new business activity was the eight war bonds issued in the Austro-Hungarian Monarchy. The greatest challenge, however, came from the peace treaties of 1919, which decreed the dissolution of the Habsburg Monarchy. The former capital of the empire, Vienna, declined from the center of a country with over 50 million inhabitants to the capital of the Austrian Republic with less than 7 million.

After the war, the survival of the population could be guaranteed only by state-subsidized imports of food. This contrasted with the decline of the production of goods and lower tax revenues as a result of the war. The solution was in increasing foreign debt and a boosted issuing of banknotes, which resulted in a considerable increase in the amount of money. This circumstance, along with the hesitant attitude of Austrian politics with regard to the economic and political reorientation of the country, led by 1922 to hyperinflation, which was worsened by a speculative wave in the Stock Exchange.[16] By then the external value of the Austrian crown had sunk to less than a fourteen-thousandth of its value before the war. The incompetence of Austrian financial policy did not end until October 1922, thanks to the League of Nations. The League organized an internationally guaranteed bond of 650 million gold crowns (*Goldkronen*) and appointed a League of Nations commissioner in Vienna, who was in charge of the Austrian budget until 1928. This created the foundation for a stabilization of the Austrian currency and monetary policy. In 1922, the Austrian National Bank (Oesterreichische Nationalbank) was created, and in 1925 the *Schilling* was introduced as a new currency with an exchange rate of 10,000 paper crowns to a new monetary unit. Afterward, the Austrian currency became one of the most stable of the interwar years, and was also called the "Alpine dollar" ("*Alpendollar*").[17]

For the banks—and for a few striking individuals—the period of inflation was the occasion for vast currency and stock speculation. Betting on the sinking or increasing of different currencies could be a source of considerable gain, and the equity capital of the enterprises had to be adapted time and again to the decreased value of money by means of a renewed issuing of shares. However, speculation went far beyond this, in that joint-stock companies were created exclusively for the purpose of speculation. As a consequence of the stabilization of the currency in 1922, this money veil disappeared. An equity bull market followed between January 1923 and March 1924, and in Vienna shares were issued with a face value of around 6.5 billion crowns. Following this, speculation turned in 1924 to vast dealings in futures betting on the decline of the French franc. This tactic failed, a serious banking crisis ensued, and the Vienna Stock Exchange descended to fundamental insignificance.

The consequences for Austrian banks were catastrophic. Whilst between 1919 and 1923 their number had nearly doubled, increasing from 180 to 358, it then decreased to 192 by 1927.[18] As a consequence of the banking crisis from 1924 onwards, many failed banks were closed and there were a number of mergers and acquisitions. This kept the number of weakened large banks small, but also led to a long-term weakness. Banks were now suffering from a double problem of costs: On one hand, they had lost the major part of their capital as a consequence of the development of inflation and had to refinance themselves expensively on Western capital markets; on the other hand, the increase in the number of employees during the period of inflation caused considerable expenses. Before the war, the ten largest Viennese banks had 5,500 employees; by 1923 this number increased to 16,000.[19] Hyperinflation had also caused the savings bank sector to lose its funds, and savings activity remained at lower levels in the following years, which is why only small amounts of capital could be raised from this side.[20]

In the 1920s, the equity capital of Viennese universal banks had shrunk to about one-fifth of its value before the war; the balance sheet totals still amounted to around forty percent. Viennese banks reacted with an internationalization and resorted to foreign capital, which was also supposed to guarantee their independence from Austrian politics. In the case of the ten largest Viennese banks, the foreign stake of share capital increased from ten percent in 1913 to thirty percent in 1923. Two banks, the Anglobank and the Länderbank, became wholly foreign-owned. In addition, there were (mostly short-term) loans from abroad. The short-term foreign liabilities of the Viennese large banks, which in 1924 still amounted to 240 million Austrian schillings, increased to 1 billion schillings by 1931. As a result, the Viennese banks in the 1920s were fully aware of having become international banks based in Vienna. The international orientation also corresponded to the business activity of the Viennese banks. As a consequence of the Peace Treaty of Saint-Germain and the nationalist legislation in the succession states, banks had to renounce or restructure their positions in these countries. Of the 143 branches the ten largest Viennese banks could boast in 1918, only nine survived by 1924. And yet, all large financial transactions ultimately went through Vienna. Western capital was often unwilling to invest directly in the succession states and preferred the mediation of Viennese banks, which had long been an integral part of the international financial system. Thus Viennese banks again developed their industrial financing in Central, Eastern, and South-Eastern Europe.[21] However, since their conditions were not competitive for first-class clients, they tended to become "lemon pickers,"[22] mainly having to accept clients with low credit worthiness.

As a consequence of this decreased credit worthiness, foreign funds could be obtained only at a high cost. Both the interest rates for foreign loans and those for the refinancing of the Austrian National Bank (bank rates) amounted to about ten percent. Because of the increase in their own expenses, banks had to add an interest margin of eight to nine percent, which is why they could not grant under eighteen percent even to their best customers, and even under these conditions the offer was limited.[23] The consequence of the structural weakening of the efficiency of the Viennese credit sector was that enterprises that did not directly belong to the banking groups could only resort to a very short and expensive supply of capital. This should certainly be regarded as one of the factors that ensured that the total economic gross investment quota in Austria in the interwar years mostly remained at a level of less than ten percent of GDP.[24]

On account of all these unresolved structural problems, the world economic crisis of the 1930s hit the Austrian banking sector particularly hard. In 1929, the Bodenkreditanstalt, which had taken over several banks in trouble, faced financial ruin. As a result of enormous political pressure, it was taken over by the Creditanstalt. As a consequence of this merger, the industrial group of the Creditanstalt increased by about half. But these were only the first signs of the actual banking crisis that would follow in 1931.

In 1931, the Creditanstalt could no longer by itself produce a balance sheet in conformity with the law. Now, under these conditions, even the largest universal bank in Austria threatened to fall victim to the world economic crisis, which would have vast consequences not only for the financial markets, but also for Austrian industry. Since—as a result of equity infusion in the 1920s—forty percent of the bank belonged to foreign stakeholders and had vast foreign liabilities, efforts were quickly undertaken, at national and international level, to rescue the bank. In May 1931, after its troubles became known, there was a run on the bank that the Creditanstalt could survive only thanks to state guarantees and considerable new indebtedness entered into with the Nationalbank. As a consequence of capital flight, the central bank's portfolio of bills increased remarkably and the currency reserves decreased dangerously.[25]

The effects of the first rescue operation put into force by the government did not last long. The Creditanstalt became a plaything of national and international politics. It was the first major bank to be in trouble during the world economic crisis, and the foreign creditors were consequently inflexible with regard to their receivables. They were certain of Britain's and France's political support and of their influence on the League of Nations and the Bank of England. This situation prompted the Austrian government to accept a general liability for the debts of the Creditanstalt, which was, however, a mere illusion, given the financial troubles of the state. As soon as the banking crisis extended to the foreign creditors' countries and it became clear that the crisis of the Creditanstalt was not an isolated phenomenon, they also found themselves having to grant considerable concessions. The reorganization of the Creditanstalt, which lasted until 1936, occurred at a substantial loss for both the foreign creditors and the Austrian state. The loss amounted to over 1 billion Austrian schillings and was sustained by the state and the foreign creditors. As a result, the financial flexibility of the state was severely limited for the following years. In January 1933, the share capital of the Creditanstalt was devalued to 1 million schillings and new capital amounting to 142 million schillings was added. Fifty-one percent of it came from the Austrian state, which also took on the bank's debts to the Nationalbank.[26] The bank was thus practically nationalized.

In 1934, the reorganization process of the Viennese banking sector came to a conclusion. The Wiener Bankverein, which survived the 1920s with comparatively little damage, and the banking activities of the Niederösterreichische Escomptegesellschaft (NEG) were merged with the Creditanstalt into the Österreichische Creditanstalt-Wiener Bankverein. As a holding company for the industrial interests of NEG, the Österreichische Industriekredit AG was created. The number of Austrian major banks had thus decreased from eight in 1919 to just one, with the exception of the Länderbank, which was French-owned.[27] Another Austrian middle-sized bank, Mercurbank, had to close its counters temporarily during the crisis in 1931 of its German parent bank, Danatbank, but was able to survive thanks to a bridge loan from the Nationalbank. After the merger with Danatbank, Dresdner Bank had at its disposal ninety-five percent of the share capital of Mercurbank.[28] At the same time, as a result of both capital flight and loss, foreign loans to Austrian banks had almost completely ceased and the foreign deposits and stakes of the Creditanstalt had been used in order to pay foreign debts. It is therefore possible to speak of an "Austrification" of the Austrian banking system. The international position of Vienna as a financial hub was almost completely lost.

"Anschluss," National Socialism and World War II

As a consequence of the annexation, the "Anschluss," of Austria to the German Reich in 1938, the situation of Austrian banks changed abruptly. The number of joint-stock banks (*Aktienbanken*) and mortgage banks (*Hypothekenbanken*) remained almost unchanged, that of savings banks (*Sparkassen*) and *Raiffeisenkassen* decreased by ten percent, that of cooperative banks (*Volksbanken*) by two-thirds, and that of private bankers by six-sevenths. As early as 1938-39, this was linked to a change in the management in the Austrian economy. In the case of the six leading banks and the fourteen major insurance companies, about two-thirds of the directors and members of the supervisory boards were replaced. The annexation of Austria to Nazi Germany in 1938 led to the extensive destruction of the Austrian private banking sector.[29] Of the 140 private banks existing at the beginning of 1938, about 100 were "Jewish-owned." Eight of these were "Aryanized," all others were liquidated. Even sixteen firms of "non-Jews" were liquidated. The Wiener Giro- und Cassenverein served as "acting director" for seventy-eight "Jewish" banks.[30] Racist or political cleansing immediately began in the banks; by early 1939, all Jewish employees had been removed. Many of them died in the Holocaust.

After the "Anschluss," the Vienna Stock Exchange played only a minor role. On 12 March 1938 it was first closed, then reopened in October of the same year after the appointment of an "acting director." Individuals who were considered "Jews" according to Nazi legislation had no access to the Stock Exchange from 11 July 1938 onwards. In August 1939, the German regulations concerning the Stock Exchange entered into force, in 1943 a trading halt was ordered, and on 4 April 1945 a renewed closure followed.[31]

The German stake of the shares of Austrian banks increased from eight to eighty-three percent between 1938 and 1944.[32] Since the Dresdner Bank had reached a dominant position within the Viennese Mercurbank as early as the 1930s, it exploited this position in order to play a decisive role in the Nazi reorganization of the Austrian banking system. Mercurbank took over the Austrian branch of the Länderbank as well as the Viennese branches of Zivnostenská banka, Società Italiana di Credito Commerciale, and Allgemeine Wechselstuben-AG Hermes and became the second-largest regional bank in the southeast of the German Reich.[33] The largest bank in the Reich, Deutsche Bank, had to content itself with participation in Creditanstalt-Bankverein (CA-BV), the industrial company of which was incorporated into the VIAG. By 1942, Deutsche Bank developed its participation in the CA-BV into a majority stake.[34] This became an essential vehicle of financial control in Central and South-Eastern Europe.[35]

The "Anschluss" and the military expansion of the German Reich clearly appeared to offer attractive opportunities from an economic point of view. "Traders follow the flag," said Eduard Hilgard, head of the insurance sector (*Reichsgruppenleiter Versicherung*) and board member of the Allianz Versicherung. After the loss of importance of Vienna as a financial hub, German capital nourished the hope of regaining a leading position in Eastern and South-Eastern Europe. Vienna hoped to become the "Hamburg of the east." It was perfectly in keeping with the intentions of their current German parent companies that the Viennese banks should take over their ancestral markets again. This plan failed with a considerable loss, because the hope of the Viennese banks to reobtain their old position in the southeast by force was a gamble on the victory of Nazi Germany.

The Reconstruction Period after 1945

The social, political, and economic situation in Austria in 1945 is no longer imaginable today: human losses as a consequence of the war, persecution, destruction, division of the country into four occupation zones, the presence of 1 million displaced persons, about 500,000 Austrian war prisoners, the requirements of political cleansing by means of denazification, and insufficient energy supply. But the worst consequence was famine, since agricultural production had dramatically plummeted. In addition, as a result of the separation from Germany and later from Eastern Europe by the Iron Curtain, the country was economically isolated. As a consequence, Vienna was disadvantaged because of its peripheral position on the eastern border.[36] However, there were considerable differences compared to 1918. Now people expressed their commitment to the Republic of Austria and attempted to reconstruct the country under these difficult circumstances. In addition, Austria could quickly acquire statehood, unlike Germany. Whilst the government in Vienna in 1945 was initially recognized only by the Soviet occupying power, after parliamentary elections in November it was recognized, from early 1946 onwards, by all the occupying powers.

The reconstruction concerned in the first place the monetary system. On 3 July 1945 the Oesterreichische Nationalbank could resume its work. At this time, its only assets were its fictional receivables to the Deutsche Reichsbank. Then the Allies restituted a part of the gold stock which had been transferred to Berlin in 1938. From 1948 onwards, the funds of the Marshall Plan played a crucial role in the foreign exchange reserve. In 1945, an extensive exchange control was introduced. Afterwards, Austria became a member of the new international organizations such as the IMF and gradually fulfilled the liberalization obligations involved, although with numerous restrictions.[37] Between 1949 and 1953, the complicated system of different foreign exchange rates was gradually overcome.[38] In 1950, Austria joined the European Payments Union, which prepared the European countries for the Bretton Woods monetary system, and in 1959 the Austrian schilling was declared convertible for foreigners.[39]

Throughout this period, the specter of inflation posed an increasing threat. Between 1938 and 1945 the volume of cash in circulation had increased from 1.2 to 8 billion reichsmark. On 5 July 1945 banks were reopened and, with the law limiting access to deposits on counters (*Schaltergesetz*), sixty percent of deposits were blocked. As early as 30 November 1945, the schilling was reintroduced. One hundred and fifty reichsmark per person were exchanged at a 1:1 rate; the rest was transferred into blocked accounts. But by 1947 the volume of banknotes in circulation doubled. With the Currency Protection Act of 9 December 1947, new banknotes were printed, certain deposits were deleted without replacement, and others were transformed into receivables toward the federal treasury. By means of an exchange operation, the volume of cash was considerably reduced: The banknotes of the year 1945 were recovered and the new schilling banknotes were introduced with a 3:1 ratio. An amount of only 150 schillings per person was exchanged at a 1:1 ratio. In order to keep the further inflationary pressure under control, employers and employees stipulated from 1947 to 1952 five wage and price-fixing agreements which marked the beginning of the Austrian social partnership. Nonetheless, prices and wages increased by 140 percent during this period, the monetary volume increased from 7.4 to 17.3 billion schillings, and the volume of loans from 2.1 to 11.2 billion shillings. It was not until 1952 that a stabilization of currency could be achieved, as a result of the government's tough austerity program and of the central bank's restrictive use of monetary policy instruments.[40] In 1955—the year of the Austrian State Treaty—a new law concerning the Nationalbank was issued, which afforded a special guarantee for the independence of bank loans from the state. Furthermore, the new areas of open market policy and minimum reserve policy were added to the instruments of the central bank.

At the Vienna Stock Exchange, securities transactions were officially reopened on 15 November 1948, although the market was impaired not least by unexplained legal framework conditions. Until well into the 1950s, the capital market was, as a consequence of the destruction of savings, unable to absorb issues. As a result, in connection with the Currency Protection Act of 1947, a two-percent federal bond came on the market, for the adoption of which, given the lack of private demand, a banking syndicate had be to created. The energy loan in 1953 achieved only mild sales among the public. Because of the lack of national long-term capital deposits, investment funds in the postwar period were raised by means of ERP counterpart funds, public and private funds, and to a lesser extent by means of credit institutions. How small the national potential for investments and how high the value of the Marshall Plan was for investment activities appear clearly from the fact that in the years 1948 and 1949 the "dollar side" alone of the Marshall Plan roughly corresponded to the entire Austrian gross investment.[41]

Also, from the point of view of banks, the situation in 1945 was initially wholly unclear. The ownership conditions were not clear for many customers; about 7,000 enterprises, therefore, had to be put under public administration. Real estate had suffered much, and the value of receivables concerning Austrian enterprises had yet to be calculated. Stakes and assets in Eastern Europe were cancelled, and receivables concerning the German Reich and German enterprises were completely uncertain. Under normal circumstances, Austrian banks in 1945 would have filed for bankruptcy. Therefore, the nationalization in 1946 of the three major banks (Creditanstalt-Bankverein, Länderbank, Hypotheken- und Creditinstitut) was ultimately a relief. Because the banking business was at any rate subject to strict government conditions, the granting of loans was, in turn, subject to public control and the central bank gave banks renewed liquidity.

The consequence of nationalization in Austria was not the emergence of public enterprises. Rather, the private form of organization (mostly stock corporations, "*Aktiengesellschaft*", abbr. "AG") continued to exist; the state had simply become a shareholder. It was important that the ministry of finance had the function of owner of the banks, whereas in the case of nationalized industry this was exerted by a special ministry of nationalization. At any rate, in this case, too, the principal of proportional representation was followed, so that the Creditanstalt was assigned to the People's Party and the Länderbank to the Socialist Party. As a result of the property regulation resulting from the 1955 State Treaty and the 1958 Property Agreement, banks could make up the balance again according to the rules. They drew up a reconstruction balance sheet for the period 1945 to 1954, which became the basis for the schilling opening balance sheet.[42] From that moment onwards it is possible to speak of a normal business activity in the context of Austrian economic tradition.

The new Austrian banking system reconstructed after 1945 had a few special characteristics. Nationalized banks had extensive industrial groups at their disposal, and in the Austrian "market economy" the banking system and large-scale industry were administered by the state. Also, the reconstruction period was marked by a tight regulation of the loan system, which partly had repercussions until the 1980s. The creation and granting of new loans was regulated by the Law on Loan Regulation of 3 July 1945 and the Loan Control Agreement of 1951. In addition, the federal government introduced a committee in charge of exerting an influence, by means of planned loan regulation, on the development of the Austrian economy.[43] In cooperation with the Oesterreichische Nationalbank, limits were fixed with regard to capital imports, the granting of loans, and so-called "*Habenzinsabkommen*" (agreement on deposit interest rates).

Development since the 1950s: Nationalbank and Stock Exchange

In the 1960s, Vienna as a financial hub continued to develop mainly in connection with the Austrian domestic market, within the framework of the Bretton Woods monetary order.[44] After the collapse of the Bretton Woods monetary system in the early 1970s, Austrian monetary policy oriented itself in accordance with a European currency basket at first, and from 1976 onwards an extensive link with the German mark followed.[45] Since the 1980s, the Oesterreichische Nationalbank (OeNB) had already completed the gradual opening of the Austrian financial hub and reacted with a flexibilization of the interest and open market policy.[46] At the beginning of the 1990s, the movement of capital was definitively liberalized.[47] Afterwards, the Austrian financial system was fully integrated into the European structure, with the adoption of the EU directive in the context of its access to the EU and the EEA in 1994-95.[48] On a national level, the Capital Market Adaptation Act of 1993 represented the essential step, which was followed by numerous other acts and amendments. The further development of the surveillance system led, after many intermediate stages, to the creation, on 1 April 2004, of a separate financial market authority as an independent public-law institution with its own legal personality.[49] In order to ensure a level playing field on an international scale, special levies for banks, duties on stock-exchange transactions and a whole series of other taxes were abolished.[50]

In 1998, the Austrian National Bank Act was adapted to the requisites of the European System of Central Banks.[51] On 1 January 1999—at the beginning of the third stage of the Economic and Monetary Union (EMU)—the euro was introduced as the common currency in Austria and eleven other member states of the European Union. The conversion took place at an exchange rate of one euro to 13.7603 Austrian schillings. The monetary policy tasks of the OeNB have thus been transferred to the European Central Bank (ECB). Decisions concerning these matters are taken by the Executive Board of the ECB. As a result, the OeNB is an integral part of the European System of Central Banks (ESCB), consisting of the ECB and the national central banks.[52]

After the creation by the mid-1950s of regular framework conditions for the capital market and the gradual recovery of savings activity, the stock exchange trade was also differentiated. In 1957, the foreign exchange trade was resumed, and in 1960 continuous trading for industrial shares began, although initially with only three stocks.[53] The stock exchange continued to suffer from a low supply, especially in the case of shares relating to the nationalization of Austrian large-size enterprises. From 1957 onwards, the attempt was made to enhance the stock market to a certain extent by means of so-called "*Volksaktien*" (people's shares). These were non-voting stakes in nationalized enterprises or in enterprises that had been acquired after 1955 from former "German property."[54] Forty percent of the capital of the Austrian Länderbank and of the Creditanstalt-Bankverein were in this form offered to Austrian citizens for purchase and the issue was several times oversubscribed.[55]

The marginal significance of the Vienna Stock Exchange appears clearly from that fact that between 1953 and 1963 only stocks with a volume of 33.7 billion schillings and shares with a volume of 2.3 billion schillings were placed.[56] An obstacle derived from legal provisions put the equity market at a disadvantage compared to other forms of finance. From the early 1950s, tax incentives for both the self-financing of enterprises and the purchase of fixed-income securities came into force, although the double taxation of shares remain untouched. As a result, there was, until the 1980s, a distortion of the capital market in favor of government issues and of the banking sector and to the disadvantage of the stock exchange trading. In 1981, 547 stock corporations were active in Austria, of which the Vienna stock list reported on sixty.[57]

The legal basis of the Vienna stock exchange was renewed in 1989 and harmonized with the EU directives in 1993. In the mid-1980s, the stock trade experienced a considerable upward trend for the first time in decades. Generally speaking, the securities trade was characterized by a development which was not least ascribable to new products such as Eurobonds, etc. Bonds lost their attractiveness compared to equity papers as a consequence of the introduction of the tax on interest earnings.[58] The international interest was also drawn to Vienna again, as a consequence of which a significant increase in revenues began in 1985-86. The privatization of nationalized enterprises, the introduction of an auction procedure for the issue of federal bonds, and the abolition of the governmental obligation to authorize issues promoted the development of the capital market.[59] With the creation of the ÖTOB (the Austrian futures and options market) in the Vienna Stock Exchange in 1991 the futures market was reintroduced. In 1997, the Wiener Börsekammer founded the Wiener Börse AG and merged it, together with the ÖTOB, into a company that was also called Wiener Börse AG.[60] Thus, a new, profit-orientated service company was created. In 1989, the first computer-supported trading system was launched, and in 1999 the Wiener Börse AG entered into a partnership with the Deutsche Börse AG. As a result, it became part of an extended international network of exchanges, which helped to increase liquidity and the demand of foreign investors.[61]

Compared to the modest volumes which prevailed until the 1970s, the Stock Exchange experienced a significant upswing from the mid-1980s onwards, especially the stock market. Annual revenues increased from 0.16 billion euros in 1984 to 31.23 billion euros in 1998. In 2002, revenues decreased to 12.73 billion euros as a consequence of the "New Economy Crisis." In 2003, an unprecedented growth began, which reached its peak in 2007 with an annual revenue of 157.88 billion euros. In 2008, revenues decreased again to around 53 billion as a consequence of the international financial and banking crisis, and increased again in 2009 to 78 billion. The capitalization of the traded shares of domestic enterprises increased from 2.06 billion euros at the close of 1984 to 46.27 billion euros in 2003, reaching its peak in 2007 with 156.33 billion euros. This amounted to an increase of over 250 percent compared to 2003. By 2007, capitalization plummeted by two-thirds to 58.14 billion euros, as a consequence of heavy losses and individual delistings.[62]

International comparisons show that the small Vienna Stock Exchange displayed from 2003 to 2007 a very dynamic development of quotations and capitalization, but was hit particularly hard by the crisis from 2008 onwards. Whilst capitalization in Vienna increased from the equivalent of 25 billion U.S. dollars in 2001 to 236 billion in 2008—that is, by 840 percent—capitalization in Frankfurt and Zurich increased only by 100 percent and in New York by forty-two percent. After quotations and stock exchange capitalization in Vienna by 2007 had increased strongly above average thanks to an extensive inflow of both domestic and foreign capital, a disproportionately severe loss marked the year 2008. In 2008, capitalization plummeted in Vienna by two-thirds, as mentioned above, whereas at the Swiss Exchange it decreased only by thirty percent, in Frankfurt and New York by forty percent.[63]

The strategic policy of the Vienna Stock Exchange consisted, from the 1990s onward, in positioning itself as a regional exchange for Austria and South-Eastern Europe.[64] To this purpose the technical infrastructure was modernized and many strategic partnerships were entered into with numerous exchanges in the region, but also on a global level. In the new millennium the Wiener Börse AG acquired, together with other capital market enterprises, majority stakes in the stock exchanges of Budapest, Ljubljana, and Prague. Since 2009, the four enterprises have signed up collectively under the umbrella brand CEE Stock Exchange Group.[65] Together with other exchanges in the region, they offer special indexes, organize collective road shows, and represent traded securities together on a global level. They attempt to establish themselves, despite the global trend toward large stock exchange mergers (e.g. NYSE Euronext in 2007), as a regional player with a specific competence for the respective market areas.

Banks and Financial Institutions

The development of the Austrian banking system from the late 1940s onward can be divided into four stages:[66]

—the recreation of institutional framework conditions until the 1950s

—a stage of growth of the loan market within the context of regulated international monetary structures in the 1960s

—a stage of strategically motivated competition until the mid-1980s

—and the internationalization and privatization from the 1980s onward.

The Austrian loan system was divided into different sectors until the 1970s: joint-stock banks (*Aktienbanken*) and bankers, savings banks (*Sparkassen*), Austrian state mortgage banks (*Landeshypothekenbanken*), *Raiffeisenbanken*, *Volksbanken*, *Bausparkassen*, and other banks. The liquidity transfer took place mainly within the sectors; peaks are covered between the major banks, central institutions, and the post savings bank (*Postsparkasse*).[67] The first task was to overcome the consequences of the war. The considerable loss in revenues and assets logically led to lower savings activity. Sight deposits recovered and reached a normal level as early as 1953. Also, the banks' share in the balance sheet total of the loan system in 1953 (forty-seven percent) was higher than before the war.[68] As a consequence of the recovery of the long-term business from the mid-1950s onwards, retail banking experienced a lasting upswing, which benefited the savings banks (*Sparkassen*), mortgage banks (*Hypothekenbanken*), and later also *Raiffeisen* banks. Savings activity now recovered and savings banks and credit cooperatives increased their market shares. This marked the recovery from the consequences of the war. For the first time, many Austrians were born in income groups with a higher demand for banking services.[69]

The second phase, roughly corresponding to the 1960s, was marked by differing growth rates of the customer groups. This was the beginning of what can be called the democratization of the loan system and the transition to bread-and-butter transactions ("*Massengeschäft*" in German). Especially private households now resorted to banking services. From this period onward, enterprises no longer paid wages and salaries in cash, thus forcing gainfully employed persons to open bank accounts. Banks promoted this development by keeping salary accounts free of charge. The first to profit from this were savings banks and credit cooperatives, since their customers traditionally came from this segment of the population. Until the early 1970s, therefore, there was virtually no competition, but simply an expansion of the banking services for the existing customer base.

Once a general availability of banking services had been achieved within the whole territory, competition intensified in the 1970s. All banks began to enter the customer area relating to competition. The benchmark of success was above all the growth of balance sheet totals, whereas profitability became less important. Banks now also dedicated themselves to bread-and-butter transactions, and savings banks and cooperatives dealt with industrial financing. As a result, the trend toward universal banks was visible in all financial institutions, and this was promoted by the legislation. In the case of cooperatives, their central institutions in particular developed into large-size banks.

During the course of intensified competition, many new branches were created and new products were offered. The total number of major institutions and subsidiary branches increased from 3,261 in 1970 to 5,143 in 1982.[70] Branches also acted as collection points for capital, since after experiencing two instances of inflation Austrian savers had become averse to risk. Households do not invest their financial reserves over a long period or in risk capital. Whilst savings were mainly invested for a short period, loans were granted mostly for a long period and the loan system has thus also to compensate the period. The financial sector thus carried the risk of the long-term commitment which savers were not ready to take on themselves.

The importance of the pension and stock market remained low, as a consequence of which the capital market became dependent on the money market. The capital market had become an inter-banking market, the financial sector interposed itself between supply and demand as mediator and grew between 1950 and 1980 six times more than the GNP. This was a direct consequence of the risk-free mass savings in lieu of capital raising by means of securities, which also had repercussions on the banks' own assets. In the 1950s, the equity capital was still low as a consequence of the war, but it increased thanks to the Bank Reconstruction Act of 1955, which admitted a new evaluation. In the 1950s and 1960s, deposits and loans grew twice as fast as the GNP; the equity capitalization could not keep up with it and in 1980 was virtually at the same level as in 1953. The stage of intensified competition, in which the industrial groups of major banks also became a heavy burden, led to a dramatic deterioration of both profitability and capital structure. The equity quota of the total Austrian banking system plummeted from 5.5 percent in 1960 to 2.5 percent in 1985. As a result, banks entered the period of concentration and internationalization from the second half of the 1980s in a much weaker condition with regard to capital structure and profitability. Nevertheless, the share of equity capital has been increasing since then, also as a reaction to Basel II from the end of the 1990s onwards.

In 1979, the trend toward the universal bank was completed also on a juridical level by means of the Loan System Act.[71] The strong state influence on the financial sector continued. This concerned not only the state-owned quotas of major banks but also the strong position of the local authorities due to their large demand on the capital market. The above-mentioned influence was visible above all in the state's promotion of savings and with regard to loans. In 1975, fourteen percent of all loans were subsidized by public sector bodies in the form of interest subsidies or cancellation subsidies. This concerned especially long-term loans for the construction of residential buildings, the promotion of exports and investments. In 1988 the proportion of subsidized loans to domestic economic enterprises and private individuals appears to have been already 41.6 percent.

From the 1980s onward, it is possible to speak of a saturation of the Austrian financial market; both balance sheet growth and economic growth decreased, and the banks, with their high supply of services and their large staff, were faced with problems of profitability. Following once again the principles of the social partnership, attempts were made to solve this also by means of agreements. In 1979, an end was put to the practice, which had been customary for decades, of regulating investments and loan conditions together within the framework of a "*Habenzinsabkommen*" (agreement on deposit interest rates). Until then, the Austrian banking sector was an oligopoly market, a "protected sector" and a heavily regulated economic sector. In 1985, another step was taken with regard to the tense economic situation, yet again in the Austrian tradition with cooperative agreements, the so-called Regulatory Agreements ("*Ordnungspolitische Vereinbarungen*"). Such agreements provided for the setting of minimum rates for interests on loans, maximum rates for interests on deposits, and the abolition of aggressive advertising methods.[72] It was not until accession to the European Union in 1995 that it became clear, at a high cost, that even informal agreements could cause sharp reactions from Brussels. As a consequence of EU integration, the Regulatory Agreements were no longer sustainable. The EU competition commissioner's condemnation of the Vienna Lombard Club in 2002 as a cartel of banks can be regarded as a reaction to this tradition. Commissioner Mario Monti called the Lombard Club "one of the most shocking cartels in the history of the EU."[73]

From the 1990s onwards, fundamental changes took place in the banking system. Legal provisions experienced a thorough "Europeanization." In 1993 a new Banking System Law replaced the old Loan System Law. The new law provided for, inter alia, risk-weighted assets. In the following years many amendments were undertaken, also in order to implement EU directives.[74] Furthermore, the Basel II provisions introduced changes with regard both to the relations between banks and their customers and to capital market behavior. The abolition of the anonymity of securities and savings accounts was fiercely debated in Austria, which happened as late as 2000.

Privatizations and Mergers

Structural change in the Austrian banking system in the 1990s was characterized by a process of concentration and internationalization. An important prerequisite was above all the privatization of nationalized banks. The Privatization Act of 1991 created the legal basis for the selling of the Länderbank and the Creditanstalt without having to involve the parliament. In the following years, the Austrian loan system was transformed as a result of mergers and regroupings. In this context the central institutions of the savings bank sector played a leading role. The expansion and concentration processes within the savings bank sector had already begun on the basis of the Savings Banks Act of 1979, which had abolished the regional principle that had been hitherto applied. Afterward, about 100 independent savings banks disappeared between 1980 and 1998. According to the Loan System Law of 1986, the savings banks (*Sparkassen*), *Raiffeisenkassen*, people's banks (*Volksbanken*), and Austrian state mortgage banks (*Landes-Hypothekenbanken*) were allowed to incorporate their banks into a stock corporation. As a result, the structural change went beyond the established sector boundaries, although the savings banks enjoyed certain competition advantages thanks to favorable guarantee constructions.[75]

In 1991, the Wiener Zentralsparkasse acquired the Länderbank, which generated significant losses due to foreign engagements, and Bank Austria was founded.[76] As the "red" Länderbank is regarded as an institute under Social-Democratic influence, the "black" Creditanstalt, which is under the influence of the Austrian People's Party (ÖVP), has not participated in the reorganization of the Länderbank. As a result of this merger, Bank Austria drove the Creditanstalt from its market leadership position in the Austrian banking sector. The Girozentrale merged with the Österreichisches Credit Institut and established the GiroCredit in 1992, thereby transforming from a top institution in the cooperative banking sector into a small Austrian universal bank. In the same year, the Bayerische Vereinsbank acquired a stake in the traditional Schoellerbank.[77] The merger of Bank Austria and GiroCredit in 1994 represented an interim solution for three years. From 1995 to 2004, the Bayerische Landesbank bought a significant stake in the Bank für Arbeit und Wirtschaft AG (BAWAG),[78] of which the Austrian Trade Union Federation (ÖGB) has been the majority owner, and the Erste Bank acquired considerable stakes in the Salzburger Sparkasse. In 1996, the DG-Bank acquired a minority stake in the Österreichische Volksbanken AG. In 1997, the acquisition of the traditional "middle class" Creditanstalt by the "red" Bank Austria caused considerable political controversy. As part of this transaction, Bank Austria was forced to sell the GiroCredit to the Erste Bank due to competitive legislation.

In the cooperative banking sector, the Raiffeisenlandesbank Niederösterreich-Wien and the Raiffeisenbank Wien merged in 1997. The Raiffeisen Zentralbank organized its activities in the reforming nations in the Raiffeisen International, which filed for a listing at the Vienna Stock Exchange in April 2005 and was regarded as one of the best-performing listed companies until 2007. In 2000, the trade union bank (*Gewerkschaftsbank*) BAWAG acquired the majority stake in the Postsparkasse (PSK)[79] as part of the last large-scale privatization in the banking sector and the Bavarian Hypo Vereinsbank (HVB) took over Bank Austria. As part of this transaction the Austrian bank was incorporated into the HVB as an asset, without any monetary flow. The merger was approved by the European Commission in November 2001—and thus the third-largest bank of Europe was established. In 2001, the complete merger of Bank Austria and the Creditanstalt was accomplished. In the following year, the new mother institution faced serious economic pressure, and in July 2003, the capital increase of Bank Austria Creditanstalt based on a stock exchange listing was implemented. The HVB together with Bank Austria was integrated into the Italian UniCredit Group, which opted for a delisting of Bank Austria from the Vienna Stock Exchange. As a consequence of these developments, the bank density in Austria has been declining since the 1990s. The number of major institutions has been reduced from 1,210 (1990) to 855 in 2009.[80] Nevertheless, Austria is still considered "overbanked." The employment level has remained relatively stable. The staff level in the Austrian banking sector increased from 74,597 employees in 1990 to 80,293 in 2008.[81]

Internationalization

Whilst domestic business has grown slowly, the internationalization of the Austrian banking sector has increased significantly over the last decades. In the 1970s, the internationalization was mainly characterized by the emergence of trust banks. Until the mid-1980s, the creation of affiliates expanded and the creation of joint ventures was typical of the end of the 1980s. In addition, the stakes in foreign banks and banking trusts increased. This development was accompanied by a shift from banking to customer business and to specialized foreign entities (e.g. leasing subsidiaries). In contrast to domestic business, where a universal banking business is pursued, the foreign business focused on a niche business. The banks followed their customers and the engagement abroad therefore expressed the increasing internationalization of the Austrian economy. The internationalization of the Österreichische Länderbank, the Girozentrale, and the Creditanstalt-Bankverein amounted to more than forty percent in the 1990s. In terms of internationalization, Austria has been ranked at the same level as the Netherlands, Ireland, and Switzerland. But the engagement abroad has not pursued only one direction, foreign financial institutes have also entered the Austrian market. In 2003, the majority stakes of twenty-nine banks were foreign-owned, foreign banks had twenty-two affiliates in Austria and 225 financial institutions pursued their business based on the freedom of services as part of the EU.

Selected banks started early to internationalize their business, but this temporarily led mainly to additional costs. The share of foreign assets as part of the balance sheet of the total number of institutes increased from one percent in 1960 to 7.7 percent in 1970 and grew further to 22.6 percent by 1985—in the case of banks and bankers even to 36.2 percent. The early foreign engagement was characterized by an international expansion, based on the establishment of affiliates in New York and London. In the 1990s, however, Austrian banks had to face the fact that they are not among the global players, especially in terms of their size. Consequently, they reinforced their focus on the domestic market and the geographically neighboring markets. In addition, the engagement abroad has turned into a domestic business based on the capital market regulations and the adoption of EU directives. This development has been facilitated by the technological revolution (computers), which enabled global financial transactions without a physical presence in big financial centers. The internationalization impacted the asset structure of the banking sector. The total amount of foreign receivables of the Austrian financial industry increased from 61.3 billion euros in 1990 to 376.5 billion in 2008. The amount of foreign payables reached 68.1 billion and 269.6 billion euros in the same years. In 2008, approximately a fifth of receivables of customers in Central, Eastern, and South-Eastern Europe was accounted for by banks based in Austria.[82]

Since the opening of the capital market in 1991 and Austrian membership in the EEA as well as subsequently the EU, the Austrian financial market can no longer be regarded as a national, Austrian financial market but as a regional, Viennese financial hub that must exist in a liberalized international market.[83] Viennese financial institutions have been facing opportunities based on the freedom of services within Europe since 1995.[84] Overall, the foreign engagement of Austrian banks can thus be regarded as business regionalization rather than globalization. This also applies to the last phase of Austrian banking history, characterized by the opening of the Eastern European economies. Due to its geographic position as well as tradition, Austria has been pursuing a very intense foreign trade with centrally-planned economies, which has also impacted banking transactions. These transactions have been facilitated by an extended system of national and export credit guarantees. The Austrian banking sector already assumed a market share of fifteen percent of the financial business in the "Eastern bloc" prior to the opening of the Eastern European market. Therefore, the Austrian economy has been able to react quickly to the system transformation in the former Eastern European countries—the banks among others were present in these markets early on and expanded their businesses faster than most competitors in terms of affiliates and stakes in existing banks, advisory services, and employee training. Especially in the neighboring countries, Austrian banks represent the market leaders today and assume an unrivaled market position.

With the opening of Eastern European markets, Austrian banks were able to ensure a strong market position by acting as "early movers."[85] Especially the Bank Austria Creditanstalt, the Erste Bank, and the Raiffeisen Zentralbank engaged significantly in these markets.[86] In 2002, approximately ten percent of the consolidated balance sheet of the Austrian banks was accounted for by transactions in Central and Eastern Europe—of these ten percent generated twenty-two percent of the revenues and even twenty-six percent of the earnings before tax. The major driver of the business results in Eastern Europe is the relatively higher margins in the interest, provision, and trade business as well as the more favorable cost structure.[87] In 2003, the Raiffeisen Zentralbank employed approximately four-fifths of its 21,000 employees in the Central and South-Eastern European countries, the Bank Austria Creditanstalt was represented by 19,000 employees in this region, and approximately 22,000 employees worked in the Eastern European affiliates of the Erste Bank.[88]

The international crisis which started in 2008 impacted the Viennese banks with varying magnitude. In the early phases of the crisis, write-offs and uncertainties in connection with the activity in the transforming countries led to anxieties, but the institutions were involved in the Western markets, which were highly affected by the crisis. In 2008, the Austrian government reacted with a national package of supporting initiatives for banks to the acute crisis after the bankruptcy of Lehman Brothers in the U.S. and the prospective tightening equity capital directives (Basel III). Several large banks leveraged in total 6.2 billion euros for national capital and guarantees for bonds amounting to 27.6 billion euros.[89] In November 2008, the Oesterreichische Clearingbank AG was established in order to support short-term transactions between Austrian banks and to improve the liquidity balance on the domestic money market.[90] The Erste Bank and Raiffeisen launched the redemption of the capital as early as 2010. Bank Austria did not leverage the above-mentioned government support and received a capital increase from the Italian holding UniCredit amounting to 2 billion euros in March 2010.[91] In the cooperative banking sector, the customer-oriented business units of the Raiffeisen Zentralbank Österreich AG and Raiffeisen International Bank-Holding AG were merged in 2010.[92]

The Österreichische Volksbanken AG generated significant losses as a result of the crisis. Its subsidiary Kommunalkredit had to be nationalized, the Investkredit, the majority rights of which were also held by the ÖVAG, was integrated more tightly within the institute, the foreign units in Central and South-Eastern Europe were identified as potential divesture units.[93] The Carinthian Hypo Group Alpe Adria faced the highest losses. This institution pursued a risky expansion strategy from the 1990s onward—among others in the countries of the former Yugoslavia—and was accused of fraudulent balance sheet preparation in 2004. In 2007, its owners (Land Carinthia, Grazer Wechselseitige Versicherung, and a private group of shareholders who generated a high profit as part of the deal) sold a stake majority to the Bayerische Landesbank. In December 2009, this institution had to be nationalized. The Hypo Group Alpe Adria received 700 million euros from the Bavarian owners during the financial crisis in 2008 and 900 million euros participation capital as part of the Austrian package of supporting capital for banks. In 2009, further capital flow followed amounting to more than 1 billion euros provided by the then owners as part of the nationalization aiming at the rescue of the bank. The Austrian state added 450 million euros, and other domestic banks provided 500 million euros. Comprehensive guarantees are taken over by the parties involved.[94] In general, the bankruptcy of Austrian financial institutions was prevented by deploying extensive public funds. The engagements of Austrian banks (and also of Bank Austria as part of the Italian UniCredit Group) in Central, Eastern, and South-Eastern Europe were sustained despite some unfavorable legal amendments in those countries (e.g. in Hungary). Financial institutions have thus proved a factor of stability for those economies and maintain their engagements in order to support and leverage the still considerable growth potentials in those countries.[95]

Notes

1. See Peter Eigner, Michael Wagner, and Andreas Weigl, "Finanzplatz: Wien als Geld- und Kapitalmarkt," in *Wien: Wirtschaftsgeschichte 1740-1938*, Teil 2, *Dienstleistungen*, ed. Günther Chaloupek, Peter Eigner, and Michael Wagner (Vienna: Jugend & Volk, 1991), 911-97.

2. Franz Baltzarek, *Die Geschichte der Wiener Börse* (Vienna: Verlag der Österreichischen Akademie der Wissenschaften, 1973), 19-53.

3. Alice Teichova, "Peripetien des Finanzzentrums Wien," in *Auf Heller und Cent*, ed. Karl Bachinger and Dieter Stiefel (Frankfurt: Ueberreuter, 2001), 529.

4. In 1851, customs between Austria and Hungary were abolished. In 1859, a trade agreement was concluded with Prussia, the commercial law was substantially liberalized, and a new railroad concession law was issued. Herbert Matis, "Leitlinien der österreichischen Wirtschaftspolitik," in *Die Habsburgermonarchie 1848-1918*, Band 1, *Die wirtschaftliche Entwicklung*, ed. Alois Brusatti (Vienna: Verlag der Österreichischen Akademie der Wissenschaften, 1973), 29-67.

5. See Siegfried Pressburger, *Oesterreichische Notenbank 1816-1966* (Vienna: Oesterreichische Nationalbank, 1966), 11ff.; Othmar Bachmayer, *Die Geschichte der österreichischen*

Währungspolitik (Vienna: Manz, 1960), 96ff.

6. John Komlos and Marc Flandreau, "Core or Periphery?," in *Auf Heller und Cent*, ed. Bachinger and Stiefel, 163ff.; Pressburger, *Oesterreichische Notenbank*, 163ff.; Evelyn Kolm, "Die Oesterreichisch-ungarische Bank im Spannungsfeld der Nationalitätenkonflikte," in *Auf Heller und Cent*, ed. Bachinger and Stiefel, 221-22; Hildegard Hemetsberger-Koller, "Die suspendierte Goldkonvertibilität," in ibid., 185ff.

7. See Charles P. Kindleberger, *A Financial History of Western Europe* (London: Allen & Unwin, 1984), 121-22; Gustav Otruba, "Die Wiener Rothschilds," *Wiener Geschichtsblätter* 41 (1968): 149ff.

8. See Eduard März, *Österreichische Industrie- und Bankpolitik in der Zeit Franz Josephs I.* (Vienna: Europa Verlag, 1968), 29ff.; Alice Teichova, "Banking in Austria," in *Handbook on the History of European Banks*, ed. Manfred Pohl (Aldershot: Elgar, 1994), 4; Herbert Matis and Fritz Weber, "Kaisertum Österreich—Donaumonarchie," in *Europäische Bankengeschichte*, ed. Hans Pohl (Frankfurt: Knapp, 1993), 324-25.

9. Andreas Resch, "Wien—die wechselvolle Entwicklung eines Finanzplatzes in Zentraleuropa," in *Europäische Finanzplätze im Wettbewerb*, Bankhistorisches Archiv, Beiheft 45 (Stuttgart: Steiner, 2006), 103.

10. John Komlos, *Die Habsburgermonarchie als Zollunion* (Vienna: Österreichischer Bundesverlag, 1983), 99-141; Michael Pammer, *Entwicklung und Ungleichheit* (Stuttgart: Steiner, 2002), 120ff.

11. Pammer, *Entwicklung und Ungleichheit*, 165-69.

12. Hans Kernbauer and Fritz Weber, "Die Wiener Großbanken in der Zeit der Kriegs- und Nachkriegsinflation," in *Die Erfahrung der Inflation im internationalen Zusammenhang und Vergleich*, ed. Gerald D. Feldman and William J. Bouwsma (Berlin: de Gruyter, 1984), 182-83.

13. Peter Eigner, "Die Konzentration der Entscheidungsmacht: Die personellen Verflechtungen zwischen den Wiener Großbanken und Industrieaktiengesellschaften, 1895-1940," PhD. diss., University of Vienna, 1997, 58ff.

14. Ivan T. Berend, "Banking and the Hungarian Economy in the 20th Century," in *Bank Austria Creditanstalt: 150 Jahre österreichische Bankengeschichte im Zentrum Europas*, ed. Oliver Rathkolb et al. (Vienna: Zsolnay, 2005), 218.

15. See Eduard März and Karl Socher, "Währung und Banken in Cisleithanien," in *Die Habsburgermonarchie 1848-1918*, Band 1, ed. Brusatti, 361-62; Eduard März, *Österreichische Bankpolitik in der Zeit der großen Wende 1913-1923* (Vienna: Verlag für Geschichte und Politik, 1981), 75.

16. Pressburger, *Oesterreichische Notenbank*, 366; Bachmayer, *Die Geschichte der österreichischen Währungspolitik*, 127; Karl Bachinger, "Eine stabile Währung in einer instabilen Zeit," in *Abschied vom Schilling*, ed. idem. et al. (Graz: Styria, 2001), 11ff.

17. The central bank regulations in turn allowed for a gold bullion standard with an one-third cover of note circulation including specific foreign currencies in the cash cover. The *Bareinlösepflicht* remained suspended. Hans Kernbauer, *Währungspolitik in der Zwischenkriegszeit*, s.l., s.a., 17ff.; Pressburger, *Oesterreichische Notenbank*, 375; Bachmayer, *Die Geschichte der österreichischen Währungspolitik*, 121ff.

18. Dieter Stiefel, "Österreich," in *Europäische Bankengeschichte*, ed. Pohl, 441.

19. *Statistisches Taschenbuch für Wien 1926*, Vienna 1926, 11.

20. For the savings banks (*Sparkassenwesen*), see Hedwig Fritz, *Geschichte*, 150 Jahre Sparkassen in Österreich Band 1 (Vienna: Sparkassenverlag, 1972); Walther Schmidt, *Das*

Sparkassenwesen in Österreich (Vienna: Reichsverband deutscher Sparkassen in Österreich, 1930); Andreas Resch, "Überleben in Zeiten der Hyperinflation," in *Auf Heller und Cent*, ed. Bachinger and Stiefel, 371-88.

21. Alice Teichova, "Banking and Industry in Central-East Europe in the First Decades of the 20th century," in *Bank Austria Creditanstalt*, ed. Rathkolb et al., 148-61.

22. Aurel Schubert, *The Credit-Anstalt Crisis of 1931* (Cambridge: Cambridge University Press, 1991), 37.

23. Fritz Weber, *Vor dem großen Krach*, Habilitationsschrift, Vienna 1991, 297.

24. Andreas Resch, "Konjunkturelle Rahmenbedingungen, investitionshemmende Politik und Arbeitslosigkeit zwischen den Weltkriegen," in *Rationalisierung und Massenarbeitslosigkeit*, ed. Günter Chaloupek, Harald Hagemann, and Andreas Resch (Graz: Leykam, 2009), 79-125.

25. Bachmayer, *Die Geschichte der österreichischen Währungspolitik*, 131-32; Bachinger, "Eine stabile Währung in einer instabilen Zeit," 97ff.; Peter Berger, *Im Schatten der Diktatur: Die Finanzdiplomatie des Vertreters des Völkerbundes in Österreich: Meinoud Marinus Rost van Tonningen 1931-1936* (Vienna: Böhlau, 2000), 164ff.; Dieter Stiefel, *Finanzdiplomatie und Weltwirtschaftskrise* (Frankfurt: Knapp, 1989); Kernbauer, *Währungspolitik in der Zwischenkriegszeit*, 285ff.; Schubert, *The Credit-Anstalt Crisis of 1931*, 141ff.

26. See Stiefel, *Finanzdiplomatie und Weltwirtschaftskrise*; Schubert, *The Credit-Anstalt Crisis of 1931*.

27. Stiefel, "Österreich," 443.

28. Gerald D. Feldman, "Die Länderbank Wien AG in der Zeit des Nationalsozialismus," in *Österreichische Banken und Sparkassen im Nationalsozialismus und in der Nachkriegszeit*, 2. Band, *Regionalbanken, Länderbank und Zentralsparkasse*, ed. idem. et al. (Munich: C.H. Beck, 2006), 259-489; Dieter Ziegler, "Die 'Germanisierung' und 'Arisierung' der Mercurbank während der Ersten Republik Österreich," in *Banken und "Arisierungen" in Mitteleuropa während des Nationalsozialismus*, ed. Dieter Ziegler, Geld und Kapital 5 (Stuttgart: Steiner, 2002), 41.

29. For the reorganization of the bank sector during National Socialism, see Gerald D. Feldman et al., *Österreichs Banken und Sparkassen im Nationalsozialismus und in der Nachkriegszeit*, 2 vols. (Munich: C.H. Beck, 2006); Peter Eigner and Peter Melichar, "Enteignungen und Säuberungen—Die österreichischen Banken im Nationalsozialismus," in *Banken und "Arisierungen" in Mitteleuropa während des Nationalsozialismus*, ed. Ziegler, 43-119; Eigner, "Die Konzentration der Entscheidungsmacht," 537ff.; Peter Melichar, *Neuordnung im Bankwesen: Die NS-Maßnahmen und die Problematik der Restitution*, Veröffentlichungen der Österreichischen Historikerkommission: Vermögensentzug während der NS-Zeit sowie Rückstellungen und Entschädigungen seit 1945 in Österreich, Band 11 (Munich: Oldenboug, 2004); Herbert Matis and Fritz Weber, "Economic 'Anschluss' and German 'Großmachtpolitik': The Take-over of the Austrian Credit-Anstalt," in *European Industry and Banking between the Wars*, ed. P. L. Cottrell, Håkan Lindgren, and Alice Teichova (Leicester: Leicester University Press, 1992), 109ff.

30. Eigner and Melichar, "Enteignungen und Säuberungen," 54-55, 63.

31. Baltzarek, *Die Geschichte der Wiener Börse*, 137ff.

32. Otto Klambauer, "Zur Frage des Deutschen Eigentums in Österreich," in *Jahrbuch für Zeitgeschichte* (1978): 148.

33. Ziegler, "Die 'Germanisierung' und 'Arisierung' der Mercurbank," 41; Feldman, "Die Länderbank Wien AG in der Zeit des Nationalsozialismus."

34. Gerald D. Feldman, "Die Creditanstalt-Bankverein in der Zeit des Nationalsozialismus, 1938-1945," in *Österreichs Banken und Sparkassen im Nationalsozialismus und in der*

Nachkriegszeit, 1. Band, *Creditanstalt-Bankverein*, ed. idem. et al. (Munich: C.H. Beck, 2006), 23-187; Matis and Weber, "Economic 'Anschluss' and German 'Großmachtpolitik,'" 109ff.

35. Harold James, "Die Deutsche Bank und die Diktatur 1933-1945," in *Die Deutsche Bank 1870-1995*, ed. Lothar Gall et al. (Munich: C.H. Beck, 1995), 381ff.

36. See Peter Eigner and Andreas Resch, "Die wirtschaftliche Entwicklung Wiens im 20. Jahrhundert," in *Wien im 20. Jahrhundert*, ed. Franz X. Eder et al., Querschnitte 12 (Innsbruck: Studienverlag, 2003), 8-140.

37. For instance, membership in the IMF only as an article XIV member. Hannes Androsch, "Zur politischen Ökonomie der österreichischen Währungspolitik," in *Das Kreditwesen in Österreich: Festschrift für Hans Kransensky zum 80. Geburtstag*, ed. Konrad Fuchs and Max Scheithauer (Vienna: Manz, 1983), 20.

38. Hans Seidel, "Die österreichische Wechselkurspolitik 1945-1953," in *Auf Heller und Cent*, ed. Bachinger and Stiefel, 501ff.; Herbert Matis, "Vom Nachkriegselend zum Wirtschaftswunder—Der Schilling im 'goldenen Zeitalter,'" in *Abschied vom Schilling*, ed. Bachinger et al., 201ff.

39. Stephan Koren, "Die Geldpolitik Österreichs im Wandel der internationalen Währungsordnung," in *Das Kreditwesen in Österreich*, ed. Fuchs and Scheithauer, 164.

40. Fritz Diwok and Hildegard Koller, *Reinhard Kamitz: Wegbereiter des Wohlstands* (Vienna: Molden, 1977), 40.

41. Hans Seidel, *Österreichs Wirtschaft und Wirtschaftspolitik nach dem Zweiten Weltkrieg* (Vienna: Manz, 2005), 294ff.; Peter Eigner, "Ein Schritt vor, zwei Schritte zurück—Die wechselhafte Geschichte des Finanzplatzes Wien im 20. Jahrhundert," in *Bank Austria Creditanstalt*, ed. Rathkolb et al., 488-93.

42. Erich Miksch, "Der österreichische Kapitalmarkt," in *Das Kreditwesen in Österreich*, ed. Fuchs and Scheithauer, 124.

43. Bachmayer, *Die Geschichte der österreichischen Währungspolitik*, 140.

44. Theresia Theurl, "Österreich," in *Europäische Bankengeschichte*, ed. Pohl, 588-89.

45. Gertrude Tumpel-Gugerell, "Der Euro—ein Ausblick," in *Vom Schilling zum Euro*, ed. Klaus Liebscher and Wilfried Seipel (Vienna: Manz, 2002), 31.

46. In the mid-1990s, the minimum balance requirement for deposits of long duration was lowered and a general reduction of the minimum rates was put through. In return, the allowability of cash assets against the minimum balance was abolished.

47. Maria Schaumayer, "Der Schilling als Beispiel für eine erfolgreiche Integration in den europäischen Wirtschafts- und Währungsraum," in *Vom Schilling zum Euro*, ed. Liebscher and Seipel, 75; Peter Mooslechner, *Der Finanzplatz Wien* (Vienna: WIFO, 1993), 31-32.

48. Herbert Schimetschek, "Finanzsystemstabilität im Umfeld liberalisierter Finanzmärkte," in *Vom Schilling zum Euro*, ed. Liebscher and Seipel, 134.

49. Anton Stanzl, "Bankenaufsicht," in ibid., 180-81.

50. Peter Eigner, "Konzentration, Privatisierung und Internationalisierung: Österreichs Banken seit den 1990er Jahren," in *Kartelle in Österreich*, ed. Andreas Resch (Vienna: Manz, 2003), 194.

51. Schaumayer, "Der Schilling als Beispiel für eine erfolgreiche Integration," 75; idem., "Die währungspolitische Bedeutung eines wettbewerbsfähigen Kapitalmarktes," *Österreichisches Bank-Archiv* (1991): 847-48; Eigner, "Konzentration, Privatisierung und Internationalisierung," 194-95.

52. See Klaus Liebscher, "Vom Schilling zum Euro—Kontinuität einer stabilitätsorientierten

Währungspolitik," in *Vom Schilling zum Euro*, ed. idem. and Seipel, 61-62.

53. Miksch, "Der österreichische Kapitalmarkt," 246ff.; Koren, "Die Geldpolitik Österreichs im Wandel der internationalen Währungsordnung," 164.

54. Baltzarek, *Die Geschichte der Wiener Börse*, 152ff.

55. Dieter Stiefel, *Verstaatlichung und Privatisierung in Österreich: Illusion und Wirklichkeit* (Vienna: Ueberreuter, 2011), 49.

56. Miksch, "Der österreichische Kapitalmarkt," 243-44.

57. Franz Vranitzky, "Der österreichische Kapitalmarkt," in *Das Kreditwesen in Österreich*, ed. Fuchs and Scheithauer, 232.

58. Stefan Kirschner, "Die Entwicklung der Wiener Börse," PhD. diss., Vienna University of Economics and Business, 2003, 104.

59. Theurl, "Österreich," 584-85.

60. Wiener Börse AG, *Geschäftsbericht 1997*, Vienna 1998.

61. Schimetschek, "Finanzsystemstabilität im Umfeld liberalisierter Finanzmärkte," 135.

62. Data: Wiener Börse.

63. Calculated on the basis of World Federation of Exchanges data.

64. See *Geschäftsberichte* of Wiener Börse AG, various vols.

65. CEESE, Vienna 2009.

66. Elementary to this: Gunther Tichy, "Drei Phasen des Strukturwandels im österreichischen Kreditapparat," *Österreichisches Bank-Archiv* (1977): 307-19; idem., "Zu einigen wichtigen Strukturmerkmalen des österreichischen Kreditapparates," ibid., 322-40. See also Hellmuth Klauhs, "Der Wettbewerb der Kreditunternehmungen," in *Das Kreditwesen in Österreich*, ed. Fuchs and Scheithauer, 296ff.; Ernst Magerl and Leo Pötzlberger, "Die Struktur des österreichischen Kreditwesens und seine rechtliche Situation," in ibid., 153ff.; Theurl, "Österreich," 590. For an analogous periodization on the basis of the development of the currency ratios, see Androsch, "Zur politischen Ökonomie der österreichischen Währungspolitik," 13.

67. Theurl, "Österreich," 586.

68. Tichy, "Drei Phasen des Strukturwandels im österreichischen Kreditapparat," 308ff.; Eigner, "Konzentration, Privatisierung und Internationalisierung," 188.

69. Karl Pale, "Die Rolle des Sparkassensektors in der österreichischen Kreditwirtschaft," in *Das Kreditwesen in Österreich*, ed. Fuchs and Scheithauer, 204ff.; Theurl, "Österreich," 589.

70. Fuchs and Scheithauer, eds., *Das Kreditwesen in Österreich*, Table 3.10, 341.

71. Theurl, "Österreich," 590.

72. Eigner, "Konzentration, Privatisierung und Internationalisierung," 193.

73. Ibid., 202.

74. Ibid., 194-95; Stanzl, "Bankenaufsicht," 179-80.

75. Stanzl, "Bankenaufsicht," 179-80.

76. For the merger, see Rene A. Haiden and Peter Haiss, "Merger Management am Beispiel der Bank Austria," in *Konzentration und Ausgliederung im Unternehmensbereich*, ed. Alois Mosser, Veröffentlichungen der Österreichischen Gesellschaft für Unternehmensgeschichte 18 (Vienna: Manz, 1996), 113ff.; and the more journalistic account by Klaus Grubelnik, *Die Rote Krake: Eine Bank erobert Österreich* (Vienna: Orac, 1998).

77. Gerhard Randa, "Österreichs Banken auf dem Weg nach Europa—kein Sonderweg," in *Vom Schilling zum Euro*, ed. Liebscher and Seipel, 155; Eigner, "Konzentration, Privatisierung und Internationalisierung," 198ff.

78. *Der Standard*, 26 May 2004; *Die Presse*, 29, 30, and 31 May 2004.

79. BAWAG and PSK merged in 2005. Starting in 2006, heavy speculative losses have been coming to light. Leading managers were imprisoned and in 2007 the bank was sold to the U.S. private equity investment firm Cerberus. *Financial Times Deutschland*, 7 May 2007.

80. OeNB data. The number of branch offices developed less evenly. It increased from 4,497 in 1990 to 4,694 in 1996 and then declined to 4,172 in 2009.

81. OeNB data.

82. Oesterreichische Nationalbank, *Finanzmarktstabilitätsbericht 16*, Vienna, December 2008, 15.

83. Georg Winckler, "Wirtschaftspolitische Rahmenbedingungen des Finanzplatzes Österreich," in *Der Unternehmer und die Banken*, ed. Edith Frauwallner and Heinz Handler (Vienna: Bundesministerium für Wirtschaftliche Angelegenheiten, Sektion Wirtschaftspolitik, 1999), 18.

84. Randa, "Österreichs Banken auf dem Weg nach Europa," 161.

85. Josef Zechner and Alexander Stomper, "Wien als Finanzzentrum Mittel- und Osteuropas," Sparte Bank und Versicherung, Wirtschaftskammer Wien, April 2003.

86. Ibid.

87. Oesterreichische Nationalbank, *Finanzmarktstabilitätsbericht 6*, 38ff.

88. *Der Standard*, 28 Apr. 2004; *The Wall Street Journal*, 19 Feb. 2004.

89. *Die Presse*, 29 May 2010.

90. Oesterreichische Clearingbank AG, Press Information, 13 Nov. 2008.

91. *Der Standard*, 13 Feb. 2010.

92. *Die Presse*, 9 July 2010; *Der Standard*, 12 Oct. 2010; <www.rbinternational.com> (15 Dec. 2010).

93. Österreichische Volksbanken-AG, *Geschäftsbericht 2009*; Österreichische Volksbanken-AG, *Zwischenbericht 3. Quartal 2010*.

94. For a brief overview, see for example *Die Presse,* 10 Dec. 2010.

95. Herbert Stepic, "Raiffeisen International: Bemerkungen eines Ostpioniers," in *Der "Ostfaktor": Österreichs Wirtschaft und die Ostöffnung 1989 bis 2009*, ed. Dieter Stiefel (Vienna: Böhlau, 2009), 47.

Konferenzplatz Wien: Vienna as an International Conference Site

Eric Frey

They are a common sight in downtown Vienna: groups of men and women in business suits with badges around their necks. They are part of the flourishing convention industry that attracts hundreds of thousands guests to the Austrian capital every year.

Since 2005, Vienna has led the worldwide ranking of cities that attract international meetings that is published by the International Congress and Convention Association (ICCA). In 2009, the last year for which figures are available, Vienna recorded 160 major international meetings, with Barcelona (135) and Paris (129) as runners-up.[1] Using a broader definition, the city government counted 882 national and international conventions in 2009 and a total of 2,569 events, including company meetings. The city is particularly popular for medical conventions that make up a fifth of all meetings and regularly attract several thousand, sometimes tens of thousands, participants.[2]

According to city figures, there were 1.373 million overnight stays by convention visitors for 2009. Even though that is only fourteen percent of all overnight stays by visitors, the share of congress business in total tourism turnover is much larger because convention visitors tend to spend one-and-a-half times as much per day as regular tourists (420 euros vs. 280 euros). The city estimates the added value of all international meetings at 736 million euros for 2009, securing a total of 15,000 jobs.[3]

Most of the revenue stems from private-sector events, including medical and other professional conventions. But the growing number of meetings related to the strong presence of international organizations also plays a significant economic role. A study by the accounting firm Ernst & Young for the Austrian foreign ministry from August 2009 reported a fifteen percent increase in the number of international conferences from 2004 to 2008 and an increase of 125 percent in the number of participants. For the year 2008, Ernst & Young estimates that these activities directly contributed 190.5 million euros to Austrian GDP; through multiplier effects, total demand increased by 1.1 billion euros.[4]

Vienna's attractiveness as an international meeting place is related to its central geographical location, the great number of historical and cultural sights, convenient transport links and relatively moderate prices for restaurants and accommodation. But the strong market position that the city achieved in such a competitive industry is mostly due to the availability of several excellent convention centers and the sustained efforts by a series of Austrian governments to turn Vienna into a center for international organizations and into an international meeting place.

These initiatives started in the 1950s, shortly after the signing of the State Treaty that gave Austria full independence, and were originally driven mostly by political calculations. But right from the start, the economic benefits of a major convention business were also part of the decision-making process. In the 1970s and 1980s, the huge investments needed to host organizations and conferences triggered a series of heated domestic political controversies, in which the economic costs and gains of these projects were judged quite differently by the Socialist-led government and the conservative opposition. The debates affected domestic popular attitudes toward international organizations and conferences, but in the end it did not damage Vienna's international standing and its ability to attract spendthrift foreign visitors. Whether Austria's political objectives were met, however, is a different question.

The Birth of an International Role

With the end of the Habsburg Empire in 1918, Vienna lost its role as an international—or just European—political and commercial meeting place. The occupation by Nazi Germany in March 1938 and the outbreak of World War II cut most international ties. The destruction by Allied bombings during World War II also destroyed a large part of the city's tourism infrastructure. Tourism recovered during the 1950s in Vienna as in Salzburg and the Alpine region, and Austrian economic planners saw tourism as a significant factor for the country's development.

But as Austrian leaders looked to attract visitors from abroad, they had another motive in mind. Shortly after the signing of the State Treaty in May 1955, the government began to focus on attracting international organizations to Vienna. The first opportunity arose with the decision at a New York conference on nuclear energy in September/October 1956 to launch the International Atomic Energy Agency (IAEA), designed as a clearing house for nuclear transactions. Austria lobbied hard for Vienna as the designated headquarters location. "Choosing Vienna as the IAEA's seat would underline Austria's neutral status and mark its re-entry into the international community after the ignominious years of 'Anschluss' and after the end of the four-power occupation."[5] Vienna was picked over Geneva, Copenhagen, and Rio de Janeiro, mostly because its neutral site so close to the Iron Curtain was seen to be well suited as a place to store large amounts of fissile material.

Already at that time there was a larger political objective behind the Austrian government's quest to host international organizations. In a footnote, IAEA historian David Fisher cites a private conversation with Heinrich Haymerle, who was then political director in the Austrian foreign ministry, in which Haymerle refers to the experience of 1938, when only Mexico protested against the German invasion and the Anschluss. "This time, by having an international organization in Vienna, the Austrian Government wanted to ensure that any repetition of its disappearance would be noticed!" Haymerle reportedly said.[6] This larger security-based rationale, also called the "Mexico syndrome," was subsequently attributed to Chancellor Bruno Kreisky, who was then state secretary in the foreign ministry, but one must assume that there was already early on a broad consensus among both diplomats and political leaders that Austria needed to attract an international presence to secure its survival as a neutral state between the two Cold War blocs.

In the summer of 1957, the preparatory staff of the IAEA moved to Vienna and was given temporary offices in the Musikakademie. The first General Conference of the agency from 1 October to 21 took place in the Konzerthaus, an art nouveau concert hall. Austria's Foreign Minister Karl Gruber presided over the meeting of fifty-two national delegations, and federal President Adolf Schärf gave the opening address.[7] It was very probably the first major diplomatic conference in Vienna since the Vienna Congress of 1814-15.

The IAEA established Vienna as a site for UN organizations, and given the central role the agency has played in international security ever since, it was a lucky draw for the city. The role of the IAEA was boosted by the Non-Proliferation Treaty that came into force in 1970 and turned the agency into the watchdog against the spread of nuclear weapons.

In 1958, key parts of the Hofburg, the 700-year old imperial palace in downtown Vienna, were turned into a public convention and event facility, the first of its kind in the city. In 1969, management was handed over to a private operating company owned by several hotel chains, a travel agency and the public casino company.

Vienna's role as an East-West international meeting place was firmly established through the summit between Soviet leader Nikita Khrushchev and the newly elected U.S. President John F. Kennedy on June 3 and 4, 1961, only the second meeting between the leaders of the two superpowers since the outbreak of the Cold War and the first one on neutral ground. According to various reports, the two administrations also considered Stockholm, Oslo, Helsinki, and Geneva as meeting places. Kennedy voiced a clear preference for Vienna, which Khrushchev accepted, in a gesture of support for Austria's policy of neutrality.[8]

The summit was the crucible for the country's ambition to become an international meeting place, and there were doubts whether the city had sufficient and adequate accommodation for the large delegations and the accompanying journalists. But with the help of some bed and breakfasts and a few overflow beds in a military barrack, all visitors found places to sleep.[9]

Most importantly, the television pictures from the summit itself, the banquet and subsequent concert in the Schönbrunn Palace and the lady's program for Jacqueline Kennedy and Nina Khrushcheva showed a glorious and peaceful city with an impressive cultural heritage. The enthusiastic reports in the Austrian press about Vienna's successful debut on the global stage indicated both a growing sentiment of national solidarity that appeared capable of overcoming the long-standing rancor between the "waterhead" Vienna and the rest of the country and also the birth of the belief that the policy of neutrality, and the international respect for this policy choice, could form the basis of a new national identity.[10]

The Road to a United Nations Headquarters

The Austrian campaign to turn Vienna into an international center gained speed in the mid-1960s. In 1965, Austria lured the Organization of the Petroleum Exporting Countries (OPEC) from Geneva to Vienna.

In November 1966, the UN General Assembly decided to locate the newly founded United Nations Industrial Organization (UNIDO) in the Austrian capital. The presence of two major UN agencies as of January 1967 made the city the third largest site of the world organization, behind New York and Geneva. On 21 February 1967, the federal government pledged to construct a new UN headquarters on an empty lot on the east bank of the Danube, the Donaupark, that could house both organizations, and an adjacent conference center. The facility was set to be let to the UN free of charge.

The project was an initiative by the conservative People's Party led by Chancellor Josef Klaus but had the full support of the Socialist Party, which was in opposition on the federal level but governed in Vienna. In subsequent years, that bipartisan consensus on Vienna's international role would break down.

An international architectural competition organized jointly by the federal and city governments ran from November 1968 to May 1969. From 280 entries, the seven-member jury picked the American architect Cesar Pelli as the winner, followed by a British and a German team. The highest-ranked Austrian was Johann Staber. All four teams were asked to modify their proposals in line with zoning and technical requirements.[11]

But on 1 March 1970, the People's Party lost the parliamentary elections and the Socialists under Bruno Kreisky formed the new government. On 18 December 1970, a multi-ministry committee chose Staber's project over the competitors. Kreisky strongly defended the decision in public appearances, in which he denied local favoritism and argued that Staber's plans were best suited for the specific needs of the UN organizations.[12] His energetic advocacy for the *Internationales Amtsitz- und Konferenzzentrum Wien* (IAKW), also known as the Vienna International Center (VIC) or UNO-City, changed the political dynamics. The project was increasingly identified with Kreisky and the Socialists and gave the People's Party room to launch a negative campaign against their own baby.

Kreisky had long argued that Austria's foreign policy and its neutrality would be best served by a strong international profile. That view was in line with his personal biography, which led him into Swedish exile during the Nazi occupation of Austria, his personal qualifications as a professional diplomat and his personal ambitions. Kreisky was fully convinced that the presence of international organizations and a high-profile foreign policy would serve as a better defense against foreign aggression, which was usually associated with the Soviet Union at the time, than a specific alliance or a strong army, several aides reported.

"Better than by the military, Austria would have to prepare against [a Soviet invasion] by political means," says Thomas Nowotny, Kreisky's personal secretary from 1970 to 1975. "It never should happen again that—as in 1938—the country should disappear with just one single, faraway country, namely Mexico, raising faint protest. The international community should have an interest in the existence and independence of Austria. Such interest could be created and maintained by an active foreign policy that rendered useful services to the international community [...] and by establishing a strong international presence in Vienna, by enlarging the number of UN and of other international organizations headquartered in Austria's capital; and by establishing the city as a venue for international gatherings."[13] Even Kreisky's effort to have General Motors build a major engine plant in Vienna was driven not only by his desire to create new jobs, but seen as "a security asset of greater value than a few supersonic fighter planes," Nowotny argues.

Nowotny's successor Georg Lennkh also referred to the "Mexico syndrome" in Kreisky's thinking about Vienna's international role.[14] But interestingly enough, there is hardly any written evidence for this foreign policy doctrine. In 1973, shortly before construction at the VIC began, Kreisky called the building "a political decision because Vienna's role as an UN center is of highest importance for Austria's neutrality and security."[15] But in the following years, as the project came under fire from the opposition and the media, he focused on the economic benefits of job creation and indirect returns of the presence of several thousand international civil servants.

Still, Kreisky's motives "were more than obvious for us, who worked in Kreisky's office," said Nowotny, and the same holds true for international observers. In a widely quoted article in October 1976, *The Times* of London called the office blocks that were going up on the bank of the Danube "the main pillar for Austrian defense" and said that they were cheaper than any modern military system.[16]

The domestic debate about the VIC and Vienna's international role, however, focused primarily on economic costs and benefits. The People's Party first criticized the non-transparent procurement process and the choice of the Staber project against the jury's decision. An investigative parliamentary committee set up in April 1971 did not come to any clear conclusions. The next target of the opposition were the skyrocketing construction costs, which rose from projected 6.5 billion Austrian schillings to nearly 9 billion schillings. In 1967, the government had presented an estimate of 600 million schillings. Meanwhile, the needed office space for the two UN organizations shrank, mostly because UNIDO turned out to be smaller than expected. Instead of 7,000 employees, the new plans assumed 4,500 people to work at the VIC, and even that number was never met. Austria started to lobby for additional UN organizations to move to Vienna to fill the empty space.

Several reports by the Austrian court of auditors (*Rechnungshof*) in 1974 were also critical of the choice of project and the lack of cost control during construction. The auditors, however, also faulted the unlimited pledge by the previous government to build a UN headquarters for free.[17]

Vienna, meanwhile, began to attract a growing number of international meetings. On 18 June 1979, U.S. President Jimmy Carter and Soviet leader Leonid Brezhnev met in Vienna to sign the SALT II Treaty on nuclear arms control, the second superpower summit after the Kennedy-Khrushchev talks. International guests numbering 1,200 attended the formal opening of the VIC on 23 August 1979, which turned Vienna officially into the third United Nations headquarters, behind New York and Geneva. Simultaneously, the UN held its first major conference in Vienna, the UN Conference on Science and Technology for Development (UNCSTD).

There was media speculation about growing tensions with Switzerland and the United States as Austria was gearing up to lure offices away from the other UN sites. An article in *The New York Times* even speculated that Vienna might be set up as an alternative home for the UN Secretariat and the General Assembly if members turned against New York for political reasons. The Vienna site was not completed yet, however. The conference center that had been part of the original plan still needed to be built.

The Controversy of the Conference Center

In March 1979, the Kreisky government approved the construction of a new conference center next to the VIC that could seat 6,000 people. The capacity was subsequently raised to 9,500 people. Architect Johann Staber received the commission without a public bidding process.

The decision was controversial from the start. The opposition People's Party said it was a waste of taxpayers' money that could not be afforded in economically difficult times. Even the People's Party knew that more conference space was needed in Vienna, but its leaders called for an alternative project closer to the city center, either an expansion of the Hofburg facilities or a major renovation of the Messepalast, the former imperial stables built by Johann Fischer von Erlach that were at the time used for trade fairs.

The government pointed to its contractual obligation toward the UN to construct an efficient conference center that could be used by the organizations at any time. Only the Donaupark next to the VIC provided sufficient space for an adequate facility, and the construction of a major new building would also create up to 5,000 jobs, it argued. Moreover, a large-scale conference center would also help to attract professional conventions and other private-sector congresses with several thousand participants.

By the late 1970s, Vienna had become an attractive place for such meetings, primarily from the medical profession, and the Hofburg was reaching its capacity limits. Organizers and hotel owners warned, however, that the participants of these conventions would not accept a location outside the inner city and would shun the new conference center. Even the government took these concerns seriously, but it felt that they were outweighed by the requirements of the UN organizations and the need for a very large center to host mammoth conventions. The construction of the U1 subway line that would cut the commuting time between the VIC and the inner city to less than ten minutes would help to overcome the worries about the geographical distance, officials argued.

Even the People's Party had long supported the construction plans, as the government never failed to point out.[18] The 1967 agreement with the UN had included a conference center. In 1972, the People's Party supported a parliamentary vote in favor of the center. Faced with the high construction costs for the VIC, a conservative parliamentarian, Fritz König, warned in 1974 that the government might postpone or even sacrifice the conference center project, thus endangering Vienna's position as congress site.[19] It is fair to say that the campaign by the People's Party against the conference center was driven by short-term political calculations and an appeal to populism rather than a long-term vision.

In November 1981, the People's Party led by Alois Mock initiated a *Volksbefragung*—a non-binding referendum—in Vienna, posing the question whether the conference project should be shelved in favor of a cheaper expansion of the Hofburg facility. A second question referred to a plan to spend more money on urban reconstruction. Ninety percent voted against the conference center, but only sixteen percent of the eligible voters participated, reflecting the call for a boycott of the poll by the Socialist city government of Vienna. Soon afterwards, the People's Party launched a nationwide *Volksbegehren* (petition drive), the most widely used instrument of direct democracy in Austria, against the project. It came under the headline "for 12,000 apartments, secure jobs in all of Austria, and against the unnecessary conference site" and was clearly designed to mobilize resentment in the provinces against the capital. That undertaking was far more successful. More than a quarter of the electorate—1.36 million voters—signed the petition between May 12 and 17, 1982. It was the largest number of signatures ever collected in such an instrument. In some regions with high unemployment more than fifty percent of the voters made the effort to sign the petition.[20]

The Kreisky government chose to ignore the initiative and argued that three-quarters of the population had not signed the petition. To counter concerns about the construction costs, the government presented a financing model in which Arab investors would bear half of the expenses, which were estimated at 4.5 billion schillings. The opposition put the cost at 7.5 billion schillings, citing the usual cost overruns and interest payments. In the end, the total bill came up only to 3.5 billion schillings, one of the few examples where a public project was completed below cost estimates.

In the subsequent months, dozens of small towns and villages where the People's Party had the majority sent letters to the chancellery calling for the money to be spent on projects outside Vienna. The communal council of Gnadenwald near Innsbruck voted nine to one for a petition to stop construction at the conference center and distribute the designated budget among all Austrian communes. Gnadenwald with 409 residents would receive 400,000 schillings and would spend the money to renovate the rectory and build a larger town hall.[21]

All these efforts did not stop the construction, but it hurt the popularity

Austria Center Vienna © IAKW-AG / Marius Höfinger

Rights that took place in June 1993 with more than 5,000 international participants. Medical conventions were even larger, attracting up to 10,000 participants and hundreds of companies that needed exhibit space. In 1997, the government reacted to the growing need and agreed to pay for another expansion.[23] In some years, up to 300,000 people a year attended events at the ACV.

Despite strong business and good capacity use, the ACV failed to turn a profit until 2004. Smaller meetings tended to create high overhead expenses that were not covered by the fees.[24] The innovative financing model that helped to reduce construction costs led to higher operating expenses for years to come, giving some retroactive credibility to the opponents of the project. Still, given the enormous indirect benefits for business in Vienna, the conference center is no longer subject to any significant controversy.

A new privately run convention center near the Prater, the Reed Messe Wien Exhibition & Congress Center, opened in January 2004 and further increased the available space for international meetings in Vienna. It is mostly used for trade fairs, but it also hosted a major international AIDS conference in July 2010 that brought a record 25,000 participants to Vienna.

The strong competition between the ACV, the Hofburg and the Reed Messe add to Vienna's attractiveness, but undercut the profitability of all conference venues. The CEO of the ACV, Thomas Rupperti, claims that a growing number of organizers refuse to pay any rent, forcing the centers to rely on commissions from hotels and businesses.[25] Several new five-star hotels along the Ringstrasse and in the inner city as well as a growing number of top restaurants signal the huge importance of the conference business for the city.

The End of the Mediator Role

In contrast to the flourishing commercial side, the political benefits of these investments grew increasingly doubtful. Vienna's importance as an international center is undisputed, and the number of international organizations climbed from eight in 1980 to nineteen in 2005.[26] With the fall of the Iron Curtain in 1989, Vienna also gained ground as a financial and corporate center. But the city no longer offered any special attraction as an international meeting place. The Vranitzky/Mock government focused on gaining entry into the European Community and did not pursue the visions of Kreisky, who saw himself as a mediator between east and west, north and south, and Israel and the Arab world. When Israel and the PLO initiated secret negotiations in 1992, it was Norway and not Austria that hosted the talks.

Vienna became the place of choice for permanent institutions that were set up by the Conference for Security and Cooperation in Europe (CSCE) in 1992. And when the CSCE was converted into the OSCE in 1995, Vienna became the site of its Secretariat and its most important offices, including its Parliamentary Assembly, fending off tough competition from Prague. The CSCE was given office space in the Hofburg and the delegations refused several offers by the city government to move the headquarters to the Austria Center. When a major fire at the Hofburg in November 1992 destroyed not only the main conference rooms, but also some of the CSCE offices, the city quickly had to find new space in the Hofburg to stop the delegations from leaving Vienna all together.[27]

Even though regular OSCE meetings take place in Vienna throughout the year, the organization does not attract a lot of international attention. When it came to high-profile international negotiations and meetings, other European cities were regularly chosen over Vienna. Neutrality, which was once an asset, appeared to have turned into a liability.

Several summits between the presidents of the United States and Russia took place in the new member countries of NATO, such as the Czech Republic, Slovakia or Slovenia. And despite the presence of the IAEA in Vienna, talks with Iran over its controversial nuclear program are usually conducted in Geneva, which is still seen as the number one negotiating place in the world. Some critics blame the government's general lack of interest in foreign policy for that development. As stated earlier, the Social Democrats gave up the foreign minister post in the coalition talks in 1986 and never asked for it again. In the People's Party, the post was held by party leaders Alois Mock and Wolfgang Schüssel until the year 2000, when Schüssel became chancellor with the help of the far-right Freedom Party. The next two foreign ministers were at least seasoned diplomats, Benita Ferrero-Waldner and Ursula Plassnik. The current foreign minister, Michael Spindelegger, was spokesman for foreign affairs in the parliamentary faction, but his foreign policy experience was quite limited when he assumed the post in 2008. After he became leader of the ÖAAB, a major inner-party organization, his attention has been often focused on domestic political issues. When Wikileaks published confidential cables from the U.S. Embassy in Vienna, which lamented the lack of interest in foreign policy by Chancellor Werner Faymann and argued that Spindelegger saw himself in his foreign missions more as a commercial salesman than a diplomat, the government protested loudly, but most domestic commentators agreed with that pointed analysis.[28]

A Different Kind of Success Story

In the second decade of the twenty-first century, Vienna can claim to be one of the most attractive cities in the world. The city regularly leads the surveys by the consulting group Mercer International among expatriate managers for quality of life, mostly for its cultural offerings, high safety and good transportation links.[29] But Vienna's international exposure is also a factor, making the city more cosmopolitan than the sometimes narrow-minded Viennese mentality would suggest. Both the presence of international organizations and the brisk conference business contributed to that fortunate development. As Austria is only surrounded by democratic countries that are members of the EU and NATO or—in the case of Switzerland and Liechtenstein—neutral, the concern for national security is no longer an issue when it comes to attracting international conferences. The benefits are not what the diplomats and political leaders of the 1950s expected, but they are no less real.

Notes

*I would like to thank the Bruno-Kreisky-Archiv, the Austrian Ministry for European and International Affairs, and the United Nations Information Service in Vienna for help to prepare this article.

1. ICCA Press Release, 19 May 2010, <www.iccaworld.com/npps/story.cfm?nppage=2175>.

2. Christoph Rella, "Wiener Kongress trotzt der Krise," *Wiener Zeitung*, 9 Apr. 2010.

3. Rathauskorrespondenz, 4 Apr. 2010, <www.wien.gv.at/rk/msg/2010/0408/013.html>.

4. "30 Jahre UNO-City: Der Wiener Magnet für die Welt," *Die Presse*, 27 Aug. 2009; and Press Release by the Austrian Ministry of European and International Affairs from 28 Aug. 2009, <www.bmeia.gv.at/aussenministerium/aktuelles/presseaussendungen/presseaussendungen-2009/spindelegger-uno-city-in-wien-ist-teil-unseres-internationalen-selbstverstaendnisses.html>.

5. David Fisher, *History of the International Atomic Energy Agency: The First Forty Years* (Vienna: IAEA, 1997), 49.

6. Ibid., 56.

7. Ibid., 59-60.

8. Martin Kofler, "Juni 1961: Das 'Wiener Gipfeltreffen' Chruschtschow-Kennedy," in *Die Augen auf Wien gerichtet: Gipfel 1961 Chruschtschow—Kennedy*, ed. Monika Sommer and Michaela Lindinger (Vienna: Studienverlag, 2005), 21-22.

9. Monika Sommer, "Eine Bühne der Weltgeschichte," in ibid., 65-66.

10. Ingrid Bauer, "Nina und Jackie—Zwei Frauen, zwei Welten," in ibid., 95ff.

11. "Die Wiener UNO-City," APA historisch—Zeitgeschichte online, <www.historisch.apa.at/cms/apa-historisch/dossier.html?dossierID=AHD_19790823_AHD0001>.

12. Protocol of the hearing at the Unido *Untersuchungsausschuss* in the Austrian Parliament, 8 July 1972.

13. Interview with Thomas Nowotny, 6 Dec. 2010.

14. *Der Standard*, 28 Aug. 2009, 9.

15. "Die Wiener UNO-City," APA historisch—Zeitgeschichte online.

16. *Arbeiter-Zeitung*, 28 Oct. 1976.

17. Letter by *Rechnungshofpräsident* Jörg Kandutsch Zl. 300-5/73, dated 21 Dec. 1973. Kreisky-Archiv.

18. See, for example, letter by Chancellor Bruno Kreisky to the town of Bisamberg, 19 Apr. 1983. Kreisky-Archiv.

19. "Konferenzzentrum wird Monsterbürotürmen geopfert," ÖVP-Pressedienst, 15 Nov. 1974.

20. "Denkmal für Kreisky," *Die Zeit*, 28 May 1982.

21. Letter by the Gemeindeamt Gnadenwald, 22 Sep. 1982. Kreisky-Archiv.

22. "Monumente eines Sonnenkönigs," *Die Presse*, 28 Feb. 2010.

23. "Edlinger sagt neue Halle für Austria Center zu," *Der Standard*, 4 Feb. 1997.

24. "Steigende Auslastung bringt Austria Center höhere Verluste," *Der Standard*, 18 May 1995.

25. "Kongresszentren matchen sich um Großveranstaltungen," *Der Standard*, 14 Jan. 2010.

26. Klaus Emmerich, *Unterwegs zum Frieden: 50 Jahre Österreich in den Vereinten Nationen* (Vienna: Ueberreuter, 2005), 136.

27. "Redoutensaal: Wien als KSZE-Standort gesichert," *Der Standard*, 18 Nov. 1992.

28. "Nein, nein und wieder nein," *Der Spiegel*, 49/2010.

29. Mercer 2010 Quality of Living Report, <www.mercer.com/articles/quality-of-living-survey-report-2010>.

OMV: A Case Study of an Austrian Global Player

Alexander Smith

The OMV Aktiengesellschaft[1] is in terms of net revenues Austria's largest corporation[2] and a major European energy company. Its oil and natural gas exploration and production activities cover seventeen countries around the globe. The Vienna-based enterprise is fully vertically integrated. It consolidates upstream and downstream operations from exploration, fossil fuel recovery, transport, and refining to marketing, distribution, and direct customer sales at its own gas stations. In addition, OMV operates in the petrochemical industry and, since 2007, in electricity generation. The Austrian oil and gas group is the leading energy corporation of East Central Europe. As such it plays an important role in European energy security.

Broadly defined, an enterprise which owns and controls assets in two or more countries is referred to as a multinational corporation (MNC) or global player.[3] A main characteristic of a MNC, which "may be privately, publicly, cooperatively, or governmentally owned,"[4] is the establishment of "local operations as a means of serving a foreign market rather than engaging in arms-length transactions with market intermediaries."[5] A global player thus is "a cluster of corporations of diverse nationality joined together by ties of common ownership and responsive to a common management strategy."[6] According to these widely accepted definitions, OMV clearly is a multinational corporation or global player. This arises, however, from the nature of the oil and gas industry, which is inherently global and affords transnational integration.[7] In this context, the MNC concept's explanatory power seems limited. To recognize OMV as multinational does not really improve our understanding of the company's idiosyncrasies. It would put the

Austrian group on equal footing with the large international oil companies, the so-called "supermajors."[8] In this article, it is argued that OMV is a globally operative major European corporation whose significance draws on its specific strategic positioning and role in European energy security.

The aim of this article is, first, to briefly trace OMV's development with its gradual internationalization from its formation to the end of Europe's division into East and West in 1990. In a second step, the company's post-Cold War well-directed strategy of expansion and its specific focus on the new markets of East Central Europe will be outlined. The third section points out OMV's leading position in Central, Eastern, and South-Eastern Europe. In the fourth part of this article, the corporation's and, thus, Austria's role in European energy security will be discussed. The final section deals with OMV's controversial ventures in Sudan and Iran.

The Internationalization of a National Oil Producer

After the end of the Second World War, Moscow laid claim to the Austrian petroleum industry as "German assets." Soviet soldiers occupied the prolific oil fields around Vienna, and, in early October 1945, the Soviets declared the seizure of large parts of the Austrian oil economy. The confiscated enterprises were transformed into the Soviet Mineral Oil Administration (SMV).[9] In accordance with the decisions made by the Allies in Potsdam in summer 1945, the "German assets" were used as war reparations. First, Moscow embarked on a strategy of dismantling Austrian industry property in its zone of occupation. The bulk of movable oil industry assets were shipped to the Soviet Union.[10] Later, the seized companies were regarded as "milk cows" and the Soviets tried to attain maximal reparations out of continuous production.[11] According to Günter Bischof, "Stalin's *top priority* in his Austrian policy was the *economic exploitation of the Soviet zone of occupation* in Austria" (emphasis in original).[12] This was especially true for Austria's profitable oil industry.

After ten years of Allied occupation, with the signing of the State Treaty on 15 May 1955, Austria retrieved its independence. On 13 August 1955, the Soviet-controlled oil industry assets were handed over to the Republic of Austria under the terms set out in the Moscow Memorandum and placed under government control. In the following year, the fully state-owned OMV mineral oil company was formed out of SMV's property holdings. After its formation, OMV was confronted with formidable operational challenges. The company's starting conditions could hardly have been more difficult. The Soviets not only left the SMV with empty coffers, but the newly created OMV also suffered from considerable deliveries (*Ablöselieferungen*) of its high-grade oil from the Matzen field to the Soviet Union.[13]

In addition, more subtle factors put a strain on the young Austrian enterprise. Its Soviet legacy, which became apparent in an outdated organizational structure, technological sophistication, and personnel administration as well as lacking environmental sensitivity,[14] and a noncompetitive entrepreneurial spirit, had to be overcome in order to turn into a modern Austrian and internationally viable company. This process was initially hampered by OMV's lacking sales organization, which is an integral part of any integrated oil firm. Only in 1965 did the Austrian parliament decide the integration of the state-owned gas station operators Martha Erdöl and ÖROP into OMV.[15] This event marked an important step for the company's further development and its transformation into a competitive European player.

In OMV's early years, domestic petroleum production not only sufficed to meet the yearly deliveries to the Soviet Union, but there was also enough oil for the Austrian refineries to run at full capacity.[16] However, with high economic growth and the increasing motorization of the Austrian society, domestic production was soon unable to keep up with the soaring demand for mineral oil products. OMV had no other choice but to open up new petroleum resources either by purchasing oil from international suppliers or by trying to obtain concessions abroad to produce its own crude. With the completion in 1960 of its modern refinery in Schwechat near Vienna, OMV created the capacity to process large amounts of domestic and imported petroleum. In the subsequent years, Schwechat was incrementally expanded and became Europe's largest inland refinery of its time.[17]

In the 1960s, OMV's crude oil imports originated from the Soviet Union, Yugoslavia, and Bulgaria and were transported by barge on the Danube River or by railway in tank cars.[18] High costs and limited capacity of these shipping methods emphasized the need for pipeline transportation. In 1967, OMV concluded contracts with international oil companies for the construction of the Adria-Wien Pipeline (AWP) to supply the Schwechat refinery—via the Transalpine Pipeline (TAL)—with crude arriving at the Trieste terminal in Italy. The AWP and the conclusion of accessory agreements are of historical significance for the Austrian mineral oil company. They have been called a "crucial condition" for OMV's prominence in the Austrian and Central European energy markets today.[19]

OMV soon did not content itself with direct petroleum imports. In the late 1960s, it joined a consortium of European oil companies under the leadership of the French major Elf-ERAP for exploration activities in

The OMV refinery in Schwechat

southern Iran.[20] But OMV was not only interested in liquid mineral fuels. For the development of an Austrian natural gas economy it made an effort to secure competitive and reliable foreign gas supply sources. It found them in the Soviet Union. In June 1968, OMV concluded as the first Western corporation a long-term agreement for the supply of natural gas with Moscow.[21] Even though at the time of the Cold War the cooperation with the communist "enemy" was highly controversial, this revolutionary deal turned out to be precedent-setting. The Austrian firm "opened the door to the West" for Russian natural gas and other Western oil and gas companies soon followed OMV's lead.[22] The major German gas company Ruhrgas, for example, met two years later "in OMV's Vienna offices to sign a similar deal with the Kremlin."[23]

OMV continued the internationalization of its fossil fuel procurement in North Africa and the Middle East by pushing—against the resistance of the international oil majors—into Algeria, Libya, and Syria.[24] In the 1970s and early 1980s, the company acquired further interests for the exploration of oil and natural gas in Ireland, Norway, Canada, Mexico, Venezuela, Egypt, Gabon, and Tunisia. Most of these investments, however, did not pay off in economic terms and failed to provide OMV with noteworthy quantities of fossil resources. Until the late 1980s, the Austrian group still invested far more in domestic than in international exploration.[25] As a consequence, by the mid-1980s oil production in foreign countries did not amount to much. The production of appreciable quantities of natural gas outside of Austria in fact did not start before 1990. Despite OMV's internationalization in fossil fuel exploration and production, in the first three decades since its formation the company's focus largely remained on the Austrian market. While in international comparison OMV was a small oil corporation at the time, in the Austrian economy it gained a key position.[26] The company's primary concentration on Austria finally ended with its important strategic reorientation in the 1980s.

As pointed out by Michaela Roiss, the new rules of procedure of 1982 initiated a reorganization of the company toward a more efficient operational management and administration. In the seminal business plan of 1983, OMV's executive board redefined the corporation's strategic goals. They included the further internationalization of the mineral oil business and its positioning as the Central European hub for oil and natural gas. This business plan marks the beginning of "the transformation process from a national provider to an internationally operative, competitive European supplier."[27] In the course of the implementation of its new strategy, OMV adopted a new cost organization (*Kostengestaltung*) in 1984 and an innovation program in 1985. The former was directed at cost reductions, staff cuts, and a more efficient administration. The latter introduced the change from an outdated functional organization to a modern divisionalization into business units.

In the mid-1980s, when global oil output started to exceed demand by far, the world petroleum business turned into a buyer's market. Tumbling prices for fossil fuels ruined the international oil companies' earnings prospects and forced them to implement cost-cutting programs. The collapse of prices is sometimes referred to as the "third oil price shock"—this time to the detriment of the producers and sellers. OMV could not escape the global trend. The reorganization measures and the slimming down of personnel of the 1980s were very important for the company's future development and economic competitiveness.

The same is true for the political decision in 1987 to start the privatization of OMV. In a first step the Austrian industry holding company (ÖIAG) took public fifteen percent of the corporation's capital stock. In 1989, another ten percent were sold to private investors. In those days OMV was in a growth phase and in the course of realizing its international expansion. In 1985, it acquired twenty-five percent of OxyLibya's assets, Occidental Petroleum's Libyan subsidiary, and founded OMV of Libya. "This acquisition was the breakthrough of the international exploration and production activities."[28]

Two years later, OMV took over Marathon Oil's Burghausen refinery in Bavaria. The investment strategy strained the group's capital position. Going public implied a more or less unrestricted access to capital markets, which allowed to adapt the company's equity base to its growth.[29]

Expansion into East Central Europe

From the late 1980s onward, OMV clearly focused its exploration activities outside of Austria. With its new exploration and production (E&P) strategy it aimed at an expansion of its global activities and a diversification of its resource base through an internationalization of upstream operations. In pursuance of its strategy, OMV massively raised its exploration budget to 1.1 billion schillings in 1991 and 1992 and restructured the division by consolidating the two exploration groups "domestic" and "foreign."[30] Henceforth, priority was clearly given to activities abroad. As a result, OMV invested in the British and Norwegian North Sea, Jordan, Malaysia, and Turkey (1988); Gabon, Indonesia's Arafura Sea, Libya, and the Dutch North Sea (1989); Indonesia's Java Sea, and Pakistan (1990); Albania, Angola, Bulgaria, and Yakutia in Siberia (1991); as well as Vietnam and Yemen (1993).[31]

The internationalization of upstream operations became immediately noticeable in the structure of OMV's petroleum production. Starting with Libya as the operating company in 1985 and the British North Sea some years later—these two acquisition were decisive for the increase of OMV's own oil as a share of the total volume traded—, in 1990 the Austrian group's foreign oil output surpassed domestic production for the first time. Since the mid-1980s, OMV gradually increased its petroleum production abroad while inland output remained stable. In 1989, the company's domestic oil and natural gas production amounted to 11.86 million barrels of oil equivalent (mboe), compared to only 6.31 mboe of foreign output. Only one year later, the relation changed dramatically in favor of the latter: While inland output remained stable at 11.98 mboe, non-Austrian production doubled to 13.09 mboe.[32] This is primarily due to OMV's acquisition in early 1990 of a five percent share in the North Sea oil field "Beryl" and its 14.38 percent participation in Conoco's "Dunlin" field, both of which added 60 mboe to the company's reserves.[33]

With the fall of the Iron Curtain in 1989-90, Europe's post-World War II division finally came to an end. This world-historical event opened up the promising markets of Central and Eastern Europe (CEE). This led to a rethinking by OMV and a strategic reorientation: While the Austrian market was saturated, the company identified the growth markets of the CEE region as a key for its further expansion.[34] OMV also intended to reach out of Austria in marketing and distribution. Therefore, it expanded its downstream business by stepping into the CEE gas station market, which promised robust growth. As formulated by former OMV chief executive Richard Schenz back then, "going international in marketing means Central Europe."[35] Before 1990, OMV established a sales organization, i.e. a gas station network, only in Austria. From then on, it gradually shifted the main focus of its marketing operations from its home market to CEE.

In the mid-1980s, OMV started to streamline its Austrian gas station network. The closure of several hundred gas sales points was the consequence. The number of filling stations operated by OMV in Austria decreased from 1,328 in 1987 to 928 in 1991, 800 in 1995, and 548 in 2000. At the same time, the company established a veritable gas station business in the CEE region. The first sales organizations were opened in 1991, when the company operated a total of twelve gas stations abroad. This number steadily augmented to ninety-eight in 1992, 274 in 1995, and 588 in 2000.[36] OMV, which started in 1989 to open stations in the company's colors and under its logo, soon ran gas stations in all countries neighboring Austria, except for Switzerland and Liechtenstein.

The (economic) opening of Eastern Europe, however, did not just create new growth opportunities for the Austrian oil and gas group. Initially, it led to a sharp decline in prices for chemicals and fertilizers—sectors in which OMV had only recently heavily invested. In 1989, it took over PCD Polymere[37] and in 1990 it acquired the major chemical group Chemie Linz. When the recession set in and world oil prices plunged—with all its negative consequences for the refinery business—OMV went into the red.[38] In 1993, the company was not yet accurately streamlined but went into expansion. This resulted in severe operating losses. In the wake of the huge drop in operations in the corporation's worst year since its formation, OMV initiated far-reaching structural changes. In a nutshell, the company aimed at a retreat to core business. The plan was to strengthen integrated oil and gas operations while reducing the chemical and petrochemical business. The reorganization also involved an intensive cost-cutting program with substantial reductions in staff. In 1993-94, the workforce was cut by twenty percent to 11,000 employees.[39]

Thanks to the immediate and insistent implementation of the rationalization measures, in 1994 OMV successfully accomplished the turnaround and went back into the profit zone. The company's success made it increasingly interesting for international investors. In the same year, the

International Petroleum Investment Company (IPIC), a subsidiary of the Abu Dhabi National Oil Company (ADNOC), joined OMV as a strategic partner. When ÖIAG launched a third offering in the course of OMV's privatization, IPIC acquired 19.6 percent by June 1994. By the end of the year, ÖIAG issued further 2.5 percent to private shareholders. The Austrian government share of OMV's capital stock thus decreased to below fifty percent for the first time. In May 1996, 14.9 percent of OMV were put on the market, reducing ÖIAG's stake to 35 percent and increasing the shares in free float to 45.4 percent.

According to Robert Denk, in the 1990s OMV managed to significantly improve its position in the E&P and marketing sectors. Thanks to its domestic restructuring and further internationalization, the company succeeded in attaining a "top position in the relevant market" and in "decisively enhancing its asset portfolio."[40] OMV's expansion strategy into the east thus was quite successful. Ten years after its adoption, the company developed into a serious competitor in Central Europe.[41] The name change in 1995 from ÖMV to the more international OMV symbolizes the "profound transformation, through which the former Austrian mineral oil administration changed into a listed group with global operating range."[42]

Towards a Leading Position in Central, Eastern, and South-Eastern Europe

In the late 1990s and early 2000s, a veritable wave of consolidation took place in the world petroleum industry. Mergers and acquisitions among the international major oil companies resulted in a reshaping of market conditions and power relations in the industry: BP swallowed Amoco, Exxon merged with Mobil, Chevron absorbed Texaco and Unocal, and Conoco joined forces with Phillips. Consolidation not only occurred among the majors. Many small and mid-sized oil companies were forced to participate in the merger battle in order to guarantee their future chances of survival in an increasingly hostile environment. A report by the Pan-European Oil Team at UBS in London already predicted in 1997 that "critical mass and global reach are vital for the industry." Moreover, it stated, "Looking further ahead, we can see consolidation as being the only survival route for the plethora of companies in central and eastern Europe, with OMV playing a prime role in the process."[43]

OMV made an effort to play an active role in the merger contest. Due to the Austrian state's stake in the company—the blocking minority is twenty-five percent plus one share—the latter was, and still is, protected against foreign acquisitions. In line with its consolidation strategy, in 1999 OMV conducted its first hostile takeover of a competitor by absorbing the Australian exploration company Cultus Petroleum in order to increase operations in Australia and New Zealand. However, with the beginning of the new millennia OMV continued to focus its expansion on its strategic growth markets of the CEE region. More specifically, with the opening of its first gas stations in Romania and Bulgaria in 1999 the Austrian company pushed south-eastward. In those days, OMV defined its strategic growth market reaching from the Black Forest along the Danube River to the Black Sea.

In 2000, OMV acquired ten percent in the integrated Hungarian oil and gas company MOL—its main competitor in its core markets. Two years later, the Austrian corporation gained a 25.1 percent stake—which was sold in 2005—in Romania's second-largest oil company, Rompetrol, and opened its first gas station in Serbia. In 2003, OMV substantially upgraded its international exploration and production and European marketing positions. It took over the international E&P business of the German Preussag Energie, purchased forty-five percent of the Bayernoil refinery complex consisting of three refineries in the Ingolstadt area, acquired 313 BP gas stations in Germany, Hungary, and Slovakia as well as 139 Avanti stations in Austria, the Czech Republic, Slovakia, and Bulgaria and opened sales points in Bosnia and Herzegovina for the first time. As a result of these acquisitions, OMV raised its total oil and natural gas production by forty-three percent—with Preussag contributing half of the increase—and expanded its gas station network by forty-five percent to a total of roughly 1,800.[44]

In December 2004, the Austrian oil and gas group acquired a controlling interest in Petrom, Romania's leading oil company and a major player in the region. This was OMV's largest acquisition in history, which "adds both upstream production and downstream assets, and makes the Austrian firm the leading player in its focus area."[45] With the takeover of Petrom, OMV's workforce climbed from 6,137 in 2003 to 57,480 one year later, and daily oil and natural gas production increased from 120,000 to 340,000 boe in the same time period.[46] Petrom added 1 billion boe and thus more than tripled the OMV group's estimated oil and gas reserves. OMV's refinery capacity had already been increased from 13 to more than 18 million tons as a result of the Bayernoil takeover. Petrom's Petrobrazi and Arpechim refineries added further 8 million tons in capacity. Between 2004 and 2005, the number of gas stations operated by the group rose to about 2,450, revenues grew by almost sixty percent to 15.58 billion euros—with Petrom contributing 3 billions—and net profits more than doubled from 690 to 1,496 million euros.[47] OMV's stock price soared by eighty-eight percent in 2004. Due to an increase in capital stock and the issuance of a convertible bond at the end of 2004, the shareholding structure changed with more than half of OMV's shares in free float.[48]

The Austrian oil and gas group's gradual expansion into the CEE region was continued in 2006. By acquiring seventy gas stations in the Czech Republic, it became the country's market leader in the downstream business. With a twenty percent market share in the Danube region by the end of the year, OMV reached the leading position in marketing in its core market. Nevertheless, the company aspired to expand further south-eastward. In March 2006, OMV entered the Turkish market by gaining a thirty-four percent stake in the country's largest fuel retailer Petrol Ofisi, which operates a network of more than 3,200 gas stations. This was a strategic step into one of Europe's most promising growth markets. OMV's then chief executive Wolfgang Ruttenstorfer saw this investment as "a bridge between our strong position in Central Europe on the one hand and the Caspian and Arab region on the other."[49] Because of their huge oil and natural gas resources, these regions are of particular interest for the company.

Turkey was defined as the third main market along with Central and Eastern Europe (CEE) and South-Eastern Europe (SEE). The country is getting ever more important as a market. Surrounded by one of the world's greatest oil and natural gas reserves in Iraq, Iran, the Caspian Sea, Azerbaijan, Kazakhstan, and Turkmenistan, its geographic location is exceptional. Turkey is a bridgehead for the transit of fossil fuels from these resource-rich regions to Europe.[50] Meanwhile, Turkey has strategic priority for OMV. From this perspective, the company's decisive increase in October 2010 of its stake in Petrol Ofisi to almost ninety-six percent is consistent with its overall strategy. OMV paid 1 billion euros for securing exclusive control of Turkey's biggest gas station operator. Alongside with Vienna for CEE and Bucharest for SEE, the company is establishing Istanbul as its third regional center to serve the Turkish market. With its market entry into Turkey and the rapid extension of its activities in the country, OMV considerably expanded its downstream target markets, now reaching from southern Germany to eastern Anatolia.

In September 2006, OMV (re)entered the strategically important Russian E&P market and extended its contracts with Gazprom for the supply of natural gas from Russia to 2027. In the same year, the company also obtained exploration licenses in Egypt, New Zealand, Norway,

Romania, and Yemen. However, the year was not invariably successful. The planned merger with the largest Austrian power company Verbund failed on political grounds. The merger would have created a giant energy company with businesses ranging from the exploration and production of fossil fuels to the supply of electricity to final consumers.

A year later, OMV started its attempt to merge with MOL, a major Hungarian oil and gas company and its main competitor in the Eastern European market. By September 2007, OMV had increased its interest in MOL to 20.2 percent—after acquiring a ten percent stake in 2000—and released a declaration of intent to merge with the Hungarian company. Because OMV is partly state-owned, this was regarded by the latter as a hostile takeover attempt by a foreign government. MOL urged the Hungarian parliament to pass a strategic companies law—widely known as "Lex MOL"—to prevent it from falling into foreign hands.[51] In further consequence, the Hungarian company began large-scale purchases of its own shares to thwart OMV's same efforts. After opposition from the European Commission, OMV abandoned in August 2008 its bid for the takeover of MOL. In March 2009, OMV sold its 21.2 percent stake in MOL for 1.4 billion euros to the Russian oil company Surgutneftegaz. Selling it for a price almost twice the market value, OMV passed on its MOL interest with a handsome sixteen percent mark-up on the price it paid two years earlier.[52]

After years of high oil prices and fat profits in the world petroleum industry, OMV had to suffer a severe drop in operational results with the advent of the world economic crisis in late 2008. Net sales declined by thirty percent to 18 billion euros from 2008 to 2009. Profits collapsed by more than fifty percent to 717 million euros. As one consequence, the company commenced streamlining its sparsely profitable Austrian filling station business. Almost one hundred gas sales points were divested. In early 2009, OMV announced its retreat from the Italian market. At the end of the year, it sold its Italian subsidiary with a network of ninety-nine gas stations in the northeastern Italian region of Triveneto. On the other hand, OMV is entering new territory by investing in electricity generation. In 2009, it started the construction of an 800 MW gas-fired power plant in Brazi, Romania. A similar plant is being built in Samsun on the Black Sea in Turkey.

OMV jumped on the opportunity the end of the Cold War offered in Eastern Europe and succeeded in gaining the leading position in its core

OMV in Comparison to Major Oil and Natural Gas Companies

	Country	Revenue 2009[a] (million USD)	Net Profit 2009[a] (million USD)	Market Value 2010[b] (million USD)	Production 2009 (thousand barrels of oil equivalent per day)	Employees 2009	State Control (percent)	PIW Top 50[c] (2008 Ranking)	Global 500[d] (2010 Ranking)
ExxonMobil	USA	310,586	19,280	316,230.8	3,932	80,700		3	3
Royal Dutch Shell	NED/UK	278,188	12,718	176,968.1	3,142	101,000		7	2
BP[e]	UK	246,138	16,578	177,609.1	3,998	80,300		6	4
Total	France	189,190	11,214	136,580.4	3,129	96,387		9	14
CNPC	China	178,426	12,796	329,259.7[f]	3,200	1,649,992	100	5	10
Chevron	USA	167,402	10,483	152,293.4	2,704	59,963		9	11
ConocoPhillips	USA	152,840	4,858	76,081.5	2,288	30,000		8	17
Eni	Italy	119,897	6,291	94,142.6	1,769	78,417	30	20	24
Gazprom	Russia	102,815	20,923	137,995.6	8,087	393,600	50.002	14	50
Statoil	Norway	80,565	3,064	73,918.9	1,962	28,736	67	27	74
OMV	Austria	25,811	1,033	13,209.4	317	34,676[g]	31.5	44	333

a Revenues and net profits of CNPC, Gazprom, Statoil, Total, Eni, and OMV were calculated on the basis of the exchange rates as of 31 Dec. 2009, i.e. USD 1 = CNY 6.8279 = RUB 30.3076 = NOK 5.7767 = EUR 0.6942.

b Values (market capitalization) as of 31 March 2010 according to the *Financial Times* Global 500 Index. For OMV, market capitalization as of 31 Dec. 2009.

c *Petroleum Intelligence Weekly's* ranking of the world's top 50 oil companies. Due to their vast reserves and high production, Saudi Aramco is no. 1 and NIOC of Iran no. 2.

d *Fortune's* ranking of the world's 500 largest corporations.

e The costs of and loss of market value due to the Deepwater Horizon oil spill disaster in the Gulf of Mexico in April 2010 are not included.

f PetroChina

g Of which 28,984 Petrom Group.

Sources: BP, Annual Review 2009; Chevron, 2009 Annual Report; China National Petroleum Corporation, 2009 Annual Report; ConocoPhillips, Building on Strengths: 2009 Summary Annual Report; Eni, Annual Report 2009; ExxonMobil, 2009 Summary Annual Report; OAO Gazprom, Annual Report 2009; OMV, Factsheet, February 2010; Royal Dutch Shell, Annual Report and Form 20-F 2009; Statoil, Annual Report on Form 20-F 2009; Total, L'Essentiel 2009-2010.

markets. It has become the largest oil and gas company of Central, Eastern, and South-Eastern Europe. Thanks to creative managerial decision-making and the consequent and systematic pursuit of its expansion strategy, OMV increased its revenues fivefold from 5 billion euros at the end of the 1990s to 25 billion euros a decade later—at least in 2008 before the slump of the world economy. Even if in its relevant downstream markets the Austrian energy group is both in size and performance a major player, in worldwide comparison it is one of the smallest companies among the international integrated majors.[53] Especially in comparison to the "supermajors," which are the so-called "Big Five" (BP, Chevron, ConocoPhillips, ExxonMobil, and Royal Dutch Shell) together with Total and Eni,[54] OMV is a small-sized corporation. This is shown by the table on the previous page that compares the Austrian major with the world's largest oil and gas companies.

OMV's and Austria's Role in European Energy Security

Compared to the major international oil companies, all of which are among the largest corporations in the world, OMV is of minor size and a seemingly minuscule player. This does not mean, however, that the Austrian enterprise is no more than a regionally established energy group without global significance. OMV skillfully positioned itself as a leading player in strategically important markets. Due to its early engagement in the European natural gas business—think of the pioneering first natural gas import contract of a Western company with the Soviet Union in 1968—OMV has secured an important role in this energy sector in Europe.[55]

Austria's favorable geographic location in the heart of Europe makes it a bridgehead between east and west and a gateway between north and south. Hence, important transit pipelines for the supply of Europe with natural gas run across Austrian territory. Austria is a central link in the European gas grid and a hub for the supply of Russian gas to Western Europe.[56] The Trans-Austria Gas pipeline (TAG) for deliveries to Italy, the Southeast pipeline (SOL) to Slovenia and Croatia, the Hungaria-Austria Gas pipeline (HAG) to Hungary, and the West-Austria Gas pipeline (WAG), which is one of the most important supply routes for Russian gas to Western Europe, are operated by OMV. Because of crucial pipelines transiting Austria like the WAG and the TAG, the company always has had a weighty say in the European gas business.[57]

OMV is in a dominant position in the strategic CEE and SEE markets and is expanding its engagement in Turkey. The company's core markets form the European Union's southern gas corridor for the delivery of natural gas from Caspian and Middle Eastern sources to Europe. OMV is playing a prominent role in the development of the EU's southern passage, which is intended to supply an important part of Europe's future energy needs and thus "is one of the EU's highest energy security priorities."[58] The central project of the southern gas corridor for Europe is the OMV-led Nabucco pipeline that would link the world's most prolific gas fields in the Caspian region, the Middle East, and Egypt to the OMV Baumgarten natural gas junction in Lower Austria. In this sense, the pipeline "strengthens the Austrian role and the OMV presence in the most important and strategic gas infrastructures."[59] As the only proposed natural gas pipeline free of Russian involvement and supplies, Nabucco aims to diversify delivery routes to Europe.[60] The project is being developed by a consortium of six European energy companies: Botaş of Turkey, Bulgargaz of Bulgaria, MOL of Hungary, RWE of Germany, Transgaz of Romania, and OMV. The Austrian company is heading the group and is operator of the project.

Political dissent among the countries involved in the project and, above all, a lack of natural gas to feed the pipeline have already delayed Nabucco.[61] At this point in time, construction of the 7.9 billion euros and 3,300 km pipe with a planned capacity of 31 billion cubic meters (bcm) per year is scheduled to start in 2012. The first gas is expected to arrive in Baumgarten in 2015.[62] The signing of the Intergovernmental Agreement in Ankara in July 2009 by the leaders of Nabucco's transit countries—Turkey, Bulgaria, Romania, Hungary, and Austria—considerably improved the chances that the pipeline will be built. In addition, the European Union firmly backs Nabucco. "Europe is united in its determination to go ahead with this key project."[63] Nabucco is a TEN-E (Trans-European Energy Networks) priority project, which proves Brussels' commitment to the construction of the pipeline. The importance of the Nabucco project for Europe's energy security is confirmed by EU documents and numerous statements by EU officials. According to former EU Energy Commissioner Andris Piebalgs, Nabucco is "the EU's most important gas supply project" and thus "essential to Europe."[64]

Among the priorities identified by the European Commission as crucial for Europe's energy security is alongside the Nabucco project also the establishment of a "diverse and adequate LNG [liquefied natural gas, A.S.] supply for Europe."[65] OMV contributes to the realization of this strategic goal of European energy policy as well. The Austrian company is leading a consortium that plans to build a 10 bcm per year LNG regasification terminal on the island of Krk in Croatia. The project "is being enthusiastically embraced by the EU."[66] Because of OMV's engagement in the Nabucco pipeline and the Krk LNG terminal, "Austria is directly involved [...] in the development of two important diversification projects."[67]

Austria is not only an important transit country for natural gas, but it is also "hosting the major gas hub in the region."[68] The Central European Gas Hub (CEGH) at Baumgarten an der March in Lower Austria is one of Europe's largest gas transmission centers. About one-third of all Western Europe's natural gas imports originating from Russia pass through the Baumgarten distribution node at the border to Slovakia.[69] In view of this fact it is hardly surprising that Austria was called by Russia's Prime Minister Vladimir Putin "the biggest, and I stress this, the most reliable transit agent for Russian gas."[70] The country thus plays through OMV an important role on Europe's energy map "as a crucial gas-supply hub for transiting Russian gas to France, Italy and Germany in Western Europe; to Hungary in Central Europe; and to Slovenia and Croatia in the Balkans."[71]

The CEGH is owned and operated by OMV, with the Vienna Stock Exchange (Wiener Börse AG) having a twenty percent stake in it. OMV has signed a cooperation agreement with the Russian state-run gas monopoly Gazprom in January 2008 for the participation of the Russians in the Central European hub. The European Commission has still to give its approval on the basis of EU competition law. Moscow promised to support OMV to expand the CEGH in cooperation with Gazprom to continental Europe's biggest gas distribution and trading platform.[72] Baumgarten therefore is not only a major natural gas junction. Since the establishment of the CEGH Gas Exchange of Wiener Börse in December 2009, it is also a stock exchange for natural gas where traders can buy and sell gas on the spot market.

As outlined above, OMV plays a prominent role in Europe's energy system: The Austrian company operates vital east-west (WAG) and north-south (TAG) transit routes for the supply of Western Europe with Russian natural gas; it is leading the EU's most important pipeline project (Nabucco) and developing Europe's southern gas corridor; it is contributing to Brussels' aim of establishing a diverse LNG supply for Europe; and, finally, it controls one of Europe's largest gas distribution nodes (CEGH). Due to its excellent and long-lasting business relations with the Russian gas monopoly Gazprom on the one hand and its engagement in the development of the EU's southern gas corridor without Russian participation on the other, OMV is contributing to two fundamental goals of European energy security strategy: the maintenance of constructive and mutually beneficial energy relations with Moscow—Europe's most important natural gas supplier—while simultaneously decreasing import dependency from Russia and improving energy security through diversifying supply sources.

OMV under Criticism

The global expansion and diversification of its exploration and production activities took OMV to political hot spots. In July 1997, the Austrian group joined the Swedish oil company Lundin Petroleum, Petronas of Malaysia, and the Sudanese Sudapet to explore for and produce petroleum and natural gas in concession Block 5A in Sudan. Keen to expand its E&P portfolio, OMV gained a 26.1 percent stake in the consortium led by Lundin. In September 2003, OMV announced its withdrawal from Sudan and the sale of its interest in Blocks 5A and 5B to India's Oil and Natural Gas Corporation (ONGC) for 105.6 million euros. The Austrian company left Sudan to focus its E&P activities in the more stable markets of its prime growth areas. The Sudanese sale freed up funds for the acquisition of a majority stake in Petrom.[73]

The decision to enter war-torn Southern Sudan, a region where a bloody civil war between the government in Khartoum and armed groups has been raging for many years, sparked severe criticism. In Europe and the Western world as a whole, international oil companies doing business in Sudan "were increasingly seen as accomplices in the mass displacement and killing of hundreds of thousands of civilians."[74] Allegations of complicity in human rights abuses were raised against the consortium members. In a report published in June 2010, the European Coalition on Oil in Sudan (ECOS) calls for an investigation of the consortium's involvement and responsibility in the Sudanese oil war. The NGO believes that Lundin, OMV, and Petronas "may have been complicit in the commission of war crimes and crimes against humanity."[75] OMV denies these allegations. The company declared in a statement that it has "integrated and consequentially implemented" international human rights standards and insists on having "fulfilled its social responsibility" in Sudan.[76]

Another international hot spot where OMV has conducted business is Iran. With the coming to power of Mahmoud Ahmadinejad in 2005, Tehran adopted a confrontational policy towards the international community regarding its nuclear ambitions. A series of United Nations Security Council resolutions sanctioning the Mullah regime document Iran's international isolation.[77] In September 2006, the United States extended the Iran Sanctions Act—formerly known as Iran and Libya Sanctions Act of 1996—until the end of 2011. This act of Congress authorizes the imposition of U.S. sanctions on foreign companies that invest more than 20 million dollars per year in Iran's energy sector. In July 2009, the EU Foreign Affairs Council imposed a tough sanctions regime on Iran aiming at energy, financial, and transport sectors. President Ahmadinejad's harsh rhetoric and military threats against Israel, his denial of the Holocaust, the regime's systematic disregard of fundamental human rights, and the country's secretive nuclear and ballistic missile programs have led Iran into international isolation.

Nevertheless, in April 2007 OMV signed a heads of agreement with the National Iranian Oil Company (NIOC) for participation in the development of phase twelve of the South Pars natural gas field in the Persian Gulf. Iran has the world's second biggest reserves of natural gas. The country's largely untapped gas resources are of highest economic interest. This is especially true for Europe with its ever-increasing hunger for the fossil fuel and Brussels' aim of diversifying its supplies away from Russia. The OMV-led Nabucco project was initially developed with Iranian gas from the South Pars field, which is the world's largest single natural gas reserve.[78]

Because of the increasing isolation of Iran and growing U.S. pressure, in the spring of 2008 Royal Dutch Shell and the Spanish Repsol YPF decided to abandon their Iranian engagements.[79] After the release of a U.S. blacklist in June 2010 of individuals and companies doing business in Iran—OMV was among the forty-one companies mentioned—Total and Eni announced they would reconsider their operations. OMV declared that it is no longer operationally active in the country.[80] The company's activities in Iran have at no time infringed on international or European sanctions. OMV was supported and defended by the Austrian government against international (and domestic) criticism. Nevertheless, doing business with the undemocratic, human rights abusing, and militaristic Mullah regime was widely regarded as unethical and, therefore, unacceptable. It was claimed by NGOs that OMV would be indirectly co-financing the Iranian nuclear program. Austrian activists accused the company of being a "silent partner of a terror regime."[81] As these examples demonstrate, becoming a global player comes with tough political choices and responsibilities in OMV's corporate mission.

Concluding Remarks

While it had once been a "sleepy government agency," OMV turned into "one of the world's strongest growing companies of the business."[82]

On the basis of its modest initial condition and the company's difficult circumstances in the past, the Austrian mineral oil corporation has been "extraordinarily successful in strategic development, growth, internationalization, and financial performance."[83] OMV developed from a fully state-owned and functionally organized minor Austrian oil producer to a modern, largely privatized, and globally active major European player in the oil and natural gas industry. It gained the leading position in Central, Eastern, and South-Eastern Europe. But not only is the company's horizontal integration remarkable. Alongside its geographical expansion, OMV is developing into a fully integrated energy group with businesses along the value chain from fossil fuel exploration and production to power generation in gas power plants and by renewables including the supply of electricity to final consumers. Through its control of the CEGH and important gas transit routes to Western Europe, OMV no longer plays a negligible role in European energy security. This is indeed an "impressive rise."[84]

As outlined elsewhere, a multinational corporation or global player is commonly defined as a company which owns and controls assets and is locally anchored in more than one country. This definition, however, seems inadequate to correctly classify OMV's role and position in the world petroleum industry. OMV is not a *Weltkonzern* in the sense of doing business on a global scale in all areas of operations and wielding considerable economic power. In contrast to the "supermajors," the Austrian company pursues a global strategy only in fossil fuel exploration and production.[85] OMV's marketing organization does not span the whole world. Its downstream markets are restricted to CEE, SEE, and Turkey. This does not, however, decrease the Austrian group's clout and important role in various strategic key markets.

Notes

1. Founded under the name "Österreichische Mineralölverwaltung AG," which means "Austrian Mineral Oil Administration, Inc.," the company changed its name to "ÖMV Aktiengesellschaft" in 1974 and to today's official title "OMV Aktiengesellschaft" (OMV AG) in 1995. In this paper, I exclusively use the corporation's current name "OMV," independent of the time period under consideration.

2. OMV is leading the business magazine *trend* Top 500 list of Austria's biggest companies. See <www.trend.at/articles/0724/580/175720/die-top-500-oesterreichs-unternehmen#> (14 Nov. 2010).

3. See United Nations Economic and Social Council and United Nations Center on Transnational Corporations, "Transnational Corporations in World Development: A Re-Examination," Commission on Transnational Corporations, 4th Session, New York, 15-26 May 1978, 158; and John H. Dunning, "The Distinctive Nature of the Multinational Enterprise,"

in *Economic Analysis and the Multinational Enterprise*, ed. idem. (London: George Allen & Unwin, 1974), 13, 15. A MNC is also called a multinational enterprise (MNE) or transnational corporation (TNC).

4. Ray Goldberg, "The Role of the Multinational Corporation," *American Journal of Agricultural Economics* 63, no. 2 (1981): 367.

5. Paul W. Beamish and John C. Banks, "Equity Joint Ventures and the Theory of the Multinational Enterprise," *Journal of International Business Studies* 18, no. 2 (1987): 2.

6. Raymond Vernon, "Economic Sovereignty at Bay," *Foreign Affairs* 47, no. 1 (1968): 114.

7. In a global industry like the world oil industry "transnational integration is a requisite of participation rather than a source of an incremental competitive advantage; it is inherent in the structure of the industry." See Stephen J. Kobrin, "An Empirical Analysis of the Determinants of Global Integration," *Strategic Management Journal* 12 (1991): 18.

8. The "supermajors" are BP, Chevron, ConocoPhillips, Eni, ExxonMobil, Royal Dutch Shell, and Total. See Amy Myers Jaffe and Ronald Soligo, "The International Oil Companies," The James A. Baker III Institute for Public Policy, Rice University, November 2007, 17, <www.bakerinstitute.org/publications/NOC_IOCs_Jaffe-Soligo.pdf> (11 Oct. 2010).

9. For detailed information on the SMV, see Walter M. Iber's recent study *Die Sowjetische Mineralölverwaltung in Österreich: Zur Vorgeschichte der OMV 1945-1955*, Veröffentlichungen des Ludwig Boltzmann-Instituts für Kriegsfolgen-Forschung 15 (Innsbruck: Studienverlag, 2011) and the review of this book in this volume. See also Hans Seidel, *Österreichs Wirtschaft und Wirtschaftspolitik nach dem Zweiten Weltkrieg* (Vienna: Manz, 2005), 429-79.

10. The bigger part of the Soviet dismantling of the Austrian industry actually was done before the Potsdam Conference. A summary listing the dismantled oil industry equipment is given in Iber, *Die Sowjetische Mineralölverwaltung in Österreich*, 49, 54.

11. Seidel, *Österreichs Wirtschaft und Wirtschaftspolitik nach dem Zweiten Weltkrieg*, 466.

12. Günter Bischof, *Austria in the First Cold War, 1945-55: The Leverage of the Weak* (Basingstoke: Macmillan, 1999), 36.

13. Under the State Treaty the Republic of Austria was committed to deliver for a period of ten years 1 million tons of oil per year to Moscow. In the end, 6.52 million tons of Austrian oil had been shipped to the Soviet Union, of which 1.3 million tons were borne by OMV. See Friedrich Feichtinger and Hermann Spörker, eds., *ÖMV-OMV: Die Geschichte eines österreichischen Unternehmens* (Horn: Ferdinand Berger & Söhne, 1996), 92. The oil was not destined for consumption in the Soviet Union but was transferred to the GDR, Czechoslovakia, Poland, and Hungary. See Iber, *Die Sowjetische Mineralölverwaltung in Österreich*, 215.

14. See Walter M. Iber and Otto Sova, "Von der Sonde 'Gösting II' zum European Player OMV: Österreichs Erdölindustrie im 20. Jahrhundert," 10 May 2009, <www.althofen.at/AvW_Museum/Geschichte_der_Chemie/Erdoelindustrie%2020%20Jh%20OMV.pdf> (15 Sept. 2010).

15. OMV obtained 100 percent ownership of Martha Erdöl Ges.m.b.H. and seventy-four percent of ÖROP Handels-AG, which was renamed as Elan Mineralölvertriebs-AG in 1968. The new OMV marketing organizations were operating almost 1,300 gas stations in Austria in the late 1960s. See Franz Mathis, *Big Business in Österreich: Österreichische Großunternehmen in Kurzdarstellungen* (Munich: Oldenbourg, 1987), 215.

16. Feichtinger and Spörker, eds., *ÖMV-OMV*, 101. In 1955, domestic oil production amounted to 3.6 million tons.

17. Iber and Sova, "Von der Sonde 'Gösting II' zum European Player OMV."

18. Feichtinger and Spörker, eds., *ÖMV-OMV*, 103.

19. Ibid., 105. OMV gained a fifty-one percent stake in the AWP, which branches off from the TAL at Würmlach in Carinthia. Furthermore, the company obtained a say in the future construction of refineries in Austria and concluded long-term deals for product purchases in Schwechat.

20. In 1969, OMV bought a five percent share in the AREPI (*Agence de Recherche et d'Exploitation Pétrolière en Iran*) consortium for the onshore exploration and production of oil along the Persian Gulf coast. The other participants were Elf-ERAP (thirty-two percent), the Italian AGIP (twenty-eight percent), the Spanish Hispanoil (twenty percent), and the Belgian Petrofina (fifteen percent).

21. According to the terms of the contract, the Soviet Union pledged to deliver over a period of twenty-three years 1.5 billion cubic meters (bcm) of natural gas per year. In the following decades, further long-term gas supply deals with Moscow followed. Since 1968, more than 160 bcm of Russian natural gas were imported to Austria. For an overview of the business contacts that led to the revolutionary 1968 deal, see Georg Rigele, "Strom—Erdgas—Atom: Drei Schwerpunkte zur Energiegeschichte Niederösterreichs im 20. Jahrhundert," in *Niederösterreich im 20. Jahrhundert*, Band 2, *Wirtschaft*, ed. Peter Melichar, Ernst Langthaler, and Stefan Eminger (Vienna: Böhlau, 2008), 427-28.

22. Herbert Rambousek, *Die "ÖMV Aktiengesellschaft"—Entstehung und Entwicklung eines nationalen Unternehmens der Mineralölindustrie*, Dissertationen der Wirtschaftsuniversität Wien 23 (Vienna: VWGÖ, 1977), 100.

23. Judy Dempsey, "OMV of Austria Aims to Become a Hub for Natural Gas," *The New York Times*, 8 July 2007, <www.nytimes.com/2007/07/08/business/worldbusiness/08iht-omv.4.6553409.html> (3 Nov. 2010).

24. Feichtinger and Spörker, eds., *ÖMV-OMV*, 166.

25. Of its exploration budget of 800 to 1,000 million schillings per year, on average only 100 million were invested for the search of crude and natural gas in foreign countries. The lion's share was budgeted for exploration in Austria. See ibid., 184.

26. Rambousek, *Die "ÖMV Aktiengesellschaft"*, 3. Rambousek noted as late as in 1977 that OMV's main focus was on the Austrian energy business (p. 200). This refers to the company's limited international orientation in those days.

27. Michaela Roiss, "Die Geschichte der österreichischen Erdölindustrie: Transformation vom verstaatlichten Versorger zu einem wettbewerbsfähigen europäischen Anbieter," PhD. diss., University of Linz, 2004, 184-85.

28. Ibid., 223.

29. David Meindlhumer, "Die Auswirkungen des ersten und zweiten Ölpreisschocks auf die ÖMV: Eine wirtschaftsgeschichtliche und finanzwirtschaftliche Betrachtung," Diplomarbeit, University of Linz, 2006, 92.

30. Feichtinger and Spörker, eds., *ÖMV-OMV*, 234. While funds had been divided equally between the domestic and foreign exploration divisions, with their fusion seventy-five percent were allocated to foreign activities and twenty-five percent to exploration on Austrian territory.

31. Ibid., 233-34.

32. See Robert Denk, *"13 %-Company": Value Management im OMV Konzern*, Controlling—Wissen & Praxis Band 3 (Vienna: WUV, 2002), 15. With the exception of the mid-1990s, these proportions remained relatively stable through the decade. In 1999, domestic output amounted to 13.89 mboe, and foreign production reached 13.26 mboe. In 2000, production in both zones equalled 14.2 mboe.

33. Roiss, "Die Geschichte der österreichischen Erdölindustrie," 223.

34. See ibid., 193.

35. Quoted in John L. Kennedy, "OMV to Focus on Restructuring, Integrated Oil Operations," *Oil & Gas Journal*, 11 Apr. 1994, 32.

36. All numbers were taken from Denk, *"13 %-Company"*, 15.

37. In 1998, PCD Polymere was sold to Borealis, with OMV acquiring twenty-five percent in the latter. Today, OMV holds a thirty-six percent interest in Borealis. The remainder is held by IPIC.

38. Feichtinger and Spörker, eds., *ÖMV-OMV*, 225.

39. Kennedy, "OMV to Focus on Restructuring," 34.

40. Denk, *"13 %-Company"*, 17.

41. Feichtinger and Spörker, eds., *ÖMV-OMV*, 236.

42. Klaus Malle, *Top oder Flop: Herausforderungen und Chancen für österreichische Unternehmen in der multipolaren Welt* (Vienna: Linde, 2009), 117.

43. Quoted in David Knott, "How to Survive the Merger Battle," *Oil & Gas Journal*, 1 Dec. 1997, 38.

44. OMV, *Was wir 2003 bewegt haben: Bericht zum Geschäftsjahr*, 25, 30. With the Bayernoil acquisition, OMV raised its share in the Transalpine Pipeline (TAL) to twenty-five percent. For this and all other OMV annual reports (*Geschäftsberichte* and *OMV in Zahlen*) referred to in this article, see <www.omv.com/portal/01/com/!ut/p/c4/04_SB8K8xLLM9MSSzPy8xBz9CP0os3hfA0sPN89Qo1BHE08DpyBTE3dfAwjQD05J1S_IdlQEAHT_Ke8!/> (12 Nov. 2010).

45. "Romania: Government Approves Petrom Privatization," *Petroleum Economist*, July 2004.

46. OMV, *Was wir 2005 bewegt haben: Der OMV Konzern in Zahlen*, 3, 5.

47. Ibid., 6, 11.

48. With IPIC's increase of its interest in OMV first to 19.2 percent at the end of 2008 and then to twenty percent in December 2009, the proportion of shares in free float has dropped to 48.5 percent, with ÖIAG's 31.5 percent stake remaining unchanged.

49. Quoted in OMV, *Wachstum im mitteleuropäischen Öl- und Gasgeschäft: Geschäftsbericht 2006*, 11.

50. See, for example, the interview with Wolfgang Ruttenstorfer by Miriam Koch, "OMV-Boss Wolfgang Ruttenstorfer: 'An meinem Sessel wird absolut nicht gesägt,'" *Format*, 27 Aug. 2009, <www.format.at/articles/0935/525/249723/omv-boss-wolfgang-ruttenstorfer-an-sessel> (19 Oct. 2010); and Chris Bryant and Delphine Strauss, "OMV Pays €1bn for Control of Petrol Ofisi," *Financial Times*, 24 Oct. 2010, <www.ft.com/cms/s/0/9f627ec2-de02-11df-88cc-00144feabdc0.html#axzz16OYZ4g7W> (25 Oct. 2010).

51. N. J. Watson, "Mol's Downstream Deliveries," *Petroleum Economist*, November 2008.

52. Derek Brower, "Surgutneftegaz Marches into Hungary," *Petroleum Economist*, May 2009.

53. Denk, *"13 %-Company"*, 18.

54. Jaffe and Soligo, "The International Oil Companies," 17.

55. Rambousek, *Die "ÖMV Aktiengesellschaft"*, 140. Already by the late 1970s, "OMV's goal to make of Austria a hub in the European gas network was successfully realized by the company" (p. 141, see also p. 204).

56. See Andrea Gilardoni, *The World Market for Natural Gas: Implications for Europe* (Berlin: Springer, 2008), 65.

57. Rambousek, *Die "ÖMV Aktiengesellschaft"*, 141.

58. Commission of the European Communities, "Second Strategic Energy Review: An EU Energy Security and Solidarity Action Plan," COM(2008) 781 final, Brussels, 13 Nov. 2008, 4.

59. Gilardoni, *The World Market for Natural Gas*, 73.

60. Christophe-Alexandre Paillard, "Russia and Europe's Mutual Energy Dependence," *Journal of International Affairs* 63, no. 2 (2010): 67.

61. The development of Nabucco primarily stalls because of lacking supply commitments by Caspian natural gas producers. Azerbaijan hesitates to make any commitments and has supply contracts with Russia. Gazprom has also secured large parts of Kazakhstan's and Uzbekistan's production. Turkmenistan drops out for the time being because of the unsettled status of the Caspian Sea and Iran is not considered a politically opportune supplier. See, for example, Oliver Geden and Andreas Goldthau, "Das Luftschloss Nabucco," *Der Standard*, 27 Jan. 2009, 31; Kirsten Westphal, "Die Nabucco-Erdgaspipeline und die Europäer," *Russlandanalysen* 176, 30 Jan. 2009, 15-16; and Heinz Kramer, "Die Türkei als Energiedrehscheibe: Wunschtraum und Wirklichkeit," SWP-Studie, S 9, Stiftung Wissenschaft und Politik, Berlin, April 2010, 6, 21-22.

62. This is the official schedule by Nabucco Gas Pipeline International, the company responsible for the project. According to Günther Oettinger, EU commissioner for energy, Nabucco will come on stream in 2018 at the earliest. See Cerstin Gammelin, "Nabucco-Pipeline kommt später," *Süddeutsche Zeitung*, 25 March 2010. RWE and Reinhard Mitschek, managing director of Nabucco, deny any delays. According to Mitschek, the project is "absolutely on track." See Interview with Reinhard Mitschek by Reuters Insider on 26 May 2010, <insider.thomsonreuters.com/link.html?ctype=group_channel&chid=3&cid=107536&shareToken=Mzo3ZTViMzQzYS0yZWRlLTRlMmYtYmJhMy1jOGFkNGU2NTBhZDc%3D%0A> (22 Nov. 2010).

63. Quote of Andris Piebalgs. See "Commissioner Piebalgs Recalls European Commitment to Nabucco Project in a Conference Held in Budapest," Press Release by the European Commission, IP/07/1338, Brussels, 14 Sept. 2007, <europa.eu/rapid/pressReleasesAction.do?reference=IP/07/1338&format=HTML&aged=0&language=EN&guiLanguage=en> (22 Nov. 2010).

64. Quoted in Ali Tekin and Paul A. Williams, "EU-Russian Relations and Turkey's Role as an Energy Corridor," *Europe-Asia Studies* 61, no. 2 (2009): 338.

65. Commission of the European Communities, "Second Strategic Energy Review," 17.

66. "Croatia: OMV to Push Ahead with LNG Plant," *Petroleum Economist*, April 2007.

67. International Energy Agency, *Energy Policies of IEA Countries: Austria 2007 Review* (Paris: OECD/IEA, 2008), 81.

68. Ibid., 76.

69. OMV, *The Baumgarten Natural Gas Station*, <www.omv.at/SecurityServlet/secure?cid=1191498070547> (22 Nov. 2010).

70. Quoted in Anita Orban, *Power, Energy, and the New Russian Imperialism* (Westport: Praeger Security International, 2008), 161.

71. M. K. Bhadrakumar, "A Pipeline into the Heart of Europe," *Asia Times*, 30 June 2007, <www.atimes.com/atimes/central_asia/if30ag01.html> (24 Oct. 2010).

72. See Janusz Bugajski, *Expanding Eurasia: Russia's European Ambitions* (Washington, DC: Center for Strategic and International Studies, 2008), 89.

73. Luke Anthony Patey, "State Rules: Oil Companies and Armed Conflict in Sudan," *Third World Quarterly* 28, no. 5 (2007): 1009. For OMV's Sudan engagement, see also Jemera Rone,

Sudan, Oil, and Human Rights (New York: Human Rights Watch, 2003), 626-29.

74. Patey, "State Rules," 1006.

75. European Coalition on Oil in Sudan, "Unpaid Debt: The Legacy of Lundin, Petronas and OMV in Sudan, 1997-2003," Utrecht, June 2010, 5, <www.ecosonline.org/reports/2010/UNPAID_DEBT_textonlyweb.pdf> (7 Aug. 2010).

76. See Ritt Goldstein, "Die OMV als Komplize bei Kriegsverbrechen im Sudan?" *Wiener Zeitung*, 15 June 2010.

77. The United Nations Security Council has passed the following resolutions punishing Iran for non-cooperation on its nuclear activities: resolution 1737 of 23 December 2006 (first round of sanctions), resolution 1747 of 24 March 2007 (second round), resolution 1803 of 3 March 2008 (third round), and resolution 1929 of 9 June 2010 (fourth round).

78. Igor Tomberg, "Iran in the European Gas Market: A Russian Point of View," Institut français des relations internationales (Ifri), October 2009, 15, <www.ifri.org/files/Energie/Tomberg.pdf> (8 Oct. 2010).

79. Ibid., 9. U.S. authorities have put pressure on American pension funds with sizeable investments in Shell and other energy companies. The idea was that the funds would force the companies to withdraw from Iran by threatening them to divest their interests.

80. See Jakob Zirm, "Energie: OMV wartet auf den Regimewechsel im Iran," *Die Presse*, 28 July 2010.

81. Matthias Küntzel, "What does Austria and OMV want?", Vienna, 9 May 2007, <www.cafecritique.priv.at/OMV-PK_engl.html> (7 Oct. 2010); and Diana Gregor, "Austria's Marriage with Iran—Support for Nuclear Program versus Historic Responsibility," Talk at The Yale Initiative for the Interdisciplinary Study of Antisemitism (YIISA), Yale University, New Haven, 4 Feb. 2010, <www.yale.edu/yiisa/dianagregorpaper2410.pdf> (8 Oct. 2010).

82. Christian Wüst, "Ölrausch im Weinviertel," *Der Spiegel*, 43/2005, 204.

83. Denk, *"13 %-Company"*, 18.

84. Malle, *Top oder Flop*, 119.

85. OMV's current E&P activities cover seventeen countries on four continents, i.e. Austria, Faroe Islands, Ireland, Norway, Romania, Slovakia, and United Kingdom in Europe; Iraq, Kazakhstan, Pakistan, Russia, and Yemen in Asia; Egypt, Libya, and Tunisia in Africa; as well as Australia and New Zealand. Additionally, the company maintains representative offices in Abu Dhabi, Ashgabat, and Tehran.

Austria and its Migrants

Rainer Münz

Habsburg Monarchy, Interwar Period, and World War II

During the nineteenth century, the Habsburg Empire was one of the most important source countries of transatlantic migration.[1] Between 1820 and 1914, more than 4 million of its citizens emigrated to the United States, Canada, and Latin America. At the same time the emerging urban and industrial centers of the Habsburg Monarchy also became prime destinations of migrants leaving agrarian peripheries and small towns. Today's telephone directories of cities like Vienna and Graz containing a large number of Czech, Hungarian, Polish, Serbian, and Slovak family names still give account of this nineteenth-century mobility within the Habsburg Monarchy.[2]

In 1918-20 the newly created Republic of Austria repatriated some 200,000 predominantly German-speaking members of former bureaucratic and military elites of the empire that saw themselves "stranded" in other successor states. During the rest of the interwar period, however, emigration prevailed. At least 220,000 non-German-speaking residents who had moved to the Alpine provinces during the monarchy returned to their home countries, which had become independent nation states in 1918. During the interwar period, some 80,000 Austrians chose overseas destinations. Most people left for economic reasons, but there also was a Jewish emigration to Palestine and an emigration of Nazi supporters to Germany. Most of the latter came back after Austria's annexation by Nazi Germany in 1938. During the following years (1938 and 1941), some 128,000 Jews were forced to leave Austria.[3] Another 64,000 perished in the Holocaust.

During Nazi rule and World War II a large number of ethnic Germans from Northern Italy (South Tyrol in particular) and Central and Eastern Europe opted for German citizenship and were partly resettled on Austrian territory. The war economy used millions of foreign workers and forced labor recruited or enslaved from territories under German control. Of them 822,000 were forced to work in Austria.[4] In 1944-45, some 1.4 million foreigners, including foreign and forced labor, surviving concentration camp inmates, allied prisoners of war, ethnic Germans, and other refugees resided on Austrian territory. After the war, most foreign labor and all prisoners of war were quickly repatriated, while many ethnic Germans remained in Austria and were joined by newly arriving expellees.

Migration and Mobility Pattern since 1945

Since 1945, modern Austria has experienced several types and waves of migration that have changed the size and composition of its population. During the postwar period (1945-49) more than 350,000 ethnic German expellees from Czechoslovakia, Hungary, and Yugoslavia found a new home in Austria. Another 100,000 displaced persons and refugees found—at least temporarily—refuge in this country.[5] In contrast to this return, migration of those who left Austria after its annexation by Nazi Germany in 1938 was small.

In the following decades Austrians emigrated in larger numbers to Germany, Switzerland, and the U.S. The main reasons were higher wages, better employment opportunities, and more attractive opportunities for university students as well as established researchers.

In 1961, Austria started to recruit temporary labor to reduce shortages on the labor market resulting from both high economic growth and reduced female labor force participation during the peak years of the baby boom.[6] Austria's approach was inspired by the German and Swiss "guest worker" model.[7] In 1961, some 1,800 Italian workers were recruited. In 1962, Austria concluded a recruitment agreement with Spain. Both attempts did not lead to larger flows of workers, as the wage differentials between the two countries and Austria apparently were not large enough, and Italians and Spaniards had the possibility to go to other Western European countries (including France, West Germany, and Switzerland). Austria then reached agreements with Turkey (1963) and Yugoslavia (1966) and established recruitment offices in both countries. At a larger scale, recruitment only picked up after a short economic downturn (1967). The "guest worker" program focused on low skilled or unskilled workers that were recruited for jobs Austrians no longer wanted to take.

Labor recruitment was stopped in 1973. There were two reasons for this: The first "oil price shock" led to an economic recession lowering the demand for additional labor; and the first Austrian baby boomers turned eighteen and started to enter the labor market.

By 1973, when recruitment was suspended, some 178,000 people from Yugoslavia and 27,000 from Turkey were working in Austria. In total, many more had come for a limited period of time as so-called "guest workers." The majority of them returned to their home countries. But the minority that remained after the recruitment stop were joined by spouses and children with similar educational background coming to Austria through family reunion. The effects are still visible when looking at the educational structure of people of Turkish and Western Balkan origins living in Austria (see Graph 7).

Due to its geographic location and its status as a neutral country, Austria long served as a major transit and receiving country for refugees from Central and Eastern Europe. This was not only true for the immediate postwar period. During crisis years of communist regimes, people came in large numbers: in 1956 from Hungary (179,000), in 1968 from Czechoslovakia (163,000), in 1980-81 from Poland (approx. 150,000).[8] The majority of these political refugees did not stay in Austria, but moved on to other Western countries or returned home. The country also served as transit hub for some 250,000 Soviet Jews who emigrated between 1973 and 1989 to Israel and the USA.

The number of refugees increased again with the unfolding of civil wars, ethnic cleansing, and mass expulsion in Croatia, Bosnia, and Kosovo. Austria gave temporary protection to 16,000 Croats, 95,000 Bosnians, and less than 10,000 Kosovars; 75,000 Bosnians were later given permanent status. A military coup in Turkey in 1990 and a civil war in this country's Kurdish areas also led to a considerable inflow of asylum seekers. The unfolding civil war in Chechnya had a similar effect. Since the year 2000, asylum claims in Austria have been decreasing to low numbers (2010: 11,022). Russian citizens (mostly from the Caucasus region) are still the largest single group.[9] All in all, about two million people found shelter, transit facilitation, temporary protection, or permanent asylum in Austria between 1945 and 2000.[10]

In the early twenty-first century, the migration pattern in Austria changed fundamentally. The Western Balkans and Turkey were no longer the main source regions, as more and more migrants came (and continue to come) from Germany and neighboring countries of Central Europe,

Graph 1: Net Migration: Immigration minus Emigration of Austrian and Foreign Citizens, 1961-2010

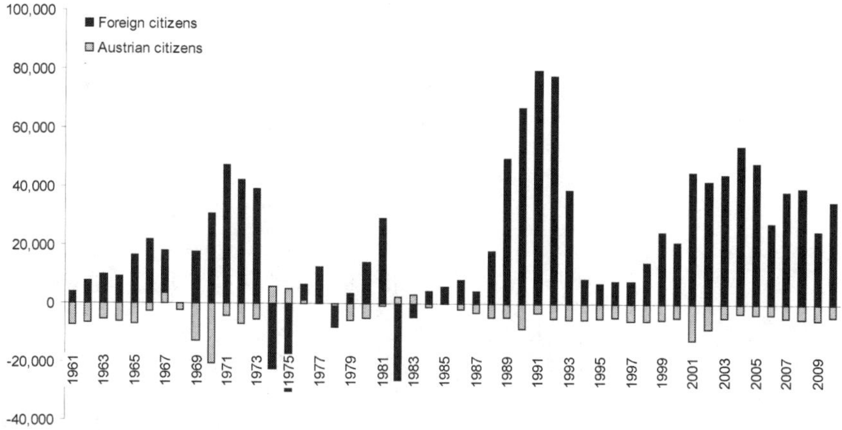

Note: Figures for 2010 are preliminary.
Source: Statistik Austria, Population statistics.

Graph 2: Gross Migration: Total Number of Immigrants coming to Austria and Emigrants leaving the Country, 1996-2010

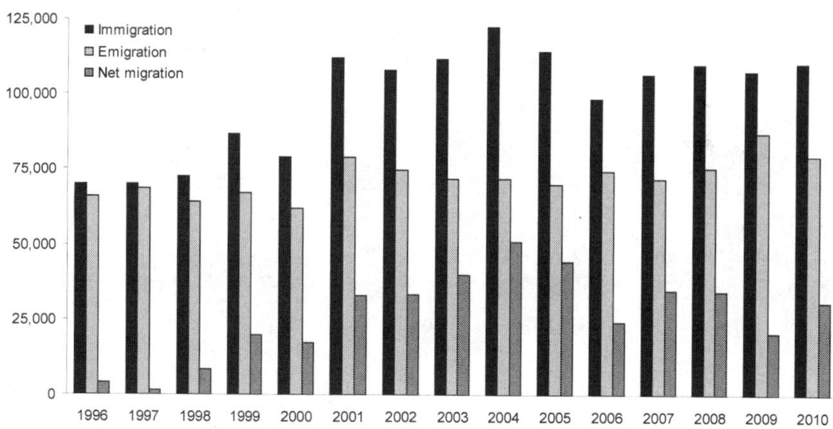

Note: Figures for 2010 are preliminary.
Source: Statistik Austria, Migration statistics.

which became EU members in 2004 and 2007. Citizens of these countries made use of their freedom to move and to establish themselves throughout the European Union. Austria became a destination of intra-European east-west mobility despite the fact that newly arriving citizens of new

EU member states only had limited access to the Austrian labor market. Germany was the only other country that also upheld this transitional regime for seven years (the maximum foreseen in the accession treaties with countries of the enlargement rounds 2004 and 2007).[11]

Four Successive Waves of Migration

Several waves of migration took place during the period 1945-2010. Annual data, however, are available only for the period 1961 to date. The following periods can be identified both in quantitative terms and with respect to the prevailing types of immigration (see Graph 1):[12]

The first wave was the result of displacement, mass expulsion, and refugee flows linked to the new geopolitical order established in 1945. All this led to a large number of people coming to reestablished Austria or transiting through this country during the period 1945-48.

The second wave started with the recruitment of supposedly temporary labor (so-called "guest workers"), which took place between 1961 and 1973. The peak year was 1971 with a net intake of 48,000 foreign immigrants. During the same period, native Austrian labor and skills continued to emigrate, with a peak net loss of -20,000 citizens in 1970. In 1974-75 the pattern reversed with 50,000 foreign labor migrants returning to their home countries and some 10,000 Austrians also returning from other countries.

The third wave (1988-93) was closely related to the fall of the Iron Curtain, the end of travel restrictions for citizens of former communist countries, and the beginning of inter-ethnic tensions, civil wars, and ethnic cleansing in the Balkans and the Caucasus. The wave peaked in 1991-92 with a net intake of 80,000 foreign nationals during both years. The net inflow during the whole period amounted to 331,000 foreign citizens. With more restrictive asylum laws and new visa requirements for citizens of Central and Eastern Europe imposed by most Western European countries, this wave came to a sudden stop.

The fourth wave started in 1999-2000 and was neither linked to proactive recruitment nor to any crisis or geopolitical change in the vicinity. This new immigration is linked to the emergence of an EU-wide migratory space leading to more intra-European mobility of students, labor, and skills. During the period 1999-2009, annual immigration fluctuated between 80,000 and 130,000 people, while annual emigration fluctuated between 60,000 and 90,000 (see Graph 2). In total, Austria recorded a net gain of 410,000 foreign immigrants during these ten years.

Between 1961 and 2010—the period for which annual data are available—a net amount of 1,080,000 foreigners immigrated and remained in Austria. During that period the net migration balance for Austrians was negative (-205,000), indicating more nationals leaving than returning. In the 1960s and 1970s, this was due to Austrian labor migrants working abroad. In recent times, there are students and researchers leaving the country. Austrian companies who have gradually become European and global players are sending managers abroad. But an important net loss is related to the retirement and return of former labor migrants. Those who have been naturalized once came as foreign nationals, but leave the country as Austrians.

Graph 3: The new Austrians: Naturalizations, 1946-2010

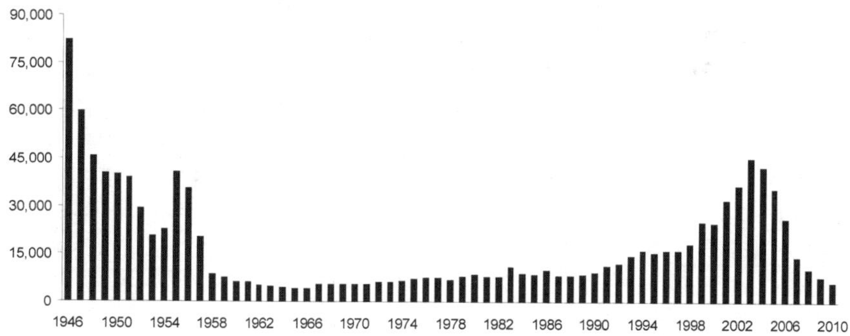

Source: Statistik Austria, Naturalization statistics.

Naturalization since 1945

In sum, Austria has naturalized 1,132,000 individuals since its reestablishment as an independent country in 1945. Naturalizations first peaked in the postwar years when war refugees and expellees living in Austria were given citizenship often based on their geographic origin and ethnicity. In contrast to Germany, which automatically extended citizenship to all ethnic German refugees and expellees living on its territory in 1949 (and to others who would still come from former German territories), Austria chose to naturalize members of this group individually. After 1957, annual naturalizations dropped to a few thousand. A second wave of naturalizations took place between 1999 and 2006, when a large number of refugees from the Balkans, Turkey, and Russia fulfilled the residency requirement of ten years and became eligible for citizenship. The peak years were 2003 and 2004, both with more than 40,000 naturalizations. Since that time Austria's citizenship laws have become more restrictive, which is one of the reasons for the rapidly declining number of naturalizations in the years 2007-10 (see Graph 3). But the low numbers—less than 6,200 in 2010—also reflect the fact that a growing number of immigrants are from other EU countries and therefore have less interest in naturalization, as the gain in status and rights is small compared to third country nationals becoming Austrian citizens.

Recent Migration Flows

Between the 1960s and the 1990s, former Yugoslavia and Turkey dominated as source countries of foreign immigrants while internationally mobile Austrians predominantly moved to Germany and Switzerland. In the early twenty-first century, Germany has become the most important source country, followed by the new EU member states.[13]

In 2009, 107,785 people moved to Austria (see Graph 4). Of them 17,566 were Germans. Two-thirds of all immigrants were EU citizens (including Austrian citizens returning to their home country). Among the remaining non-EU immigrants were roughly 15,800 asylum seekers, 10,000 persons joining family members already living in Austria, 6,000 foreign students, and 4,000 workers filling skills shortages. The largest group of non-EU immigrants was people from Western Balkan states (11,454). During the same year (2009), 87,189 people left Austria (see Graph 5). The largest group were Austrian citizens (21,067) followed by Germans (10,398) and other EU citizens.

Graph 4: Who came in 2009? Immigrants by Citizenship (N=107,785)

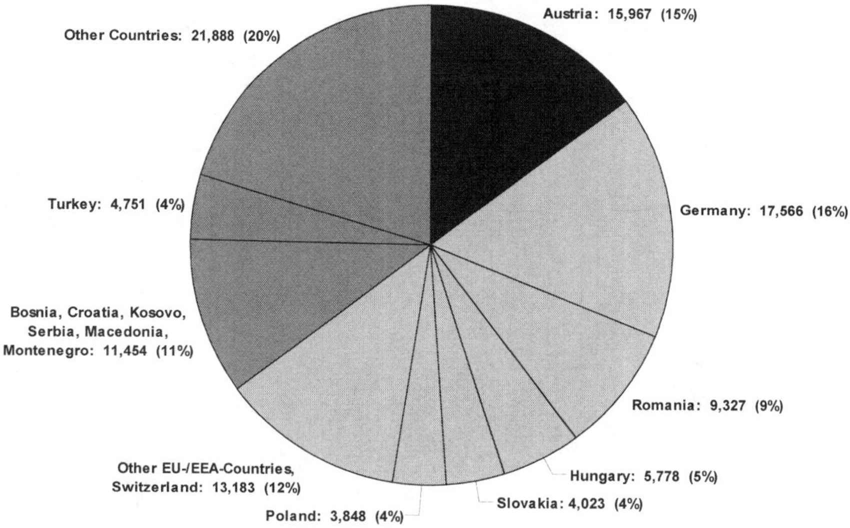

Source: Statistik Austria, Migration statistics.

Graph 5: Who left in 2009? Emigrants by Citizenship (N= 87,189)

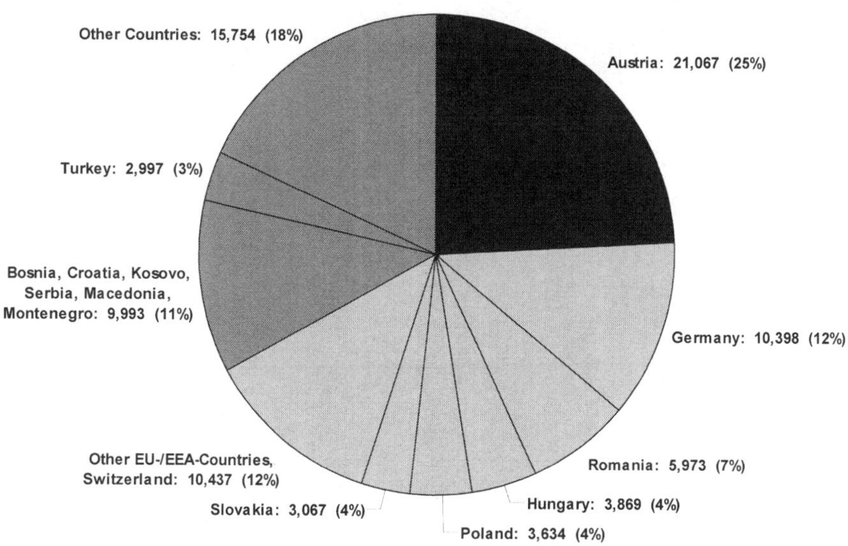

Source: Statistik Austria, Migration statistics.

Austria's Migrant Population

In 2009-10, Austria had a total population of 8.3 million; of them, 1.1 million were born in another country (representing thirteen percent of total population). Their Austrian-born children (385,000) represent another 4.7 percent of total population. In official statistics, both groups together are labeled as "population with migrant background" (see Table 1). Regional concentration is highest in Vienna, where twenty-seven percent of the population is foreign-born. Second in line is Vorarlberg with fifteen percent foreign-born. In

Table 1: Who has "Migrant Background"? Austria's Resident Population by Place of Birth (First/Second Generation)

<table>
<tr><td rowspan="3">Population in private households
8,262,101
100.0%</td><td colspan="2">Population without "migrant background"
Austrian-born parents
6,794,000
82.2%</td></tr>
<tr><td rowspan="2">Population with "migrant background"
Foreign-born parents
1,468,101
17.8%</td><td>1st migration generation
Foreign-borns
1,082,624
13.1%</td></tr>
<tr><td>2nd migration generation
Austrian-borns
385,477
4.7%</td></tr>
</table>

Note: Population living in private households (according to the labor force survey), annual average 2009.
Source: Statistik Austria, Labor Force Survey (Mikrozensus) 2009.

Table 2: Who is a "Foreigner"? Austria's Resident Population by Citizenship and Place of Birth (First Generation)

<table>
<tr><td rowspan="4">Total population as of Jan 1st 2010
8.375.290
100,0%</td><td rowspan="2">Austrian citizens
7.480.146
89,3%</td><td colspan="2">Austrian-borns
6.952.559
83,0%</td></tr>
<tr><td>Foreign-borns
527.587
6,3%</td><td rowspan="3">Persons of foreign origin (Foreign citizens plus foreign-borns)
1.422.731
17,0%</td></tr>
<tr><td rowspan="2">Foreign citizens
895.144
10,7%</td><td>Austrian-borns
129.881
1,6%</td></tr>
<tr><td>Foreign-borns
765.263
9,1%</td></tr>
</table>

Note: Total population (according to population registration), as of 1 Jan. 2010; as people not living in private households are also included the total population shown in Table 2 is larger than in Table 1.
Source: Statistik Austria, Population register.

southeastern Austria (Burgenland, Carinthia, Styria) the foreign-borns only represent six to eight percent of total population, well below Austrian average.

Some 0.9 million people living in Austria are foreign nationals (eleven percent of total population). The majority of them are foreign-born (765,000). But an increasing number of Austrian-born children grow up as foreign nationals (130,000) (see Table 2).

Today the most important source country of people with migrant background living in Austria is neighboring Germany (213,000) (see Graph 6). Second in line are Serbia (which in Austria's official statistics is still shown together with Kosovo and Montenegro; in total 208,000), Turkey (183,000), Bosnia (131,000), and Croatia (70,000). Among the new EU member states, Romania (63,000) and Poland (59,000) are the most relevant source countries. It is important to note that this ranking is not influenced by naturalizations, as it counts immigrants and their children by origin regardless of citizenship. The highest proportion of naturalized immigrants could be found among immigrants from the Czech Republic. But in absolute terms the largest numbers of naturalized immigrants were born in Germany, Serbia (plus Kosovo and Montenegro), and Turkey.

Graph 6: Which Origins have Austria's Foreign-born Population? Countries of Origin (First Generation, 2010), in thousands

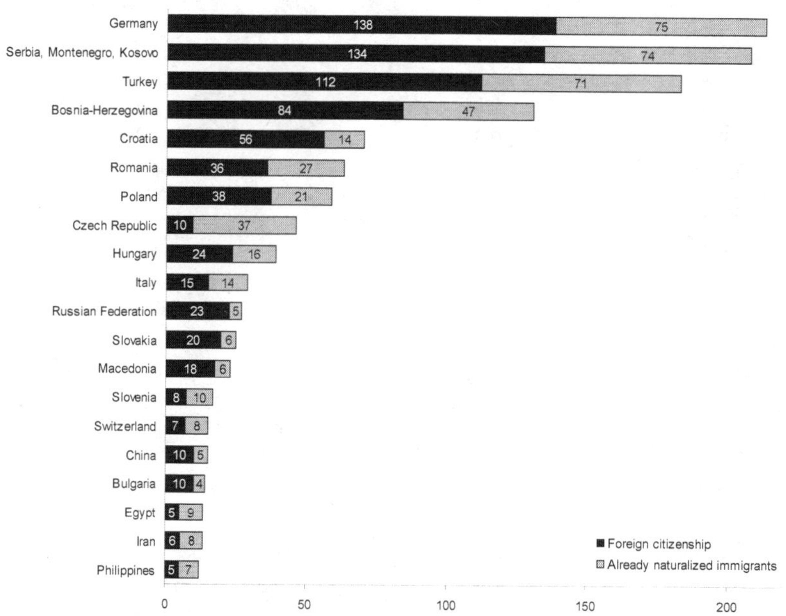

Source: Statistik Austria, Population statistics.

Graph 7: National Origins and Education: Highest Grade Completed; Population Age 25-65, 2009

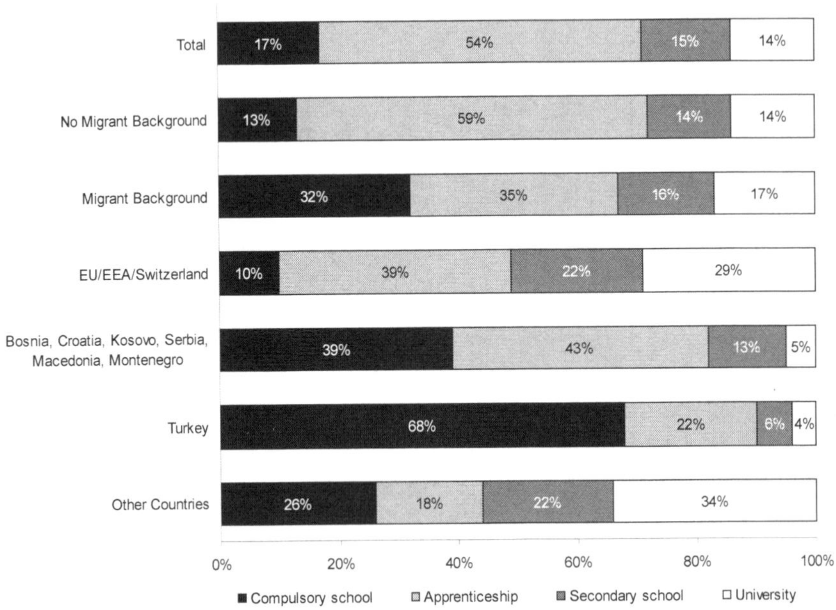

Source: Statistik Austria, Labor Force Survey (Mikrozensus) 2009.

Education

The educational background of the foreign-born population living in Austria differs significantly from that of native-born Austrians (see Graph 7). Both people with university degrees (seventeen percent) and with only compulsory school levels (thirty-two percent) are overrepresented among immigrants. People who have come from other EU countries (twenty-nine percent), Eastern Europe, the Americas, and Japan (thirty-four percent) have a much larger share of university graduates than people from Turkey (four percent) and the Western Balkans (five percent). Conversely, sixty-eight percent of all Turkish immigrants and thirty-nine percent of all immigrants from the Western Balkans only have finished compulsory school.

To a certain degree, the lower educational attainment is passed on to the next generation. This becomes apparent when looking at the educational careers of eighth graders. In 2008-09, some fifteen percent of those with family languages other than German going to lower secondary schools finished their education at that level (or left school without having passed the eighth grade successfully). Another five percent repeated the eighth grade. Most of them have dropped out of the educational system one year later. Only five percent of children living in German-speaking households and attending lower secondary schools took the same early exit.

In grammar schools, children of the same age rarely drop out. But in 2008-09 some seven percent of all eighth graders with family languages other than German had to repeat class as compared to less than four percent of the pupils speaking German at home.

Austria's educational system foresees a common curriculum only between grades one and four. At age ten children are selected for grammar schools (*Gymnasium*), giving access to higher education, and lower secondary schools (*Hauptschule*, *Mittelschule*, *Sonderschule*) that rather prepare for vocational training starting after the eighth grade. In urban agglomerations most children of native Austrian background attend grammar schools while children of non-German speaking immigrants rather end up in lower secondary schools.

Table 3: Who Continues and Who Doesn't? Educational Careers of Eighth Graders by Family Language and Type of School (2008-09)

	Lower secondary school		Grammar school	
	German family language	Non-German family language	German family language	Non-German family language
Repeat eighth grade in year 2008-09	0.8%	4.6%	3.7%	7.1%
No further education in year 2008-09	4.5%	14.9%	1.0%	2.7%

Source: Austrian Federal Ministry of Education, Culture, and Arts; Statistik Austria, Educational statistics.

Employment

In contrast to the 1960s and 1970s, when almost all adult migrants were employed, as the majority of them had been recruited for particular jobs, the labor force participation of today's migrants is lower than that of native-born Austrians. The participation rates are lowest for migrants from Turkey and their adult children (men: sixty-six percent, women: thirty-nine percent). But migrants from the Western Balkans and their adult children (men: seventy-one percent, women: sixty-one percent) and from EU countries (men: seventy-eight percent, women: sixty-two percent) also have participation rates below those of native-born Austrians (men: seventy-eight percent, women: sixty-nine percent) (see Graph 8). Conversely, unemployment rates are much higher among citizens of Turkey (2009: fourteen percent) and Western Balkan countries (eleven percent) than among Austrian citizens (seven percent).[14]

Available data show a mismatch between job requirements and skills among employed migrants. There is a rather strong relative allocation of highly educated migrants to work in medium- and even in low-skill jobs and of migrants with medium skills in low-skill jobs. During the first years after arrival, language problems could explain part of the mismatch. At the same time, migrants find it difficult to get either their qualifications properly recognized or they face barriers to entry (temporary or longer-term) which bar them from doing the jobs for which they would otherwise be formally qualified.[15]

Graph 8: National Origins and Labor-Force: Labor-Force Participation Rate; Population Age 15-65, 2009

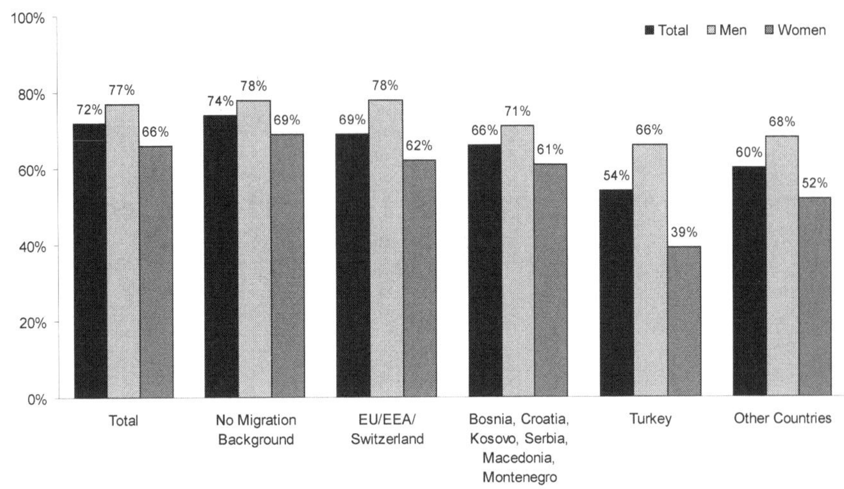

Source: Statistik Austria, Labor Force Survey (Mikrozensus) 2009.

Graph 9: National Origins and Unemployment: Unemployment Rate; Population Age 15-65, 2009

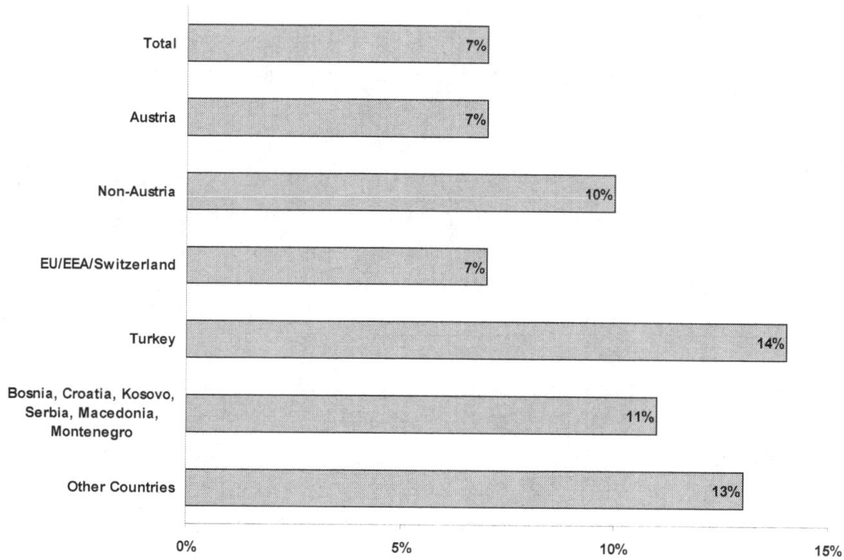

Source: Statistik Austria, Labor Force Survey (Mikrozensus) 2009.

Conclusions and Outlook

During the nineteenth century, the predominantly German-speaking and Catholic Alpine provinces of the Habsburg Monarchy became ethnically and religiously diverse through immigrants coming from non-German-speaking parts of the empire: Czechs, Poles, Croats, Jews, Ukrainians moved to the emerging urban and industrial centers of Upper and Lower Austria (including Vienna) and Styria. Ethnic Italians from Trentino moved to Vorarlberg. These migrants were Austrian citizens coming from neighboring provinces, but perceived as strangers. Local populations partly reacted with a growing German nationalism, anti-Slavic sentiments, and an increase of traditional Christian anti-Semitism. The newcomers were confronted not only with prejudices, but also pressed to assimilate in order to be accepted. Many Jews became Catholic or Lutheran. During the first half of the twentieth century, the diversity inherited from the nineteenth century almost completely disappeared. Many migrants of Slavic origin returned to their home countries once they had become independent states as a result of the postwar order established in 1918-20. Jews were forced to leave after 1938 or perished in the Holocaust. Most Austrian Roma shared the same fate. In return, Austria received large numbers of ethnic Germans, making its society more homogenous.

It was the recruitment of labor during the 1960s and 1970s that brought people from Turkey, Bosnia, Serbia, and Kosovo to Austria. Most of them came from regions that did not play any role in nineteenth-century migration flows. Without recruitment, they would probably not have thought about working in Austria. The establishing of a new geopolitical order in Europe after the fall of communism and the gradual emergence of an EU-wide labor market reversed the migration pattern again. Austria now mainly attracts immigrants from neighboring EU countries. For the first time, Germany plays the most important role, but other EU migrants come from regions of Central Europe that where on the "migration map" already during the nineteenth century.

During the twenty-first century, Austria and its neighboring countries will be confronted with demographic aging caused by longevity and a low number of children per family. This will also lead to shortages of labor and skills. Part of the answer to this development will be a more proactive migration policy as immigration from the geographic vicinity is likely to decline with increasing wages and living standards in neighboring EU countries. And Austria will have to compete with other countries also looking for skilled and attractive migrants.

Notes

1. For further details on Austria's migration history during the Habsburg Empire, see Heinz Fassmann, "Migration in Österreich 1850-1900," in *Demographische Informationen 1986* (Vienna: Austrian Academy of Sciences, 1986), 22-31; idem. and Rainer Münz, *Einwanderungsland Österreich—Historische Migrationsmuster, aktuelle Trends und politische Massnahmen* (Vienna: Jugend & Volk, 1995); and Gerda R. Neyer, "Auswanderungen aus Österreich: Ein Streifzug durch die 'andere Seite' der österreichischen Migrationsgeschichte von der Mitte des 19. Jahrhunderts bis zur Gegenwart," in *Am Rand der Utopie*, ed. Horst Schreiber et al. (Innsbruck: Studienverlag, 2005), 14-26.

2. Michael John and Albert Lichtblau, *Schmelztiegel Wien* (Vienna: Böhlau, 1990).

3. For further details on refugees entering or leaving Austria, see Gernot Heiss and Oliver Rathkolb, eds., *Asylland wider Willen: Flüchtlinge in Österreich im europäischen Kontext seit 1914* (Vienna: Jugend & Volk, 1995), 122-39.

4. Detlef Brandes, Holm Sundhaussen, and Stefan Troebst, eds., *Lexikon der Vertreibungen: Deportation, Zwangsaussiedlung und ethnische Säuberung im Europa des 20. Jahrhunderts* (Vienna: Böhlau, 2010); Versöhnungsfonds, "Zwangsarbeit in Österreich 1938-1945," Vienna, 2005, <www.versoehnungsfonds.at/upload/doc/86/Broschuere.pdf>.

5. Brandes, Sundhaussen, and Troebst, eds., *Lexikon der Vertreibungen*; Heiss and Rathkolb, eds., *Asylland wider Willen.*

6. In contrast to the U.S., the European baby boom only started after 1955 and ended in the late 1960s.

7. For further details on Austria's migration policy since the 1960s, see Fassmann and Münz, *Einwanderungsland Österreich*; Karin König, "Das österreichische Migrationsregime von 1945 bis heute," in *Staatsarchitektur: Vor der Information,* ed. Jo Schmeiser et al. (Vienna: Otto Sares, 1998), 150-55; Michael Jandl and Albert Kraler, "Austria: A Country of Immigration?" Migration Information, 2003, <www.migrationinformation.org/Profiles/display.cfm?ID=105>.

8. The Polish refugees are the only ones fully visible in available migration statistics as most of them came in November-December 1980, but left in 1981 (see Graph 1).

9. Information provided by the Federal Ministry of the Interior.

10. For more details see Rainer Münz, Peter Zuser, and Josef Kytir, "Grenzüberschreitende Wanderungen und ausländische Wohnbevölkerung—Struktur und Entwicklung," in *Österreichischer Migrations- und Integrationsbericht: Demographische Entwicklungen*, ed. Heinz Fassmann and Irene Stacher (Klagenfurt/Celovec: Drava, 2003), 20-61.

11. Kristof Tamas and Rainer Münz, *Labour Migrants Unbound? EU Enlargement, Transitional Measures, and Labour Market Effects* (Stockholm: Institute for Future Studies, 2006).

12. For more details see Münz, Zuser, and Kytir, "Grenzüberschreitende Wanderungen und ausländische Wohnbevölkerung."

13. See also OECD, *International Migration Outlook: SOPEMI 2010* (Paris: OECD, 2010), 191-92.

14. Unemployment rates are only available by citizenship, but not by migrant background.

15. Michael Landesmann, Robert Stehrer, and Mario Liebensteiner, *Migrants and Economic Performance in the EU15: Their Allocations across Countries, Industries, and Job Types and their (Productivity) Growth Impacts at the Sectoral and Regional Levels*, WIIW Paper, Vienna, February 2010.

Austria and Central Europe

Emil Brix

At least since the sixteenth century the position of Austria on the geopolitical map of Europe has always been a consequence of its position and self-definition as either a German or a Central European power. But until the rise of ethnic political legitimization in the nineteenth century, the Habsburg Empire with its growing territorial reach in eastern and south-eastern Europe had little need to make decisions between a leading political role in the German-speaking area and its growing role as a multinational empire which comprised various language groups and peoples with different cultural and religious affiliations. In the second half of the nineteenth century, Austria became Central European not by conviction but by default. In times of growing ethnic-political demands, the multinational Habsburg Empire was either doomed or it would have had to clearly formulate a new integrating idea. The old dynastic principle did not suffice to keep a large Central European political entity with about ten languages spoken together.

Following military defeat against Prussia in 1866, the dissolution of the multinational Habsburg Monarchy in 1918 and the catastrophe of the Second World War, which saw the definite end of the concept of Austria being a "second" or even a "better" German state, in the middle of the twentieth century Austria had the task to reinvent itself again. Austria became a "neutral" country, which meant that the country looked west in political and economic terms, and only in cultural terms were special relations with Central European neighbors to the east partly maintained and, in the 1980s, slowly enlivened. Due to its position on the Iron Curtain, which strictly separated Western Europe from the communist East after 1945, it was only after the end of communist regimes in 1989 and the piecemeal integration of all Central European countries into the European Union that Austria could again become part of Central Europe. Critics of Austria's reformulation of common Central European interests have hinted at the fact that Austria after 1989 used the notion of Central Europe mainly to reinforce Austrian identity[1] and to make way for Austrian economic expansion in Central and South-Eastern Europe. What is certainly correct about such a criticism is that the notion of Central Europe has since its inception in the nineteenth century mainly been interpreted by its protagonists as a rather vague means to create an imagined community and as a response to needs of economic competitiveness.

In Austria, even in the last years of the Cold War period, the notion of Central Europe was not a very popular concept. Only some liberal intellectuals and parts of the ÖVP (mainly liberal and Christian-democratic party elites), who felt that Austria loses out by turning the doctrine of "neutrality" into a rejection to connect with historical traditions and into a somewhat isolationist worldview ("*Schicksalslosigkeit*"), promoted Central European activities. The Social Democrats, trade unions, and parts of the tabloid press were more reluctant, as they feared for the possible impact of these discussions on the delicate postwar Austrian system of consensus orientation and extensive state regulations (including the labor market). Diplomats and Austrian foreign policy circles feared that their special role of providing a meeting place for East and West and their breathing space for a "good neighborhood policy" with the neighboring communist countries might be reduced. Overall, the public viewed an Austrian role in "*Mitteleuropa*" with suspicion.[2]

Austria's dilemma during the years of the peaceful revolutions in Central Europe and the dissolution of Yugoslavia was even more obvious. It was due to the changes in the Soviet Union and its consequences for a relaxation of East-West tensions that in summer 1989 Austria could apply for membership in the then European Community (today European Union). From that time onwards, joining the EC was on top of the Austrian national agenda. A short-lived euphoria about the fall of the communist regimes in neighboring countries was soon replaced by concerns about migration, the labor market, security issues, and a rather diffuse concern that Austrian Central European initiatives might hinder or delay Austria's European ambitions. Therefore, for Austrian foreign policy Central Europe played only second fiddle to EC membership. Joining the European Union in 1995 did not fundamentally change the cautious public mood or Austrian foreign policy orientations. It is only now when the EU enlargement towards Central and South-Eastern Europe is already realized or, in the case of the Balkan countries, accepted as a common objective of the Union that regional Central European cooperation becomes more popular.

For the whole region the notion of "Central Europe" has a varied history. Austria is therefore in this context no exception. In the context of the operative space of smaller states in Central Europe, the present-day role is still mainly seen as a consequence of the discourses of the 1980s about common cultural traditions which transcended European East-West divisions. The identity aspects of this notion are beginning to move from being an argument for differentiation from the East towards being an argument for differentiation from the West. For member countries of the EU such as Austria, the Czech Republic, Slovakia, Poland, Hungary, and Slovenia the notion "Central Europe" is increasingly used as an internal and external identity option which is seen as a possibility to increase political operative space. Due to the persistence of "culture-orientated rhetoric" a geographically neighboring smaller country such as Switzerland (but not Liechtenstein) has neither an interest nor a real possibility to use the notion as a political option. For all other countries in the region the increasing renewed political interest in "Central Europe" as a cultural and political notion (identity container) is an expression that they still search for political options (positioning discussions) within an enlarged European Union.

To discuss the political relevance of the notion, it is worth looking at the changing protagonists of Central European discourses from the 1980s to the present day. The general picture is unequivocal and corresponds to similar historical revolutionary processes. In the 1980s the protagonists of "Central Europe" were liberal intellectuals. Immediately after 1989, some of their lines of argumentation were taken up by politicians (mainly by intellectuals who had become politicians), but these discussions soon became subdued by the interest to join NATO and the European Union, and today Central European policy-making has become a field for civil servants.

History of the Notion "*Mitteleuropa*"

Although from the end of Middle Ages onwards the idea of Central European cooperation has been a political option for smaller political entities between Western European and Eastern European (Ottoman and Russian) spheres of influence, it was only in the nineteenth century when the notion "Central Europe" became a political and economic argument.

The nineteenth-century use of the term concentrated on the idea of a free trade area under German domination. Before the establishment of Central and Eastern European nation states, "Central Europe" was mainly a way to describe the degree of German influence in the region. Tony Judt summarized this situation by writing: "Until 1945, the term Central Europe had a peculiarly Germanic ring to it."[3] After the establishment of the German Empire in 1871, the German term "*Mitteleuropa*" came to be known as a term describing German imperial ambitions to dominate the area on its eastern borders. In 1915, the liberal German economist Friedrich Naumann conceptualized in his book *Mitteleuropa* the German imperial idea. He gave the projection of a new economic and political order for Europe. *Mitteleuropa* should be an economic union of states in which Germany was to play a central role.[4] As a political option for small states, it was only in the twentieth century after the First World War that the newly established independent states started to develop Central European options, which were meant to help these states against the growing foreign policy pressures of Germany and Russia. But the major characteristic of the interwar period was that for none of the states concerned "Central Europe" was more than an additional option in their attempts to find partners among the large European powers.[5] After 1945, the political space for small states no longer depended on Germany, but for all practical purposes the communist build-up of the Warsaw Pact resulted in a similar exclusion of operational space for Central European states. This created an ideological division which by the 1960s had come to be seen as being unalterable, thus leaving for Central European discussions only cultural options.[6]

The Cultural Debates of the 1980s

The theoretical background for cultural options could be found in the concept of three different European regions that had first been developed in the interwar period. The idea of a distinct Central European region had from the very beginning much to do with the wish to create a political perspective that was neither distinctly East nor West (István Bibo, Jenó Szúcs[7]). Before 1989, this perspective was only an option for opposition groups (with the exception of Austria, where Central Europe under the heading "good neighborhood policy" had become a topical issue already in the early 1980s)[8] and could develop only in the 1980s as a consequence of growing economic disadvantages of the communist economic system.

Regarding the arguments that were stressed by intellectuals behind the Iron Curtain when they formulated a Central European policy to fight communist reality, there were three clearly differentiated strands of reasoning. For writers such as Milan Kundera, the symbolic use as a cultural protest against "Easternization" and against attempts to create an Eastern uniformity should help to position the East Central European countries in a Western European tradition. Others such as Václav Havel used "Central Europe" to legitimize the option of parallel opposition societies, which should speak out against the non-democratic reality ("living in truth") and ask for good governance. The third discourse was concerned with questions of political culture. György Konrad was among those intellectuals who pleaded for "anti-politics." This was the beginning of a renewed discussion about civil society (based on liberal and/or communitarian values).

These three discourses (symbolic relevance, good governance, civil society) seem to have long-term relevance for small state policies. Before 1989, the notion of a common Central European culture was used as a reminder of how unreal a European separation into East and West is. Nowadays, democracy and market economy are accepted all over Europe and the continent is no longer divided by fundamental principles but rather by "national interests." How can small states along the former East-West divide adapt their policies to this changed situation in Europe? Especially the transition countries cannot rely on any concepts of European solidarity which go beyond the principal political support for an enlarged European Union. In the language of national interest, it is difficult to convince the population of a "rich" country why it should share its well-deserved wealth with a "poor" country. To stress the advantages of European security, stability, and long-term economic effects is not sufficient. These are "cold" projects, which can hardly create feelings of solidarity between communities. Immediately after 1989, the feeling of solidarity certainly helped to overcome the idea of two separate Europes.

Thus some of the basic messages of "Central Europe" that were directed at the public at large are still appropriate: Central European culture is a constant reminder of how unreal a European separation into East and West is. Nowadays, Central Europe is also a reminder of the impact of culture on the concept of Europe. As Central Europe cannot be found on the political maps of Europe it can only be made an issue as a cultural construct. Small states use the idea to create a specific image of their country as a cultural landscape of an astounding vitality and diversity that crosses state and ethnic borders. In a longer perspective Central Europe is a region which is interrelated by common cultural traditions and where amidst current political change Central Europeans themselves always projected their common cultural geography to a wider world.

The end of Eastern European communism brought not only political and economic change, but also gave new life to cultural traditions which transcend national borders and the conformity of modern life. In the 1980s, the cultural dissent of intellectuals recreated the idea of Central Europe as a common cultural area that supports demands for democratic change. At the beginning of the twentieth century, many cultural and intellectual innovations came from places like Vienna, Prague, Budapest, Cracow, or Trieste. Before the peaceful revolutions of 1989, intellectuals coming from these cities protested against cultural conformity imposed by the political separation into East and West by referring to the pluralistic values of Central European culture. Today, now more than twenty years after the end of the Iron Curtain, the cultural scene in this region has developed into a force which often critically responds to master ideas of ethnicity, heritage, and market.

Some of the cultural sensitivities that developed in confrontation with the constant pressures and chances of changing social realities survived. The plurality of cultural life in the Central European countries has always been part of Western imagination; artists and intellectuals who fled from the totalitarian regimes kept the idea of cultural plurality alive also by shaping the cultural life in their countries of exile. It was in the 1980s when intellectuals such as Milan Kundera, Václav Havel, György Konrad, and Claudio Magris stressed the significance of personal human experience. It was from this part of Europe where the plurality of modernist thinking started (see Steven Beller's article in this book).

Many of the European writers and intellectuals who started in the 1980s the discussions about "Central Europe" as a means of protest against the Easternization of a substantial part of Europe have since then changed profession or their places of living. Karl Schwarzenberg left Austria and became strongly involved in Czech politics (as foreign minister and founder of a new political party). Wladyslaw Bartoszewski returned from Bavaria to Warsaw and is still today in a government position. Adam Michnik became editor of the largest Polish daily newspaper. Timothy Garton-Ash became a respected Oxford academic. Erhard Busek left politics and became president of an Austrian NGO active in the field of Central and South-Eastern European cooperation. The global impact of their ideas lies in present-day geopolitical thinking which took up many of their ideas of the continued relevance of history, geography, and the "soft power" of culture (including religion) for international relations.

Changes of Cultural Contents or Perceptions?

How much did the end of the East-West divide change our outlook on Central Europe? Some years ago, a *New York Times* critic wrote about Central European filmmaking: "The great majority of the movies made in the region since 1990 have been eminently forgettable."

One of the many definitions of Central Europe says that all people from this region laugh and weep not only about the same jokes and tragedies but that they prefer to do both at the same time. In the Western mind there is still the question whether this is true or just another Central European joke. Maybe this is what Václav Havel meant when he called Central Europe a "kingdom of the spirit."

When Milan Kundera's influential and impassioned political essay *The Tragedy of Central Europe* appeared in 1983 while the author was in exile in Paris, it challenged the balance of power of the day and struck a chord with Central European intellectuals who felt betrayed by the political separation of East and West in Europe. Ultimately, the controversies which this article evoked helped change the course of European history for the better. Kundera envisaged Central Europe as a displaced region—"with the exception of little Austria"—languishing under Russian domination. Now, almost thirty years later, the area is part of a different world. But it is worth reconsidering what Kundera had to say and examining what has become of the ideas he championed and the ideas he criticized.

Considering what might be the Europe that mattered for Romanians, Hungarians, Czechs, and Poles, he declared that "Europe" does not represent a phenomenon of geography, but a spiritual notion synonymous with the word "West." In his view, after 1945, the central part of Europe, historically "tied to ancient Rome and the Catholic Church," had been kidnapped by the East, although culturally it had remained in the West. In Kundera's view, the East meant, above all, Russia: "In Central Europe, the eastern border of the West, everyone has always been particularly sensitive to the dangers of the Russian might." Most present-day discussions about Europe are less outspoken, but Kundera touched a sensitive point when he hinted at how Russia might be perceived differently from a certain vantage point when he described how "on the eastern border of the West—more than anywhere else—Russia is seen not just as one more European power but as a singular civilization, an other civilization." In all fairness, one might suggest that it was not Soviet Russia but Nazi Germany that tore up the structures and the hopes of the small Central European countries between Germany and Russia.

By advocating a Central European solidarity, Kundera wanted to turn the disadvantages of small-nationhood into an asset: "Boxed in by the Germans on one side and the Russians on the other, the nations of Central Europe have used up their strength in the struggle to survive and to preserve their languages. Since they have never been entirely integrated into the consciousness of Europe, they have remained the least known and the most fragile part of the West—hidden, even further, by the curtain of their strange and scarcely accessible languages." But it was from this "fragile" part of Europe where many cultural innovators of the early twentieth century emerged (Freud, Schoenberg, Kafka, Wittgenstein, and many others). Kundera perceived in this extraordinary creative explosion the outline of a cultural configuration that could be called Central European, but without implying political boundaries: "Central Europe is not a state: it is a culture or a fate." He described a cultural configuration that seemed to contain and preserve the idea of Europe as such, and possibly its future. His conclusion summed up the struggle of Central European intellectuals in the 1980s (with more political fervor than literary detachment): "Europe hasn't noticed the disappearance of its cultural home because Europe no longer perceives its unity as a cultural unity."[9]

Since 1989, it is obvious that Central Europe is a constant and for the West sometimes incomprehensible reminder of European cultural values. Kundera had stopped taking part in these discussions already in 1986. The following quotation was his last comment on the topic:

> CENTRAL EUROPE. Seventeenth century: The enormous force of the baroque imposes a certain cultural unity on the region, which is multinational and thus polycentric, with its shifting and indefinable boundaries. The lingering shadow of baroque Catholicism persists there into the eighteenth century: no Voltaire, no Fielding. In the hierarchy of the arts, music stands at the top. From Haydn on (and up through Schoenberg and Bartók) the centre of gravity of European music is there. Nineteenth century: A few great poets, but no Flaubert; the Biedermeier spirit: the veil of the idyllic draped over the real. In the twentieth century, revolt. The greatest minds (Freud, the novelists) revalidate what for centuries was ill known and unknown: rational and demystifying lucidity; a sense of the real; the novel. Their revolt is the exact opposite of French modernism's, which is antirationalist, antirealist, lyrical (this will cause a good many misunderstandings). The pleiad of great Central European novelists: Kafka, Hasek, Musil, Broch, Gombrowicz:

> their aversion to romanticism; their love for the pre-Balzac novel and for the libertine spirit (Broch interpreting kitsch as a plot by monogamous Puritanism against the Enlightenment); their mistrust of History and of the glorification of the future; their modernism, which has nothing to do with the avant-garde's illusions.
>
> The destruction of the Habsburg Empire, and then, after 1945, Austria's cultural marginality and the political nonexistence of the other countries, make Central Europe a premonitory mirror showing the possible fate of all of Europe. Central Europe: a laboratory of twilight.[10]

Such a cultural and ideological definition of Central Europe lost most of its relevance with the end of the ideological divide of Europe. For the new Central European states, the first years after 1989 could be seen as a time when the cultural notion "Central Europe" had become irrelevant. The glorious but vague dreams of Central Europe were a vision fulfilled which could be replaced by more pragmatic issues. Among these issues the metaphor "return to Europe" indicated a major orientation towards European integration. What came to be seen as most important was the institutional and economic change, the build-up of new national sovereignty, the preparation of new transregional options (NATO, EU) and the development of bilateral options.

But already in the early years of transformation there was a strong indication that European politics had to take into account that—without ideological divisions—identity aspects of policy-making had tremendously gained ground and had become a viable option for populism in political parties irrespective of their position in the political spectrum. This returned interest in symbolic politics had a specific Central European ring to it. Community and identity building in the transition countries partly relied on cultural reconstruction processes, which comprised discourses on traditions of plurality, on historical legitimacy, on aspects of ethnicity and on the possibility to make use of Western images of "Central Europe."

Issues and Interests: Central Europe after 2000

Before 1989, "Central Europe" was mainly an intellectual metaphor of protest against the Easternization of the string of communist countries to the west of the Soviet Union and neither concrete policy issues nor pragmatic day-to-day forms of cooperation within the region could be developed. This fact proved to be a stumbling block for any attempts to build after 1989 issue-orientated Central European cooperation. For the transition countries the main political priorities were seen in the field of domestic institutional change and European integration issues for which regional identities did not play any role in the political competition.

Early attempts of regional cooperation comprised the Central European Initiative (CEI) and the Visegrad Cooperation. Both initiatives are based on the idea of a common cultural identity. Whereas the CEI soon integrated a large number of member countries, the Visegrad group remained an attempt to coordinate politics between Hungary, Poland, the Czech Republic, and Slovakia (before 1992 Czechoslovakia). The CEI never became politically relevant. Only the Visegrad group remains viable because for the four member countries the economic and political advantages of regional cooperation have become a commonly shared view. The idea of political competitiveness of the region also increases the chances for other less formal groupings, such as the "Regional Partnership" (between the Czech Republic, Slovakia, Poland, Hungary, Slovenia, and Austria), which Austria initiated in 2001.[11] Whereas the Visegrad group established some common institutional infrastructure, the Regional Partnership works only on the basis of regular meetings of foreign and home office ministers and sector-orientated high-level meetings of officials (i.e. the directors of the cultural departments of foreign ministries coordinate their cultural diplomacy and initiate common cultural projects in the framework of a "platform culture Central Europe").

Attempts to merge existing regional groupings, or at least to formulate clear mandates for each group, have been discussed at various times in order to increase the political impact of regional cooperation for decision-making processes in the European Union. Some of the countries involved (Poland, Czech Republic) support Central European political cooperation only as a foreign policy option among others—as a flexible instrument for consultation in specific political issues.

A major shift towards a returned interest in regional cooperation became evident after the countries in the region had officially started the EU integration process. Central European identity started to become a lobbying instrument that especially countries such as Hungary, Slovenia, Slovakia, and Austria prominently supported. This was partly an attempt of pre-accession positioning. Since then, many forms of pragmatic cooperation make use of the notion "Central Europe" or "Danube Region" (such as research cooperation, city networks, ecological projects, infrastructure projects).

In conclusion, it is possible to say that the perception of a common Central European region is increasingly being used by smaller states as a policy instrument for defining their European position and for building regional ad hoc coalitions for specific political issues. In the case of Austria, Slovakia, and Hungary there is a growing shared conviction that "Central Europe" will remain their major foreign policy option. During the last few years, Slovene foreign policy also has made a remarkable shift towards Central European cooperation. The extent to which Central Europe is still interpreted as a cultural discourse has some negative effects on its political significance, because bilateral relations between smaller Central European states have to take into account historical conflicts and national stereotypes that form a clear part of the discourse.

Central Europe will continue to be an invitation to listen to an imaginary cultural landscape. Artists have developed a highly personal and sensual approach, which expresses an intellectual reflection of the social reality as well as of the historic developments in this region. Belonging to a specific style or a formal group is less important than portraying individual experiences. There is a continuing very strong reference to literary and historical traditions. But, surprisingly, it was the EU membership of Austria and the other countries of the region that reopened the political discourse about regional Central European cooperation.

For Austria, Central European cooperation within the EU and close cooperation with South-Eastern Europe (and also the Ukraine) in coordination with Central European partners is a most rational political option. After almost a hundred years of disintegration of the region, there appears to be a rare chance that all countries concerned share common political, economic and cultural interests. And for the time being neither Germany nor Russia shows much strategic interest to turn the tables toward the old games of imperial outreach into the region. Evidently, Central Europe gained this new lifeline from EU integration and from the prospect of further enlargement. In its position on EU policies and on the future of the EU, Austria has to keep this in mind when looking for like-minded countries in the European project.

Geopolitical questions of the role of this region did not disappear simply by cutting through the barbed wire. Every step of European integration raises new questions about our understanding of Europe. Where are its borders? What makes us feel European? How do we construct our identities? How do we identify our loyalties? For these questions it is worth revisiting Central Europe. In Austria the idea that this country forms part of Central Europe may by now already have become mainstream thinking, which is no small political achievement, but some of the consequences of this position have yet to be realized in everyday political relations with our old and new partners.

Notes

1. Charles S. Maier, "Whose Mitteleuropa? Central Europe between Memory and Obsolescence," in *Austria in the New Europe*, ed. Günter Bischof and Anton Pelinka, Contemporary Austrian Studies 1 (New Brunswick: Transaction, 1993), 16.

2. Günter Bischof and Emil Brix, "The Central European Perspective," in *Europe and the Superpowers: Essays on European International Politics*, ed. Robert S. Jordan (London: Palgrave Macmillan, 1991), 231.

3. Tony Judt, "The Rediscovery of Central Europe," in *Eastern Europe...Central Europe... Europe*, ed. Stephen R. Graubard (Boulder: Westview Press, 1991), 24.

4. Lonnie R. Johnson, *Central Europe: Enemies, Neighbors, Friends* (New York: Oxford University Press, 1996), 165-66.

5. Jacques Le Rider, *Mitteleuropa: Auf den Spuren eines Begriffes* (Vienna: Deuticke, 1994), 138-40.

6. See Karel Bartosek, "Probleme einer Defintion," in *Europa und Mitteleuropa? Eine Umschreibung Österreichs*, ed. Andreas Pribersky (Vienna: Sonderzahl, 1991), 112-13.

7. Jenó Szúcs, *Les Trois Europes* (Paris: L'Harmattan, 1985).

8. See Erhard Busek and Emil Brix, *Projekt Mitteleuropa* (Vienna: Ueberreuter, 1986).

9. Milan Kundera, "The Tragedy of Central Europe," *New York Review of Books* 31, no. 7 (1984): 33-38.

10. Milan Kundera, *The Art of the Novel* (London: Faber and Faber, 1986), 124-25.

11. Some commentators interpreted the Austrian proposal for a "regional partnership" as a direct response to the so-called "EU-14 sanctions" of 2000 against the VP-FP coalition government. See Michael Gehler, *Österreichs Außenpolitik der Zweiten Republik: Von der alliierten Besatzung bis zum Europa des 21. Jahrhunderts*, vol. 2 (Innsbruck: Studienverlag, 2005), 1019.

The Europeanization of Austrian Political Culture: Austrian Exceptionalism Revisited

Fritz Plasser and Gilg Seeber

Austria still represented a special case in the concert of Western democracies in the 1970s. In view of the remarkably high voter participation by international comparison, the concentration of votes on two dominant mass parties, the above average share of organized party members, the perpetuation of great-coalitional governments as well as the structural pillarization and segmentation of the electorate in political *Lager*, the political system of Austria has been described as "one of the most stable of the competitive systems studied."[1] Latent corrosion and structural erosion processes, however, began to raise doubts as to the hyperstability of Austria's political system,[2] which have been articulated in the 1980s ever more expressively.

The collapse of stable party allegiances and traditional *Lager* mentalities as the spread of latent protesting attitudes and diffuse anti-party affects indicated to a deep-seated change of Austrian politics.[3] The appearance of new, populist actors in the electoral arena and new polarizing cleavages accelerated the reduction of Austrian specifics and the adjustment to the normality of Western European democracies, which has been described with concepts like *de-Austrification*,[4] *mainstreaming*,[5] *Westernization*,[6] *Europeanization*,[7] *Americanization*,[8] and recently *globalization*. Actually, it was still possible up until the 1980s to speak of an Austrian *exceptionalism* compared to Western Europe as a whole, which not only characterized the institutional logic of the political process in a remarkable way, but also the political culture of the Austrian population.[9]

One specific trait of Austria's postwar political culture was exceptionally high turnout rates. The mean turnout at national parliamentary elections during the first decades after the war has only been higher in Belgium and Luxembourg—both are countries under mandatory voting regimes—compared to Austria.[10] But Austria did not only count to the countries with the highest participation at national elections, it was also a country with the strongest institutional affiliations with both parties and organizations. More than seventy percent of the voters still had a strong identification with a political party during the 1960s—every fourth one was a party member, and about two-thirds were strongly or moderately affiliated with parties, unions, or political interest groups. Consequently, Verba, Nie, and Kim drew the conclusion from their Seven Nation Study 1969 that "if we consider the proportion in the top category of institutional affiliation, Austria stands out."[11] This special position of Austria was not limited to the high voter participation and the strong institution affiliations of the Austrian electorate. The Austrian exceptionalism was also explainable by central qualities of the political system—Austria's neutrality and Austria's corporatism, called "social partnership"[12]—and characterized the political culture in the first postwar decades.[13]

But this Austrian exceptionalism also had its ambivalent sides. Marsh summarized a central trait that characterized Austria's political culture even up to the early 1970s: "The Austrian case is particularly interesting because they recorded the lowest system responsiveness score above but now record the highest level of political trust. It is a strange stance to take. They feel that officials and politicians ignore them but can be trusted to do what is right and care for a common collective good. It is a uniquely Austrian idea."[14] The paradox Austrian version of a high-trust society has first been examined in international comparison within the frame of the Political Action Study in the early 1970s. Whereas the study found Austrians generally to see "their government as having low responsiveness and their individual potential for influence as low in both an absolute and relative sense, this did not appear to lead to a serious feeling of dissatisfaction with the policy performance of the government."[15]

The Austrian government's high performance evaluation presented a marked contrast to that of the other nations. One explanation for this was found in "the uniqueness of the Austrian setting at this time. Unlike the other Western societies that faced political turmoil and social and economic disruption, Austria was the picture of peace and tranquility. Indeed, Austria seemed little affected by the major currents that swept across Europe and the United States."[16] The strikingly passive posture of Austrians, their passive trust in political elites and institutions harmonized with a high degree of political content and personal well being. "Austrians seem caught in a benign time-warp,"[17] which best described the way Austrians experienced life during the 1970s with the metaphor of the "island of the blissful."

During the 1980s, the Austrian high-trust society was slowly replaced by distrust, anti-party resentments, anger, and protest. Already in the middle of the 1980s, Austria showed—right after Italy—the highest share of party-weary voters, whereby an increasingly militant criticism of politicians and parties as well as a growing impression of a general failure of politics produced a polarizing mixture of protest motives, which found considerable resonance particularly in the lower strata of society, leading to an increasing electoral support of the right-wing populist FPÖ under Jörg Haider.[18] The political culture of distrust neutralized the core pillars of Austrian exceptionalism: Stable party affiliations were dissolving, the share of party members was reduced, the voter participation decreased, the share of volatile voters increased radically, whereby the dealignment of an once hyperstable party system first of all substantially weakened the electoral position of both leading parties.[19]

Table 1: Dealignment in Austria, in Percent

	Turnout	Party Identification	Party Changers	Party Members
1975	92.9	65	3	23
1979	92.2	63	7	22
1983	92.6	61	10	22
1986	90.5	60	16	23
1990	86.1	49	17	18
1994	81.9	44	19	15
1995	86.0	49	22	14
1999	80.4	51	18	13
2002	84.3	55	24	15
2006	78.5	53	26	12
2008	78.8	44	28	11
Change 1975-2008	-14.1	-21	+25	-22

Source: GfK Austria, Political Surveys 1975-2008.

The Austrian exceptionalism, however, was not only challenged by increasing discontent, weariness, and a right populist momentum, but also weakened through considerable and lasting ceasures. The Waldheim Affair 1986, which culminated in the watchlist decision 1988, at first polarized the older and younger generations, but consequently also led to a tendential break with the "myth of victimization," which had dominated Austria's official self-image during the first decades after the war.[20] In 1989, the fall of the Iron Curtain radically changed the geopolitical position of Austria and finished the postwar history of an exposed, neutral, small country situated on the breaking line of the East-West Conflict. Exogenous and endogenous factors of change had lasting effects upon the political culture of Austria. During the 1990s began a stepwise drifting apart of two political cultures: A citizen culture with high subjective political competence and only moderate discontent was confronted with a subculture of discontent with strong feelings of lack of political influence accompanied by massive weariness and distrust.[21]

In the middle of the 1990s, almost every second citizen believed that politics were mostly failing and about one-third was dissatisfied with the performance of Austrian democracy. Criticism was mainly directed to the mutual blockades between the governing grand coalition partners, scandals and affairs, as well as widespread anti-foreigner resentments, which were intentionally reinforced and instrumentalized by the right-wing populist FPÖ. The culmination of this development was reached during the parliamentary elections of 1999, when the combination of diffuse weariness, discontent with the performance of the grand coalition, and the wish for political changes made the FPÖ to the second strongest party.[22] The temporary turbulences in voting behavior and the collapse of traditional voting patterns especially among blue-collar voters shifting towards the FPÖ left their traces. As a consequence, Austrian electoral behavior had temporarily—at the height of the right-wing populist impact at the national parliamentary elections in 1999—distanced itself from European electoral trends, it again approximated Western European standards and patterns thereafter[23] as comparable right-wing parties in several European democracies were also successful in mobilizing protest votes.

The most influential weakening of Austrian exceptionalism occurred in 1995 following the accession of Austria to the European Union. Austria is meanwhile one of twenty-seven member states of the EU and tied to collective decisions of the European Union through a complex regime of rules and treaties. At the same time, the EU membership also opened up a new field of political-cultural tensions, which is expressed in a comparatively strong EU skepticism among considerable parts of the Austrian population. The confidence of Austrians in the institutions of the European Union is low, only in the United Kingdom are resentments toward the EU even more pronounced than in Austria compared to the original fifteen EU countries. Fifteen years after joining the EU, a majority of Austrians present themselves as "ambivalent" Europeans. Disappointed expectations in the membership, critically evaluated decisions of the EU, fears of economic and social consequences of the already executed and still planned expansions, political and cultural problems of identification as well as solid campaigns of populist acting Austrian politicians as well as influential tabloids throw their shadows upon the relationship of Austrians to the European Union and also have consequences for the domestic discussion. To what extent the political culture of Austria has been Europeanized during the last fifteen years and Austria developed to a "mainstreamed" democracy compared to other European countries, is subject of the following chapters, which are based on the data of international comparative studies like the European Values Survey (EVS), the European Social Survey (ESS), the World Value Survey (WVS), and Eurobarometer Surveys.

1. Political Involvement—Revisited

According to Almond and Verba, mainly two classes of political orientation are required for a good functioning and the stability of democracies: political involvement and the political support.[24] The degree of political interest is thereby seen as an indicator for the mental participation of the population in politics, whereby the actual level of political interest strongly varies by European comparison and is rather low in general.[25] A comparatively low interest in politics, a lower readiness for a participation in unconventional political behavior than in other countries, and the highest share of inactive citizens internationally in regard to more informal modes of political participation—these were most striking results of the Political Action Study in the early 1970s, which first analyzed the political repertoire of political participation of Austrians as part of a study in several countries: "Comparing Austria with other advanced industrial societies, especially the USA, a certain expression of political inactivity can be discovered. Characteristic of the political culture of Austria is a rather small degree of participation. This phenomenon is connected with intensive feelings of political inefficacy, e.g., the lack of trust in an individual's capacity to efficiently influence processes of political decisions."[26] In the early 1970s, for instance, only fifty percent of Austrians were very or fairly interested in domestic affairs, while forty-seven percent showed hardly any or no interest at all. In the following years, the degree of political interest also stagnated and—according to the data of the World Value Survey—in 1990 only fifty-four percent of the Austrian population were interested in political events. Compared to the neighbors Germany and Switzerland, the political interest of Austrians was significantly lower.[27] During the 1990s, a partial mobilizing impact was noted in Austria, the share of persons strongly interested in politics increased and the degree of political interest approached the European average.[28] Regarding political interest, Austria is in the meantime positioned within the upper middle of European countries. Only in Germany is the political interest of the populations higher than in Austria. However, political interest is far below the European average in Spain and Italy.

Table 2: Interest in Politics, in Percent

	Very or fairly interested	Not very or not at all interested
Germany	69	31
Austria	60	40
Netherlands	60	40
Switzerland	59	41
United States	59	41
Denmark	50	50
France	48	52
Sweden	44	56
Finland	43	57
Great Britain	42	48
Italy	40	60
Spain	35	65

Question: "*Would you say that you are very interested, fairly interested, not very interested or not at all interested in domestic affairs of your country?*"
Source: EVS 2008, WVS 2005, GFS 2009.

Political interest is one of the suppositions that the citizens will become politically active in case of need. This is the case when the citizens have the feeling that they can understand political contents and influence the making of politics. This attitude, which is described as a feeling of political competence and political efficacy, is viewed as the central condition for an active citizen's democracy.[29] In the early 1970s, comparative data from the USA, Great Britain, the Netherlands, and West Germany showed that in Austria feelings of political inefficiency were strongly present.[30] Regarding the feeling of political powerlessness, the resignative estimation of the own chances to exert political influence and the impression of distance of political elites to the citizens, Austria was even in the late 1980s only surpassed by Italy, where low trust in the personal political competence was met by a pronounced distrust in the "*classe politico.*"[31] During the early 1990s, the trend data showed a moderate increase of civic competence among Austrians, whereby the feeling of political efficacy was still less pronounced than in Germany or Switzerland.[32] During the middle of the 1990s, the civic competence of the Austrian population corresponded according to the data of the Eurobarometer (1995/45) with the average of the fifteen EU members at that time. Only in Luxembourg and in Denmark were the possibilities of subjective influence of citizens on their governments estimated higher than in Austria. Newer data, however, questioned the impression of a continuously increasing civic competence of the Austrian population.[33] Recently, three of four Austrians doubted that the government, the parties, and the political elites took the problems of the population seriously and considered them in their decisions: an empirical *déjà vu* of the findings of the Political Action Study from the early 1970s, according to which Austria and Italy belonged to those countries where the sense of political powerlessness and lack of influence was especially widespread.[34]

In an international comparison the considerable weaknesses of the civic competence of Austrians, which in the meantime are not a problematic specificity of the Austrian political culture anymore but overshadow the relationship between citizens and political elites in several West European democracies, must be seen in a different light.[35] While in Switzerland still at the end of the 1980s every second citizen was convinced of his personal political possibilities of taking influence, as well as every third in West Germany and in every fourth one in Austria, the civic competence of the Swiss population significantly decreased over time. In 1989, only forty-three percent of the Swiss believed to have no impact upon the decisions of the government, but in 2006 this share reached sixty-two percent and approached the situation in Austria or Italy, where seventy and eighty percent, respectively, indicated feelings of political inefficacy. The situation in Austria and Italy has also recently been approximated by the estimates of the German population, of which a majority is also convinced that they cannot influence the actions and decisions of their government.[36]

While Austria recorded during the early 1970s by international comparison the lowest system responsiveness score, this exceptional position of Austria changed thirty years later. According to the data of the

European Social Survey, the responsiveness of the political elites is in the meantime evaluated in a similarly critical way as in Austria as well as in Spain, Germany, or France. A positive evaluation of the responsiveness of politicians is, however, found in Denmark, Finland, the Netherlands and in Switzerland. Regarding the evaluation of the affinity of politicians to their citizens, Switzerland still occupies a top position among European democracies and belongs to a group including the Nordic democracies and the Benelux countries, while citizens of Germany and Austria as well as Italy, Spain, and France see their political elites disconnected from the wishes and needs of ordinary people.[37]

Table 3: Evaluating Responsiveness of Politicians, in Percent

	Politicians in general care what people like me think:	Politicians interested in votes rather than people's opinions:
	hardly any or very few politicians care	nearly all or most just interested in votes
Spain	68	74
Germany	64	64
Austria	61	71
France	57	n.a.
Great Britain	46	60
Netherlands	38	47
Finland	37	46
Switzerland	37	44
Denmark	32	32

Question: *"Using this card, do you think that politicians in general care what people like you think? Would you say that politicians are just interested in getting people's votes rather than in people's opinions?"*
Source: ESS 2002/3.

Over time there were only few changes regarding the third characteristic of political involvement of the Austrian population worked out by the authors of the Political Study thirty-five years ago: the narrowed repertoire of political participation when compared internationally. For instance, one of the core findings of the Political Action Study carried out in 1974 was that in Austria modes of political participation exceeding the act of voting were rather restricted.[38] This finding has been confirmed several years later in a broad study about the political actions of Austrians.[39] A study conducted in 1989 dealing with political participation reached similarly discouraging results. At the end of the 1980s, the political repertoire of participation of the Austrian population only differed very little from the patterns in the early 1970s.[40] Mostly comparable results were also found in the several studies from the 1990s.[41] In view of citizen-centered forms of participation, the repertoire of political participation of the Austrian population only changed slightly during the last decades and only differs in nuances from the passive, party-dominated culture of participation of the late 1960s.[42] Only every tenth fits the normative picture of the "*super citizen*" who largely uses the potential political modes of participation available to him. Every second one behaves mostly passive and limits his civic engagement to the participation in elections, the use of political information in the media, and occasional discussions about politics.

In view of the narrow repertoire of political participation, the strong impetus of activation and mobilization observed in other European countries only seems to have touched Austria marginally.[43] This is also confirmed by data of the European Values Survey 2008, according to which the Austrian population uses informal modes of political participation still less often than the populations of other Western democracies.

Table 4: Political Action

	percent who have signed a petition	percent who have attended lawful demonstrations	percent who have joined in boycotts
United States	70	15	19
France	68	45	16
Denmark	67	34	18
Great Britain	66	15	14
Switzerland	65	26	14
Germany East	58	35	4
Germany West	57	26	13
Finland	55	16	24
Netherlands	53	22	12
Italy	51	38	12
Austria	49	16	9
Spain	41	39	8

Question: "*I'm going to read out some different forms of political action that people can take, and I'd like you to tell me, for each one, whether you have actually done any of these things, whether you might do it or would never, under any circumstances, do it.*"
Source: EVS 2008, WVS 2005.

While Austria in the 1990s still had a much higher voter turnout compared to most other countries in Europe, these turnout rates declined at the following elections. On a European list of voter turnout between 1950 and 1990 Austria ranked second.[44] Twenty years later Austria only ranks ninth. In Malta, Luxembourg, Belgium, Cyprus, Denmark, Sweden, Liechtenstein, and Italy turnout at recent parliamentary elections was higher than in Austria. Also, at the recent elections to the European Parliament (2009) the voter participation in Austria (forty-six percent) was only slightly above the average voter participation in the twenty-seven EU member countries (forty-three percent). But Austria has not only lost its top position regarding a high voter turnout; while the comparatively high voter participation together with the highest share of party members in Western Europe still had been a strong characteristic of the relationship between citizens and politics in Austria, this leading position has also changed. The share of party members in Austria lies with roughly eleven percent only slightly ahead of Switzerland and Finland now. Also regarding party affiliations Austria approached the Western European average by now.[45]

Yet, there are certain indications that civic society structures are developing in Austria, too. According to comparative analyses, Austria, just like Sweden, Denmark, and West Germany, does count to those European countries where participative structures are generally thriving, if—besides core political activities—the cooperation in voluntary organizations or the share of those who are engaged socially in an informal way are also considered.[46] In spite of the existing doubts regarding the responsiveness of political elites, the increased distrust toward politicians and the widespread sense of political inefficiency, Austria does range—together with Switzerland and Germany—in the upper category of political participation in Europe.[47]

2. Political Trust—Revisited

A characteristic attribute of the political culture of the Austrian population has been its high trust in central institutions of the political system. Being a high-trust society, Austria differed significantly from other European countries, which partly suffered from veritable crises of confidence. While in other Western democracies the growing share of critical citizens, disenchanted democrats and growing civic disengagement was discussed with concern,[48] the level of political trust of the Austrian democracy remained largely intact.[49] The erosion of stable party affiliations and affective loyalties left traces in the confidence of Austrians to central institutions of the party state; yet, a still quite high level of trust is rendered judicial institutions like the police and the courts as well as administrative institutions, even though this level of trust lies generally below the one measured in the 1990s.[50]

The trust in institutions developed quite differently in the European countries since the beginning of the 1980s, especially regarding trends, patterns, and attitudes to the central institutions of the party state and to judicial institutions. In view of the average levels of trust in the parliament and judicial institutions, Austria ranks on top of the EU member countries together with Finland, Luxembourg, Sweden, and the Netherlands.[51] Austria and especially Switzerland are better positioned regarding the support of political institutions and actors compared to Germany, which still belonged to the top level of European countries during the late 1980s.[52] An example of a high-trust society is, however, not Austria anymore, but Switzerland, whose population is characterized by an especially positive attitude toward their political institutions and actors by comparison with other European countries.

The authors of the Political Action Study saw the proof for Austrian exceptionalism in the high trust of Austrians in their government.[53] The above average degree of political trust in the government found in the early 1970s can also be registered in an international comparison over thirty years later. According to Norris, the net change in European confidence in government varied in direction and size by country,[54] whereby the trust in institutions among the population of Scandinavian countries was clearly more stable and higher compared to other countries of the European Union in every phase. The Netherlands, Luxembourg, and Denmark are still counting to those countries in which strong majorities trust their national governments. On the other side, Italy and France are part of those countries where the trust in national governments lies far below the European average. The values for Austria are found constantly in the upper areas and lie at every point of measure just above the European average since 1997. The constantly high trust of Austrians in the national government has been touched less by the effects of the international crisis of the financial and capital market and the resulting measures of budgetary consolidation than in other countries. While between 2009 and 2010 dramatic losses of trust in governments could be observed in Greece, Spain, Portugal, and Ireland, the trust of Austrians in their government only decreased slightly.

Table 5: European Trust in National Government, 1997-2010, in Percent

	1997	2002	2005	2007	2010	1997-2010 net change
Netherlands	69	65	40	73	47	- 22
Luxembourg	65	76	76	66	66	+ 1
Denmark	59	60	61	67	50	- 9
Portugal	52	52	33	46	20	- 32
Greece	50	41	44	41	25	- 25
Austria	48	53	46	57	54	+ 6
United Kingdom	48	36	41	34	26	- 22
Spain	46	51	47	52	20	- 26
Ireland	44	47	41	41	21	- 23
Finland	42	59	64	75	49	+ 7
Sweden	41	59	35	55	57	+16
France	38	32	25	36	25	- 13
Germany West	34	43	30	52	31	+ 3
Germany East	32	40	24	37	32	0
Italy	29	39	35	37	25	- 4
Belgium	16	49	47	62	22	+ 6
Total	44	49	43	52	36	- 8

Question: "*I would like to ask you a question about how much trust you have in certain institutions. For each of the following institutions, please tell me if you tend to trust it or tend not to trust it.*" The national government—proportion responding "Tend to trust."
Source: Eurobarometer Surveys 1997-2010.

Similarly stable and above the European average is the confidence of Austrians in their own parliament. The values for Austria lie in the upper segment, and the trust in parliament is only constantly higher in the trend data in the Netherlands, Luxembourg, Denmark, and Sweden. However, there are noticeable differences between countries. In 2010, seventy-two percent of the Danes trusted their parliament, while only twenty-one percent of the Spanish population and twenty-six percent of the Italians trusted their national legislative institutions. Overall, the trust of Austrians in parliament is higher than the one of the German population in their parliament, and much higher than the trust of U.S. citizens in their Congress.[55] Even though the Scandinavian countries approach the type of a high-trust society more than Austria does, the above average capital of trust which is rendered the central institutions of government still remains a characteristic attribute of Austria's political culture.

As far as the trust of Austrians in their system of justice, the police, or political parties is concerned, the values are situated in the upper middle. Only in Denmark, Finland, and Switzerland is the trust in the judiciary system higher than in Austria. In a transatlantic comparison, the levels of trust in Austria regarding the judiciary system, the police, and political parties largely correspond with those found in the United States. However, the American Congress is confronted with considerable problems of credibility and trust, while Austrians trust their legislative constantly on a high level. In the European average, the low trust of Austrians in their political parties is in no way remarkable "since this orientation could weaken for many reasons, including the growth of more educated and rational voters choosing parties based upon policies and performance, rather than habitual loyalties toward specific parties, without meaning that citizens have necessarily lost faith with the party system as a whole."[56]

Table 6: Confidence in Institutions, in Percent (a great deal or quite a lot)

	Justice System	Police	Political Parties
Denmark	87	91	44
Switzerland	75	82	25
Finland	73	92	16
Sweden	70	74	28
Austria	65	73	15
Germany West	61	76	15
United States	57	70	15
Netherlands	57	69	33
France	55	75	16
Great Britain	53	67	14
Germany East	44	65	10
Spain	42	68	18
Italy	37	77	13

Question: *"Please look at this card and tell me, for each item listed, how much confidence you have in them, is it a great deal, quite a lot, not very much or none at all?"*
Source: EVS 2008, WVS 2005.

Even though the crisis of confidence from which several European countries are suffering for years so far has not reached Austria, the political trust in institutions over time has remained largely consistent in Austria and clearly lies above the European average. Austrian exceptionalism still has given up its position against a West European normality: Austria is not any longer the European role model of a high-trust society—this position is taken by the Scandinavian countries and Switzerland—yet it is found in the upper top of European democracies where the majority of the population basically trusts the central institutions of their governments.

3. Support for Democracy

The generalized support for democracy as a form of government has been stable and firmly anchored in Austria for decades. Nine out of ten respondents on the average are explicitly defending democracy as the better form of government.[57] This acceptance of the democratic order is in West European comparison only better distributed in Sweden, Denmark, and Luxembourg than in Austria.[58] On the whole, Austria is—together with West Germany and Switzerland—part of those European countries in which the public supports the democratic idea to an especially high degree.[59]

Table 7: Support for Democracy, in Percent: "Democracy better than any other form of government"

	agree strongly	agree	disagree/ disagree strongly
Denmark	76	23	1
Austria	59	37	4
Sweden	59	36	5
Germany West	56	40	4
Switzerland	55	42	3
Spain	52	44	4
Italy	52	44	5
France	52	42	6
Finland	42	53	5
Netherlands	40	53	7
Great Britain	36	57	7
Germany East	33	57	9

Question: *"I'm going to read off some things that people sometimes say about a democratic political system. Could you please tell me if you agree strongly, agree, disagree or disagree strongly?"*
Source: EVS 2008.

Table 8: Evaluation of the Democratic Regime, in Percent: "Having a democratic system"

	very good	fairly good	fairly bad	very bad
Denmark	86	13	1	0
Sweden	70	24	5	1
Italy	64	33	2	1
Switzerland	60	37	2	1
Spain	58	39	2	1
Austria	55	37	5	3
France	52	40	6	2
Germany West	48	44	6	2
Great Britain	46	40	10	4
Finland	45	47	7	1
United States	45	40	11	4
Germany East	38	50	12	1
Netherlands	37	55	7	2

Question: *"I'm going to describe various types of political systems and ask what you think about each as a way of governing this country. For each one, would you say it is a very good, fairly good, fairly bad or vary bad way of governing this country?"*
Source: EVS 2008, WVS 2005.

The basically positive attitude of Austrians toward democracy is also expressed by an above average portion of the population content with the performance of democracy. In a West European comparison, the satisfaction with democratic performance is only higher in Luxembourg, Denmark, and the Netherlands than in Austria. According to Eurobarometer data, two-thirds of the European public express on the average satisfaction with the workings of democracy in their own country. In eleven of the fourteen nations under comparison these attitudes became more positive from 1995 to 2010.[60] Satisfaction with democracy is remarkably low in France, Greece, and Italy and even their satisfaction with democracy has grown since the early 1990s. In a comparison between countries, Austria lies in the upper segment, whereby the gap between the general support of democracy and contentedness with its actual functioning is larger in Austria than for instance in Germany or Switzerland.[61] On the other side, the public's satisfaction with the working of democracy agrees with the evaluations of the functioning of democracy by the political elites. There is agreement between the democratic attitudes of the elites and the positive orientations

Table 9: European Satisfaction with Democratic Performance, 1995-2010, in Percent

	1995	2000	2005	2010	1995-2010 net change
Denmark	83	77	92	91	+ 8
Luxembourg	76	79	82	90	+14
Ireland	70	79	71	56	-14
Netherlands	69	77	71	72	+ 3
Germany West	68	64	58	72	+ 4
Austria	61	56	68	76	+15
Spain	55	76	67	58	+ 3
Belgium	55	63	65	62	+ 7
Great Britain	48	69	61	58	+10
France	48	64	52	51	+ 3
Germany East	48	41	29	52	+ 4
Portugal	42	50	41	40	- 2
Greece	41	52	53	49	+ 8
Italy	20	36	43	44	+24
Total	56	62	61	62	+ 6

Question: *"On the whole, are you very satisfied, fairly satisfied, not very satisfied, or not at all satisfied with the way democracy works in your country?"*
Proportion responding "fairly" or "very" satisfied.
Source: Eurobarometer surveys 1995-2010.

Table 10: Satisfaction with Democratic Performance, in Percent: Political Elites vs. Citizens

in percent are very or fairly satisfied	Political Elites*	Citizens**	Gap
Sweden	92	81	-11
Denmark	90	91	+ 1
Germany	88	69	-19
Finland	85	69	-16
Switzerland	81	65	-16
Austria	77	76	- 1
France	77	51	-26
Spain	75	58	-17

*Survey of N=1,171 leading members of national governments, national parliaments, or party politicians in eight European countries.
**Representative surveys.
Source: *Project Political Communication Cultures in Europe (2008).
**Eurobarometer 2009, GFS 2009.

of the population like it can only be found by comparison—on an above average level—in Denmark and Sweden. The strongest discrepancies in the evaluations by political elites and citizens are found in France and Spain, where the populations evaluate the performance of democracy significantly more critically compared to the political elites of their countries.

In view of the pronounced acceptance of democracy as the preferred form of government, the above average content with the actual performance of democracy as well as the high trust in central institutions of the democratic system of government, the political culture of the Austrian population largely represents a civic democracy in the meantime. In a typology of political culture of the EU member states, Gabriel includes Austria together with Denmark, Finland, Luxembourg, the Netherlands, and Sweden in a group of countries approaching the example of a civic culture as introduced by Almond and Verba.[62] In a cluster analysis conducted on the basis of data of the European Social Survey and the European Values Survey, Austria is also positioned—together with Switzerland and the Scandinavian countries—in the top group of countries with an extraordinarily positive relationship of citizens to democracy.[63] Similar results are reached by an aggregated analysis of the Eurobarometer data, according to which civic attitudes are only met more frequently in the Scandinavian countries as well as Luxembourg than in Austria. Austria ranges in regards to the civic orientations of its population together with Germany and the Netherlands in the upper middle segment of European countries. The lowest levels of civic orientations are found in the southern European countries, whereby a considerable north-south drift is found regarding political-cultural attitudes on the whole.

Within the last twenty years, the political culture of the Austrian population has largely approached the European country average. In some aspects of political culture, meanwhile, Austria counts in the top group of countries in which civic orientations are especially widespread. This is first of all true for the acceptance of democracy as the preferred form of government as well as for the high trust in central institutions of the governing system. Even the traditional weaknesses of the political culture of Austria—the comparatively weak feelings of political efficacy, a somewhat narrow repertoire of political participation as well as the impression of lacking responsiveness of the political elites—are in the meantime compared to other European countries less exceptional as just twenty years ago.[64] The political-cultural mainstreaming of Austrians moved Austria into the upper middle segment of European democracies. Central characteristics of Austrian exceptionalism have either dissolved or are playing only a subordinate role.[65]

Figure 1: Positioning Austria's Political-Cultural Orientations in Comparison

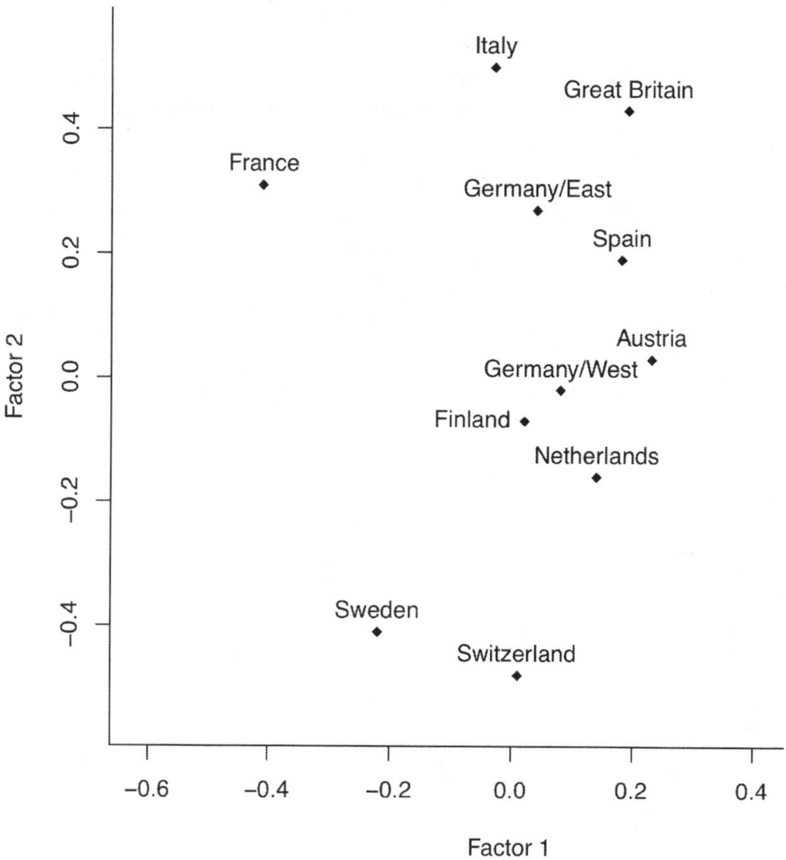

Note: Mean factor scores based on a factor analysis including indicators of political interest, political action, confidence in institutions, attitudes towards democracy, and national pride. Two factors have been extracted from individual level data by principal component analysis and rotated by the varimax method with Kaiser normalization. Total variance explained is forty-three percent. Higher scores for factor 1 indicate less political activism, while higher scores on factor 2 indicate less confidence, less favorable attitudes towards democracy, and less national pride.
Source: EVS 2008.

Figure 1 visualizes some of the main findings in the previous sections. It uses the European Values Study as a data source and is based on an exploratory factor analysis of individual level indicators of political interest, political action (signing a petition, joining in boycotts, attending lawful demonstrations, joining unofficial strikes, and occupying building/factories), confidence in institutions (justice system, political parties, and government), attitudes towards democracy (satisfaction with democracy, and democracy as the best political system), and national pride. By extracting two factors, it turns out that lack of interest in politics is reflected in larger scores in both dimensions, more intensive involvement shows as smaller scores of factor 1, while smaller values of factor 2 indicate higher confidence in institutions, as well as more favorable attitudes toward democracy and more national pride. The scattergram reproduced in Figure 1 shows mean scores for each country. Austria is located toward the right of the display, i.e. has, on the average, a lower degree of participation in informal political activities, while it is found right in the center according to factor 2, indicating average levels of confidence in political institutions, support for democracy, and national pride when compared to the other European countries. To what extent the Europeanization of Austria's political culture can also be found in the attitudes to the European Union, or whether Austria represents a special case among the West European EU member countries, is the topic of the last part of this essay.

4. Euroskepticism in Austria

While the Austrian citizen politics largely adopted Western European standards, Austria still represents an unusual case regarding the attitudes of the population to the European Union. With the exception of Great Britain, the Euroskepticism in no other Western European country is equally pronounced as in Austria.[66] Fifteen years after joining the EU, the relationship of the Austrian population to the European Union is still overshadowed by emotional distance, skepticism, and criticism, which is expressed by a below average support of the EU, her institutions and political decisions.[67] According to new data of the Eurobarometer surveys, Austrians associate much more negative evaluations with the European Union than the average European citizen does. In no other member country—with the exception of Great Britain—are assumed negative consequences of the membership so centrally placed as in Austria. The average Austrian citizen associates with the EU primarily the euro (sixty-two percent), waste of money (fifty-two percent), an increase of criminality (fifty percent), bureaucracy (forty percent), growing unemployment (thirty-seven percent) and—rather positively—the control of the frontiers (thirty-seven percent). Concerning negative connotations, the Austrian values lie significantly above the EU average; regarding positive associations, clearly below.[68] There is also pronounced discontent among Austrians with the functioning of democracy within the European Union. Only thirty-eight percent of the population are satisfied with the democratic performance within the EU, while sixty-six percent are dissatisfied. In no other member country is the difference between satisfaction with the democracy in the own country and with the democracy in the European Union as great as in Austria. Furthermore, two-thirds doubt that Austria could influence important decisions of the EU, and seventy percent of all Austrians live under the impression that the bigger countries and their interests have more weight within the European Union compared to the smaller member states. With the exception of Great Britain, no Western European member country evaluates the membership as critically as Austria, but this does not mean that the Austrians question the membership in the EU as such or would favor a stand-alone position like Switzerland.

The remarkable degree of skepticism of Austrians regarding institutions and decisions of the EU can only partly be based on feelings of inferiority by citizens of a small country attempting to hold on to their national sovereignty. Resistance against the transfer of national competences to the European Union can also be registered in other countries independent of their size. Also utilitarian explanations of the Austrian Euroskepticism, which relate the cost of membership with the disappointed expectations of economic advantages, only explain partial aspects of the skeptical attitude toward the EU. Apparently not only political and economic factors contribute to EU skepticism but also cultural prejudices toward the opening of Austrian society to Europe. In no other country among the original fifteen EU member states was the resistance toward the planned and in 2004 executed eastern enlargement of the European Union so pronounced as in Austria.[69]

Table 11: Evaluation of EU Membership 2010, in Percent

	our country's membership is a good thing	our country has benefits from membership
1. Luxembourg	70	68
2. Netherlands	69	68
3. Denmark	66	76
4. Ireland	66	77
5. Belgium	64	66
6. Spain	59	60
7. Sweden	54	52
8. Germany	50	48
9. Italy	48	47
10. Finland	45	54
11. Greece	44	61
12. France	44	51
13. Portugal	43	54
14. Austria	36	41
15. Great Britain	29	36
Total	52	57

Questions: *"Generally speaking, do you think that our country's membership in the European Union is a good thing?"*
"Taking everything into account, would you say that our country has benefits from being member of the European Union?"
Source: Eurobarometer 73 (Spring 2010).

The reasons for this were not exclusively found in economic factors such as the assumed cost of the expansion, but were also founded upon considerable fears of increasing migratory movements, since in Austria on the whole economic as well as cultural resentments toward a growing immigration are widely present. It is only for a minority of Austrians imaginable that cultural and religious diversity could also be an enrichment for society. According to data of the European Values Survey 2008, sixty-nine percent of Austrians believe that the migrants would contribute to an increase of criminality, sixty-six percent see migrants as a burden for the social system, fifty-six percent believe that the share of immigrants represents a threat for society, and forty-eight percent are convinced that the newcomers would take work away from their own population. Exactly half of the respondents expressed the opinion that the Austrian culture and way of life would be undermined by the migrants.[70] For the majority of Austrians, the process of European integration has apparently gone too far already; however, just in these attitudes toward European integration, the biggest difference between the population and the political and economic elites can be found in Austria compared to other EU countries. In no other EU member country is this elite-public gap between an integration-skeptical population and integration-friendly elites as pronounced as in Austria.[71]

The widespread EU skepticism, economically motivated prejudices toward immigrants, and feelings of cultural threat as well as anxieties to lose the traditional Austrian lifestyle are the characteristics differentiating Austria from the other member countries of the European Union, who view the consequences of the progressing Europeanization much more positively. In the Europeanization of the political culture, Austria's approximation to Western European standards of citizen politics represents a positive development. A remarkably subject-oriented culture changed to an average European citizen culture over the years. But cultural traditions of Austrian exceptionalism, such as introversion and tendencies to seclusion of a largely homogenous small-state society existing over decades, remain of latent authoritarian dispositions[72] as well as a pronounced national pride compared to other European countries, which also provides a potential for chauvinistic resentments toward non-Austrians,[73] defining the limits of Europeanization in Austria, which will still have to be overcome if Austria wants to move toward a truly European civic culture.

Notes

1. Kenneth Janda, *Political Parties: A Cross-National Survey* (New York: The Free Press, 1980), 318.

2. Fritz Plasser and Peter A. Ulram, *Unbehagen im Parteienstaat* (Vienna: Böhlau, 1982).

3. Fritz Plasser, *Parteien unter Stress* (Vienna: Böhlau, 1987).

4. Anton Pelinka, "Die Entaustrifizierung Österreichs: Zum Wandel des politischen Systems 1945-1995," *Österreichische Zeitschrift für Politikwissenschaft* 25, no. 1 (1995): 5-16.

5. Anton Pelinka, "Austrian Exceptionalism," *Austrian History Yearbook* 33 (2002): 1-14.

6. Günter Bischof and Anton Pelinka, eds., *The Americanization/Westernization of Austria*, Contemporary Austrian Studies 12 (New Brunswick: Transaction, 2004).

7. Heinrich Neisser and Sonja Puntscher Riekmann, *Europäisierung der österreichischen Politik: Konsequenzen der EU-Mitgliedschaft* (Vienna: WUV, 2002).

8. Fritz Plasser, "Assessing the Americanization of Austrian Politics and Politicians," in *The Americanization/Westernization of Austria*, ed. Bischof and Pelinka, 235-54.

9. Fritz Plasser and Peter A. Ulram, "Politischer Kulturvergleich: Deutschland, Österreich und

die Schweiz," in *Staatsbürger oder Untertanen? Politische Kultur Deutschlands, Österreichs und der Schweiz im Vergleich*, ed. idem. (Frankfurt: Peter Lang, 1991), 17-48; and idem., *Das österreichische Politikverständnis: Von der Konsens- zur Konfliktkultur?* (Vienna: WUV, 2002).

10. Mark N. Franklin, *Voter Turnout and the Dynamics of Electoral Competition in Established Democracies since 1945* (Cambridge: Cambridge University Press, 2004), 11.

11. Sidney Verba, Norman H. Nie, and Jae On Kim, *Participation and Political Equality: A Seven Nation Comparison* (Cambridge: Cambridge University Press, 1978), 110.

12. Pelinka, "Austrian Exceptionalism."

13. Wolfgang Mueller, "Kalter Krieg, Neutralität und politische Kultur in Österreich," *Aus Politik und Zeitgeschichte* 1-2 (2009): 11-19.

14. Alan Marsh, *Political Action in Europe and the USA* (London: Macmillan, 1990), 167.

15. Samuel H. Barnes et al., *Political Action: Mass Participation in Five Western Democracies* (Beverly Hills: Sage, 1979), 490.

16. Ibid., 417.

17. Marsh, *Political Action in Europe and the USA*, 168.

18. Plasser and Ulram, *Das österreichische Politikverständnis*, 112; and idem., "Bürger und Politik in Österreich," in *Deutschland, Österreich und die Schweiz im neuen Europa: Bürger und Politik*, ed. Oscar W. Gabriel and Fritz Plasser (Baden-Baden: Nomos, 2010), 155.

19. Plasser, *Parteien unter Stress*; Peter Gluchowski and Fritz Plasser, "Zerfall der Parteibindungen in Deutschland und Österreich," in *Wahlen und politische Einstellungen in Deutschland und Österreich*, ed. Fritz Plasser et al. (Frankfurt: Peter Lang, 1999), 3-29; Wolfgang C. Müller, Fritz Plasser, and Peter A. Ulram, "Party Responses to the Erosion of Voter Loyalties in Austria," in *Political Parties and Electoral Change*, ed. Peter Mair, Wolfgang C. Müller, and Fritz Plasser (Thousand Oaks: Sage, 2004), 145-78; Fritz Plasser and Gilg Seeber, "Austrian Electoral Behavior in International Comparison," in *The Changing Austrian Voter*, ed. Günter Bischof and Fritz Plasser, Contemporary Austrian Studies 16 (New Brunswick: Transaction, 2008), 150-78; and Fritz Plasser and Peter A. Ulram, "Electoral Change in Austria," in *The Changing Austrian Voter*, ed. Bischof and Plasser, 54-78.

20. Pelinka, "Austrian Exceptionalism."

21. Plasser and Ulram, "Bürger und Politik in Österreich," 154.

22. Plasser and Ulram, *Das österreichische Politikverständnis*, 112.

23. Plasser and Seeber, "Austrian Electoral Behavior in International Comparison," 169.

24. Oscar W. Gabriel, "Citizen Politics—Das Konzept und seine wissenschaftliche Bedeutung," in *Deutschland, Österreich und die Schweiz im neuen Europa*, ed. idem. and Plasser, 14.

25. Jan W. van Deth, "Politisches Interesse," in *Deutschland und Europa: Ergebnisse des Social Survey 2002-2003*, ed. idem. (Wiesbaden: VS Verlag, 2004), 275-92.

26. Leopold Rosenmayr, ed., *Politische Beteiligung und Wertwandel in Österreich* (Vienna: R. Oldenbourg, 1980), 303.

27. Plasser and Ulram, "Politischer Kulturvergleich," 43.

28. Plasser and Ulram, *Das österreichische Politikverständnis*, 35.

29. Oscar W. Gabriel, "Politische Einstellungen und politische Kultur," in *Die EU-Staaten im Vergleich*, ed. idem. and Sabine Kropp (Wiesbaden: VS Verlag, 2008), 201.

30. Rosenmayr, ed., *Politische Beteiligung und Wertwandel in Österreich*, 47; and Marsh, *Political Action in Europe and the USA*, 167.

31. Plasser and Ulram, "Politischer Kulturvergleich," 28.

32. Plasser and Ulram, *Das österreichische Politikverständnis*, 197.

33. Plasser and Ulram, "Bürger und Politik in Österreich," 160-64.

34. Barnes et al., *Political Action*; Rosenmayr, ed., *Politische Beteiligung und Wertwandel in Österreich*; Marsh, *Political Action in Europe and the USA*.

35. Russell J. Dalton, *Citizen Politics: Public Opinion and Political Parties* (Washington, DC: CQ Press, 2008).

36. Oscar W. Gabriel and Fritz Plasser, "Deutschland, Österreich und die Schweiz im europäischen Vergleich," in *Deutschland, Österreich und die Schweiz im neuen Europa*, ed. idem., 270.

37. Ibid.

38. Rosenmayr, ed., *Politische Beteiligung und Wertwandel in Österreich*, 24.

39. Roland Deiser and Norbert Winkler, *Das politische Handeln der Österreicher* (Vienna: Verlag für Gesellschaftskritik, 1982), 225.

40. Plasser and Ulram, "Politischer Kulturvergleich," 19.

41. Fritz Plasser and Peter A. Ulram, "Politische Involvierung und politische Unterstützung in Österreich," in *Wahlen und politische Einstellungen in Deutschland und Österreich*, ed. Plasser et al.; and idem., *Das österreichische Politikverständnis*.

42. Plasser and Ulram, "Bürger und Politik in Österreich," 166.

43. Dalton, *Citizen Politics*; Ronald Inglehart and Christian Welzel, *Modernization, Cultural Change, and Democracy: The Human Development Sequence* (Cambridge: Cambridge University Press, 2005); and Bruce E. Cain, Russell J. Dalton, and Susan Scarrow, *Democracy Transformed? Expanding Political Opportunities in Advanced Industrial Democracies* (Oxford: Oxford University Press, 2006).

44. International Institute for Democracy and Electoral Assistance, *Voter Turnout in Western Europe* (Stockholm: IDEA, 2004), 56.

45. Plasser and Seeber, "Austrian Electoral Behavior in International Comparison."

46. Oscar W. Gabriel and Kerstin Völkl, "Politische und soziale Partizipation," in *Die EU-Staaten im Vergleich*, ed. Gabriel and Kropp, 294.

47. Gabriel and Plasser, "Deutschland, Österreich und die Schweiz im europäischen Vergleich," 281-82.

48. Susan J. Pharr and Robert Putnam, eds., *Disaffected Democracies* (Princeton: Princeton University Press, 2000); Russell J. Dalton, *Democratic Challenges, Democratic Choices: The Erosion of Political Support in Advanced Democracies* (New York: Oxford University Press, 2007); and Pippa Norris, *Democratic Deficit: Critical Citizens Revisited* (New York: Cambridge University Press, 2011).

49. Hermann Denz, "Staat und Zivilgesellschaft: Widersprüche, Verwerfungen, Bruchlinien," in *Die Konfliktgesellschaft: Wertewandel in Österreich 1990-2000*, ed. idem. et al. (Vienna: Czernin, 2000), 194; Plasser and Ulram, "Bürger und Politik in Österreich," 176; and Christian Friesl, Thomas Hofer, and Renate Wieser, "Die Österreicher/-innen und die Politik," in *Die Österreicherinnen: Wertewandel 1990-2008*, ed. Christian Friesl et al. (Vienna: Czernin, 2009), 216.

50. Plasser and Ulram, "Politische Involvierung und politische Unterstützung in Österreich"; idem., *Das österreichische Politikverständnis*; idem., "Bürger und Politik in Österreich"; Oscar W.

Gabriel, "Sozialkapital und Institutionenvertrauen in Deutschland und Österreich," in *Wahlen und politische Einstellungen in Deutschland und Österreich*, ed. Plasser et al., 147-89; and Oscar W. Gabriel et al., *Sozialkapital und Demokratie: Zivilgesellschaftliche Ressourcen im Vergleich* (Vienna: WUV, 2002).

51. Gabriel, "Politische Einstellungen und politische Kultur," 197.

52. Gabriel and Plasser, "Deutschland, Österreich und die Schweiz im europäischen Vergleich," 283-85.

53. Marsh, *Political Action in Europe and the USA*, 167-68; Rosenmayr, ed., *Politische Beteiligung und Wertwandel in Österreich*, 303.

54. Norris, *Democratic Deficit*, 108.

55. Ibid.

56. Ibid., 118.

57. Plasser and Ulram, "Bürger und Politik in Österreich," 180.

58. Bettina Westle, "Aspekte politischer Kultur im internationalen Vergleich—Legitimitätsvorstellungen und Legitimitätsurteile," in *Politische Kultur*, ed. Westle and Gabriel (Baden-Baden: Nomos, 2010), 308.

59. Gabriel and Plasser, "Deutschland, Österreich und die Schweiz im europäischen Vergleich," 276-77.

60. Norris, *Democratic Deficit*, 168.

61. Gabriel and Plasser, "Deutschland, Österreich und die Schweiz im europäischen Vergleich," 276.

62. Gabriel, "Politische Einstellungen und politische Kultur," 207.

63. Gabriel and Plasser, "Deutschland, Österreich und die Schweiz im europäischen Vergleich," 291.

64. Ibid.

65. Pelinka, "Austrian Exceptionalism."

66. Anton Pelinka, "Austrian Euroscepticism: The Shift from the Left to the Right," in *Euroscepticism: Party Politics, National Identity and European Integration*, ed. Robert Harmsen and Menno Spiering (Amsterdam: Edition Rodopi, 2005), 207-27.

67. Peter A. Ulram and Fritz Plasser, "Ungeliebt, aber unverzichtbar: Die Österreicher und die EU," in *Europa als Prozess: 15 Jahre Europäische Union und Österreich*, ed. Roman Pfefferle et al. (Vienna: Lit, 2010), 99-113.

68. Eurobarometer 73: Public Opinion in the European Union, Spring 2010.

69. Jan Stankovsky et al., *On the Eve of EU Enlargement* (Vienna: Signum, 1998).

70. Christian Friesl, Katarina Renner, and Renate Wieser, "'Wir' und 'die anderen'—Einstellungen zu Fremden und Fremdenfeindlichkeit in Österreich," *SWS-Rundschau* 50, no. 1 (2010): 13.

71. Wolfgang C. Müller et al., "Der Elite-Public Gap in der Europäischen Integration," in *Europa als Prozess*, ed. Pfefferle et al., 122-23.

72. Oliver Rathkolb and Guenter Ogris, *Authoritarianism, History and Democratic Dispositions in Austria, Poland, Hungary and the Czech Republic* (Innsbruck: Studienverlag, 2010).

73. Michal Krzyzanowski and Ruth Wodak, eds., *The Politics of Exclusion: Debating Migration in Austria* (New Brunswick: Transaction, 2008).

Austria's Dismal EU Membership: From Enthusiasm to Ambivalence

Sonja Puntscher Riekmann

Introduction

Austria's application for EU membership coincided with the end of the Cold War and the demise of the Soviet Empire. The debate about membership, mainly driven by economic reasons, had flared up several times before, but only in the second half of the 1980s geopolitics opened a real window of opportunity for putting aside the arguments about Austria's neutrality that had so far precluded membership. The application documents were handed in on 17 July of the mythical year 1989, whereas membership started on 1 January 1995. However, Austria's European perspective remained contested. Not only did the rising Freedom Party (FPÖ) switch from a pro- to an anti-European stance, but also the Social Democratic Party (SPÖ), leading the grand coalition with the People's Party (ÖVP), was split over the issue. And so were the trade unions as well as interest organizations representing employees and small enterprises. Moreover, the relatively young Green Party was skeptical about the EU's democratic standards and thus campaigned against membership, albeit for different reasons than the Freedom Party. Against these odds the grand coalition pursued its project with determination and thus the referendum on membership in 1994 became a success for Europe: More than two-thirds voted in favor, by far the best result in that accession series comprising also the Nordic countries. As a matter of fact, Norway rejected membership for the second time, whereas Finland (sixty-one percent yes votes) and in particular Sweden (fifty-two percent yes votes) showed less enthusiasm.

In the following years, however, the Austrian ardor withered. According to Eurobarometer opinion polls[1] on the question whether membership is a good thing, approval already reached a first-time low in 1997 (thirty percent). Since then harsh pendulum swings were registered, while on average positive answers were always fifteen points below the EU average. While low scores were expectable in 2000 when the installment of the conservative radical right coalition provoked "diplomatic measures" of the other fourteen member states against the Austrian government, the scores were somewhat astonishing in spring 2004. However, six months later approval jumped up to forty-five percent, and fell again to thirty-six percent one year later. In 2008, at the peak of the financial crisis, similar pendulum swings can be observed with regard to the question whether a country has on balance benefited from the Union: Forty-seven percent of Austrians answered positively in 2008 (plus eleven percent compared to the previous survey), and in 2010 this score fell again to forty-one percent,[2] and only twenty-six percent were of the opinion that the EU is "going in the right direction."[3] At the same time, according to a national poll, two-thirds of the population seemed convinced that the effects of the current financial crisis can only be staved off in cooperation with the Union.[4] Turnouts in European elections may be considered another significant indicator regarding popular attitudes towards the EU: Starting from a remarkable 67.7 percent in 1996, turnout fell to forty-nine percent (1999) and 42.4 percent (2004), while rising to almost forty-six percent in 2009 lingering above the EU average of forty-three percent.[5]

One can interpret these data in terms of normalization. In many EU member states we witness similar developments, contradictory stances looming large almost everywhere. However, they influence the stances of Austrian governments whose consensus on the EU shows clear signs of erosion, which in turn impinges upon popular attitudes. Whereas in pre-accession times the grand coalition advocated membership against popular fears and skepticism eventually overriding them, the post-accession period is marked by insecurities and pendulum swings in the mood of elites as much as of citizens. This reality, though, can also be analyzed against the backdrop of European developments, such as the struggle for a European constitution from 1999-2004 and the negative referenda in France and the Netherlands in 2005. Moreover and ironically, the Treaty of Lisbon, rid of the constitutional parlance and in line with past treaty revision, did not fare any better, as it was voted down in the Irish referendum of 2008. Together with the international financial and economic crisis these instances of EU's constitutional and identity crisis contribute to fueling Austrians' disgruntlement.

In Austria, both treaties—the Constitutional Treaty and the Treaty of Lisbon—have been ratified by the parliament, a referendum being ruled out on legal terms. The overwhelming majority of legal experts denied the need for another referendum that is constitutionally required only in the case of a fundamental change of the Austrian constitution. However, with some sixty-one percent of voters in favor of a national referendum, unsurprisingly the two radical right parties FPÖ and BZÖ took up the issue. And this provoked a change of mind also in the incumbent Social Democratic Party. In a public letter, the Social Democratic Chancellor Alfred Gusenbauer together with the new party leader and his successor Werner Faymann promised the Austrian public to subject all future treaty revisions to referendum. Interestingly, though, this promise was neglected in 2010 during the discussion of the first treaty change creating the constitutional basis for the financial stability mechanism. If under strict conditionality, the new Article 136, para 3 TFEU allows for bailouts until now forbidden by Article 125.[6] A salient issue in net payers' countries such as Austria, it could hardly be qualified as a minor change. However, in the relevant EU Main Committee of the Austrian parliament, Chancellor Faymann argued that such an amendment does not entail any further transfer of national competency and, thus, could be ratified without referendum.[7]

This paper aims at analyzing the "special relations" of Austria and Europe *first* in a brief historical retrospective on the reasons guiding the accession process. It will, *second*, try to explain the pendulum swing from enthusiasm to disappointment due to political and socio-economic developments. It will, *third*, give an account of the debates on the Constitutional Treaty and its follow-up, the Treaty of Lisbon, by unraveling the discursive conundrum of pragmatic endorsement, ignorance, populist criticism, outright rejection, and colliding visions of the Union ranging from further deepening to a complete overhaul in terms of variable geometry. It is the thesis of this essay that Austria is still struggling to define its role in the Union. It seems to be driven by illusions of national grandeur and by fears of remaining isolated at the same time. In reaction to such public mood, governments and political parties are continuously oscillating between crude pragmatism and Euroskepticism. This is, of course, not just the case in Austria, but owing to its political and socio-economic history before and after World War II the Austrian case is marked by special facets.

Austria's Struggle for EU Membership

Austria's history of relations with the European Union began as early as the 1950s.[8] Once full independence was achieved in 1955 after the conclusion of the State Treaty establishing Austria's neutrality, the grand coalition formed by the People's Party and the Socialist Party began talks about joining the European Coal and Steel Community. Interestingly, the initiative came from the Socialist Party, the People's Party being more cautious, while these stances reversed later on. Such talks took place in the shadow of the Cold War, the Soviet Union being very critical about Austria's *rapprochement* towards the "Western bloc." The same held true for Austria's membership in EFTA, which the Soviet Union did tolerate in the end. EFTA, on the other hand, sought its own rapprochement towards the EEC. Owing to the critical French position on relations with the United Kingdom, this move clashed with the refusal of France and the Commission to enter negotiations with EFTA. In the 1960s, Austria's European policy was not only hampered by domestic debates on the issue of neutrality but also and even more so by the dynamics in the EEC such as the failure of British membership (1963) rejected by de Gaulle. Envisaging a new "*Ostpolitik*," de Gaulle opposed Austria's aspirations in the name of smooth relations with the Soviet Union.[9] Moreover, in 1967 Italy blocked further association talks with Austria as long as the issue about its northern province South Tyrol/Alto Adige was unresolved. In 1969, the pertinent agreement on conflict resolution procedures cleared the way for the free trade agreements between EFTA and the EEC (excluding agricultural products) in 1972. By then also the Soviet Union, seeking to normalize its relations with the EEC, had attenuated its opposition.

The 1970s were the apotheosis of the Social Democratic era, marked by "Austro-Keynesianism,"[10] the flourishing of social partnership and corporatism, and the modernization of the society and political institutions through democratic, legal, and social reforms. In terms of foreign policy, Chancellor Bruno Kreisky governed with an absolute majority until 1983, diverting his course from Europe to the world at large, the Middle East being the most important case in point. In any event, many observers perceived that decade as a period of stagnation in the European integration process. Whilst the EEC was described by the newly coined term "Eurosclerosis," Austria bathed in the reputation of being an "island of the blessed," an attribute created by Pope Paul VI during a visit of the Austrian president to the Vatican in 1971. The island, though, was less blessed than generally assumed due to economic difficulties resulting from the oil crisis and, as a consequence, rising unemployment. The Austro-Keynesian answer was still de rigueur, but doubts about its sustainability were also rising. In the general election of 1983, the Socialist Party lost its absolute majority, and Bruno Kreisky handed the chancellery over to his uncharismatic heir, Fred Sinowatz, who formed a coalition with the small Freedom Party. The latter, while having far-right roots, as many of its members and functionaries had been active National Socialists, at that time showed a serious will to develop political liberalism, taking the German FDP as role model. However, this reform took the party to the brink of electoral insignificance. By the mid-1980s, Jörg Haider conquered the party leadership and gave it a new face by a double-edged strategy: While still flirting with the old far right, he combined anti-Semitism and xenophobia with economic modernism challenging traditional Austrian corporatism. Later anti-Europeanism became part and parcel of this strategy, which was all the more peculiar as the Freedom Party already in the 1950s had advocated EU membership. Due to this alarming shift of the Freedom Party in 1986, the new Social Democratic Chancellor Franz Vranitzky broke the coalition,[11] called for a general election, and thereafter formed a grand coalition with the People's Party that had stayed out of government since 1970.

At the same time, another political actor came into being: the Green Party. Emerging from a number of social protest movements pervading the late 1970s and the early 1980s, it did surprisingly well in local elections and finally in the national election of 1986. The Greens and the "new" FPÖ, as well as the Liberals created in 1993 as its splinter group after a row about the future course of the party, all were the unmistakable instance of a deep change in the Austrian party and corporatist system. In the following decade, the so-called big parties continuously lost voters who became as volatile as in other European states. In the last national election of 2008 they both received less than thirty percent of votes and hence also lost the two-thirds majority necessary for constitutional revision. In only two years from 2006 to 2008, the grand coalition shrank from almost seventy to fifty-five percent of votes. In the period crucial for EU membership the coalition still commanded impressive majorities of eighty-four percent (1986) and seventy-four percent (1990); however, the seeds of decline began to bud thereafter. In 1994, the year of the EU referendum, the grand coalition was reduced to mere 66.2 percent and had to make important concessions to the opposition in the negotiation of the constitutional law defining the relations with the Union.

Enthusiasm and Disappointment

Austria's accession to the European Union started in an atmosphere of large consensus. As aforementioned, in spite of two parties opposing EU membership in the referendum of 1994, sixty-six percent of the electorate voted in favor of it. The grand coalition rallied behind this truly common project and campaigned forcefully and convincingly for what was considered *the* major step in Austrian history since the State Treaty leading to independence in 1955. Campaigns though were also operating with questionable exaggerations regarding economical gains for everybody, whereas more cautious outlooks on the socio-economic future were ignored and critical stances regarding the democratic deficit were dispelled as negligible. Moreover, the Freedom Party under Jörg Haider campaigned against membership with such absurd arguments that they could hardly convince even their own electorate. The socio-economic developments producing winners and losers as well as the competition regime governing the single market were largely shunned by the government. The Green Party, while campaigning for Europe but against the existing EU on issues regarding the democratic deficit, was latently split in two factions, one advocating reform from within and the other from outside the Union. After the positive referendum, their spearhead of the no vote, Johannes Voggenhuber, immediately accepted the popular decision and became one of Austria's most prominent members of the European Parliament engaged in the two conventions establishing the Charter of Fundamental Rights as well as the Constitution for Europe.

In this context, the constitutional changes negotiated by the political parties in the Austrian parliament in 1994 were remarkable. The law accompanying EU membership endowed the parliament with considerable powers in defining the position of the government in a given policy field. Owing to the loss of the constitutional majority in the 1994 elections, the grand coalition had to concede to the opposition parties, in particular the Freedom Party and the Greens, a number of rights of information as well as of imposing binding decisions on the ministers when acting in the Council.[12] The European Union was given a most prominent place in the Austrian constitutional law, which was to regulate European decision-making of national actors in a much more extensive way than any other national constitution in Europe.[13] Participation was not only guaranteed to the national parliament but also, owing to Austria's federalism, the regional governments, in case European legislation affected their competencies. Regarding Austria's status of neutrality, the provisions concerning the

European Common Foreign and Security Policy are particularly relevant: *First*, owing to the distrust between the Social Democratic and the People's Party in this respect, participation in European decision-making presupposes a consensus of the chancellor and the minister of foreign affairs. It was indeed assumed that in the foreseeable future these two actors would stem from these two parties. *Second*, European military policies, including the sending of Austrian troops abroad, were linked to the co-decision of the national parliament.[14] However, the enthusiasm of the opposition was curbed soon thereafter, the grand coalition having regained the constitutional majority and hence the discipline of their MPs to refuse their consent to decisions binding the ministers.[15]

After accession, popular enthusiasm dwindled continuously. When promises about economical gains did not materialize for everybody, the EU was easily identified as the main culprit. Moreover, in the following years the consensus within the grand coalition began to erode as both parties incrementally lost popular support, whereas the Freedom Party soared, becoming the second strongest actor and surpassing, if only by a tiny majority, the People's Party in the general election of 1999. When the latter decided to refuse the offer of the Social Democratic Party to continue the old coalition and instead coalesced with the far-right Freedom Party, Austria entered a new political era. This holds true in several respects.

First, Chancellor Wolfgang Schüssel broke the taboo regarding the Freedom Party that, in spite of its electoral success, until then had never been considered a possible partner by any political force in Austria, not even by the People's Party itself, which in the past had defined Jörg Haider as acting outside the "constitutional ark." In particular after the intensive debates since the 1980s about Austria's role during the Nazi period, Haider's crude xenophobic nationalism as well as his repeated toying with the Third Reich, such as praising its employment policy, had become unbearable. For a better understanding of the issue, it is important to dwell briefly on the political context of the time. In that period, a number of contradicting phenomena surfaced simultaneously: During the candidacy of the former UN Secretary General Kurt Waldheim for president of Austria, a discussion broke loose about his role in World War II and evolved into a far more general debate about Austria's role in the Third Reich. Finally, the government's negotiations to join the EU conspicuously coincided with a declaration of Chancellor Franz Vranitzky in the national parliament about Austria's complicity in the Nazi crimes, including apologies to the victims (1991) for whom a reparation fund was established in 1994. Hence, a new consensus about the past seemed to pervade the nation which was, however, perturbed by Haider's uninterrupted electoral success. In 1999, Haider's efforts were crowned by Wolfgang Schüssel's government coalition. The result was a wave of protest within and without the country. Austria's image of the "island of the blessed" had finally crumbled, when under the leadership of Jacques Chirac the other fourteen members of the EU decided to take diplomatic measures against the Austrian government. These legally ill-conceived measures never resulted in any really serious steps and were quickly suspended after a report of three "wise men" led by the Finnish President Martti Ahtisaari on whether the government had infringed Article 6 of the EU Treaty. Despite some critical remarks on the FPÖ's political stances regarding minorities and democratic standards, the authors of the report concluded that serious and protracted infringements had not occurred. They recommended amending of Article 7 of the EU Treaty to provide for better procedures regarding sanctions.[16] However, Austrian citizens largely perceived these measures as sanctions against the whole people.[17]

Second, and perhaps owing to this development, Austria's political elite was less and less capable of defining a pro-active role in the European arena and thus gradually yielded to an increasingly reactive perspective on EU affairs. Scapegoating the Union for unpopular decisions became an important facet. Moreover, the ministers of the Freedom Party, torn between government duties and anti-Europeanism, showed a lamentable performance in Brussels. There was, indeed, an impressively frequent turnover of Freedom Party ministers throughout the whole coalition period.

Third, and concomitantly, the Austrian government had a hard time dealing with the next enlargement toward its neighbors in Central and Eastern Europe. Dreams about playing a special role as mediator or even champion of enlargement were thwarted by the accession countries that declined the invitation to the "regional partnership" launched by the Minister of Foreign Affairs Benita Ferrero-Waldner. Domestically, economic elites, in particular banking and oil industries, welcomed the opening of the Iron Curtain,[18] whereas smaller enterprises and their workforces felt threatened by potential labor migrants willing to take up jobs at much lower wages. Thus, the negative implications of a coalition with the xenophobic Freedom Party proved difficult and could only be quenched by fighting for longer transition periods regarding the opening of the Austrian labor markets. These arrangements hardly prevented migration, yet they created a space of illegality that made life particularly cumbersome for migrant workers in the healthcare sector where they are indispensable. Since then, all Austrian governments engaged in a dubious debate about further enlargement toward the Western Balkans and Turkey. While the former government, in which Wolfgang Schüssel served as minister of foreign affairs, in 1999 had agreed at the European Council summit in Helsinki to give Turkey accession status, this stance became ever more difficult to maintain in the coalition with the Freedom Party. Thus, in public, the accession perspectives of Turkey were downplayed by repeating time and again that membership is not on the horizon for the next twenty years. With regard to the Western Balkans, clear preference was given to Croatia, whereas the Austrian government remained rather silent about other potential candidates, at least in public.

It is against this backdrop that Austria's position within the Union (including Austrians' disaffection with the Union) is to be analyzed. There is, however, another reality to be considered: Whereas Austria's political and economic elites had decided to apply for membership mainly driven by economic interests, the Austrian economy had to face a major overhaul in preparation for and after accession. Doubts are raised by academics whether even elites were well aware of the implications stemming thereof. As one economist put it: "The desire to actively participate in the European integration process was absolutely subordinate, at least in economical thinking. Austrian politics was less motivated by the idea of framing and supporting European political solutions than by the will to avoid discrimination in the pursuit of national interests."[19] However, this narrow approach was not sustainable in the long run: The European "economic constitution" (*Wirtschaftsverfassung*) demanded a new political culture due to its focus on competition, macroeconomic stability and structural reforms inspired by supply-side economics. Compliance with this orientation presupposed a clear break with the structures created since World War II. Austro-Keynesianism was no longer considered a recipe of success but rather a hindrance to modernization. It is also noteworthy that Haider's protest against the established order had been a protest against the incrustations of Austrian corporatism.[20] Once the process of liberalization had been started through the implementation of the *acquis communautaire*, he could easily, if paradoxically, harvest new voters by addressing the losers of that process. In the decade after accession, Austria's economic performance was rather impressive owing not only to liberalization and new rules of competition but also to the opening of the neighboring markets in Central and Eastern Europe.[21] However, many perceive redistribution as uneven, whereas the effects of the financial crisis that hit some Austrian banks hard are still to be seen. At the time of writing, the picture is ambivalent: Unemployment rose considerably in 2009 when in May it was thirty percent higher (6.3 percent) than in May 2008. Yet, it decreased from an average 7.1 percent in 2009 to

6.9 percent in 2010.[22] There are, of course, controversial interpretations of these data. However, by and large, Austrian unemployment is considerably below EU average.

Owing to the intensive engagement of the Austrian banking system in a number of new member states in Central and Eastern Europe, the financial and economic crisis seemed to produce a change of mentality regarding the Union. Suddenly, a majority of sixty-six percent perceived the EU as the savior in difficult times.[23] Not even the Freedom Party was putting membership in doubt, whereas the Social Democratic Party softened its advocacy of compulsory referenda for all future treaty revisions. However, during the European election campaign of 2009, the Freedom Party launched a debate on Europe's cultural roots exploiting anti-globalist and xenophobic sentiments looming large in the electorate. Moreover, the leftist populist EP candidate and former journalist, Hans-Peter Martin, exploited anti-establishment attitudes by denouncing in his pamphlets published regularly in the *Kronen Zeitung*, Austria's widespread yellow press, EU bureaucracy in general and the EP in particular as a hoard of corruption. It is noteworthy that the letter promising referenda for all future treaty revisions written by the former Chancellor Gusenbauer together with the incumbent head of government Faymann was also published in the *Kronen Zeitung*.

Intriguingly, the discursive hegemony deployed by the late editor of the *Kronen Zeitung* seems to be a constitutive element of strategic thinking in large parts of the Austrian political establishment. As a matter of fact, the notorious letter written after the Irish negative referendum was not addressed to the Austrian citizens but to the editor himself. It started by paying tribute to the Irish no vote that the Social Democratic Party is to respect "without any restrictions and reservations." It promised to take the feelings of unease and the criticisms against the EU seriously. In particular, the party wished to engage itself in the promotion of a European social union, yet what followed was again the well-known pleading for nationalist protectionism with particular regard to the labor market. At the heart of the letter, though, lay the aforementioned promise of subjecting "future treaty revisions encroaching upon Austrian interests" to a referendum. Such a provision should also apply to the accession of Turkey "that would overstrain the existing structures of the EU." The authors concluded that they "want to work at a Europe which is oriented towards the needs and desires of the people living on the continent, in order to restore their confidence in this great unification act."[24]

As will be shown by the next chapter, in the ratification debate on the Treaty of Lisbon that took place before the above quoted letter was published, positions of the Austrian political parties are marked by intriguing contradictions and swings.

Treaty Ratification in the Light of Negative Referenda in France, the Netherlands, and Ireland

After accession, all treaty revisions were ratified by the Austrian parliament. And so was the Treaty establishing a Constitution for Europe, on which all members of the Austrian parliament voted yes, except for one representative of the Freedom Party. Thus, the critical debate on the Treaty of Lisbon that actually enshrined most of the provisions of the Constitutional Treaty has not been so much about the treaty itself as about the necessity to redefine the Union in the light of the negative votes in the referenda in France and the Netherlands in 2005.

A comparison of the two debates in parliament about the Constitutional Treaty in May 2005 and the Treaty of Lisbon in April 2008 offer some intriguing insights into the mostly reactive attitudes of Austrian members of parliament and government. The first debate occurred before the negative referenda in France and the Netherlands and unfolded in a largely pro-European atmosphere to which also the far-right Freedom Party contributed. Obviously, the Freedom Party being "captured" in the government could hardly deviate from the general line of the coalition. Moreover, just one month before, in April 2005, the party had split into two parts. As a matter of fact, the Freedom Party ministers and a number of parliamentarians had formed the so-called BZÖ (*Bündnis Zukunft Österreich*, i.e. Union for the future of Austria) under the leadership of Jörg Haider, whereas the rest together with all but one regional party organization remained in the Freedom Party, whose new leader became Heinz-Christian Strache. In the following years and against all odds created by the schism, Strache's FPÖ enjoyed considerable electoral success in national and regional elections. Meanwhile, the BZÖ struggled for survival. Only in Carinthia, where Haider until his death in 2008 had repeatedly been governor,[25] could the BZÖ impressively win in the election of March 2009.

In the debate on the Constitutional Treaty all parties seemed to converge on supporting the reforms, even if speakers pertaining to the different parties accentuated different aspects. The representatives of the People's Party, Chancellor Wolfgang Schüssel and Wilhelm Molterer as head of the group in parliament, strongly endorsed the treaty as a major achievement and claimed the credit for specific provisions that Austria had fought for, such as the social clause, the role of social partners, the safeguard of local public services and of water provisions.[26] The leader of the Social Democratic opposition party, Alfred Gusenbauer, while stressing the general value of European integration, mentioned the growing EU skepticism as a result of too little and not too many EU competencies. Due to this deficiency, the EU would be unable to satisfy the peoples' interests. He also discussed the democratic deficit as a result of an institutional setup that differs from national democracies and, thus, he pleaded for a future reform to reconstruct the national model at the European level. Interestingly, his claim was to install a European government that citizens could vote out of office in case of discontent.[27] On the whole, he supported the Constitutional Treaty as a precondition for better EU politics. Touching upon the issue of a national referendum, Gusenbauer denied such claims that he considered dangerous, but he advocated a Europe-wide plebiscite.[28] To the great astonishment of the domestic audience three years later, in his function as Austrian chancellor, Gusenbauer reversed his stance by signing the notorious letter to the editor of the *Kronen Zeitung*.

The head of the BZÖ group, while supporting the Constitutional Treaty, focused on issues of security emerging from migration, terrorism and international organized crime, whereby these classical topics dear to the far right were considered to be appropriately tackled by the Constitutional Treaty. Moreover, he stressed the preservation of veto rights in important fields and praised the Charter of Fundamental Rights that would prevent groups from calling for sanctions against a government, as had happened in Austria in 2000.[29]

The representatives of the Green Party in general supported the Constitutional Treaty as an instance of progress in terms of democracy and efficiency, albeit they voiced some criticism regarding military and security provisions as well as the EURATOM Treaty, a traditional Green topic based on Austria's history with nuclear energy.[30] As EURATOM had been settled outside the Constitutional Treaty, its ratification did not meet further opposition. In the end, a number of initiatives concerning the issue of a Europe-wide referendum on further treaty revisions were presented by different groups and approved by an overwhelming majority. And so was the Constitutional Treaty with one dissentient vote only.

The picture was quite different during the debate on the Treaty of Lisbon. First, the political landscape had changed. In the so-called grand coalition, the Social Democratic Party took the helm again. However, both parties had to bear considerable losses in the election of 2006, and thus, coalition negotiations had proved difficult. The Social Democratic Party made important concessions to the People's Party that acquired important portfolios such as the ministry of finance, foreign, as well as economic and labor affairs. Despite Chancellor Gusenbauer's attempts of justification, he could not conceal his lack of clout and hence from the outset suffered from the odium of weak leadership. He came under heavy pressure from his own party, where behind the scenes important actors began to prepare for his fall that became true only eighteen months later.

The Freedom Party, now in opposition and on the way of consolidation due to growing electoral success, returned to its clear Euroskeptical stance, albeit with new nuances. Its boisterous leader Heinz-Christian Strache no longer advocated a simplistic anti-Europeanism. Gradually the EU became perceived not only as a common area of security to be shielded against migration, organized crime, and terrorism but also as a cultural sphere: Oddly enough Strache, presiding over a party that in religious terms had always been rather agnostic, suddenly started to invoke Christian Europe against Muslim citizens and migrants. However, more urgent than that appeared the need for a national referendum on the Treaty of Lisbon. The general thrust of all interventions made by the Freedom Party concerned the lack of legitimacy of the EU to be redressed by a national referendum.[31] In particular, the Freedom Party considered the Treaty of Lisbon as encroaching upon the national constitution in a way to fundamentally change the latter. Centralization and formation of a European state were the key terms, whereas Austria's neutrality was said to vanish under new treaty.[32] The much smaller BZÖ, now also in opposition, while sharing the Freedom Party's position on the referendum, advocated a new and comprehensively changed "fundamental treaty" based on the old idea of "core Europe." For that matter, the BZÖ coined the term "Europe of modules" in which the net payers were to form the inner core or module. Of course, Austria should be part of it. In what the BZÖ called a "Treaty for Europe," territorial, financial, and cultural boundaries should be clearly defined also in the light of Europe's absorption capacity in regard to further enlargement.[33]

Taking a pragmatic approach, the Green members of parliament stressed that the importance of the Treaty of Lisbon appeared somewhat exaggerated, but they acknowledged the progress in terms of democracy and efficiency. In regard to the crucial question of a national referendum, the party line was to endorse European-wide referenda.[34]

Expectably, the parties of the grand coalition were in favor of ratifying the Treaty of Lisbon, the new provisions of which were appraised by all speakers. While Ursula Plassnik, minister of foreign and European affairs, in public had time and again highlighted the fact that the treaty contained ninety-five percent of the provisions enshrined in the Constitutional Treaty and hence did not represent anything fundamentally new, in the parliamentary debate she argued that to play a global role the Union had to be deepened. Even if the Treaty of Lisbon was not perfect, it was the first common work of twenty-seven member states. She appealed to the citizens' positive spirit in order to make a significant impact on the European level. In line with the People's Party position, she rejected a national and advocated a Europe-wide referendum that, so she regretted, had been rejected by other member states.[35]

In this context, the position of Chancellor Alfred Gusenbauer was perhaps the most interesting. While supporting parliamentarian ratification of the Treaty of Lisbon as an historical moment, the chancellor challenged the opposition leader Strache on the issue of a national referendum by pointing to the large majority that had voted "yes" on accession. He criticized Strache for inciting popular fears and accused him of pursuing an exit agenda. He pointed, moreover, to the fact that the Treaties of Amsterdam and Nice had also been ratified by the parliament. That is, so he resumed, a perfectly normal procedure.[36] The two-thirds majority for treaty ratification was easily reached again in this case, as in the ratification of the Constitutional Treaty, but with different results: of 178 votes cast, 151 were positive and twenty-seven negative.

Two months later, after the Irish "no" in June 2008, things changed. With supporters of a national referendum gaining ground, the Social Democratic leadership prostrated itself before the populist discourse of the Freedom Party that since long had made inroads into the Social Democratic electorate. The chancellor and the designated head of the party thus wrote the aforementioned letter promising a referendum on all future treaty revisions. This turn was one of the People's Party reasons to break up the unloved coalition and to call a new election in September 2008. However, the electoral outcome did not fulfill the People's Party's hopes: It remained second in spite of Social Democratic losses. The only winner was the Freedom Party, whereas the expectations of the Greens were thwarted, too. After a long period of slow but steady growth under the party leader Alexander van der Bellen, the Greens had to face losses in several regional elections and stagnation at the national level. Thus, the party suddenly also qualified its position on the EU, its new leader Eva Glawischnig declaring the Treaty of Lisbon dead and advocating a more critical position in regard to the EU. This stance provoked a row within the party and in particular with the MEP Voggenhuber, who was denied the position as leading candidate in the European elections of 2009 by the party congress. He withdrew, and the party lost more than three percent of the votes.

One last point of the current Austrian-EU relations is noteworthy: The novel provisions for EU decision-making enshrined in the Treaty of Lisbon required implementation at the national level in particular with regard to the simplified procedure of treaty change and the powers granted to national parliaments in the control of subsidiarity and proportionality. In this respect, the Austrian legislator has adapted the constitution with some dubious outcomes. Legal scholars criticize systemic inadequacies in procedural and institutional terms that might entail constitutional and political problems in the future. Moreover, it is unclear how the national parliament will cope with the requirements of scrutinizing EU law-making without the creation of new structures and new resources.[37] For that matter, however, the national parliament instead of breaking new ground chose trodden paths by delegating genuine parliamentarian tasks to the executive, thus undermining its own new powers from the outset.[38] Whereas it is true that the much-lauded enhancement of national parliaments as one important step towards reducing the EU's democratic deficit has hardly seen appropriate implementation in many member states, Austria's long tradition of violating the separation of powers principle is to continue also in this case.

Conclusions

In a peculiar way, Europe plays an important role in Austrian politics. Citizens, however, seem to perceive the Union less as an arena in which the country could proactively play the game, but rather as an encroaching foreign power to be contained if not fought off. There is little debate about the process of integration and the positions taken by the political establishment therein. It would also be rather difficult to ascertain what such positions are. Besides general commitments to European integration as we may read in the government's agreement, it is difficult to discern distinctive projects. The two presidencies of 1998 and 2006, for example, were well-managed semesters in which the Austrian government took up certain aspects of the predecessor's agenda and sometimes could drive the debate to positive conclusions (e.g. in the much controversial question of the Services' Directive) by exerting its power as honest broker.[39]

On the other hand, European legislation eventually colliding with Austrian regulations is seen as an unfriendly act.[40] The government tending to scapegoat Brussels in case of popular criticism exacerbates this perception. The media play a special role as well: While ignoring the Union most of the time, they tend to exaggerate negative implications of

European policies, the *Kronen Zeitung* being a special point in case. The presence of an ever stronger radical right party imposing its critical EU discourse onto its competitors adds to the Austrian conundrum. However, the financial and economic crisis seems to trigger a change of mentality as recent opinion polls demonstrate.[41] It may, though, be a sign of fear rather than of satisfaction. Thus, it is also difficult to assess future reactions to the implications of the Treaty of Lisbon that finally entered into force on 1 December 2009 after the positive referendum in Ireland. In particular, the new role of national parliaments as conceived by the treaty will pose some hard questions in regard to the preparedness of the Austrian parliament to tackle the tasks stemming thereof. While the concept of subsidiarity remains dear to all parties, there is little preparation for the implementation of the specific control functions of national parliaments enshrined in the Treaty of Lisbon. In this respect, the Constitutional Convention (2003-05), which was set up to discuss the overhaul of the Austrian constitution, represents an interesting instance of what may be called the European absentmindedness of Austria's political establishment. The convention, obviously moulded on the European Convention of 2002, while discussing at length the needs for substantive constitutional reforms shunned reflections upon the implications of European law for the Austrian legal order.[42] The convention was terminated in 2005 without results and the issue has not been taken up since.

In conclusion, Austria's EU membership is marked by intriguingly contradictory aspects. Popular sentiments oscillate between pragmatism and disaffection, between "permissive consensus and constraining dissensus."[43] Political elites tend to exploit (or incite) both sentiments: In the shadow of permissive consensus, ruling parties try to obfuscate their practices in EU politics, whereas opposition parties, in particular the radical right, aim at reaping or stimulating the constraining dissensus.[44] This, however, does not only happen in Austria.

Notes

1. Standard Eurobarometer 70/2009.
2. Standard Eurobarometer 73/2010.
3. Standard Eurobarometer 70/2009.
4. Sozialwissenschaftliche Studiengesellschaft, Press Conference, Vienna, 22 Dec. 2008.
5. <www.europarl.eu/parliament/archive/elections2009/en/Austria>.
6. I will not dwell upon the details of the rows on bailout or no bailout the Europeans have fought since the Greek crisis. Suffice it to say that the first grants conceded by the EU were based on Article 122, para 2 TFEU, thus circumventing the no-bailout clause of Article 125.

Besides protests from different member states and political actors, this has also led to legal actions before the German Constitutional Court whose ruling is to be expected in the spring of 2011. See also Sonja Puntscher Riekmann, "Europas Verfassung nach Lissabon: Europäische Politik in der Finanz- und Wirtschaftskrise zwischen Pragmatismus und Legitimation," in *Rechtsfragen der Implementierung des Vertrags von Lissabon*, ed. Thomas Eilmansberger, Stefan Griller, and Walter Obwexer (Vienna: Springer, 2010), 497-525.

7. Parlamentskorrespondenz Nr. 1032, 16 Dec. 2010; <www.parlinkom.gv.at/PAKT/PR/JAGR_2010/PK1032/>.

8. For the history of Austrian-EU relations, see Paul Luif, *On the Road to Brussels: The Political Dimension of Austria's, Finland's, and Sweden's Accession to the European Union* (Vienna: Braumüller, 1995), 185-99; and Michael Gehler and Rolf Steininger, eds., *The Neutrals and European Integration 1945-1995* (Vienna: Böhlau, 2000), 465-701.

9. In this context, another story is noteworthy: it was the then Foreign Minister Bruno Kreisky to launch the debate about how to organize relations between EFTA and the EEC in view of a possible British EEC membership. He pleaded for a coordinated approach of the remaining EFTA members. In a meeting in Vienna (1961), several points limiting the rapprochement were formulated (such as the power to making international treaties, neutrality-related decisions in the case of war or grave international crises, safeguarding of crucial supplies). However, when the British request of membership had been turned down, Sweden and Switzerland withdrew from this initiative, whereas Austria continued its efforts to reach an association treaty with the EEC. The different interpretations of this position notwithstanding, the story is interesting in that it differs from public discourses of the following decades in which the Austrian foreign policy was less European than globally oriented. See Luif, *On the Road to Brussels*, 186-87.

10. Helmut Kramer, "Österreichs Wirtschaftspolitik im Rahmen der EU," in *Europäisierung der österreichischen Politik: Konsequenzen der EU-Mitgliedschaft*, ed. Heinrich Neisser and Sonja Puntscher Riekmann (Vienna: Wiener Universitätsverlag, 2002), 267-94; Hans Seidel, "Austro-Keynesianismus," in *Wirtschaftspolitische Blätter* 29, no. 3 (1989): 11-15; Gunter Tichy, "Vom Glanz und Elend des Austro-Keynesianismus," in *Austro-Keynesianismus—Festschrift für Hans Seidel zum 65. Geburtstag*, ed. Peter Mitter and Andreas Wörgötter, Wirtschaftswissenschaftliche Beiträge 38 (Heidelberg: Physica Verlag, 1990), 76-101.

11. See Sonja Puntscher Riekmann, "The Politics of 'Ausgrenzung,' the Austrian Nazi Past, and the European Dimension of the New Radical Right," in *The Vranitzky Era in Austria*, ed. Günter Bischof and Anton Pelinka, Contemporary Austrian Studies 7 (New Brunswick: Transaction, 1998).

12. Theo Öhlinger, "Die Europäisierung der österreichischen Verfassung," in *Europäisierung der österreichischen Politik*, ed. Neisser and Puntscher Riekmann, 81-99.

13. This position is no longer unique, in particular after the ruling of the German Constitutional Court on the Treaty of Lisbon in 2009.

14. Theo Öhlinger, "Art. 23c bis 23f B-VG," in *Österreichisches Bundesverfassungsrecht: Textsammlung und Kommentar*, ed. Karl Korinek and Michael Holubek (Vienna: Manz, 1999); Stefan Griller, "Die GASP und das Ende der immerwährenden Neutralität," in *Rechtsfragen in der Anwendung des Amsterdamer Vertrages*, ed. Waldemar Hummer (Vienna: Manz, 2001), 261-80.

15. For the rise and fall of the use of these rights, see Johannes Pollak and Peter Slominski, "Influencing EU Politics? The Case of the Austrian Parliament," *Journal of Common Market Studies* 41, no. 4 (2003): 707-29. The authors hold that "From a legal point of view the Austrian Parliament has in its hands an exceptionally strong instrument for influencing and controlling the government's EU policy. However, it refrains from using it, at least with regard to adopting binding opinions. Whereas, in the beginning, the willingness to employ the new instrument was

rather high, this changed dramatically during later years when traditional modes of party politics were reestablished. Meanwhile the instrument is not used primarily to participate in the legislative process, but rather as an informational tool, mostly by the opposition, to control governmental performance in EU-related matters" (p. 723).

16. Report by Martti Ahtisaari, Jochen Frowein, and Marcelino Oreja, in *Eine europäische Erregung: Die Sanktionen der Vierzehn gegen Österreich im Jahr 2000: Analysen und Kommentare*, ed. Erhard Busek and Martin Schauer, Schriftenreihe des DDr.-Herbert-Batliner-Europainstituts Band 8 (Vienna: Böhlau, 2003), 538-67.

17. For interesting analyses of the whole affair, see the contributions in ibid.

18. See the articles by Andreas Resch and Dieter Stiefel as well as by Alexander Smith in this volume.

19. Helmut Kramer, "Österreichs Wirtschaftspolitik im Rahmen der EU," 275 (my translation).

20. Sonja Puntscher Riekmann, "La dimension européenne du phénomène Haider," in *La crise autrichienne de la culture politique européenne*, ed. Jacques Le Rider and Nicolas Levrat (Brussels: P.I.E.-Peter Lang, 2004), 135-50.

21. Empirical studies show higher national growth rates in the first years after accession and after enlargement, but normalization thereafter. As to the liberalization and competition effects economists are skeptical about their real impact on the national economy: it seems to be high in some sectors, but lower in most others. See Fritz Breuss, "Wirtschaftliche Effekte der EU-Mitgliedschaft in Finnland, Österreich und Schweden," in *Österreich, Schweden, Finnland: Zehn Jahre Mitgliedschaft in der Europäischen Union*, ed. Paul Luif (Vienna: Böhlau, 2007), 235-65.

22. "Arbeitslosigkeit im April um 3,3 Prozent gesunken," *Die Presse*, 1 May 2010, <diepresse.com/home/wirtschaft/economist/562169/Arbeitslosigkeit-im-April-um-33-Prozent-gesunken> (12 Feb. 2011). These figures result from traditional Austrian statistics. According to European statistics that rely on different counting methods, figures are much lower.

23. Österreichische Gesellschaft für Europapolitik/IFES, *Das Europäische Parlament und die Europawahlen im Meinungsbild der österreichischen Bevölkerung*, Vienna, May 2009.

24. *Kronen Zeitung*, 28 June 2008 (my translation).

25. First from 1989-91, when he had to step down for his positive remarks about Hitler's employment policy, and second from 1999-2008, the year of his death.

26. Stenographisches Protokoll der 109. Sitzung des Nationalrates, 11 May 2005, 44.

27. Ibid., 46.

28. Ibid., 47.

29. Ibid., 47-48.

30. In 1978, in a national referendum Austrian citizens voted against the first and only nuclear power plant, thus terminating any further nuclear energy policy.

31. Stenographisches Protokoll, 55. Sitzung des Nationalrates der Republik Österreich, 9 April 2008, 74-81. In his speech Strache concludes that the incumbent coalition fears the people who, however, have an appropriate feeling of what is right and what is wrong. As the denial of a referendum turns right into wrong, Strache considers resistance a duty. He then proposes a motion for a resolution in which he spells out the need for a referendum. The motion though did not reach the majority.

32. Ibid., 80.

33. Ibid., 119.

34. Ibid., 94-98.

35. Ibid., 120-22.

36. Ibid., 97-101.

37. Stefan Griller, "Ausgestaltung der Mitwirkung des Parlaments in Österreich," in *Rechtsfragen der Implementierung des Vertrages von Lissabon*, ed. Eilmansberger, Griller, and Obwexer, 441-66.

38. Ibid., 462.

39. Johannes Pollak and Sonja Puntscher Riekmann, "The Austrian Presidency: Pragmatic Management," *Journal of Common Market Studies* 45 (2007): 7-16. For the presidency of 1996, see also Sonja Puntscher Riekmann, "Management gegen Vision: Zu einem falschen Widerspruch der österreichischen Ratspräsidentschaft," *Die Union* 1998/2.

40. For instance, when it became clear also to the general public that Austrian university law collided with EU anti-discrimination provisions, the incumbent government formed by the People's Party and the Freedom Party reacted by attacking the European Court of Justice. The government tried to conceal that the problem had been lingering since accession, whereas Austria had been given several years to correct the contradiction. Chancellor Schüssel criticized not only the relevant ECJ ruling but questioned the role of the court in general. See *Wiener Zeitung*, 7 Aug. 2009.

41. Österreichische Gesellschaft für Europapolitik/IFES, *Das Europäische Parlament und die Europawahlen im Meinungsbild der österreichischen Bevölkerung*, Vienna, May 2009.

42. Ewald Wiederin, "Bund und Länder: Tut jeder, was er kann, und kann jeder, was er muss?", in *Baustelle Bundesstaat: Perspektiven der Weiterentwicklung des politischen Systems Österreich*, ed. Friedrich Michael Steger (Vienna: Braumüller, 2007), 23-29.

43. Liesbet Hooghe and Gary Marks, "A Postfunctionalist Theory of European Integration: From Permissive Consensus to Constraining Dissensus," *British Journal of Political Science* 39, no. 1 (2008): 1-23.

44. During the second Austrian Council Presidency held in 2006 the coalition of the People's Party with the BZÖ in order to avoid potential dissensus had continuously to strike a balancing act. This led to the choice for an utterly pragmatic approach: the presidency was well prepared (as was the case in 1998) by the bureaucracy, but it was void of inspiring moments. See Pollak and Puntscher Riekmann, "The Austrian Presidency."

FORUM

The Globalization of Austrian Studies

Introduction

Günter Bischof

In the late 1980s, I began to attend the annual meeting of the *German Studies Association* (GSA). The GSA has been bringing together scholars from the U.S. and around the world to present their new research on the *German-speaking* world (Germany, Austria, Switzerland) from the fields of history, literature, cultural studies, and political science. As an Austrian working on postwar Austria, the GSA was the only venue to attend in the U.S. as a PhD student (and later as a professor) to meet the community of scholars dealing with the German-speaking world in the broadest interdisciplinary fashion. Apart from the annual meetings of the *Modern Austrian Literature and Culture Association* (MALCA), there was no regular venue for "Austrian Studies" in North America where Austrianists met. While Habsburg scholars would also attend the *American Association for the Advancement of Slavic Studies* (AAASS) and the *American Association for Slavic, East European, and Eurasian Studies* (ASEEES), they would have less interest in the Republic of Austria. By the same token, individual papers on Habsburg and Austrian history, literature, and culture might be read at the *American Historical Association* (AHA) and the *Modern Language Association* (MLA) as well as professional meetings of art historians and musicologists, yet these meetings would never focus on German Studies per se. The American conception of "German Studies" is based on the German language, so there has never been a need for a conference on Austrian Studies, since "German Studies" fully embraced the smaller unit.

There were times in the 1980s and 1990s when Austrian officialdom had a hard time accepting this American/international notion of German Studies. Even though the Austrian Cultural Institute in New York gave some token support to Austrians attending the GSA, there was also the effort to investigate whether an "Austrian Studies Association" might be started in the U.S. I was present at a meeting in the Diplomatic Academy in Vienna in 1994 when Professor Gerald Kleinfeld, the founder and long-term executive director of the GSA, vigorously defended the American tradition of German Studies as language-based, including the study of all areas where German was spoken. Professor Kleinfeld, who himself had started his career as a Fulbright student in Vienna, held his own vis-à-vis the skeptical Austrian officials who were oblivious of American scholarly traditions and practices. The GSA remained and has become more than ever the organizational home of German Studies in the United States, including the study of Austria and Switzerland. In recent GSA conferences among 1,000+ participants there have been regularly between 100 and 200 scholars dealing with Austrian topics. A growing number of young Austrian scholars are attending the GSA meeting and the Austrian Cultural Forum in New York has fully embraced the GSA and supports young Austrian scholars in attending the conference.

I suspect these *official* Austrian efforts in the 1980s/1990s to foster a separate arena of "Austrian Studies" in the U.S. had much to do with identity politics. Postwar Austrian identity formation always has been largely state-directed and -inspired. Officials in the Ministries of Education and Foreign Affairs—in good old patriarchal Josephinian manner—acted as guiding lights about how Austrians were to conceive of themselves.[1] Whereas an Austrian identity separate from Germany was in a process of formation after World War II and into the 1970s, by the 1980s it had come under siege. The "Waldheim Affair" in 1986 and the ascendancy of the right-wing populism of Jörg Haider and his assault on the "grand" SPÖ-ÖVP coalition challenged the entire postwar consensus. Ever since 1945, this grand coalition of the two strongest political parties helped forge political and economic stability on which the creation of postwar Austrian identity was building. Also, the elite consensus of the postwar foreign policy doctrine of "Austria as first victim of Hitlerite Germany" was shattering in the discourses about Waldheim's and Austrians' role in and contribution to the Nazi war of expansion and extermination.[2] All these factors seemed to produce new doubts in Austria's postwar identity, which had been built on this out-of-date victim narrative. Some people on the Ballhausplatz seemed to have felt that a new effort was needed therefore to reinvigorate Austrian identity by supporting an Austrian Studies that was independent of German Studies. Like in the 1850s, when top Habsburg officials began to push the serious scholarly study of Austrian history through the foundation of the *Institut für Österreichische Geschichtsforschung* (Institute of Austrian Historical Research), the state's officialdom aimed at directing the study of the past to forge identity.

Had the officials, who were then pushing the notion of a separate "Austrian Studies," the results of this FORUM on "The Globalization of Austrian Studies" in their hands, they probably would not have bothered. If this FORUM about both the *presence* and the *practice* of the scholarly study of Austria from around the world tells us anything, it is the fact that "Austrian Studies" has never existed anywhere among some of the major national traditions as a scholarly field separate from German and/or European Studies, be it in the Asia-Pacific region or the Euro-Atlantic world. In all these national scholarly traditions, Austria is subsumed together with Germany (and German-speaking Switzerland) in the field of "German Studies" and/or "European Studies"; or, like in the case of Japan, it originated out of Eastern European Studies. Jacques Le Rider defines the French practice straightforwardly: "*the Etudes germaniques' conceives of itself as the cultural studies of various German-speaking cultural spheres*" [my emphasis]. The study of the language and culture of the Germanic world drives the study of its history and polity. All these national perspectives tell us that Habsburg Studies have been part of the study of European empires and Europe, just like the study of the two post-World War I and post-World War II Austrian Republics have been part of the study of the Habsburg succession states, e.g. Central and Eastern European and European Studies in the larger sense. Since Austria and most of the Habsburg succession states have joined the European Union after the end of the Cold War (however, apart from Slovenia, not the post-Yugoslav succession states), German Studies have increasingly become part and parcel of the larger field of comparative European Union Studies, particularly in the social sciences.

In the academic world, the first chairs established to teach and research the German-speaking world were chairs in *German literature* (at the Sorbonne as early as 1901, in Peking in 1918, in Sydney in 1938). Leading Austrian literary greats have always been part of the teaching canon in German literature. Surprisingly, in China Stefan Zweig follows Goethe as the most favorite author writing in German. In all these national traditions specific universities drove the study of Habsburg/Austria within the context of German and European Studies: Harvard, Princeton, Columbia, Minnesota-Twin Cities in the U.S., and Oxford, Cambridge, as well as the Universities of London and Exeter in Great Britain; the Sorbonne in France; Sydney in Australia; whereas in China the study of Austria was pushed by the Chinese Academy of Social Sciences. In all of these national traditions, some leading scholars acted as the major *impresarios* pushing Austrian Studies: Felix Kreissler and Jacques Le Rider today in France; Francis Carsten, A.J.P. Taylor, Edward Timms, Ritchie Robertson, R.J.W. Evans, and Peter Pulzer in the U.K.; Archibald Cary Coolidge, William Langer, Arthur May, Sidney Fay, Robert A. Kann, Istvan Deak, John Boyer, and Carl Schorske along with his many students such as Gary Cohen today in the U.S.; Feng Zhi, Du Wengtan, and Yin Xuyi in China. Some of these scholars had made Jewish Studies their principal focus and greatly enriched that field. In Mao's China a focus on Otto Bauer, Karl Kautsky, and Austrian Marxist thought has garnered particular interest. In Japan, European history was subsumed in Western history, organized as a research field in 1904 at the Imperial University in Tokyo. Interest in the Habsburg lands was first organized through an Association of East European History (started in 1975), before scholars initiated a separate Association for Habsburg Studies in 1987.

Two other factors have been crucially important to the study of Habsburg/Austria abroad. Both *Austrian Jewish refugee scholars* from the Nazi era and *Austrian cultural diplomacy* have been major engines and promoters of Austrian Studies in the world. It is highly ironic that no cohort did more to research and teach the world about the subtleties of Austrian history, literature, and culture than the Jewish refugees of the 1930s, who had been chased out of their homeland ignominiously. They either saw the handwriting on the wall and left before the Anschluss, or were forced to leave after the Anschluss in March 1938 to save their lives. Anglo-American universities were richly rewarded in hosting and embracing this amazingly talented group of refugees. In the U.S. and U.K., Habsburg and German Studies would not be what it is today without Robert A. Kann and Egon Schwarz, Alfred Pribram, Peter Pulzer, and many others and the many students that they mentored. Even in distant China the sizable Jewish World War II refugee community of Shanghai has left a considerable legacy.

The Ministry of Foreign Affairs in Vienna (and in earlier times the Ministry of Education) has been supporting the study of Austria abroad through its Austrian Cultural Institutes (today called the Austrian Cultural Forums [ACF]). The ACF's like to say that they are representing a "cultural superpower" with their programs of bringing the very rich cultural traditions and productions of Austrians from the past and the present to the world. The ACF's regularly stage cultural performances; they also support scholarly activities within their means (this journal also has been supported by the ACF in New York since its inception). During times of domestic crises and international isolation—such as during the "Waldheim Affair" in 1986 and after the formation of the Schüssel government in 2000, when the right-wing FPÖ joined the ÖVP in a coalition government—these Austrian representations abroad had to defend the government's perspective of events. When the Foreign Ministry sent "special ambassadors" abroad in 1986 to defend Waldheim, these efforts were pooh-poohed by critics abroad. As Le Rider tells us, Austria's defiance and defensiveness over Schüssel's coalition government in 2000 did not come across well in France (and elsewhere) and hurt Austria's image. Both Waldheim's weak-kneed defenses of "just having done his duty" in the German Wehrmacht, or Schüssel, whose party had scored only a quarter of the vote, defending the "democratic will" of the Austrian people, were unpersuasive to the world.

Austrian Studies abroad has been contributing major research for a subtle understanding of Austria's past and present roles in the world for a long time. Gary Cohen argues correctly, I think, that American scholarship on Metternich's foreign policy has been defining the field for the past two generations. Similarly, William M. Johnston's monumental *The Austrian Mind: An Intellectual and Social History 1848-1938* (1972) helped launch the serious study of Austrian intellectual history both in the U.S. and in Austria (as David Luft's review of Johnston's *Der österreichische Mensch* argues in this volume), and probably also inspired significantly the "fin-de-siècle Vienna boom" of the 1980s (see Steven Beller's essay in this volume). As Peter Pulzer suggests, Evans and other British scholars made similarly signal innovative contributions to Habsburg Studies. How much these scholarly contributions have been accepted into the canon of Austrian scholarship is another question. In Austria, the field of *Österreichkunde* is often self-absorbed, staid, and unreflective of foreign scholarship on Austria. The charge of the "provincialism" of Austrian history writing is one that one hears from Austrian scholars on a regular basis.[3] It is rare to hear Austrian scholars describe Anglo-American contributions to the study of Austrian history as a "breath of fresh air."[4] In the past twenty years or so, a lot of scholarly reflection has been expended on the scope and purview of Austrian history. During "Austria's" more than 1,000-year existence, its territorial expanse and its resulting cultural-ethnic composition have changed so drastically that it is hard to define the field of "Austrian history" with any precision.

In other words, the "global" Habsburg Empire during the time of Charles V was a very different entity from the "Austrian" empire of Francis Joseph, or the Republic of Austria after the collapse of the Habsburg Monarchy in 1918.[5] We hope that this FORUM will further complicate that definitional effort but also show that there exists an enormous interest in all four corners of the globe in an engaging study of Austria and its multiple pasts. Austrian Studies have engendered serious academic interest around the world for a long time and in this sense have fully gone global.

To give our contributors a starting point for their probing of specific national traditions of Austrian Studies, we have sent out a short questionnaire. Readers of this FORUM can follow the questionnaire through Julie Thorpe's first contribution, since she chose to answer the questionnaire in a straightforward manner. The rest of the contributors chose to answer these questions in essay form. We welcomed both approaches and hope to add future national perspectives to this FORUM on the presence of Austrian Studies in the world. We consider this only the beginning of mapping Austrian Studies around the globe.

Notes

1. Peter Thaler, *The Ambivalence of Identity: The Austrian Experience of Nation-Building in a Modern Society* (West Lafayette: Purdue University Press, 2001); Ernst Bruckmüller, *The Austrian Nation: Cultural Consciousness and Socio-Political Process* (Riverside: Ariadne Press, 2003).

2. Heidemarie Uhl, "From Victim Myth to Co-Responsibility Thesis: Nazi Rule, World War II, and the Holocaust in Austrian Memory," in *The Politics of Memory in Postwar Europe*, ed. Richard Ned Lebow, Wulf Kantsteiner, and Claudio Fogu (Durham: Duke University Press, 2006), 40-72 (see esp. 61ff.); and Günter Bischof, "Victims? Perpetrators? 'Punching Bags' of European Historical Memory? The Austrians and Their World War II Legacies," *German Studies Review* 27, no. 1 (2004): 17-32.

3. See the introduction and the essays in Martin Scheutz and Arno Strohmeyer, eds., *Was heißt "österreichische" Geschichte? Probleme, Perspektiven und Räume der Neutzeitforschung*, Wiener Schriften zur Geschichte der Neuzeit 6 (Innsbruck: Studienverlag, 2008).

4. Karl Vocelka speaks of the heart-warming ("*wohltuend*") "wide horizon" that historians of Austria have demonstrated writing from outside of Austria. Reinhard Stauder notes that the broad synthetic histories of Austria are usually penned in the English-speaking academic world. See ibid., 30, 45.

5. Ibid. Introduction and passim; see also Richard G. Plaschka, Gerald Stourzh, and Jan Paul Niederkorn, eds., *Was heißt Österreich? Inhalt und Umfang des Österreichbegriffs vom 10. Jahrhundert bis heute*, Archiv für österreichische Geschichte 136 (Vienna: Verlag der Akademie der Wissenschaften, 1995).

Austrian Studies in Australia

Questionnaire: "The Globalization of Austrian Studies"

Julie Thorpe

Does the scholarly community in your country/region use the omnibus term "Austrian Studies," or is Austria part and parcel of "German Studies"?

It is part of German Studies if it is mentioned at all in the curriculum!

For an exceptional case, see University of Melbourne, Department of German, Swedish, and Russian, which has an Austrian cultural studies expert on staff, Birgit Lang: <www.german-swedish.unimelb.edu.au/staff/Birgit_Lang/index.html>.

What are the prevalent foci of Austrian Studies in your country/region: history, political science, cultural studies (Austrian literature, music, the arts, film)?

The curricular foci include history (almost exclusively WWII), literature, philosophy, and music.

A more recent trend has been the development of European Studies and European Integration Studies, as well as the various centers funded by the European Union. These centers host visiting scholars and dignitaries from Austria, and liaise with the Embassy of the Republic of Austria in Canberra. For example, see the Australian National University's Centre for European Studies: <ces.anu.edu.au>.

Is there a scholarly tradition of German/Austrian Studies in your country/region? How far back does it date?

The German language has been taught at Australian universities since the 1850s (the University of Sydney is the oldest university in Australia, founded in 1850). The first chair of German at the University of Sydney was established in 1938.

Newer Australian universities since the 1960s have also established a tradition of German Studies. The first German chair at Monash University (founded 1958) was Leslie Bodi, appointed in 1962. (For a history of German at Monash University see <arts.monash.edu.au/german/history.php>.)

Is Austrian Studies in your region/country understood more or less as "Habsburg Studies," or does post-Habsburg Republican Austria play a significant role in the dominant understanding of Austrian Studies?

The Habsburg period is largely covered only in music and some survey undergraduate history courses that cover nineteenth-century intellectual and political history. Post-Habsburg Republican Austria does not figure at all in twentieth-century history except for the period of Nazi Germany. Twentieth-century Austrian literature is taught in some universities (Melbourne), but not consistently across Australian universities.

Other traditions that have some link to Habsburg Central Europe are taught at some Australian universities where there is a diasporic community. For example, Macquarie University (Sydney) has a Croatian Studies Center located in the Department of International Studies: <www.eurolang.mq.edu.au/croatian>.

What institutions (universities, cultural institutes, orchestras, opera societies, literary/arts/music societies, etc.) have promoted and furthered German/Austrian Studies?

Aside from universities and the embassy, the Austrian émigré community has also supported Austrian Studies through hosting cultural and sporting events at the Austrian Clubs in each capital city. See the Austrian Associations of Australasia website: <www.austrian-associations.com>.

How much are academics in your country/region interested today in observing recent political, cultural, and social developments in Austria?

I would say there is scarce academic interest in Austria other than the handful who work on Austrian history and culture.

Is there a specific date, event, dominant founding figure in your country/region that initiated the study of Austria as an academic field? Or as a tradition in the arts or musical arena?

Not that I am aware of.

Who are the major representatives of and contributors to Austrian Studies in your country today?

As mentioned above, the Austrian Embassy, Europe centers, and a few scattered academics contribute to Austrian Studies in Australia, though not in a defined intellectual or institutional tradition.

What role has Austrian cultural/public diplomacy played in promoting Austrian Studies in your country/region?

As above, the embassy in Canberra and consular representatives in other Australian cities promote Austrian politics, history, and culture through public events and the work of the Europe centers most recently.

Is there a public awareness of Austria as a separate political entity in your country today, or is it viewed through the German or European Union lenses?

No, it is viewed through the prism of Germany and the EU.

Did Austrian immigrants to your country/region play a key role in promoting Austrian Studies?

The clubs that Austrian immigrants founded were largely separate from the university sector, but more recently there is an outreach to the cultural and diplomatic representatives through the EU centers.

Austrian Studies in the United States

Gary B. Cohen

The United States enjoys a distinguished tradition of research and teaching relating to Austria, the Habsburg Monarchy, its successor states, and traditions. One must grant that, thanks to the organization of American higher education and the patterns of development for various scholarly disciplines, many scholars who have worked on topics relating to Austria and the former Habsburg lands might not describe themselves as specialists in Austrian Studies. Between 1900 and World War II, there were historians who worked on Austrian or Habsburg topics, literature scholars who studied Austrian authors, and occasionally political scientists and economists who wrote on Austrian politics, law and state institutions, or economics. Still, with much less field specialization in the humanities and social sciences than was to develop after 1945, these scholars typically taught and wrote in broader fields of European history, German or comparative literature, or European and international politics. Many treated Austrian topics as only particular aspects of larger concerns.

This was most obviously the case in literature studies, where Nestroy, Grillparzer, and Stifter, or later Hofmannsthal have occupied honored places in the pantheon of great writers in German and were studied on much the same basis as other writers from the German-speaking world. This continues even today for many literary scholars who consider themselves primarily *Germanisten* and for whom the Austrian or perhaps Bavarian or Prussian context and formation of one or another writer is often not the first concern in the analysis of the literary oeuvre. In recent years, however, the advent of the new historicism in literary and cultural studies has caused many scholars in these disciplines to treat more deeply than before issues of time and place in the lives and works of particular writers. Still, there are many members of American-German and German Studies programs today who take up Stifter or Hofmannsthal, for instance, primarily in a broader context of the German language or European literature of their times rather than more narrowly in an Austrian optic.

Among historians, Archibald Cary Coolidge (1866-1928), who was professor of history in Harvard College from 1908 to his death, epitomized the best expertise on the history of the Habsburg Monarchy and Central and East Central Europe that one might find in the United States during the early twentieth century. Graduated from Harvard in 1887, he also studied at the University of Berlin and the Ecole des Sciences Politiques in Paris and earned a doctorate at the University of Freiburg in Germany 1892. Although highly knowledgeable about Austria and Central Europe, he was very much a generalist scholar of European history. During the 1890s he served in American legations and embassies in St. Petersburg, Paris, and Vienna. At the end of World War I, the U.S. State Department asked him to head up the East European section of the research group, "The Inquiry," established to prepare U.S. diplomats for the Paris peace conference. The State Department sent him to Russia in 1918 to survey conditions there and then in 1919 to Vienna to report on the lands formerly part of the Habsburg Monarchy. At Harvard he taught general courses on European history as well as more specialized ones on northern and eastern Europe, the Far East, and Russia.

Generalist scholars of European history like Coolidge or Arthur J. May, who taught at the University of Rochester for nearly forty years after the mid-1920s, dominated historical studies of Austria and Central Europe in the United States through the 1930s. Coolidge's own Harvard graduate students figured prominently among those who assisted him in the research for "The Inquiry" at the State Department and as members of the fact-finding Coolidge Mission in Central Europe in 1919. A number of Coolidge's students later became leading figures in American studies of Central Europe in the 1930s and 1940s, including at Harvard the German history specialist Sidney Fay and the diplomatic historian William Langer; at the University of Minnesota the historian of nineteenth-century Germany and Central Europe, Lawrence D. Steefel; and at the University of California, Berkeley, the Czech, East European, and Russian history specialist, Robert J. Kerner. The pioneer in America of studies of the Habsburg Monarchy in the early modern era was Henry F. Schwarz, whose *The Imperial Privy Council in the Seventeenth Century* (Cambridge, MA, 1943) remains a classic contribution to understanding how the Habsburg sovereigns began to create more robust institutions to govern their own domains.

Social scientists in the United States before the 1930s devoted much less attention to Austria and the other lands of the Habsburg Monarchy than did historians, but Oszkár Jászi, educated as a political scientist at the University of Budapest, taught history and politics at Oberlin College for several decades after 1925. There he wrote the first major English-language analysis of the fall of the monarchy, *The Dissolution of the Habsburg Monarchy* (Chicago: University of Chicago Press, 1929). Texas-born Charles A. Gulick, who taught economics at the University of California, Berkeley, from 1924 until his retirement in 1963, began research in 1930 on a major study of the first Austrian Republic, which was eventually published in 1948 in two massive volumes under the title *Austria from Habsburg to Hitler.*

The settling in the United States during the 1930s and 1940s of many refugee intellectuals from Central Europe led to a great increase in American studies of Austria and the other former Habsburg lands in a range of disciplines. A growing number of native-born American scholars joined them over the succeeding decades, and by the late 1950s a substantial cohort of scholars had emerged in American college and university faculties whose research, at least, focused on Austrian and Central European history, culture, and society, even while their teaching ranged over a wider range of European and international topics. Carleton J. H. Hayes at Columbia University was a classic generalist in modern European history, but he pioneered historical studies of nationalism in the United States. From his seminars in the 1930s and 1940s came a number of dissertations on Austrian and Central European history, including that of a young 1939 émigré Austrian lawyer who decided to become a historian in the United States, Robert A. Kann. R. John Rath finished his doctorate in the Columbia University history program in 1941, went on to write on the Habsburg Monarchy in the nineteenth century and the Dollfuss era of the first Austrian Republic and founded the *Austrian History Yearbook* in 1965. Central European émigrés who came to the United States in the 1930s, 1940s, and early 1950s, such as the historians Robert Kann, Hans Kohn, Klemens von Klemperer, Radomír Luža, and Otokar Odložilik contributed to a rich flowering of teaching and publications on Austria and Habsburg Central Europe through to the 1970s. A significant cohort of literature scholars joined them, including Heinz Politzer, René Wellek, Egon Schwarz, and Harry Zohn, as well as a smaller number of political scientists, economists, and sociologists.

The experiences of the Great Depression and then the cataclysm of World War II deeply affected not only the immigrant scholars who studied

Robert A. Kann (1906-1981), professor of history at Rutgers University, New Brunswick, NJ

and taught about Austria and Central Europe in the United States but also the growing number of American-born colleagues who came to prominence in the 1950s and 1960s. Many of these began their undergraduate or graduate education before the Second World War and deepened their interest in Central Europe during the course of the war. Archibald Coolidge's student and successor at Harvard, William Langer, helped mold a whole generation of American specialists on German, Austrian, and Central European history, politics, and society by recruiting graduate students and junior professors, not only from Harvard but other American universities as well, to fill the ranks of the research and analysis branch of the Office of Strategic Services (O.S.S.). Carl E. Schorske, who studied with Langer at Harvard, Eugene Anderson, Leonard Krieger, and Henry Cord Meyer, to name but a few, were all involved with various aspects of U.S. military intelligence during World War II.

A wave of increased specialization in the curricula of American collegiate and university history departments had begun already in the 1930s and accelerated after World War II. In the meantime interest in comparative and international politics increased substantially in political science departments; the Cold War greatly reinforced that interest. These developments offered expanded opportunities for teaching and research on Austria and the other former Habsburg lands of Central Europe, although many of the individual scholars were appointed as specialists in European history or politics more broadly and may well have been trained by scholars who were not Austrian or Central European specialists. Robert Kann, of course, became a major scholar of Austrian and Central European history; and during his long tenure at Rutgers University from the late 1940s to the mid-1970s, he was able to train many historians in his areas of interest. In Rochester, Arthur May trained doctoral students interested in Austria and modern Central Europe as well. For the medievalist S. Harrison Thomson at the University of Colorado, the history of Central and East Central Europe from medieval times to the modern era was only one of several of his major interests. He had studied at the Charles University in Prague in the 1920s and during his years at Colorado from 1936 to 1964 trained a long line of scholars of medieval and early modern Western and East Central European history. Paul Bernard and William E. Wright, for example, both specialists on eighteenth-century Austrian and Habsburg history, numbered among Thomson's students. Paul W. Schroeder, Bernard's long-time colleague at the University of Illinois, completed his doctorate at the University of Texas, Austin, in 1958, during John Rath's time there. He began his scholarly career with a study of Metternich's diplomacy in the 1830s and went on to become an internationally respected expert on nineteenth- and early twentieth-century European diplomatic and international history. Indeed, one can argue that the two leading scholars of Metternich's diplomacy in the world during the 1960s were American-born historians, since Schroeder was joined by Enno E. Kraehe, a doctoral student of Steefel's at Minnesota, who published the first volume of his classic work *Metternich's German Policy* (Princeton: Princeton University Press) in 1963. Kraehe inspired thousands of students during a teaching career of forty-three years beginning in 1948 at the University of Kentucky and continuing at the University of North Carolina, Chapel Hill and the University of Virginia.

The great expansion of American higher education in the 1960s and the rising expectations for research activity among college and university faculty spurred much growth in the humanities and social sciences and with it increased publication and teaching about Austria and Central Europe at institutions across the country. No longer was work in this specialty concentrated heavily in the Ivy League universities, the largest of the Big Ten universities, the University of Chicago, and the University of California, Berkeley. Well-trained young scholars in history, literature studies, and some of the social sciences came out of the now much expanded number of major graduate programs with interests in Austria and Central Europe. Many of these went on to concentrate their research for much of their careers in those areas, even if their teaching interests might be broader. It is hard to get precise numbers for the professors engaged in this work around the U.S., but it appears that historians are still the largest single group by discipline. Many of these have expertise on the Habsburg Monarchy and the successor states in general. With the growth of interest in post-1945 studies in the American historical profession since the 1970s and the end of the Cold War division of Central Europe in 1989, the numbers of historians in American colleges and universities interested in East Central Europe since 1918 has grown substantially. The number of American scholars working on the history or politics of the Austrian Republic today is rather smaller. The American political scientists who are interested in Austria work in either comparative politics or international relations and typically deal with Austria as part of multistate comparisons.

After the historians, the next largest group of scholars interested in Austria who are teaching in American colleges and universities today are those in literature, art history, music, film, and other cultural studies. The founding of the Modern Austrian Literature and Culture Association (MALCA) in 1961, originally as the International Arthur Schnitzler Research Association, and the continuing development of its conferences and journals testifies eloquently to the strength of literary and cultural studies regarding Austria in the United States as well as internationally. Most of the American scholars in these fields find their professional homes in departments of German, modern languages and literatures, cultural studies, art, and music. A number of the larger Slavic programs in American universities include specialists in the languages, literatures, and cultures of the Habsburg Monarchy's Slavic-speaking successor states. The increasing vogue since the 1960s of the art, music, and literature of Vienna and Austria more broadly around 1900 has given a particular boost in the United States, as in Western Europe, to academic studies of the Austrian and Central European contributions to the birth of modern culture at the beginning of the twentieth century.

American scholars and students interested in Austria and Central Europe have found assistance and support in a number of scholarly and cultural institutions devoted to Austrian affairs that have developed since the 1950s. Building on private initiatives and various less formal initiatives, the Austrian Foreign Ministry established an Austrian Cultural Institute in New York in 1955. This was formally the cultural office of the New York consulate, but soon renamed as the Austrian Forum, it developed into a formidable institution in its own right. Today, the Austrian Cultural Forum occupies a landmark twenty-four floor structure in midtown Manhattan designed by Raimund Abraham and offers a rich program of concerts, exhibits, literary readings, and lectures. Speakers, musical ensembles, and exhibits sponsored by the Forum travel around the United States.

In 1977, a grant of endowment from Austria helped the University of Minnesota to establish the Center for Austrian Studies on the Twin Cities campus. Within a few years, R. John Rath moved the *Austrian History Yearbook* from Rice University to Minnesota. The Minnesota Center has promoted new scholarship about Austria and Central Europe in a range of disciplines in the humanities, social sciences, international business, and the fine arts through a vigorous program of publications and regular international conferences. It also sponsors organized research projects and exchange programs with a number of Austrian universities and works to connect scholars, students, and an international community to scholarly, intellectual, and cultural resources in Austria, Central Europe, the EU, and Minnesota.

In 1997 the University of New Orleans founded CenterAustria to manage UNO's rapidly growing joint activities with the Leopold-Franzens-Universität Innsbruck and to develop contacts with other Austrian universities and institutions. CenterAustria sponsors a large exchange program between UNO and Innsbruck as well as scholarships, symposia, public lectures, and exhibits on Austrian and Central European topics in New Orleans. Since 1992 CenterAustria, together with its partners in Innsbruck, has published the annual volumes of *Contemporary Austrian Studies*. Both the Minnesota Center and CenterAustria in New Orleans have collaborated with their Canadian counterpart, the Wirth Institute for Austrian and Central European Studies at the University of Alberta, founded in 1998, to co-sponsor conferences, lectures, and publications.

The German Studies Association offers other important resources for American scholars interested in Austria and the other former Habsburg lands of Central Europe. The German Studies Association prides itself in being a multi- and interdisciplinary association of scholars who work in German, Austrian, and Swiss history, literature, cultural studies, political science, and economics. Its annual conferences, attended by hundreds of scholars from North America, Europe, and other parts of the world, and its scholarly journal, *The German Studies Review*, include scholarly papers on Austrian topics. The quality and range of the presentations on Austrian-related topics at the annual GSA meetings and of the articles published by American scholars in *The German Studies Review*, like those published by Americans in the *Austrian History Yearbook*, *Contemporary Austrian Studies*, *Slavic Review*, and *Modern Austrian Literature*, testify eloquently to the intellectual strength and breadth of Austrian Studies in the United States today. The number of scholars interested in Austria and Habsburg Central Europe may be fewer than those interested in Germany and France, but for at least half a century they have been a respected and well-established part of academic life in the United States.

Austrian Studies in the United Kingdom

Peter Pulzer

While many of the scholars who research, publish or teach on Austrian topics in Britain are also interested in the wider culture or history of Central or Western Europe, "Austrian Studies" occupy a recognized place in British academia, with some institutionalization in specialized university centers and publications. The best definition of the scope of Austrian Studies in the UK is that given by the Year Book *Austrian Studies*, now in its eighteenth year of publication. Its remit covers the German-language culture of former areas of the Habsburg Empire, such as Prague and the Bukovina, as well as the work of people of Austrian origin living abroad. Austrian interaction with other linguistic and ethnic groups—the Jewish communities of Austria-Hungary, for example—will also be taken into account. The editors define culture widely, to include psychology, philosophy, political theory, music, theater, film and the visual arts, with a *de facto* emphasis on literature and music. Historical and political topics make fairly rare appearances, except insofar as they provide contexts for cultural phenomena.

The existence of a specialist journal indicates that, in contrast with the historical and political coverage of Austria, literary and cultural studies are well structured on a national basis. *Austrian Studies* was founded in 1990 by two eminent scholars, Edward Timms, then at Cambridge and later professor of German at the University of Sussex, best known for his two-volume biography of Karl Kraus; and Ritchie Robertson, now Taylor Professor of German at the University of Oxford. It is now based at the University of London, closely associated with the Ingeborg Bachmann Centre for Austrian Literature, which is in turn affiliated with the Institute

Peter Pulzer, Gladstone Professor Emeritus of Government and Public Administration and Fellow, All Souls College, University of Oxford

of Germanic and Romance Studies in the University of London's School of Advanced Studies. A major independent enterprise was the critical edition of the works of Franz Kafka for S. Fischer by the late Sir Malcolm Pasley, who was also instrumental in securing a large number of Kafka's papers and manuscripts for the Bodleian Library at Oxford. Academics who specialize in Austrian literary topics generally operate within departments of comparative literature or departments of German, especially since they do not necessarily restrict themselves exclusively to *Austriaca*. Journals available to them, apart from *Austrian Studies*, include *Oxford German Studies*, *London German Studies*, and the *Modern Languages Review*.

In contrast, historians and political scientists with Austrian interests tend to operate more in the individualist tradition characteristic of British academics. Collaboration between them is at best informal. Given the centrality of the Habsburg territories and the Holy Roman Empire in European history, this also means that their interests reach further back than that of most literary scholars. A number of outstanding monographs, some with a biographical slant, illustrate this tendency, e.g. Robert Evans, *Rudolf II and his World* (1973), Peter Dickson, *Finance and Government under Maria Theresia* (1987), and Derek Beales, *Joseph II, Holy Roman Emperor 1741-1790* (1987-2009). Evans in particular has published extensively on Habsburg and Central European topics and has been widely translated. Despite these impressive standard works, the emphasis in historical and political work is on the last 150 years. A preoccupation with the Dual Monarchy goes back a long way, associated above all with R.W. Seton-Watson and his followers, as well as L.B. Namier and his pupil, A.J.P. Taylor. Interwar phenomena, such as Red Vienna, the *Heimwehr* and plans for Danubian federations have all attracted the attention of eminent scholars, e.g. Francis Carsten's *Fascism in Austria* and his documentary collection *The First Austrian Republic*, and Jill Lewis's *Fascism and the Working Class in Austria 1918-1934*. These, like many other works on the period, are the outcome of a general concern with interwar history and extremist political movements, rather than an exclusive concentration on Austria. The presence in Britain of refugee scholars from Austria, e.g. Alfred Pribram and Ernst Wangermann, was undoubtedly influential.

For understandable reasons there has been consistent interest in Austrian affairs during and after the Second World War, the tone of which has fluctuated. During the 1960s and 1970s comment was predominantly laudatory. Austrian political stability was compared favorably with the conflicts of the interwar years and the record of Austrian economic planning and industrial relations seemed to be more impressive than that of Britain. A good example of this type of verdict was *Austria 1945-1972* by Elisabeth Barker, a long-time correspondent for *The Economist*, as well as articles by Peter Pulzer, who taught politics and modern history at Oxford. A more critical tone emerged in the 1980s, as the Austrian economy began to falter, as Austrian foot-dragging on compensation to victims of National Socialism was attracting more attention, and as old ghosts were reappearing in the persons of Kurt Waldheim and Jörg Haider. Another factor was the influence of a new generation of Austrian scholars, such as Anton Pelinka, Peter Gerlich, Wolfgang C. Müller, and Friedrich Stadler, who took a more critical view of events in their country than their predecessors. Newcomers to Austrian political studies were Robert Knight, whose publication of Austrian cabinet minutes on compensation questions, *Ich bin dafür, die Sache in die Länge zu ziehen...*, caused more of a stir in Austria than in

Britain, and Kurt Richard Luther, currently professor at Keele University, who moved from a general interest in federalism and party systems to specialization in the FPÖ. In addition, coverage of Austria came from experienced journalists, following the example of G.E.R. Gedye's *Fallen Bastions* (1939). Gordon Brook-Shepherd of the *Daily Telegraph* wrote on the Anschluss, as well as producing biographies of Dollfuss, the Emperor Karl I, and Empress Zita; Richard Bassett of *The Times* on *Waldheim and Austria* (1998); and Hella Pick of *The Guardian* a nuanced study, *Austria: Guilty Victim* (2000). The individualistic character of much of this work means that there are no dedicated British-based outlets for research on history and politics. Instead, scholars publish in general political science and historical journals, including those in the United States or, in the case of collaborative Austrian-British projects, Austria.

A major stimulus to interest in Austria came from the presence in Britain of up to 30,000 Austrian refugees from National Socialism, the great majority of them Jewish, after 1938. This resulted in the creation of a number of bodies which, while not strictly scholarly, helped to publicize matters Austrian. The Austrian Centre, in existence from 1939 to 1947, raised the profile of anti-Nazi Austrians among both refugees and the British public; it also spawned the politically-oriented Free Austria Movement (Charmian Brinson et al., *Out of Austria: The Austrian Centre in London in World War II* (2008)). Longer-lived bodies include the Anglo-Austrian Society, whose long-time general secretary, Walter Foster, had come to Britain with the *Kindertransport*, and the Anglo-Austrian Music Society. This raises the question to what extent any interest in Austrian culture or scholarship should come under the heading of "Austrian Studies." Performances of Haydn, Mozart or Schubert are, after all, part of mainstream musical life. Work on Ludwig Wittgenstein and the Vienna Circle is integral to the study of modern philosophy. There were, however, some aspects of Austrian creativity that gained attention through the presence in Britain of artists of the caliber of Oskar Kokoschka and Marie-Louise von Montesiczky, writers like Elias Canetti and Robert Neumann, Erich Fried, and Jacov Lind, as well as eminent musicians, musicologists and art historians. British scholars joined in the postwar worldwide fascination with the Viennese *fin de siècle* and the Austrian *avant-garde*, as in Peter Vergo's *Art in Austria, 1898-1918* (1975) and Deryck Cooke's writings on, and editions of, Gustav Mahler.

The role of refugees necessarily raises the place of Jewish-Austrian studies, of which Britain has become one of the leading centers. Two organizations in particular are central to this enterprise. One is the Leo

Baeck Institute (LBI), founded in 1955 with institutes in Jerusalem, New York, and London to perpetuate the cultural and political legacy of the Jews of German-speaking Europe. The London Institute has been headed since 1997 by Peter Pulzer. Its remit necessarily includes Austria, as can be seen from the contents of its Year Book, published in London. The other is the Centre for German-Jewish Studies at the University of Sussex, founded by the biographer of Karl Kraus, Edward Timms. Both have offered lectures and organized conferences on Austrian-Jewish topics. Major monographs associated with the LBI include *The Rise of Political Anti-Semitism in Germany and Austria* (1964, 1988) by Peter Pulzer, who has also contributed to Austrian-edited symposia as well as a postscript to the 2008 reprint of Hans Tietze's *Die Juden Wiens*, and *The Jews of Vienna and the First World War* (2001) by David Rechter. The Sussex Centre specializes, inter alia, in the refugee experience, including the *Kindertransport*. Other resources include the Year Book of the Centre for German and Austrian Exile Studies at the University of London and BARGE (British Archival Materials Relating to German-Speaking Refugees).

A compilation in 2005 showed that "Austrian Studies" scholars were active in twenty-five British universities, as well as in other institutions, such as museums. The stimuli for such geographically scattered activities were varied and in some cases accidental, arising out of a teacher's influence, professional or social contact with refugees, travel or political preoccupations. Increasingly, however, they could not be understood without the active and enthusiastic support of successive Austrian ambassadors and the Austrian Cultural Institute (now Forum), with their imaginative and ambitious programs of events. To a significant extent, the clienteles and publicists for such programs have consisted of émigrés with roots in Central Europe. As they fade from the scene, new strategies will be needed to maintain the momentum.

Austrian Studies in France

Jacques Le Rider

The *Etudes germaniques* only evolved in France as a separate university discipline at the turn of the century. Ernest Lichtenberger started teaching at the Sorbonne in 1901, while Charles Andler did so as of 1905. At the turn of the century, the French humanities and cultural studies were still entangled in the "*crise allemande de la pensée française*," labeled as such by Claude Digeon and sparked by the outset of the Franco-Prussian War in 1870-71. The rather positive picture and interpretation of German culture thus far suddenly turned bleak. Ever since the era of Madame de Staël, French intellectuals had conceived the German-speaking Germania as one. Berlin, Weimar, and "*midi de l'Allemagne*" had not been considered significantly different from each other. Ever since the "roaring thunder" of Sadowa-Königgrätz (Hradec Králové) and the proclamation of the German Reich in 1871, the French Germania experts (historians, literary scholars, and linguists) started to focus on the differing aspects between Germany (mostly reduced to Prussia) and Austria. The *identité culturelle autrichienne* was then employed as a positive counterweight to the fearsome Prussiandom.

This tendency even intensified after World War I, with the French being in favor of prohibiting the Anschluss. The French cultural diplomacy was anxious to promote Austrian identity, and it resorted to corresponding Austrian self-perceptions (as outlined by Hofmannsthal, for instance). After World War II, the tradition to do research on Austria continued to be an integral part of the *Etudes germaniques*. One could even claim that the term of *Etudes germaniques* customarily used in France at the time enabled the circumvention of the concept of *allemand*. The *Etudes germaniques* conceives itself as the cultural studies of various German-speaking cultural spheres. The *Etudes autrichiennes* enjoyed highest reputation and outreach in the 1980s: It was not just experts in German and Austrian Studies who eagerly translated and commented on the literary avant-garde from Handke to Bernhard, but many more. The interdisciplinary wave of rediscovering turn-of-the-century Vienna modernism caused enthusiasm among an even broader public for Austria's contribution to European culture, literature, arts, and science ever since the nineteenth century.

All of the key focus areas mentioned in the question [history, political science, cultural studies (Austrian literature, music, the arts, film)] are well represented in "Austro Science." It is Austrian film only that is somehow less visible compared to German film. This is probably due to the declining significance of Austrian film production ever since 1938. However, Michael Haneke's popularity and reputation in France has decisively contributed to emphasize the unique features of "Austrian film."

There is a clear continuity to be observed ranging from the Habsburg history all the way to the First and Second Republics. The monumental breaches of tradition in 1919 (Treaty of Saint-Germain-en-Laye), 1938 (dissolution of Austria and integration into the Nazi Reich), 1945 and 1955 are also clearly highlighted.

The universities played a very significant role (German Studies as Austrian Studies, history, philosophy) at the time. The music of Mozart, Gustav Mahler, and Arnold Schoenberg's school widely contributed to maintaining a steady interest in Austrian arts. The role of the *Institut autrichien*, today called the *Forum culturel autrichien* located in Paris, remained significant all the way to the 1990s. However, there were some factors that diminished the weight of this cultural institute: The competition arising from the Goethe Institutes and the various institutions of the close German-Franco cultural cooperation; the steady decrease in operative funds, which did not just affect the Austrian cultural institutes in Western Europe, but also the French cultural institutes in Austria; and the decentralized cultural cooperation between scientific, cultural, and arts institutions (universities, concert and opera houses, museums and galleries, film festivals, etc.) all contributed to marginalizing the mediating role of the foreign cultural institutes. It was ultimately the fact that the Austrian cultural institute was politically attached to the Vienna foreign ministry, which caused a further strain on foreign cultural politics in times of crises, such as the one in 2000.

The interest in current political, cultural, and social developments in

Austria very much depends on the state of the economy. When the coalition between the Austrian Freedom Party and the Austrian People's Party was founded in 2000, attention was entirely focused on Vienna. The media turned to each and every expert who had something to say about Haider, Austria's lack of coming to terms with her past, right-wing "populism," and Austrian Euroskepticism. All this seems to be forgotten today. The sensational news on the formation of a coalition government between the conservatives and the "right-wing extremists" has become a Europe-wide banality, just to mention Italy, the Netherlands, France (where the right-wing extremist Le Pen was able to win over the socialist Jospin, in order to face a head-to-head with Chirac), and Central Europe, where the outrage caused in 2000 turned into a normal phenomenon.

Apart from that, the former Austrian model of social partnership, which stood as an example for the whole of Europe during the Kreisky era, completely lost its credibility. It was retrospectively interpreted as a "proportional system," which mainly led to a standstill of democratic talk in times of the grand coalition. I am afraid that there are currently few French people who are informed or at least wish to be informed about Austrian politics. Interest in Austrian culture seems to have declined in 2010 compared to twenty years ago, with some names (Elfriede Jelinek, Michael Haneke, etc.) still enjoying popularity.

The decisive era was the time between the Austria-Prussian War in 1866 and the establishment of the German Reich in 1871. It was during this time that the difference between Germany and Austria became manifest in all circles of French culture.

Austrian cultural diplomacy was successful in times of French enthusiasm for Austrian culture. It was not able to achieve a lot in times of declining interest for Austria (outside of *Etudes germaniques*), and even less when the French image of Austria darkened as a result of temporary irritations (for example, during the time of European "sanctions" on the coalition government between the Freedom Party and Austria's People's Party).

The key persons in restoring the *Etudes autrichiennes* within the French *Etudes germaniques* after World War II were Richard Thieberger (born in 1913 in Vienna, went to France in 1934 to start his career as a German assistant at a lycée in the French town of Reims) or Felix Kreissler (born in 1917 in Vienna, emigration to France in August of 1937). There are still many linguists and literary scholars of Austrian origin who teach at French *Départements* or *Instituts d'Etudes germaniques*.

Austrian Studies with Chinese Characteristics? Some Observations*

Ke-chin Hsia and Fei-Hsien Wang

"Austrian Studies" is an unfamiliar term in the Chinese-speaking world. Though Austria had long entered the consciousness of the Chinese, not the least since it was identified as one of the "eight imperialist invaders" in the wake of the Boxer Rebellion of 1900, there is no clear evidence that Austrian Studies was or is a banner under which research, teaching, and other intellectual activities have been pursued. German Studies (or more narrowly, *Germanistik*), on the other hand, has long been institutionalized in the Chinese academic establishment. As early as 1918, the great educational reformer Cai Yuanpei, himself having spent several years at the University of Leipzig, set up a *Germanistik* unit (later department) in the Peking University.[1] More often than not, scholarly or cultural interests in things Austrian or Habsburg have been considered part of the more global "German Studies" or "German culture." It is the impression of this report's authors that most in the Chinese-speaking academic communities do not recognize Austria as a distinct and separate field of study, though they do know—oftentimes vaguely—that Austria has its own history and cultural heritage. And they also recognize that these Austrian specificities could not be fully represented by a common "German" tag. The reputation of Austria as a highly-desired tourist destination perhaps helps in this regard, but geopolitical reality dictates that a present-day small country in the crowded house that is Europe does not attract much attention of its own on the other side of the globe.

Is there something, then, we can call Austrian Studies in the Chinese-speaking world? Or at least some accumulation of past intellectual labor that can be seen as such? We think the answer is a qualified yes. There are also signs that some Chinese scholars are trying to carve out "Austrian literature" as a research field in its own right within, if not separate from, the older, all-inclusive *Germanistik* circle (more on this later). The following is some preliminary observations on the origins, characteristics, and achievements of the more sustained intellectual engagement with Austria and things Austrian in China (and occasionally, in Taiwan). This report does not and cannot claim to be exhaustive or even comprehensive;[2] it is aimed to provide a starting point for more systematic reflections and comparisons on Austrian Studies across the world. We do, however, attempt to ground our findings in the larger context of modern Chinese history. We believe this will make these perhaps exotic (to the Western world) efforts more intelligible and revealing.

The three areas where most sustained academic interests in Austria (broadly understood) in the Chinese-speaking world are: Austro-Marxism and the Austrian social democracy; modern Austrian literature; and Austrian Jews living or active in modern China.

As a major communist power with global ambitions after 1949, it is not a surprise that the Chinese had a strong interest in intellectual traditions of the European left. However, the incessant "campaigns" and reeducation programs prescribed to intellectuals, aiming at achieving thorough control of them under the often revised, but ruthlessly enforced ideological orthodoxy of Marxism-Leninism-Mao Zedong thought, did not seem to foster a welcome environment for more vigorous research in and discussion on socialist and Marxist theories and theorists. Working on theorists not included in the officially-sanctioned genealogy of revolutionary prophets/fountains of truth carried high risk, as the direction of the political wind could change very rapidly. But a historical contingency opened a narrow window for a more systematic engagement with non-sanctioned Marxist theories. Austro-Marxism was one of them.

The Chinese clash with the USSR after the death of Stalin was the catalyst. Under the banner of "anti-Revisionism," it was decided in 1960 that the Chinese Communist leaders needed to know more about the "incorrect" Marxist theories in their struggle against the USSR, and these "incorrect" theories should be translated into Chinese as "negative examples" and studied. Trotsky was on top of the translation list, because China and the USSR hurled his name as a term of abuse at each other. The writings by other condemned Marxists like Karl Kautsky and Eduard Bernstein saw the light of the day, too, as part of this Chinese preparation for the fight over the leadership of world communism. Sponsored by the

Chinese Communist Party's Propaganda Department, some Austro-Marxist writings, especially those by Otto Bauer, were translated in the series known as "internal circulation-only" "grey books" that were available only to pre-approved higher-echelon party cadres and designated experts.[3]

The first among them was Bauer's *Der Weg zum Sozialismus* (1919), available in Chinese translation to a select audience in 1964. The Cultural Revolution, which began in 1966, slowed and then temporarily halted the project because many on the project staff were condemned as "bourgeois," "Revisionist," or "Opportunist" thanks to their proximity to the "incorrect" writings.[4] But the work resumed after 1971. Translations of Bauer's *Bolschewismus oder Sozialdemokratie* (1920) and *Der "Neue Kurs" in Sowjetrussland* (1921) were published in 1973 and 1977, respectively. 1978 saw the publication of a more inclusive Bauer anthology, *Baoweier yanlun* with selections branching out to include his musings on the nationality question and other strategic or tactical issues faced by the Austrian Social Democrats.[5]

In addition to translation, there has been a small but steady stream of research on the Austro-Marxist theories since the 1970s. One of the leading translators and editors of the "Revisionist" Marxism in the aforementioned project, Yin Xuyi, published "Aodili makesi zhuyi" ("Austro-Marxism") in the journal of the Party's Central Compilation and Translation Bureau, *Dangdai shijie yu shehui zhuyi (Contemporary World and Socialism)*.[6] It was a general introduction to the main theorists and their theories, and a competent effort at that. Appearing in the early years of the post-Mao reforms, however, the author cast this first introduction in a strongly partisan and judgmental frame, and repeatedly cited Lenin as the authority to emphasize that Austro-Marxists were centrist "Reformists" and "Opportunists" disguising themselves with revolutionary rhetoric. Despite Yin's rather level-headed presentation of Austro-Marxist ideas, he concluded that "their line and strategy did great damages to the revolutionary struggle of the Austrian working classes and thereby eased German and Austrian Fascists' way to victory. [...] The fact that the Austrian Social Democracy collapsed under the fascist terror proved the fantastic nature of their theory of 'peaceful transition' and the falsehood of their theory of 'defensive violence;' it ultimately proved the bankruptcy of Austro-Marxism."[7]

This mix of competent presentation with obligatory, strongly-worded bashings of unorthodox theories and theorists was preserved in a watered-downed version in later writings on Austro-Marxism.[8] To some extent the reason for this can be sought in the context in which the interest in Austro-Marxism was developed in China in the first place. Austro-Marxism was not seen as an *Austrian* or a historical phenomenon worthy of serious attention in its own right, but as one of the rival Marxist traditions to be studied, judged, and combated. Practical needs in proving and justifying ideological orthodoxy of the party line have shaped how Chinese scholars read the Austro-Marxist writings. No matter how much interest in Austro-Marxism originated from less partisan perspectives, or even from the more academically-oriented theoretical or historical curiosity, it was not easy to avoid overt political or ideological (negative) associations of Austro-Marxism in the Chinese context.

As China's market-oriented reforms and rapid incorporation into the larger capitalist world order unfolded in the 1990s, interests in non-Marxist-Leninist alternatives in the traditions of the left grew exponentially. Theories of democratic socialism and the experiences of Western European social democratic parties received much attention.[9] In the wake of this more general interest, Austria receives a very rare monographic treatment in Chinese. Wang Haixia's *Aodili shehuiminzhudang yanjiu (A Study on the Austrian Social Democratic Party)* appears in 2003, and provides a comprehensive overview of the Austrian Social Democratic Party since 1945. In contrast to earlier work on Austrian Social Democrats, a more approving tone permeates the author's assessment of their post-1945 achievements. Otto Bauer even gets a few praises. But in the end, the ideological "correct line" has to be reiterated, Lenin has to make a few appearances, and the author cannot resist to show the Austrians' "limitedness," "misconceptions," "mistakes," and "wishful-thinking."[10] Whether it is out of the author's genuine conviction or a sense of obligation to do what is expected, the generally sympathetic picture of the Austrian Social Democracy in Wang's book is thus marred by this cacophonous injection of party-line platitudes.

A more relaxed political and intellectual atmosphere makes it possible for Wang to devote a whole book on the "incorrect" Austrians. It also spurs the republication of Bauer translations in 2008. The enlarged Bauer anthology contains not only all the aforementioned "grey books"-era titles, but also newly translated pieces.[11] Added the translation of Rudolf Hilferding's *Das Finanzkapital* (1910) a decade earlier,[12] it seems that in the wake of China's violent economic modernization and rapid social transformation, non-Leninist Marxist alternatives fascinate some Chinese readers more than ever. What is new now is that Austro-Marxism is studied less as intramural rival or enemy. What remains unchanged, however, is that the interest is still very much geared toward the practical relevance of the subject matter, as both Wang and the publisher of the series in which the new Bauer anthology appears justify the studying and publishing of these unorthodox—to the Chinese Communists—traditions by emphasizing their values in offering useful references and inspirations to the development of "Socialism with Chinese Characteristics"—the current party line—and the growth of the party in a new age.[13]

Readers in the Chinese-speaking world have long enjoyed Austrian authors' outputs. Arthur Schnitzler's dramas and *Novellen* were translated into Chinese as early as the 1920s.[14] Stefan Zweig has been popular since 1941, when his fiction (*Amok*) was published in Chinese for the first time. He became more so after the late 1970s, when many of his *Novellen* and biographies were translated. He is the second-most translated author writing in German in China, following only Goethe.[15] In Taiwan, since the heydays of literary and philosophical existentialism in the 1960s, Franz Kafka has been a staple for any Taiwanese reader who reads European literature. Rainer Maria Rilke is always considered a connoisseurs' poet, and has asserted important literary influence in both China and Taiwan since the 1940s and 1970s, respectively.[16]

With this robust interest in Austrian authors as the natural base, academic research on them in China has been active since at least the 1980s (to our knowledge there is no equivalent development in other Chinese-speaking places). Hugo von Hofmannsthal, Rilke, Kafka, and Robert Musil have received major treatment by Chinese scholars since the 1990s, and the Institute of Foreign Literature in the Chinese Academy of Social Sciences in Beijing has been the home base of many of the scholars involved in this endeavor.[17] It was also the first and long-serving chair of the institute, Feng Zhi, a leading Chinese *Germanist* and noted poet and translator, who first called attention to Austrian literature as a field of study in its own right in a national *Germanistik* conference in 1990.[18] To advocate Austrian literature near the end of his life was a long and distinguished career coming to full circle, as Feng had been one of the major promoters and translators of Rilke in China since the early 1930s, and his own poems are prime examples of how a European poet influenced modern Chinese poetry.[19]

In 1998, Han Ruixiang and Ma Wentao published the first history of the twentieth-century Austrian (and Swiss-German) literature written by Chinese authors.[20] Does this mean that the Chinese research on Austrian literature had matured to the extent that a history of Austrian literature could be written from a Chinese perspective in 1998? According to one commentator, it was not the case, and it still isn't. Ye Jun, himself a member of the aforementioned institute, says that the study of Austrian literature in China remains focusing on decontextualized analysis of individual texts.

Furthermore, a Chinese-authored "history of Austrian literature that can stand up to high academic standards remains to be written," and "translation of Austrian literary works has been stagnated." He suggests that Chinese scholars studying Austrian literature adopt a broader understanding of what "Austria" and "Austrian literature" mean—from the Habsburg Monarchy to its successor states, including today's Austria—and to frame their research within the contexts of both literary and intellectual histories. He also urges his colleagues to be more aware of the historiography of research in Austrian literature, and be more self-conscious in connecting their own research to the dialogues in the international academic community.[21]

To scholars working in North America or Europe, Ye's last recommendation may sound a bit redundant. But for Chinese scholars working on non-Chinese topics, it is a relatively recent aspiration after independent developments of scholarly traditions—if there is any to speak of in specific disciplines—in relative isolation for decades. Ye's call echoes the eagerness of the present Chinese academic community to "go international." But in the end, how much the popularity of Austrian authors in the Chinese-speaking world will be translated into substantial and, perhaps more important, original scholarly research in Austrian literature remains to be seen.

On historical studies of Austrian-related topics, the Chinese-speaking world's efforts can been characterized as one-sided. Only the research on Austrians in China and the Austro-Chinese relationship has produced some substantial results. On topics which have no direct connections with China or the Chinese, quality scholarship is absent.[22] In this regard, the Chinese-speaking world has only the translations of Erich Zöllner's *Geschichte Österreichs: Von den Anfängen bis zur Gegenwart* in the late 1970s (published in 1981) in China and Carl E. Schorske's *Fin-de-Siècle Vienna* in Taiwan to show for.[23]

The Zöllner translation especially marked the gradual normalization of Chinese intellectual activities following the Cultural Revolution, as the previous major publication on Austrian history in mainland China was a translation of the communist author Eva Priester's strongly partisan *Kurze Geschichte Österreichs* (1946, 1949) from the abridged Russian version. The Chinese translation faithfully retained the trimmings of the Russian version, where Priester's "deficiencies" is not historical-materialist and her failures to follow the analyses supplied by Engels, Lenin, and Stalin were identified and commented on in the long preface and footnotes.[24] In contrast, in the 1981 translation of Zöllner, there was not a word of political caveat—

which, with few exceptions, was obligatory in any Chinese translation of Western historical writing until at least the early 2000s—in the Chinese publisher's preface or the translators' postscript. More surprising still, the Chinese publisher and translators had only good things to say about the book; their only worry was that the translation may not have fully conveyed Zöllner's erudition. The reason for this rare, unreserved endorsement remains a mystery.

The first Chinese-authored history of Austria of any note was probably Zhao Tangshou's *Aodili wenhuashi* (*A Cultural History of Austria*). It was written for the general public. Sometimes it reads like an in-depth tourist guide. But in its last chapter, the book summarized what interests Chinese scholars the most so far: cultural exchanges between the Austrians and the Chinese. Zhao's book was invaluable in providing sketches of generations of Austrian Sinologists stretching back to the nineteenth century, among other things.[25] This Chinese specialty in Austrian Studies has been generating some interesting work on topics such as the Chinese participation in the 1873 Vienna Expo (the first time Imperial China participated in an international exhibition officially)[26] and Austro-Hungarian WWI prisoners of war who ended up in China.[27] But the most substantial and sustained Chinese scholarly engagement on this front is to be found in the study of Jewish experience in modern China, and for our present purpose more specifically, that of Austro-German Jewish refugees in Shanghai.

In 1933, Central European Jews, fleeing the Nazis, began to stream into Shanghai, the only major city in the world where no prior application or visa was needed to enter or stay, thanks to the complex legal jurisdictions over the city. Their numbers increased significantly between 1937 and 1939. By December 1941, there were approximately 25,000 Jewish refugees staying in Shanghai, most of them from Germany and Austria. These German-speaking Jews developed active associational, religious, commercial, and cultural activities despite difficult circumstances. A "Little Vienna"—as it was called by both the refugees and the locals—emerged around Chusan Road in the Hongkew area, where Viennese-style coffeehouses and shops with German signs dotted the streets. Austrian Jews and Viennese traditions played prominent roles in the cultural life of the refugee community in particular and the larger Shanghai Jewish community in general.

The study of Jewish refugees in 1930s and 1940s Shanghai actually began from outside of China. David Kranzler's impressive 1976 book even became the point of departure and source of information for many later Chinese works.[28] But a group of Chinese scholars, mostly based in Shanghai, and especially those led by Pan Guang at the Center of Jewish

Studies Shanghai (est. 1988), have been doing an impressive catch-up since the 1980s. It was especially the case after the normalization of the diplomatic relation between China and Israel in 1992; the first major Chinese work on Shanghai Jewish history came out in that year.[29] Since then, Chinese scholars have not only translated relevant research and memoir pieces from other languages,[30] but also produce monographs and essay collections on the social history of Shanghai Jewish communities,[31] Jewish publications in Shanghai,[32] Jewish cultural elite in Shanghai,[33] and musical life of Shanghai Jews.[34] They also publish more general works on the history of Shanghai Jews in the past 150 years.[35] Archivists even found some interesting documents about the Chinese Nationalist government's 1939 plan to set up a permanent Jewish settlement in southwest China to accommodate Jewish refugees from around the world during and even after the end of the war.[36]

On the specifically Austrian component of this line of recent Chinese scholarship, there are two concentrations of interest: Austrian music and Austrian Jewish artists, and individual Austrian Jews who made special contributions to China.[37] The former is exemplified by Tang Yating's detailed work on Jewish musical life in Shanghai, which vividly documents the popularity of Viennese operettas in the Hongkew ghetto (established in February 1943) and the prominence of Austrian-Jewish artists in religious ceremonies, cabaret, classical music, theater, dance, folk music, and all other kinds of live performances—including *Heuriger Abend*—in wartime Shanghai. The latter concentration can be seen in the oft-cited names that grace most of the Chinese works on Jews in modern China: painter Friedrich Schiff, movie director husband-and-wife duo Jakob and Louise Fleck, architect Rudolf Sömjen, reporters Hans Shippe and Ruth Weiss, physicians Jakob Rosenfeld and Richard Frey, psychiatrist Fanny Gisela Halpern, and comparative philologist Erwin Reifler.

It must be added that not all of them went to China as refugees in the first place. Dr. Halpern, a student of Julius Wagner-Jauregg, for example, was invited by the Chinese government in 1933 to help the Shanghai Medical School build up its clinical psychiatry program and train its students. But attracting the most attention among all Austrians has been a refugee from Vienna (and by way of Buchenwald), Dr. Jakob Rosenfeld. He arrived in Shanghai in August 1939 and joined the Communist New Fourth Army in 1941. Dr. Rosenfeld served in the People's Army throughout the Sino-Japanese War and the Chinese Civil War, treating patients while training medical orderlies. He befriended several important Communist generals, became a party member in 1942, and held a position equivalent to a general. After decades of relative neglect—probably due to various forms of xenophobia in post-1949 China—following his premature death in 1952, Dr. Rosenfeld's standing in the pantheon of the Chinese Revolution and the Chinese Communist Party rises dramatically. Since the 1990s, there are multiple Chinese biographies of this "great friend of Chinese people."[38] Both Dr. Rosenfeld's own writings and his German biography by Gerd Kaminski have been translated.[39] As a leading scholar of Jewish experience in China puts it, Dr. Rosenfeld becomes "the symbol of selfless devotion of internationalism" and "an ever tightening link between the Chinese, Austrian and Israeli peoples."[40]

The hagiographic reincarnation of Dr. Rosenfeld in the Chinese narratives is symptomatic of the current Chinese interest in Shanghai Jews in general and Austrian Jews in particular. Jewish Studies in China has been marked by strongly utilitarian functions since its emergence in the 1980s. As Pan Guang makes it clear, "this topic has important practical significance in opposing racism and fascism, furthering friendly relations between the Chinese and the Jewish peoples as well as with others, and preserving peace in the world,"[41] and "it also plays a unique role in furthering the continued opening up of China and developing relations between China and" other nations.[42] The Chinese Jewish Studies thus serves simultaneously the needs to 1) broaden cultural/heritage diplomacy, especially with the state of Israel and Jewish communities around the world, by emphasizing and capitalizing on the previously suppressed or forgotten common connections, and 2) show to the outside world and the Chinese people themselves about post-Mao China's resolve to reform and its willingness to embrace its—again, previously suppressed or even denounced—cosmopolitan past.

The utilitarian functions behind most of these Chinese works, which can be called a "friendship" historiography, do not preclude them from being sound and solid pieces of scholarship. But they do affect the emphasis and the depth of discussion on certain aspects. For example, the mandated mission to highlight the friendly, mutually-sympathetic relation between Jewish refugees and the Chinese people has led Chinese scholars to reiterate in every possible place the lack of "indigenous anti-Semitism" in China, and usually recite the exact same words and identical sentences in doing so. But they almost always look the other way when it comes to the unavoidable inter-community tensions, conflicts, and everyday criminalities resulted from resources competition under very difficult wartime circumstances. Chinese scholars also stay mum most of the time about the spillover of imported or imposed anti-Semitism into certain Chinese minds, and about the implications of anti-Semitic coloring of the more mundane everyday conflicts. In their stead, they inject inconsequential stories about how the Chinese Communist Party's cultural heroes (but not others) were opposed to the Nazi persecution of Jews. In this regard, the older Western works, such as Kranzler's, remain the more informative and reliable source for a social history of Shanghai Jews and their interactions with the Chinese. "Friendship" historiography simply does not suffice.

Another example is the conspicuous silence about the experiences of Jews who stayed in China after 1949. Though recent works have become more forthcoming about why the greatest majority of Shanghai Jews—even many who originally wanted to stay beyond 1949—ultimately chose to leave China, they are still quite defensive, and prefer to focus on how grateful the remaining Jews were to the People's Government before they left. Likewise, in recounting the biographies of Austrian Jews who were committed to the cause of the "New China," their stories as written by Chinese scholars usually jump directly from the early 1950s to the post-Mao reform era—if these "friends of the Chinese people" were still alive—and skip the intervening decades altogether. Careful readers can still detect from between the lines, or from some occasional slips, that some of these "internationalist" heroes had encountered different degrees of difficulties before or during the Cultural Revolution, if they were lucky enough to escape personal tragedies suffered by other, more "common" people of Western descent.[43]

Chinese scholars have been more willing to explore topics that were used to be neglected or off-limits. Their writings also become less overtly judgmental when it comes to the questions of what foreigners did in pre-1949 China; now they can talk about Sephardic Jewish business magnates in Shanghai in a relatively neutral way.[44] In the case of Shanghai Jews, their diligence has produced many meticulously documented results—though repetitiveness is a problem that can no longer be overlooked—in the "friendship" historiography. The practical functions the field serves from the very beginning and the larger political environment researchers work in, however, continues to have limiting effects on how far Chinese scholars can go in the foreseeable future. Without a sincere Chinese *Vergangenheitsbewältigung*, there will always be eye-catching blank pages.

This report focuses on three branches of Austria-related intellectual pursuits that we believe to have been the most productive and intriguing. The first, the Austrian Left, and the third, China-related Austrian topics (and more specifically Austrian-Jewish history in China), both reflect and serve the political orientations and needs of their days. This common characteristic has been constant, no matter which direction the political wind was and is blowing. However, after several missing decades, the Chinese academic community is moving toward a more active and more scholarly engagement with non-Chinese topics. What we can call Austrian Studies—even if it is not a concept in use in the Chinese-speaking world—is growing in China. When the Chinese government puts its weight on a select topic, such as Shanghai Jews, tangible results upon which further, more in-depth and more scholarly research can be based come out quickly. The Chinese Austrian-Studies-in-the-making has benefitted from it, and there is no reason to doubt whether this situation will continue despite the mixed blessings of the often top-down agenda-setting and mission-defining.

It will certainly take some time before Chinese-speaking scholars can succeed in solidifying their efforts in Austrian Studies with truly original work on topics that are not directly China-related. It probably will take even longer for their international colleagues to notice and embrace any of their potential contribution on this front—and only if it is available in German or English. The Chinese reading public's love of Austrian literature bodes well in this regard, as it can self-generate a more sustained and spontaneous intellectual pursuit for a long time.

But in the shorter term, what kind of Austrian Studies topic Chinese-speaking scholars have the potential to excel in, and could therefore participate directly and quickly, in an original and substantial way, in the international academic community's dialogue? We venture to suggest one possibility to end this report.

Given the command of the Chinese language and the already existing interest in the China-related Austrian topics, the Chinese reception, perception, expectation, exploitation (in all its meanings), consumption, and the evolution thereof of Austria past and present as well as Austrians and Austrian things, seem to be a promising problem set for Chinese-speaking Austrianists to work on. This focus also could capitalize on the recent push for transnational studies from within the international German Studies community, thereby making Chinese contributions more readily visible outside of the Chinese-speaking world.[45]

What we suggest, therefore, is not some repackaged old-style studies on Austrian-Chinese or German-Chinese relation—focusing on diplomacy, economic ties, or prominent intellectual-cultural-political figures—already in existence.[46] These topics have their place and value, but beyond excavating more "facts," they do not hold much innovative or analytical promise. What we suggest is an approach that focuses on *the perception, reception, and consumption of a foreign culture, real or imagined.* The key is to examine the phenomena themselves along with the mechanisms through which Austria and Austrians become part of the Chinese consciousness, especially those mediated by popular culture and mass consumerism. The roles of the Austrian government, corporations, and individuals as well as their Chinese counterparts are of course an integral part of the story of these mechanisms and processes.

To put it differently, we suggest a truly transnational subject of study: how Austria or Austrians become part and parcel of individual Chinese person's mental cosmos and help shape his/her understanding of the world and his/her behavior as consumer in a globalizing marketplace.[47] The very popularity of Empress Elisabeth, or more precisely the obsession with the Sisi myth—thanks to Romy Schneider's films—in the officially anti-feudal, revolutionary proletariat China since the late 1980s, and the almost reflexive association of Austria—much more so than any other country—with classical music in Taiwan, are just two examples waiting for imaginative analysis. There will be more if we look for them.[48] Of course, this is only the first step. But we believe it can be a good first step.

Notes

* In this report, we follow the East Asian norm by listing East Asian person's family name before given name. Non-East Asian names and ours are still listed given name first. All transliteration is in the pinyin system.

1. Ye Jun, "Shijia yishi yu yiguo duixiang—Zhongguo xueshu shiye li de aoguo wenxue zhi chengli," *Tongji daxue xuebao shehui kexue ban* 17, no. 4 (2006): 2.

2. For example, we do not include the persistent discussion on the Austrian School of Economics in post-Mao China. It is partly due to our belief that in the Chinese context the "Austrian School of Economics" has become a code word for many things other than Austria or economic theories. The Chinese usage of the term needs its own analyst.

3. About the publishing of "grey books," see "Huipishu, huangpishu: Yidai ren de jingshen shiliang," 14 July 2008, <news.xinhuanet.com/book/2008-07/14/content_8542369.htm> (29 Dec. 2010). For a more detailed account on the "grey books" and its literature counterparts, "yellow books," see Shen Zhanyun, *Huipishu, huangpishu* (Guangzhou: Huacheng chubanshe, 2007).

4. "Huipishu, huangpishu."

5. Editor's preface to Otto Bauer, *Baoweier wenxuan* (*Otto Bauer Anthology*), ed. Yin Xuyi (Beijing: Renmin chubanshe, 2008), 1-2.

6. Yin Xuyi, "Aodili makesi zhuyi," *Dangdai shijie yu shehui zhuyi* 3 (1981): 112-29.

7. Ibid., 128.

8. For example, Chen Lin, "Aodili makeshi zhuyi gaishu," *Dangdai shijie yu shehui zhuyi* 4 (1991): 7-13; idem., "Qiantan Aodili makesi zhuyi yu minzhu shehui zhuyi zai lilun shang de luoji lianxi," *Dangdai shijie yu shehui zhuyi* 2 (1992): 65-69. Song Yunxia, "Shehui minzhu dang yu minzhu shehui zhuyi," *Lilun xuekan* 2 (1990): 37-38.

9. Translations of European and American writings and Chinese-authored pieces on related topics are too numerous to mention here. Austria is frequently featured in these studies.

10. Wang Haixia, *Aodili Shehuiminzhudang Yanjiu* (Beijing: Beijing guangbo xueyuan chubanshe, 2003). See, for example, pp. 43-46, 49, 80, 88, 96 when Lenin is cited.

11. Bauer, *Baoweier wenxuan*, 1-2.

12. Rudolf Hilferding, *Jinrong ziben: ziben zhuyi zuixin fazhan de yanjiu*, trans. Fumin et al. (Beijing: Shangwu yinshuguan, 1994).

13. Wang, *Aodili Shehuiminzhudang Yanjiu*, i, iii, 200-03; "Renmin wenku chuban qianyan," in Bauer, *Baoweier wenxuan*, i-ii.

14. Feng Zhi, "Qiantan aodili wenxue," *Waiguo wenxue pinglun* 3 (1991): 25.

15. Translator's note to the first edition (1991), in Stefan Zweig, *Zuori de shijie: yige ouzhouren de huiyi (Die Welt von Gestern)*, trans. Shu Changshan et al.(Guilin: Guangxi shifan daxue chubanshe, 2004), 348-49.

16. Ye, "Shijia yishi yu yiguo duixiang," 4. On Rilke's popularity and reception in China, see the very informative website dedicated to all things about Rilke translation and research in China, *Lierke zhongwen wang* (with its original German title *Übertragung und Forschung über Rainer Maria Rilke*), <rilkecn.com/default.asp> (4 Jan. 2011). In Taiwan, the influential poetry journal *Li* (*Bamboo Hat*) dedicated an entire issue to Rilke, and the most important Taiwanese Rilke translator Li Kuixian, himself a leading poet, contributed an essay "Lierke zai taiwan" (Rilke in Taiwan), *Li*, 163 (1990): 127-37.

17. For a list of current and former CASS researchers who publish on Austrian literature, see <foreignliterature.cass.cn/chinese/NewsInfo.asp?NewsId=1070> (accessed 30 Dec. 2010).

18. Feng, "Qiantan aodili wenxue," 25.

19. Zhang Songjian, "Lierke zai zhongguo: chuanbo yu yingxiang chutan, 1917-1949," from *Lierke zhongwen wang*, <rilkecn.com/text.asp?ID=1688> (accessed 4 Jan. 2011).

20. Han Ruixiang and Ma Wentao, *20 shiji aodili ruishi deyu wenxueshi* (Qingdao: Qingdao chubanshe, 1998).

21. Ye, "Shijia yishi yu yiguo duixiangi," 2, 5-7. The quote is from p. 5.

22. Journal articles on Austrian history that appear in China often lack either substance or originality, or both. Even the ones published by leading academic journals do not fare much better. Perhaps the isolated development of the Chinese world history community is partly to blame; the old party lines on the "correct" understanding of world history certainly did not help. Another possible reason is the belated—and still ongoing—development of formal and informal academic standards and norms in the historical profession.

23. The former is based on the fourth edition of the Zöllner book. It is translated by Li Shumao, Du Wentang, and Lin Rongyuan, and published by *Shangwu yinshuguan* in Beijing. The latter is translated by Huang Yuwen and published by Taipei's *Maitian chubanshe* in 2002, years after the Japanese translation appeared (1983). Moreover, the Schorske book is translated and read not as an Austrian Studies title. It is marketed to and received by the Taiwanese historical profession and other Taiwanese humanities scholars as an example of innovative cultural-intellectual history.

24. Eva Priester, *Aodili jianshi*, trans. Tao Liang and Zhang Fu (Beijing: Sanlian shudian, 1972). Even so the book was still labeled as "internal-circulation only," readers were exhorted on the title page that if they decided to cite it, they should reference "the original version." The reason for this was not clear. However, the publisher never made it clear what "the original version" meant: Was it the German original? Or the abridged Russian translation on which the Chinese

translation was based? Actually, down to the present day the ill-developed citation/reference practices and standards still plague the mainland Chinese academic community, as attested by many contentious controversies over accusations of plagiarism in recent years.

25. Zhao Tangshou, *Aodili wenhuashi* (Beijing: Beijing daxue chubanshe, 2002).

26. Hao Yanhong, "Daqing wangchao yu aodili weiyena shibohui—yuanzi qinggong dangan de jizai," *Dangan chunciou* 8 (2010): 15-17. This article comes out in the journal's special issue on World Expos in celebration of the 2010 Shanghai Expo.

27. Li Xuetong, "Zhanfuying zhong de meihao shiguang," *Kanlishi* 6 (2010): 78-83; Li Xuetong and Gu Weiming, eds., *Zhongguo deao zhanfuying* (Fuzhou: Fujian jiaoyu chubanshe, 2010).

28. David Kranzler, *Japanese, Nazis, and Jews: The Jewish Refugee Community of Shanghai, 1938-1945* (New York: Yeshiva University Press, 1976). Kranzler began his research in the 1950s.

29. Tang Peiji et al., *Shanghai youtairen* (Shanghai: Shanghai sanlian, 1992).

30. For example, the Chinese translation of the Kranzler book came out in 1991. Translation of memoir pieces can be found, for example, in Pan Guang and Li Peidong, eds., *Youtairen yi shanghai* (Shanghai: Shanghai zhengxie wenshi ziliao bianjibu, 1995).

31. Wang Jian, *Shanghai youtairen shehuishenghuoshi* (Shanghai: Shanghai cishu chubanshe, 2008).

32. Rao Lihua, *Shanghai youtai jishibao yanjiu* (Beijing: Xinhua chubanshe, 2003).

33. Xu Buzeng, *Xunfang youtairen* (Shanghai: Shanghai shehuikexueyuan chubanshe, 2007).

34. Tang Yating, *Shanghai youtai shequ de yinyue shenghuo* (Shanghai: Shanghai yinyuexueyuan chubanshe, 2007).

35. More scholarly: Pan Guang and Wang Jian, *Yigeban shiji yilai de shanghai youtairen: youtai minzu shi shang de dongfang yiye* (Beijing: Shehuikexue wenxian chubanshe, 2002); and the bilingual picture book that targets the international lay audience: Pan Guang, ed., *Youtairen zai shanghai* (Shanghai: Shanghai huabao chubanshe, 1995, 2005 rev. ed.).

36. Bi Chunfu, "Chongqing guomin zhengfu anzhi taowang youtairen jihua chouyi shimo," *Minguo dangan shiliao* 3 (1993): 17-21. The plan amounted to nothing more than some preliminary promotions because of the lack of sufficient funding.

37. For example, Xu Buzeng, "Cong weiyena dao shanghai—Ji jiwei cengjing zai shanghai shenghuo guo de aodili youtairen," *Shanghai dangan* 5 (1992): 52-55.

38. Huang Yao and Zhang Huixin, *Yige daxie de ren: Luo shengte zai zhongguo* (Beijing: Jiefangjun chubanshe, 1992); Zhonggong linyi diwei dangshi ziliao zhengji weiyuanhui and Zhonggong junanxian weiyuanhui, eds., *Luo shente zai zhongguo* (Jinan: Shandong renmin chubanshe, 1992); Wang Xianglian and Sun Jianhong, *Luo shengte* (Beijing: Zhonggong dangshi chubanshe, 2005); Ma Zhixin, *9615 hao qiutu* (Beijing: Zuojia chubanshe, 2005).

39. Gerd Kaminski, ed., *Zhongguo de dashidai: Luoshengte zaihua shouji, 1941-1949*, trans. Du Wengtan (Beijing: Zhongguo shehui kexue chubanshee, 2003). The translation of Gerd Kaminski's Rosenfeld biography is published as *Luo shengte zhuan*, trans. Du Wentang and Li Chuansong (Beijing: Lüyou jiaoyu chubanshe, 1995). Its original title is *General Luo genannt Langnase: Das abenteuerliche Leben des Dr. med. Jakob Rosenfeld* was published in 1993.

40. Xu, *Xunfang youtairen*, 176, 178.

41. Pan and Wang, *Yigeban shiji yilai de shanghai youtairen*, 1.

42. Pan, ed., *Youtairen zai shanghai*, 119. The quote is taken from the English original of this bilingual book.

43. The story of Fanny Ebner, an Austrian who married a politically problematic Chinese husband but stayed in China after 1949, has been made into a feature film, *Am anderen Ende der Brücke* (dir. Hu Mei, 2002). Unlike some other non-Chinese spouses, she survives the turmoil.

44. The contrast is most obvious between the still accusatory and judgmental tone of Tang et al., *Shanghai youtairen* (1992) and the generally neutral, sometimes even grudgingly admiring one in Wang, *Shanghai youtairen shehuishenghuoshi* (2008).

45. The German Studies Association in the United States, for example, has been organizing and encouraging dedicated German-Asian panels at its annual conference for several years. The 2008 GSA presidential address is a discussion on "Transnational Approaches and Their Challenges." The German academic community's "transnational turn" begins even earlier.

46. For example, though its individual points can be challenged or are in need of revision, Gerd Kaminski and Else Unterrieder's encyclopedic *Von Österreichern und Chinesen* (Vienna: Europa Verlag, 1980) as a whole is hard to replace.

47. And of course, vice versa: how China and the Chinese become (or fail to become) part of an Austrian's mental cosmos? How does it shape his/her behavior as a consumer? This is especially pertinent amid the current global "China fever."

48. An example in this vein—though not exactly an Austrian topic—is a first journalistic sketch on psychoanalysis in contemporary China: Evan Osnos, "Meet Dr. Freud: Does Psychoanalysis Have a Future in an Authoritarian State?" *The New Yorker*, 10 Jan. 2011, 54-63.

The State of Austrian/Habsburg Historical Studies in Japan

Atsushi Otsuru

The Foundation of Studies of Western History in Japan: An Absence of Austria

Ever since the Meiji Restoration, Japan aimed at a rapid modernization by absorbing Western culture and technology. In the field of the studies of history, Ludwig Riess was invited from Germany to found the Department of History at the Imperial University (currently, the University of Tokyo) in 1887. In the following year, the Department of Japanese History was added. In 1904, Imperial University reorganized these departments and placed courses on Japanese, Chinese, and Western history under the Department of History. These three courses represented the following respective roles: Japanese history promoted the national ideology, Western history provided models to follow for Japan, and Chinese history was regarded as the object of colonial control. This categorization into three areas—Japanese, Oriental, and Western history—continues to dominate the Japanese academism to date. Among the three, Western history was given a privileged status since the West was the model for Japan to learn from and played the role of enlightening the nation of the findings.

In the early twentieth century, Kumezo Tsuboi, the author of the high school Western history textbooks wrote as follows:

> The nineteenth century found constitutionalism at the state level and corporatism at the societal level. While many states confronted with each other, a global society was formed. The

> transportation and communication system came to be established, and most of the world came under the rule of Europe. Industrious nations promoted academism and industry, accumulated wealth, strengthened military forces, explored the territory, and absorbed the lazy nations. England, Germany, France, Russia and the United States all took this course. They were strong enough domestically, thus poured the power externally to compete with each other in the fields of academism, industry and transportation. This is so-called imperialism.[1]

Western History, by showing the direction for Japan to take, was given a privileged status, but the study of Austria and the Habsburgs was completely absent from what was regarded as Western history.

One century later, in 2010, *A World History for the Second-Time Readers* (Mouichido Yomu Yamakawa Sekaishi) was published. This is a history book for the general public based on the standard high school textbooks of the late twentieth century. In this book, Europe of the late nineteenth century that Tsuboi had described above is explained as follows:

> Advanced industrial nations such as England and France shifted the source of income to interest from abroad by exporting capital, in addition to exporting goods and gaining overseas markets. Meanwhile the late-coming capitalist nations such as Germany, the United States, and Japan set aside their domestic market with protectionism. Monopolistic capitalism such as cartel, trust, or *Konzern* was formed and the state, hand in hand with the monopolistic capital, advanced abroad with military forces in their back. As a result, American or German industrial production exceeded that of England since the 1890s, and the competition over colonization (division and re-division) intensified among the great powers.[2]

Such description certainly reflected the experience of the twentieth century. For example, the First World War was attributed to the competition over colonization among the great powers, and reference was made to the authoritarian nature of "late-coming" capitalism. However, these two descriptions a century apart surprisingly share a common viewpoint, i.e. understanding the development of each nation's capitalism, such as those of England, France, Germany, the United States, Russia, or Japan, independent of the rest of the world, even though the term "Western history" or "world history" was used. And the history of Austria or the Habsburgs is again completely missing from the latter description.

Having said so, we can observe a definite change both in the academism and in the historical mindset of the nation. In order to understand what change has occurred, let us now examine the Japanese historiography in the post-World War II period.

Japanese Historiography after World War II: The Introduction of Austrian History to Japan

The defeat in World War II brought a great change upon Japanese historiography. Among others, *Tenno*-centered Japanese history and Chinese history from the ruler's viewpoint went through a fundamental change. On the part of Western history, we sought a new model to follow in place of German history, which ended up in the tyranny of Nazism. British history was considered an ideal model, with an affluent society and democratic politics. By integrating Max Weber's ideal types theory and Karl Marx's primitive accumulation of capital theory, Hisao Otsuka attached great importance to the British productive middle class. His theory had a predominant influence on the Japanese historiography for some time. Besides the British model, the postwar revolutionary movement in Japan attracted attention to Soviet history. Having experienced the democratic reforms under the U.S. occupation, Japanese historiography also paid attention to American history. Austrian history, however, was not sought after as a model in Japanese historiography once again.

Toward the end of the 1960s, Japan experienced student revolts just like other developed countries. Students and young intellectuals were engaged in criticizing authoritarian politics and academicism. Marxism was not free from criticism. Chikara Rachi wrote *From the Opposite Shore* in 1978. He challenged Marxism by describing the Viennese Revolution in 1848 from the viewpoint of the minorities of the Habsburg Empire. These minorities were the very people who had been negatively mentioned as anti-revolutionary by Friedrich Engels.[3]

In the second half of the 1960s, the context for the study of the Habsburg Monarchy also shifted. The 100th anniversary of *Ausgleich* (1867) offered opportunities to reconsider the historical role of the monarchy. A lot of academic meetings were organized and attended by historians from both Eastern and Western Europe, which was exceptional at that time. Such new trends in Habsburg history were properly introduced to Japan by Toshitaka Yada.[4] He was initially interested in German history and then shifted his field of interest to Austrian history. Most of the succession states to the Habsburg Monarchy belonged to the Eastern Bloc during the Cold War.

For them, the reconsideration of the Habsburg history was an integral part of reforming communism. While the Prague Spring was interrupted by the military intervention of Warsaw Pact countries, its ideas were transplanted to Hungary.

Ivan Tibor Berend and György Ránki represented the new trends of economic history in Hungary. Under their influences, Shingo Minamizuka founded the Japanese Association of East European History in 1975.[5] Before long, a subcommittee for the history of the Dual Monarchy was organized under the auspices of this association. Though small in number, this subcommittee was the first institutional organization for both Habsburg and Austrian history in Japan. After a while, in 1987, it developed into the independent Association for Habsburg Studies. This association included two types of historians. On the one hand, there were those historians whose major interest had been German history such as Toshitaka Yada and Hideki Masutani.[6] On the other hand, there were those historians who had been interested in one of the succession states, learned its language, and then expanded their interest to the Habsburg Empire by tracing back the history. Under the auspices of the association, studies of both Habsburg and Austrian history have made a great progress.

Scholarly Works Published in Recent Years

Atsushi Otsuru published *Habsburg Monarchy: A Laboratory of the Multicultural Society* in 1995.[7] The book deals with the nationalities questions in the Austrian half of the monarchy after the *Ausgleich*. According to its Fundamental Law of 1867, every ethnicity should have equal rights to preserve and cultivate its own nationhood and language. Focusing on the process of the establishment of a minority school in a Moravian city, the author designated the Habsburg Monarchy as a "laboratory" of the multicultural society.

Mari Nomura's book *Jews in Vienna: From Fin de Siècle to Holocaust* deals with the rise of anti-Semitism in Vienna.[8] During World War I, Vienna saw a great influx of Galician Jews. They were exotic enough to be alienated even by the established Viennese Jews. This alienation of Galician Jews caused, the author argued, the rise of anti-Semitism in Vienna.

Yoshiko Yamanouchi wrote *Habsburg Cultural Revolution* in 2005.[9] She considered the rapid influx of knowledge and information in everyday life of the common people of Vienna during the age of Emperor Josef II as a cultural revolution. Masaru Baba's *Austria-Hungary and the Balkan Wars* was published in 2006.[10] Based on archival research, he analyzed the foreign

Cover of Atsushi Otsuru's Habsburg book (2007), design by Tamon Yahag
©Atsushi Otsuru

policy of the monarchy during the Balkan wars. His thesis was that having been disappointed with the European concert, the monarchy was inclined to intervene with arms, and this policy shift paved the way to the Sarajevo assassination.

Yoshihisa Hattori published *Conflict and Resolution in the Austrian Alps* in 2009.[11] Based on the records of court rulings, he analyzed the conflict resolution process in Tyrol under Maximilian I. Jun Kohno wrote *Habsburg Monarchy and Ottoman Empire: Emergence of New Politics* in 2010.[12] Confronted with the menace of the Ottoman army, the lords of the Holy Roman Empire were forced to discuss the necessity of levying new taxes, which led to the emergence of new politics, the author argued.

Kazuhiro Takii's *Hirohumi Ito: An Intellectual Politician* was published in 2010.[13] Ito was one of the most prominent politicians in the Meiji era and is now also regarded as a drafter of the Meiji constitution. Contrary to the commonly-accepted view that Ito was influenced by Rudolf von Gneist while staying in Berlin, the author emphasized the influence of Lorenz von Stein on his constitutional theory.

As stated above, the studies on Austrian/Habsburg history in Japan are still young as an academic field. However, an increasing number of scholars are joining this field. One of the factors behind this rapid growth is the depth of the Austrian/Habsburg history itself in Japan. Once you are interested in research in this field, numerous materials are available in Japanese. For example, Iwakura Mission sent to the United States and Europe in the early Meiji period happened to observe the Vienna exhibition. Among the detailed description of the exhibition, we can find the rare historical record of the Ring Street under construction. Most of the works by Ivo Andrić, L. von Sacher-Masoch, Jaroslav Hašek, Franz Kafka, Hugo von Hofmannsthal, Karl Kraus, and Stefan Zweig have been translated into Japanese. Japanese scholars' research on such intellectuals as Sigmund Freud, Hans Kelsen, Carl Menger, Josef Schumpeter, and Ludwig Wittgenstein also have made much new information available to us. Especially important is the Menger collection at Hitotsubashi University. This collection is valuable not only to the studies on the great Austrian economist Menger, but also to the studies on Austrian/Habsburg history in general.

Japanese Habsburg and Austrian Studies in the Future

At the beginning of the 1980s, social historians insisted that historians should dig the ground where they stand. At that time, I wondered what a Japanese historian specializing in Austrian history should do. I am now teaching European history at the University of Kobe. Kobe was struck by a strong earthquake in 1995. Since then, members of our Department of History became engaged in recovering historical materials damaged by the earthquake. Then we started to make use of these historical materials for the sake of local residents. In this process historical documents recording a POW camp during World War I were discovered. This POW camp was located in Aonogahara near our university, and those interned there were mainly Austro-Hungarian POWs. Fortunately, I literally found the Habsburg Monarchy under my feet.

A World of the Aonogahara POW Camp: Austrian POWs during World War I was published in 2007.[14] In 2009, an exhibition on the Aonogahara POW camp was held in the Austrian Staatsarchiv. For the opening ceremony of the exhibition, our university's orchestra played the music pieces which had been performed by the POW orchestra at that time.

Recently, it was proven that the pictures in the manor house of Eggenberg in Graz were the pieces of the painting on a Japanese folding screen. They vividly show the landscape and everyday life of Osaka at the beginning of the seventeenth century. Have there been any interchanges between Austria and Japan? Everywhere in the world, seeds for Austrian Studies are waiting to be dug up.

Notes

1. Kumezo Tsuboi, *Chugaku Seiyorekishi Kyokasho Ge-kan* (High School Textbook of Western History II) (Tokyo: Bungaku-sha, 1904), 200.

2. *Mouichido Yomu Yamakawa Sekai-shi* (A World History for the Second-Time Readers) (Tokyo: Yamakawa-shuppann-sha, 2010), 203.

3. Chikara Rachi, *Muko-gisi Kara-no Sekai-shi* (From the Opposite Shore) (Tokyo: Mirai-sha, 1978).

4. Toshitaka Yada, *Hapusuburuku Teikoku-shi Kenkyu* (A Study of Habsburg History) (Tokyo: Iwanami-shoten, 1977).

5. Shingo Minamizuka, *To-o Keizai-shi Kenkyu Josetsu* (An Introductory Study of the Economic History of Eastern Europe) (Tokyo: Taga-shuppan, 1985).

6. Hideki Masutani, *Bira-no Naka-no Kakumei: Uiin 1848* (The Viennese Revolution 1848 and its Leaflets) (Tokyo: Tokyo University Press, 1987).

7. Atsushi Otsuru, *Hapusuburuku-no Jikken: Tabunka-kyoson wo Mezashite* (Habsburg Monarchy: A Laboratory of the Multicultural Society) (Tokyo: Chu-o Koron-sha, 1995).

8. Mari Nomura, *Uiin-no Yudaya-jin: 19 Seiki-matsu Kara Horokosuto Zenya Made* (Jews in Vienna: From Fin de Siècle to Holocaust) (Tokyo: Ochanomizu-shobo, 1999).

9. Yoshiko Yamanouchi, *Hapusuburuku-no Bunka-kakumei* (Habsburg Cultural Revolution) (Tokyo: Kodan-sha, 2005).

10. Masaru Baba, *Osutoria=Hangarii to Barukan Senso: Daiichiji Sekai-Taisen Eno Michi* (Austria-

Hungary and the Balkan Wars: A Road to World War I) (Tokyo: Hosei University Press, 2006).

11. Yoshihisa Hattori, *Arupusu no Nomin Hunso: Chu-Kinsei no Chiiki Kokyo-sei to Kokka* (Conflict and Resolution in the Austrian Alps) (Kyoto: Kyoto University Press, 2009).

12. Jun Kohno, *Hapusuburuku to Osuman-Teikoku: Rekishi wo Kaeta Seiji no Hatumei* (Habsburg Monarchy and Ottoman Empire: Emergence of New Politics) (Tokyo: Kodan-sha, 2010).

13. Kazuhiro Takii, *Ito Hirohumi: Chi no Seiji-ka* (Hirohumi Ito: An Intellectual Politician) (Tokyo: Chu-o Koron-sha, 2010).

14. Atsushi Otsuru, *Aonogahara Huryo-Shuyosho no Sekai* (A World of the Aonogahara POW Camp: Austrian POWs during World War I) (Tokyo: Yamakawa-shuppan-sha, 2007).

BOOK REVIEWS

William M. Johnston, *Der österreichische Mensch: Kulturgeschichte der Eigenart Österreichs* (Vienna: Böhlau, 2010)

David S. Luft

William M. Johnston's *The Austrian Mind: An Intellectual and Social History 1848-1938* (Berkeley: University of California Press, 1972) was a major contribution to the emergence of Austrian intellectual history as a field in both the United States and Austria. In his new book on the Austrian tradition, Johnston argues that Austrian elites did not come to consciousness of what was distinctive about Austrian culture until the last years of the empire and the interwar years. The title, *Der österreichische Mensch*, refers not to the Austrian people in a sociological way, but to a type: the term might be translated as the Austrian human being or the Austrian person (or man), perhaps even as the "idea" of the Austrian person, all of which suggests why Johnston decided to write this cultural history of Austria's distinctiveness in German rather than English. He focuses on the period between 1914 and 1938 and on the way the end of the monarchy awakened interest in the characteristic qualities that had made it successful for so long. The accounts he writes about emphasize the educated officials and officers who helped to constitute the Austrian *Mensch*, especially their habitus of "conciliation, patience, and conservatism" (p. 20).

For this sense of the Austrian person Johnston coins a new term, "the Theresian human being or type," drawing on hints from Hugo von

Hofmannsthal and Friedrich Heer (both perceptive commentators on Austrian history)—and in intentional contrast to the more common usage of the term "Josephinist." Maria Theresia's reign (1740-1780) marked the beginning of modern Austria—and, oddly enough, she was arguably the founder of what came to be known a century later as Josephinism: the Austrian tradition of bureaucratic reform and modernization. On this theme Johnston cites Hofmannsthal's essay from 1917: "What we call Josephinism is sharper in outline and easier to understand: the Theresian is by far stronger, more mysterious and more fateful. In it was a summary of the essence of Austrian society, which has remained essential for what followed."[1] Johnston discusses the essays of twenty-five commentators on Austrian cultural history, presenting them in chronological order and by individual essay. He draws from writers between 1911 and 1967, from Robert Musil and Robert Müller to Friedrich Torberg and Herbert Eisenreich, to assemble his thesis about the kinds of human beings who made Austria possible and were themselves made possible by Austria.

Johnston's history of the retrospective awareness of this tradition emphasizes what he calls the Hassinger-Lhotsky paradigm, highlighting two figures who will be unfamiliar even to many Austrian historians. He argues that Hofmannsthal's ideas, because of their abstractness, have very little scholarly value, and he underscores new approaches in the mid-1920s, first in Oskar A. H. Schmitz's coining of the term "*der österreichische Mensch*" and then in the following year in Hugo Hassinger's elaboration of this idea in *Die Tschechoslowakei: Ein geographisches, politisches und wirtschaftliches Handbuch* (Vienna, 1925). Johnston regards Hassinger's formulation of this theme as the essence of the Habsburg myth as well as the essence of his own book: "These conciliatory people were represented in no small number among [Austria's] statesmen, in the nobility, in circles of officers and officials, in the clergy, among artists, scholars, and merchants [...], primarily among the Germans, but also among non-German Austrians" (cited by Johnston, pp. 198-99). Johnston argues that both Austria and Europe as a whole were slow to appreciate their debt to this "work of compromise and mediation," which allowed the West to enjoy "much of its undisturbed development" (p. 203). Johnston regards Hassinger as the first and only commentator to understand the social function of the Austrian person until Alphons Lhotsky explored this idea forty years later. In an article from 1967, Lhotsky built on Hassinger's work and seems to have drawn on Oskar Benda's ideas as well (pp. 287-88). According to Johnston, Benda's distinctive contribution (drawing on Otto Hintze) was to emphasize the contrast of political traditions within the Habsburg Monarchy between Austria and Hungary after 1700. For Johnston it is the theme of "social capital" that links these three writers and their appreciation of the loss of this human type to the peoples of Central Europe after 1918. "Can it really be that the Habsburg Empire went under because of the lack of a name for its bearers of culture?" (p. 203) Johnston does not quite argue this or attribute this thesis to anyone else, but this is characteristic of the hypothetical tone of his argument. He seems to mean that this Austrian type failed to sufficiently appreciate its own significance or to assert its own distinctive qualities.

Johnston argues that Hassinger and Benda were the only commentators who included non-Germans in this type, but he does not demonstrate this or refer in this context to Hofmannsthal's emphasis on the close connection between Bohemia and Austria. Hofmannsthal's interest in the German role in the Habsburg Monarchy and in Eastern Europe does not imply that other nationalities played no role, just as Hassinger's description of this type does not tell us how common or how effective the type was historically. It is interesting that Hassinger's methodological advance should have appeared in a book on the new Czechoslovakian state, which recalls the emphasis of Hofmannsthal and Franz Grillparzer on the close historical connection between Austria and Bohemia. The Theresian *Mensch* and the link between Bohemia and Austria are major themes from Hofmannsthal in Johnston's book, yet Johnston is generally critical of Hofmannsthal. One theme Johnston might have developed more explicitly is the distinction between those who find in the history of Austria and the Habsburg Monarchy the germ of an idea of reconciliation and those who believed that the empire itself was actually the embodiment of this idea.

Johnston emphasizes his analytic categories, but his main contribution is to draw our attention to these unfamiliar texts and to the historical linkages among them, and he coins the term "*Quellenauffrischung*" to translate the French term *resourcement*. Johnston's book is itself an example of the *resourcement* he recommends—bringing to the attention of Austrians the history of the origins of the ideas about the Austrian *Mensch* before the national identity discussions of the 1970s. *Der österreichische Mensch* may actually understate the significance of its theme by assuming that only German speakers and especially Austrians can really appreciate it. Americans, in part thanks to Johnston's work, have been fascinated by Austrian themes for the past fifty years, which also raises the question of "*der amerikanische Mensch*" and the degree to which Americans project their wishes and ideology on Austria. At least since the 1960s, American society has been dealing with the issues these writers addressed, and we can perhaps still learn from Hofmannsthal and his contemporaries. Johnston's book is important above all for locating and emphasizing this discourse. His account of these writers is often critical, but also repetitive and over-analyzed. The texts he discusses are frequently disappointing, and this material would have benefited from a more compressed treatment. His book addresses an important theme, but mainly as a retrospective idea, an interpretation, one might even say as a project for Austrian historians to investigate and try to understand.

Notes

1. Hugo von Hofmannsthal, "Maria Theresia," in *Gesammelte Werke: Reden und Aufsätze II: 1914-1924* (Frankfurt: S. Fischer, 1979), 452.

John W. Boyer, *Karl Lueger (1844-1910): Christlichsoziale Politik als Beruf: Eine Biografie* (Vienna: Böhlau, 2010)

Peter Berger

It took more than two years to convince Emperor Francis Joseph I of the political wisdom of appointing the notorious populist and demagogue Karl Lueger mayor of Vienna. Between 1895 and 1897 Lueger's bid for power, based on a string of electoral victories of his Christian Social Party, was stubbornly opposed by the sexagenarian monarch, and by Austrian Prime Minister Kasimir Badeni. When the inaugural ceremony finally took place on 20 April 1897, Lueger told the attending crowd that he saw it as his duty as incoming head of the communal government *to oppose the influence of foreigners upon all matters Viennese in a measured, yet determined way*. His words were interpreted as a warning directed against Hungary's political leadership (whose strong dislike of Lueger had caused it to scheme against his mayoral appointment), but also as yet another thinly veiled expression of Christian social Jew- and Slav-bashing. With hindsight, Lueger's thirteen-year tenure as burgomaster of Vienna (he used to refer to himself immodestly as "*Herr von Wien*") seems to have been a blessing rather than a nightmare for most of the capital city's approximately 2 million inhabitants, whether established residents or migrants from all corners of the Habsburg realm. Instead of continuing as the irresponsible polemicist and rabble-rouser, a role he had played as an opposition leader throughout the 1880s and early 1890s, Lueger now adopted the stance of an enlightened administrator of his "paternal city" and a founder of sorts of metropolitan Vienna who, much to the chagrin of his more radical "Christian" colleagues in the City

Council, knew how to utilize Jewish bank and industrial capital as well as Czech manpower for the benefit of urban development.[1]

John W. Boyer is *the* acknowledged expert on the Christian social movement in Austria from its early stirrings after 1848 until 1918, when the collapse of the Dual Monarchy profoundly changed the nature of Austrian political Catholicism. Based on two earlier works, *Political Radicalism in Late Imperial Vienna* (Chicago 1981) and *Christian Socialism in Power* (Chicago 1995), Boyer's recently published biography of Karl Lueger seems to vindicate Marc Bloch's observation that the true historian, a cannibal of sorts, cannot in the long run resist the smell of human flesh.[2] Boyer himself is a bit half-hearted in his attempt at "personalizing" the story of Austrian Christian Socialism. His Lueger book contains as much (or more) structural historiography as it is an inquiry into an individual's personality and career. Also, instead of underlining a "biographical turn" in his scholarly interest, Boyer justifies his new volume in pointing at its inclusion of a chapter on post-World War I political Catholicism in republican Austria—with the prelate-chancellor, Ignaz Seipel, playing the "flesh-and-blood" part in an otherwise highly analytical piece of scholarship.

Little is known of Karl Lueger's childhood years. He was born into a lower middle class family, his father being a janitor first at Vienna's distinguished grammar school, the *Theresianum*, and later at the Viennese Polytechnic Institute. A gifted amateur engineer, father Lueger enjoyed the privilege to attend lectures of some of the Polytechnic's professors, and occasionally even took examinations. Karl's much beloved mother Juliane, a devout Catholic, ran a tobacconist's shop. Probably owing to his father's connections Karl was admitted to the *Theresianum* despite his humble origins, and proceeded to win the recognition not so much of his fellow pupils as of his teachers, who acknowledged the boy's extraordinary talent and diligence. From 1862 onward, Lueger studied at the law faculty of the University of Vienna, earning his doctoral degree in January 1870. The bar exam followed in 1874, and soon thereafter young *Herr Doktor* Lueger threw himself into a lawyer's career. He took a certain pride in recruiting his clientele among artisans and small shopkeepers, the kind of people on whose support he would later build the Viennese Christian Social movement. Lueger never married, and his good looks notwithstanding he seems to have had few relations with women, or succeeded in hiding them from the public. As a politician depending on electoral backing, Lueger believed that his handsome-bachelor image (his nickname was "*Der schöne Karl*") counted for much of the female support for himself and the Christian Social Party. A generation later, Hitler would defend his celibate lifestyle along similar lines.

According to Professor Boyer, Lueger was ideally suited for the leadership of an anti-liberal, petty bourgeois, grass-root protest movement in a city firmly controlled by its liberal upper bourgeoisie. As a twenty-six-year-old PhD candidate, he already assaulted the elitist franchise system applied in Austria both on the state and the communal levels. In post-1867 Vienna, those entitled to vote fell into three categories (*Wahlkörper*). Category one included all (male) owners of real estate or businesses whose yearly tax contribution equalled or exceeded 500 or 100 guilders, respectively—as well as top civil servants, army personnel, and high-ranking clerics liable to a salary tax (*Besoldungssteuer*). Category two comprised the same social groups, but here the required annual tax payments were lower: 100 guilders for owners of real estate, and fifty guilders for entrepreneurs. Academics also cast their vote in the second voting class, hence its name, "*Intelligenzkurie.*" The third category of voters included all taxpayers who delivered more than an annual ten fl. From 1885 onward, the minimum contribution required for membership in the third voting class was lowered to five fl., and in 1900, a fourth voting class was introduced, partly overlapping with the already existing ones, and enfranchising every male person registered as a resident of the capital for at least three consecutive years. Even so, the number of potential voters remained small (approximately 230,000) if compared to metropolitan Vienna's fast-growing population of about 1.4 million in 1890, when the circle of outer suburbs/*Vororte* got formally incorporated into the city limits. Class suffrage—or, in the words of Boyer, the refusal to grant artisans and shop owners even a minimum of political rights—no doubt helped cement liberal domination of Vienna's city parliament, and hence was a favored target for the polemic of opposition forces such as the "Democrats," a left-leaning splinter group of defected liberals, and later the Christian Socials and the Social Democrats.

When Karl Lueger entered the realm of politics, he won a seat for the Liberal Party in the 1875 election for the Vienna City Council. Later, he also became a liberal deputy to the *Reichsrat*, the Austrian lower chamber. But he soon parted ways with mainstream liberalism, and affiliated with the above-mentioned Democrats—a decision Professor Boyer deems crucial for the history of Viennese political life. Genuine concern for the underprivileged, disenfranchised "little folk" may have been the driving force behind Lueger's apostasy, but it is also obvious that his venomous criticism of the aristocratic Cajetan Felder, grand old man of Vienna's Liberals and mayor of the town (1868-78), did much to make Lueger's position within the Liberal Party untenable. For the Democrats, Lueger and a young Jewish physician called Ignaz Mandl developed a political program based on the economist Wilhelm Neurath's ideas of "ethical collectivism," and emphasizing, inter alia, the need to crush the monopoly of Vienna's privately-owned transport and energy companies, hotbeds of inefficiency and corruption. The intellectual capacities of Mandl, whose missionary zeal made him a dreaded political infighter, left a lasting impression with Lueger. Both men represented what Carl E. Schorske has called the sharper key in Viennese communal politics, their shirt-sleeve opposition rhetoric directed both against Catholicism and "Jewish" capitalism being without precedent in the records of the distinguished City Council.

Lueger's flirtation with anti-clericalism did not outlast his personal acquaintance with a group of Catholic social reformers led by Karl von Vogelsang, a German-born former Protestant and editor of the conservative newspaper *Vaterland*, Prince Alois Liechtenstein, nicknamed "the Red Prince," an ardent advocate of social legislation in favor of the village poor, and Franz Schindler, moral theologian at the University of Vienna. The four met at a time when the democratic movement ceased to be Lueger's spiritual home. Frustrated by a bitter intra-party feud over his nomination for the post of second vice mayor of Vienna (in the end another candidate was elected), Lueger began to style himself as the popular tribune of a new coalition of fiercely anti-liberal, anti-capitalist, religious, and anti-Semitic forces, campaigning under the name of United Christians, and later as Christian Social Party. The United Christians made their first official appearance in 1888, three years after suffrage was granted to everyone paying at least five guilders per annum in income tax. These "*Fünfguldenmänner*," together with the fourth voting class in Vienna, were chiefly responsible for Lueger's consecutive (and ever more impressive) victories at the polls, until his party finally crushed both Liberals and Democrats in the decisive communal elections of 1895-97.

Like many scholars before him, John W. Boyer asks how genuine Lueger's expressions of his *Weltanschauung* were, and in particular whether he was a truly religious man and deeply convinced anti-Semite. For Boyer, Lueger's clerical attitudes and his Jew-bashing were inextricably combined. He could not have permitted himself to be *either* clerical *or* anti-Semitic, since in both respects his profile seemed too washy. Far from being a Catholic zealot or even outwardly religious, Lueger perfectly realized the credibility bonus accorded to his political experiment through the adoption of Vogelsang's and Schindler's Catholic social theory. His alliance with Catholicism seemed thus motivated primarily by the utilitarian aspect. As a Jew hater Lueger appeared more authentic than as a clerical—but a lot less rancorous, and consistent, than his fellow politician Georg von Schönerer, leader of Austria's pan-German movement. Schönerer was clearly a racist, while Lueger's anti-Semitism centered on the economic aspect. But it is fair to say that the ruthless anti-Semitic language of both men helped to "unleash destructive instincts,"[3] and paved the way for the Nazi's later success with the Viennese masses.[4] Writers sympathetic to Lueger have made the point that he *employed* anti-Semitic rhetoric rather than *enjoyed* it—and that some of his lieutenants (like a certain Bielohlawek) were far more radical than Lueger himself, who entertained friendly relations with members of the Jewish community.[5] Boyer agrees in principle, but repeatedly stresses how hypocritical, unfair and offensive Lueger's demagoguery must have appeared to most of Vienna's Jewish bourgeoisie that saw itself, with much justification, as one of the supporting pillars of Austro-Hungarian statehood.[6]

Lueger the politician may be hard or even impossible to acquit before the tribunal of history,[7] but his achievements as an urban modernizer were beyond any doubt. Professor Boyer even speaks of an "urban revolution" happening in Vienna between 1897 and 1905, and indeed Lueger's hands-on approach to communal matters was revolutionary if compared with the much more restrained political style of his liberal predecessors Andreas Zelinka, Cajetan Felder, or Julius Newald. Far from being a promoter of *welfare* in the sense of a transfer of resources from the privileged members of society to the poor and handicapped, Lueger was nonetheless a social reformer concerned with broadening the public sector of services (transportation, water, electricity, gas, health, schools, etc.) for the benefit of the resident taxpayer. His municipal socialism, inaugurated in 1896, when Vienna's new gas works went into construction, and continued with the communalization (and electrification) of the tramway system and the founding of a municipal mortgage bank, was, despite its name, driven by the motive of profitability. The gains of the public sector, in Lueger's concept, served to alleviate the pressure of taxation for the common man, or at least to prevent it from rising. Unlike the liberal era in Vienna (and unlike the 1920s, when the city was firmly in Social Democratic hands), Lueger's period of tenure was not characterized by grandiose construction projects such as the *Ringstrasse* palaces or giant municipal flats, *Karl-Marx-Hof* style. The Christian Social City Council, however, commissioned the impressive old-age home and almshouse complex of Lainz, and a number of churches—Otto Wagner's *Kirche am Steinhof* being the most outstanding example. It had a 150-mile aqueduct built (the second *Hochquellwasser-Leitung*), which brought fresh spring water from the southeastern Alps to end Vienna's notorious water shortage. Finally, under the aegis of the able urban planner Heinrich Goldemund, reforestation in the Vienna woods became a centerpiece of Lueger's municipal reform program, compensating on the esthetical level for the lack of monumental architecture. To promote the Christian arts, Vienna was accorded a new theater (*Kaiser Franz Joseph-Jubiläums-Theater*), which explicitly banned Jewish authors and actors from its stage. The boycott lasted until 1902, when the house went bankrupt, and afterwards reemerged as *Volksoper*. Now its repertory was dotted with operas and *Singspiele*, often written by Jews and performed by Jewish artists.[8]

Lueger died of diabetes in 1910, and received almost as grand a funeral as Emperor Francis Joseph in the middle of World War I, six years later.[9] At the time of his death, his Christian Socials looked very different from what they had been in the 1890s. At the instigation of Lueger's right hand, trained historian Albert Gessmann, the party had put out feelers towards Lower Austria and the Alpine provinces to cooperate with local Catholic conservative leaders. Anticipating universal male suffrage, which was introduced in Austria in 1906 and strongly supported by the Christian Socials, Gessmann hoped to win the votes of the farming population in addition to those of the party's traditional urban clientele (houseowners, shopkeepers, artisans, and the lower strata of the civil service). The results of the 1907 Reichstag election, in which the Christian Socials came out as a strong second behind the Social Democrats, vindicated Gessmann's strategy. Following the formal merger of Christian Socials and Catholic conservatives in June 1907, the new Catholic *Reichspartei* even became the largest faction in parliament, with a few deputies more than Viktor Adler's Austro-Marxists. The increasing weight of the rural element within the party coincided with a shift in its programmatic emphasis from anti-capitalism to anti-Marxism. In its ambition to represent the literate and propertied classes faithful to the Austrian state (as opposed to the "homeless" proletariat), the Christian Socials of Lueger's last years slowly but perceptibly restrained their criticism of "big business," as well as their rowdy anti-Semitism, and markedly improved their relations with conservative court circles and with the shadow cabinet of Francis Joseph's designated heir, archduke Francis Ferdinand.

The departure of its charismatic leader threw the Christian Social Party into a turbulent struggle for Lueger's succession. In his political will, Lueger had named Richard Weiskirchner, formerly head of Vienna's municipal bureaucracy (*Magistratsdirektor*), as his favorite candidate for the post of mayor of Vienna. Weiskirchner's title was challenged by Gessmann, and three years (and an interim tenure of the first deputy mayor, Josef Neumayer) had to pass before Weiskirchner got finally installed at the helm of the City Council. The parliamentary election of 1911, called a year earlier than originally scheduled, ended in disaster for the *Reichspartei* whose campaign was orchestrated by Albert Gessmann. In Vienna alone, more than 30,000 votes were lost, mainly to the Social Democrats. But just a few months later, when municipal elections in the fourth voting class were held, many of the defected lower middle class voters returned into the party's fold. Under Weiskirchner in 1913 and 1914, Vienna was run much along the same technical lines as under Lueger, but the new mayor's public statements differed from those of his predecessor in at least two respects. A long-time deputy of the *Reichsrat* and secretary of trade under Prime Minister Bienerth (1908-11), Weiskirchner saw himself as a Catholic bridge builder to Austria's liberal haute bourgeoisie, and hence did not eschew manifestations of solidarity with leading figures of the liberal camp. Also, he was openly pro-industry and pro-big business: a slap into the face of Christian Social anti-Semites for whom "capitalist" and "Jewish" were synonyms. Following the outbreak of World War I, and the explosion of anti-Jewish feelings (connected with the arrival in Vienna of tens of thousands of refugees from Russian-occupied Galicia and a string of corruption scandals involving Jewish suppliers of the army),[10] Weiskirchner's party was to pay dearly for his "tactical" liberal posture.

With the loss of the war came the end of Christian Social political supremacy over Vienna. As mayor of the city, Weiskirchner in 1919 yielded place to a Social Democrat, Jakob Reumann. With the exception of 1934-45, all Viennese burgomasters to this day were Social Democratic (or Socialist) nominees. It is one of the theses of Professor Boyer's book that the Catholics' post-1918 defeat at the hands of the democratic left amounted to something like a reenactment of the crushing of the Viennese Liberals by Christian Socialism in the mid-1890s. But unlike the Christian Socials, who after their triumph learnt to coexist with, and to a certain extent emulate, the remaining champions of liberalism in the state bureaucracy, academe, or business, the Social Democrats, advocates of the proletariat, were too much the antipodes of bourgeois polite society (as represented by political Catholicism of Seipel's fundamentalist brand)[11] to allow for mutual convergence. Consequently, the history of the interwar Republic of Austria, a creation of its antagonistic red and black parties as much as of the peacemakers of Saint-Germain, was one of "cold" and ultimately of hot civil war—the latter followed, within less than five years, by Austria's destruction at the hands of Hitler.

Was there a leader in twentieth-century Austria who could justifiably claim to be Lueger's spiritual heir? If anything, the pragmatic political style of "handsome Karl" resembled the tactical suppleness displayed by the Austrian People's Party's figureheads Julius Raab and Leopold Figl after 1945, says Boyer. Prior to World War II, he admits that Dollfuss, the chancellor turned dictator, might be seen as being (if only remotely) in the Luegerian tradition of a Catholicism restrained by strategic considerations. For Professor Boyer, there is definitely no line connecting Lueger with Adolf Hitler—the latter's plaudits for Lueger in *Mein Kampf* notwithstanding.

Shortly before or during the year 1909, Austrian writer Felix Salten (*Bambi*), an occasional commentator for Vienna's liberal daily paper, *Neue Freie Presse*, predicted that Lueger's novel-like life would be transformed into an immortal piece of literature by some author of a not too distant future.[12] John W. Boyer's *Karl Lueger* may not prove immortal, but it certainly should remain a reference biography for decades to come. Equally important, the book testifies to the enormous, but often contested potential for survival of the Habsburg Monarchy during its final decades—a potential based, not least, on the thriving civic and political culture of autonomous municipalities like Lueger's Vienna. It was not before the destruction of municipal freedom at the hands of a war-ridden state and military bureaucracy that Austria-Hungary disappeared from the map of Europe.

Notes

1. A remarkable instance of Jewish generosity with respect to Lueger's communal projects was the donation of Rothschild land for the construction of Vienna's second freshwater pipeline. See Anna Ehrlich, *Karl Lueger: Die zwei Gesichter der Macht* (Vienna: Amalthea, 2010), 157ff.

2. Fernand Braudel et al., *Der Historiker als Menschenfresser: Über den Beruf des Geschichtsschreibers* (Stuttgart: Wagenbach, 1995).

3. Carl E. Schorske, *Fin-de-Siècle Vienna: Politics and Culture* (Cambridge: Cambridge University Press, 1981), 145.

4. Albert Fuchs, *Geistige Strömungen in Österreich 1867-1918* (Vienna: Löcker, 1978), 60.

5. Steven Beller, *Vienna and the Jews 1867-1938: A Cultural History* (Cambridge: Cambridge University Press, 1989), 195.

6. Arthur Schnitzler, among others, heaped scorn on Lueger's ingratiation with the Jewish "aristocracy," but also on those Jews who deliberately overlooked his hypocritical behavior. See Ehrlich, *Karl Lueger*, 98-99.

7. The writer Albert Fuchs accuses Lueger of having committed "one act of despotism after the other" while he was mayor of Vienna. Besides actively discriminating against Social Democrats, Jews, and Czechs who applied for jobs in the city administration or the communal school system, Lueger's visions concerning the future of the Habsburg Empire were much less progressive than it is often believed, says Fuchs, *Geistige Strömungen in Österreich*, 60ff.

8. Ehrlich, *Karl Lueger*, 164-65.

9. On Lueger's municipal reforms, also see Paul Hofmann, *The Viennese: Splendor, Twilight, and Exile* (New York: Anchor Press, 1988), 143-44.

10. A notorious case was that of Josef Kranz, a banker charged with purchasing beer for the armed forces. Eduard März, *Österreichische Bankpolitik in der Zeit der großen Wende* (Vienna: Verlag für Geschichte und Politik, 1981), 222-23.

11. In John W. Boyer's view, the fundamentalism of the priest, Ignaz Seipel, who was Christian Socialism's overpowering figure from the early 1920s until his death in 1932, amounted to a complete rebuttal of Lueger's flexible (or even opportunistic) stance.

12. Felix Salten, *Das österreichische Antlitz: Essays* (Berlin: S. Fischer, 1910), 127-42.

Peter Ruggenthaler and Walter M. Iber, eds., *Hitlers Sklaven—"Stalins Verräter": Aspekte der Repression an Zwangsarbeitern und Kriegsgefangenen: Eine Zwischenbilanz* (Innsbruck: Studienverlag, 2010)

Thomas R. Grischany

The anthology *Hitlers Sklaven—"Stalins Verräter"*, edited by Peter Ruggenthaler and Walter M. Iber, endeavors to shed more light on a hitherto under-researched subject of the history of twentieth-century Europe, namely the fates of the persons who became forced laborers in Germany during the Second World War. The book deals only with the forced laborers from the Soviet Union, who accounted for almost half of the estimated up to 13.6 million laborers employed during the war. As the book's title suggests, they became "victims of two regimes"; their odyssey was not limited to their forced labor employment, but continued after the war with their repatriation and countless repressions suffered in the Soviet Union, which is also the proper focus of the book. The tome is the final result of a yearlong research project by a team of international scholars, funded by various Austrian government agencies and presented at a conference in December 2006. The research rests extensively on previously inaccessible holdings in Russian archives—especially regarding the files of the State Defense Committee GOKO—and various non-Russian archives, as well as private correspondences and memoirs.

The first section contains, as prehistory so to speak, a generic article on forced laborers in the Third Reich from the Soviet Union (Pavel Polian), and one that specifically addresses laborers from the Baltic states due to their special status as non-Slavs (Kārlis Kangeris). Both contributions provide important background information on the topic, such as basic numbers and terminological clarifications, for example regarding the application of the term "*Ostarbeiter*."

The second section examines the legal and administrative basis for the repatriation process (Nikita Petrov/ Ruggenthaler/ Natal'ja Lebedeva) as well as the practice in six regional studies on Estonia (Ranno Roosi), Latvia (Heinrihs Strods), Lithuania (Kristian Burinskaitė), Belarus (Anatolij Šarkov/Dieter Bacher), Western Ukraine (Ruggenthaler/Halyna Starko/ Roman Dubasevych), and Northern Caucasus (Igor' Krjučkov).

The article on the legal and administrative basis of the repatriation process by Petrov, Ruggenthaler, Lebedeva, and Michail Prozumenščikov can be regarded as the centerpiece of the anthology. It describes meticulously the procedures of filtration, i.e. the examination of the repatriates (who were divided into the six categories of soldier and officer POWs, collaborators, civilians, inhabitants of border areas, and orphans), which took place in transition camps at the borders as well as in filtration camps in the Soviet hinterland, the composition of the filtration committees (from the People Commissariat/Ministry for State Security NKGB/MGB, the People Commissariat/Ministry for Internal Affairs NKVD/MVD, and the military counter-intelligence SMERŠ), and the purposes and political considerations behind the actions, such as returning unsuspicious soldiers to the armed forces and exposing traitors, who were then handed over to the secret police of the NKVD.

Although the Soviet state distinguished between forced and voluntary laborers—civilians, especially in the early years, were also recruited on a voluntary basis— it distrusted all repatriates, whether POWs or civilians; they were registered and constantly monitored even after their return, and could be forced to work in order to rebuild the economy of the USSR until their final destiny was decided. However, most scholars think that POWs were generally treated worse, since they were indiscriminately regarded as traitors who should have fought to the death. The Soviet leadership was particularly interested in repatriation of people from Baltic and Caucasus regions since emigration had been especially strong from those regions. It also strove to get hold of former Soviets in Western occupation zones and countries, especially those who were considered "hostile elements." In December 1946, the filtration process of the repatriates was "by and large" concluded. The number of remigrants steadily declined until 1953, and sputtered in the late 1950s. The whole repatriation process was finished in

1962, but amnesties took turns with trials against collaborators well into the 1970s.

The tenor of the six regional case studies can be summarized as follows: In reaction to Soviet repressions, significant numbers of displaced persons had left the territories falling into the Soviet sphere of power after 1939-40—in turn, the populations in these territories were highly involved in the Shoah—and then again with the advance of the Red Army in 1944-45. The legal status of many of these persons, especially the Balts, was unclear due to the occupations of 1939-40, and there existed no international laws that protected them against forced repatriation. A great number of Estonians and Latvians had found refuge in Finland and especially Sweden, and the extradition of these refugees (together with German Wehrmacht soldiers) from Sweden to the Soviet Union is the topic of an excursus by Peter Fritz.

The situation in the filtration camps was dominated by strong propagandistic efforts to promulgate a positive image of the Soviet Union. Formally, the repatriates were promised support like financial aid and job placements, but this was more of an attempt to coax the return of those who were still abroad, for in reality the repatriates' treatment was more characterized by various punishments for their alleged "treason," like the confiscation of houses or "voluntary" labor stints, and other means to cleanse them from the "shame" of having been a forced laborer for Germany, like collaboration with the NKVD against anti-Soviet forces. In Lithuania and Western Ukraine, anti-Soviet activities amounted to an outright yet little-known guerrilla war against Soviet forces, in which repatriates were found on both sides. The private correspondences between repatriates and family members and friends who refused or were undecided on whether to return played a prominent role in the struggle over the former forced laborers, since the Soviet government tried to influence the letter writers and even resorted to falsifications.

The third section deals with former forced laborers who stayed in Austria or migrated to other parts of the world. The article by Iber and Ruggenthaler describes Soviet repatriation activities in their occupation zone but also in the Western zones, leading to tensions with the Western Allies in this microcosm of the emerging Cold War, and also covers the topic of naturalization and further emigration. In an excursus, Stefan Karner addresses the extradition of Cossacks and Vlasov soldiers from the British occupiers to the Soviet Union. The last contribution, again by Bacher, exemplarily contains the biographies of three Western Ukrainian forced laborers, the stories of which illustrate the broad spectrum of reasons for staying: typically the beginning of a new life (usually after having started a family), the dire prospects for improvement in the Soviet Union, and memories of Soviet repression, which had often led to voluntary labor service in the first place.

Taken together, the thirteen contributions constitute a substantial complementation of the research at hand. Until now, for instance, no studies on the repatriation of forced laborers to Western Ukraine, Latvia, Lithuania and Northern Caucasus existed. On the other hand, the project also highlights how much and which kind of research still needs to be done. But the work is in any case a standard reference for every scholar interested in the topic of repatriation of the *Zwangsarbeiter*.

The only downside of this impressive wealth of information is the occasionally disjointed organization and presentation of the material, a typical and hard to avoid flaw of publications that come out of conferences. Long passages overflowing with insights and data are interspersed with short segments which, due to the lack of substantial new findings, are either irrelevant, too superficial, or highly repetitive. The latter particularly applies to the regional case studies: The significance of private correspondences, for example, is emphasized for almost every region to such an extent that it could have been treated as a distinct chapter. The excursuses could have largely been integrated into the other texts, and the annex, which contains highly fascinating excerpts of memoirs from forced laborers, remains somewhat detached from the body of the book. All this could have been avoided if the single contributions had been edited into one coherent text.

The greatest question mark—and incentive for future research—that stands out amid the many raised, and for the most part answered, questions, seems to be the difference in the treatment of civilians and POWs, which is greatly emphasized by most authors only theoretically; ultimately we learn little about the actual differences, such as that POWs did not receive restitutions like the civilians in the 1990s. On p. 72, for instance, numerous cases of forced labor for repatriates are mentioned; however, it is not clear on what grounds the Soviets imposed these punishments on civilians and POWs alike. The blurriness of the line between civilians and POWs could be connected to Krjučkov's statement that the voluntary recruitment of laborers by Germany was much more successful than was admitted after the war. I expect more research along these lines to come, and it will automatically redirect a strong focus back on the first part of the double victimization in the form of a critical reassessment of the "forced" aspect of forced labor in the Third Reich.

Claudia Kuretsidis-Haider and Winfried R. Garscha, eds., *Gerechtigkeit nach Diktatur und Krieg: Transitional Justice 1945 bis heute: Strafverfahren und ihre Quellen* (Graz: CLIO, 2010)

James J. Weingartner

The term "transitional justice" represents a rather loose concept that has entered our vocabularies over the past two decades or so. It denotes efforts by national societies that have experienced gross abuses of human rights in the context of war and/or dictatorship to foster internal harmony and democracy and, perhaps most importantly, to do justice to both victims and oppressors following the termination of conditions that had given rise to profound injustices. These objectives, of course, are not always easy to reconcile with one another. The focus of this volume is on one of the vehicles of transitional justice—the trial and punishment of those accused of violations of human rights.

Although the subtitle might lead the reader to expect a broad survey of such investigations and prosecutions during the period following World War II, and there have been many, the actual contents of the book are quite limited. The volume contains papers originally presented at a conference held in 2008 in Vienna on the occasion of the tenth anniversary of the founding of the *Zentrale österreichische Forschungsstelle Nachkriegsjustiz*, and the focus of most of its contents is distinctly German-Austrian, dealing largely with the crimes of the Third Reich and postwar responses to them, but with occasional attention paid to other examples of transitional justice.

Given the diversity of its contents, this book does not lend itself well to a unified review; consequently, the essays it contains will be very briefly (and, I fear, inadequately) summarized.

The papers in the first segment of the book are the broadest in their perspectives. Wolfgang Form provides a useful analysis of the concept of transitional justice and its components, and offers an overview of efforts to implement it in the near century since the end of World War I. In a wide-ranging essay, Otto Trifterer explores multiple approaches to the challenge of *Vergangenheitsbewältigung*, with emphasis on the degree to which criminal proceedings can contribute to coming to terms with a troubled national past. Astrid Reisinger Coracini discusses the influence of post-World War II war crimes trials conducted by national courts (as opposed to the International Military Tribunal at Nuremberg) on contemporary international law. Roland Miklau draws our attention to the challenges inherent in trying defendants for war crimes and crimes against humanity, especially the problem of ensuring impartiality, and sees major progress in the recent establishment of international courts, in particular, the permanent International Criminal Court.

Peter Steinbach's essay is an assessment of the postwar West German legal approach to overcoming the Nazi past through assessing individual responsibility for its crimes. Steinbach concludes that, while the effort cannot be considered a resounding success, neither was it a failure. Moreover, he points out, the process was conducted within a constitutional framework that respects human rights, providing a model for other societies seeking to overcome the consequences of systemized criminal pasts. A very different perspective is adopted by Wolfram Pyta. In a densely argued and theoretically engaging essay, he explores the power of the prosecution of perpetrators of the Shoah to embed consciousness of the Holocaust in collective memory. Looking ahead to the point in the near future at which both perpetrators and survivors will have disappeared from the scene, Pyta looks to historical fiction based on the trials of Holocaust perpetrators—already exemplified by Peter Weiss's play *Die Ermittlung* and law professor Bernhard Schlink's novel *Der Vorleser* (widely translated and made into a movie)—to serve as the primary vehicles of Holocaust collective memory.

Subsequent contributions are less speculative. Witold Kulesza offers analyses of two post-World War II trials of Germans for crimes against humanity conducted by Polish authorities—those of Hans Biebow, former administrative chief of the Lódź (Litzmannstadt to the German occupiers) ghetto, and Arthur Greiser, wartime *Reichsstatthalter* of the western Polish territory annexed to Germany as the *Wartheland*. After summarizing prosecution evidence and defense arguments, the author concludes that the trials were fair and that they, along with other Polish trials of German war criminals, constitute important contributions to European legal culture. This, however, is asserted rather than demonstrated.

A sharp diversion from the primarily German-Austrian focus of the collection is Martin F. Polaschek's contribution dealing with South Korea's struggle with the psychic residues of forty years of Japanese control and occupation between 1905 and 1945. Many readers might find this essay particular intriguing, describing as it does an effort at transitional justice that is relatively unfamiliar to Westerners. The South Korean example is anomalous in that little was attempted until almost sixty years following the end of World War II. This was due in large part to the fact that leading figures in postwar South Korea's authoritarian regimes were themselves implicated in collaboration with the Japanese occupiers. Polaschek sees parallels between the South Korean experience and Austria's long-deferred confrontation with its Nazi past.

Klaus Marxen's essay returns the reader to the German experience, although to a more recent and less virulent fragment. Marxen discusses the post-reunification prosecutions of offenses committed under the communist regime of the DDR and explores the degree to which these proceedings contributed to the objectives of transitional justice and the further evolution of the concept. In an angry contribution, Hermann Frank Meyer offers a narrative of horrendous crimes against civilians committed by Austrian-German troops in the course of anti-partisan operations in South-Eastern Europe during World War II and presents an indictment of war crimes justice in postwar Germany and Austria. Although, while in Greece alone "1,000 Lidices" had allegedly occurred, very few of the suspected perpetrators of war crimes in the Balkans were punished or even brought to trial.

In his essay, Stefan Klemp explores an often-asked question: "Do trials of Nazi war criminals make any sense today?" Most of Klemp's contribution is, like Meyer's, a lament for the alleged failure or unwillingness of German authorities to bring to trial and convict more criminal suspects against whom the evidence seemed strong. But he argues that it is still important to attempt to bring now very old men to trial, not only for the sake of justice, but also to expand the historical record of Nazi criminality. He urges historians to work in support of this effort. Efraim Zuroff adds a short but ferocious indictment of what he believes to be Austria's "abysmal record" in prosecuting perpetrators of the Holocaust. He writes about the submission to Austrian authorities by the Wiesenthal Center (whose Jerusalem centers he heads) of a list of forty-seven former members of SS and police units involved in war crimes, of whom none have thus far been brought to justice. Zuroff cites an unnamed "senior prosecutor" as having explained that suspects were asked if they had been involved in war crimes. If they denied their participation, the cases were dropped. Unfortunately, no source for this damning information is provided.

The concluding three essays in this book address the subject of documentary sources in their relationship to transitional justice. Joachim Riedel discusses the value to historians of sources generated by criminal investigations and trials, but also warns of their limitations. Riedel concludes with a description of the holdings of the *Zentrale Stelle der Landesjustizverwaltungen zur Aufklärung nationalsozialistischer Verbrechen* in Ludwigsburg, whose former deputy director he is. Lorenz Mikoletzky, general director of the Austrian State Archives in Vienna, notes the cooperation of the institution he heads with the Austrian Ministry of Justice and the non-state *Forschungsstelle Nachkriegsjustiz*. Dick de Mildt closes this collection with an essay applying the mammoth documentary series *Justiz und NS-Verbrechen*, of which he is co-editor, to the current trial in Munich of the ninety-year-old John Demjanjuk. On the basis of many previous trials by German courts, which resulted in acquittals of low-ranking *Befehlsempfänger* on the grounds of *Befehlsnotstand*, de Mildt predicts a similar outcome for Demjanjuk (according to recent news releases, a verdict is expected by March 2011).

The essays contained in this book are a combination of the thought-provoking and the mundane. They will be of value primarily to those interested in World War II German-Austrian war crimes and crimes against humanity and their punishment (or lack thereof), although most will find few surprises. A wider perspective that included comparisons among a broader range of national experiences with transitional justice would have made this a more stimulating collection.

Walter M. Iber, *Die Sowjetische Mineralölverwaltung in Österreich: Zur Vorgeschichte der OMV 1945-1955* (Innsbruck: Studienverlag, 2011)

Alexander Smith

At the end of the Second World War, Austria was the third-largest oil producer in Europe after the Soviet Union and Romania. Austria's petroleum reserves and oil industry facilities, concentrated in the country's northeast, represented a precious treasure for the Soviet occupational force. When the Red Army entered the "Ostmark" in the spring of 1945, Moscow was already well-informed about Austria's resources and economic potential. Walter M. Iber argues in his recent study on the Austrian oil industry during the Soviet military occupation from 1945 to 1955 that Moscow from the very beginning focused on the exploitation of these rich petroleum resources in the Vienna Basin. This became evident when Soviet soldiers immediately occupied the oil fields of Lower Austria after the invasion, confiscated large parts of the petroleum industry as war booty, and started to dismantle heavy machinery and drilling rigs. The facilities were shipped to and rebuilt in the Soviet Union, whose industry had been devastated by total war against Hitlerite Germany.

Iber's book is structured in four sections. The first two provide a brief overview of the significance of petroleum in the Soviet postwar foreign policy as well as the development of the oil industry in Austria until 1945. These chapters are most useful to the reader in explaining the historical and political contexts in which Moscow pursued its specific economic policy toward Austria. In the postwar world, dominated by great power politics, the newly reestablished Republic of Austria played a rather insignificant role. Vienna depended on the diplomatic intentions of the four occupation powers, which often decided over its head. Since Stalin was not willing to risk a war with the Western powers over Austria, while the country's Communist Party (KPÖ) was rejected by the people in a disastrous defeat in the first parliamentary elections, in November 1945 it became evident that Austria would go a different path than its eastern neighbors who had fallen under exclusive Soviet tutelage. Due to these restrictions, the Soviet policy during the time of occupation aimed at the economic exploitation of Austria as a form of reparation for the destructive National Socialist war of aggression against Moscow. In describing Austria's impotent and at times hopeless position between the interests of the Western powers and the Soviets in the emerging Cold War, Iber's book recounts the struggle of the powerless Austrian government in defending the country's economic foundation and securing it from the Soviet "looters."

The third chapter represents the main part of the book. It describes the establishment of the Soviet system of plundering Austria's resources in general and the development, characteristics, and economic decline of the Soviet Mineral Oil Administration (SMV) between 1945 and 1955 in particular. After the powers agreed during the Potsdam Conference that all "German assets" in its Austrian zone of occupation would fall into Soviet hands, Moscow changed its strategy from dismantling and shipping oil equipment abroad to economic exploitation of the seized property. Getting the prolific Austrian oil fields back into production seemed to better serve Moscow's economic interest. The Soviets took advantage of the Allies' neglect to clearly define what exactly constituted "German assets." They simply interpreted all property as "German" that was in German possession at the end of the war and for which the National Socialists paid some kind of compensation. Any arbitrary interpretation was welcomed to seize control of the Austrian oil fields. When it supported their interests, the Soviets even defined Austria as the legal successor of the Third Reich, for in official language it had been "liberated" from Nazi Germany. Once the provisional Renner government in Vienna refused to create a joint Austro-Soviet enterprise (Sanafta) to get the oil into production, in September 1945 Moscow decided to go it alone and formed the SMV. The Soviet occupying force had absolutely free hand in economic affairs in its eastern Austrian zone of occupation. Regardless of the highly contested views concerning the legal status of the Austrian oil industry, the Soviets moved a large portion of the oil produced by the SMV out of the country.

Alongside these larger political dimensions and the economics of the Soviet occupation in Austria, Iber also delineates the main characteristics and daily routine of the SMV workforce. The Soviet enterprise maintained plant security guards—the communist *Werkschutz*—which acted as an armed quasi-paramilitary organization of several hundred members. Its task was the protection of the factory equipment and the oil fields but also surveilling those employees that did not belong to the KPÖ. Soviet propaganda in the "*Russenbetriebe*," first of all through a factory newspaper but also by way of lectures, exhibits, cinema shows, and stage plays, aimed at consolidating a communist spirit and influence in the enterprises. Even though the SMV operated as a stronghold of the KPÖ, this massive propaganda onslaught failed to turn the greater part of the workforce to communism. By 1954, fifty percent of the SMV employees were still either without party affiliation or members of the Socialist, Christian conservative, or even nationalist parties.

By 1952, the maladministered SMV and USIA (Administration for Soviet Property in Austria), with their inefficient and bloated administrative organizations, faced serious financial trouble. This led to mass layoffs in the following year. During the later occupation period, the SMV was unable to properly exploit the Lower Austrian oil fields and failed to reach the planned production targets. The refineries in operation had become technically outdated and produced poor-quality gasoline. To remain competitive on the Austrian market, the SMV was forced to improve the quality of its motor fuels. When the Soviets eventually started to invest into the ailing enterprise, the economic downfall of the SMV became unavoidable. These investments came too late; the Soviet economic establishments in Austria had been run down. Iber's book vividly outlines the inefficiency of the Soviet centrally planned economic system. It failed to adapt to the demands of the market, was utterly incapable of innovation, and produced products of poor quality. The SMV became a showcase of the continuous failure inherent in the communist command economy. Part of the enterprise's profits in earlier years stemmed from the withholding of taxes and custom duties from the Austrian treasury.

The last section of the book focuses on the return of these Soviet-controlled industries to the Republic of Austria and the challenging transformation of the SMV into ÖMV, the Austrian Mineral Oil Administration controlled by the government. The death of Stalin in 1953 led to a softening of the Soviet policy toward Austria. The withdrawal of the Soviet occupational forces actually suited Moscow because the economic exploitation of Austria was no longer profitable. For the Soviets, the return of the Austrian oil industry represented in fact an opportune moment to get rid of the rundown enterprises and, on top of that, to make a handsome profit. This paved the way for the conclusion of the Moscow Memorandum of April 1945 and the regaining of Austria's independence with the State Treaty of May 1955. The Soviet Union eventually pocketed 7.3 billion schillings with its signature. Iber argues that the Soviet willingness to return the oil complex to Austria derived from purely economic reasons. In the negotiations in Moscow over the transfer of the oil sector, the Austrian delegation emerged as the clear loser. Vienna could have attained a much better deal. On the basis of Soviet documents, Iber reveals that Moscow had been willing to restitute the Austrian oil establishments for petroleum deliveries (*Ablöselieferungen*) of 4.1 million tons over a period of six years. In the Moscow Memorandum, however, Austria agreed upon the delivery of 10 million tons, which was later reduced to 6 million. Iber maintains that in consideration of the Soviet account, Austria paid 1 billion schillings too much for getting back its oil industry.

According to Iber's calculations, the total costs of the Soviet occupation for Austria—i.e. industrial removals, profits by SMV, USIA, and DDSG (Danube Steamship Co.), reparations, payments for returned assets, and occupation costs—amount to 1.41 billion dollars, which roughly corresponds to 16 billion euros today. Around one-third of this huge occupation "loot" came at the expense of the oil sector. In total, the SMV had been producing 17.8 million tons of petroleum in Austria. Fifty-three to fifty-six percent of it had been exported to the Soviet Union or Eastern Europe, respectively. In light of these figures, Iber comes to the conclusion that the Soviet Union practiced "oil robbery on a grand scale" (p. 71). Earlier research based on Austrian and U.S. sources by Günter Bischof and Hans Seidel had calculated total "reparations" to the Soviet Union of 1.33 billion and 1.46 billion dollars, respectively.[1] Since Iber's calculations predominantly draw on Soviet sources not available to Bischof and Seidel, they represent an important and most interesting advance to the under-researched economic aspects of the Allied occupation of Austria.

Iber's lucid study concludes that the Soviet seizure and exploitation of the Austrian oil industry was not all bad for the country. The Soviet occupation enabled the later establishment of an Austrian-controlled oil and natural gas business. With the transfer of the oil sector in 1955 to the Austrian authorities, the Soviets also handed over their complete control of the industry. After the war ended, the Western powers had been trying to reinstate the former property rights of their petroleum companies, which had dominated the Austrian oil economy prior to the annexation of the country to the Third Reich. Soviet opposition, however, prohibited the Western Allies from restoring the property rights of the interwar period. Consequently, American and British oil companies did not regain a foothold in Austria. It was these specific circumstances that allowed for the exclusive Austrian control of the oil sector and the spectacular rise of the state-owned OMV to a leading European oil and natural gas corporation.[2]

The book is solidly researched and well-documented with source materials from numerous Austrian and international archives. Of particular interest are the Russian sources that shed new light on Soviet occupation policies. Iber's analysis is to the point and abstains from lengthy digressions. The study is packed with important new information from Soviet archives and interesting facts often backed by figures and illustrated with tables. It is astonishing how much information Iber was able to stuff into some 200 pages of text (main text excl. preface, summary, and appendix). This compactness, however, comes at the expense of narrative fluidity. Even though Iber uses straightforward language that often eludes traditional Germanic academic writing, his dense factual account may not appeal to the general reader. But he has made a major contribution to the study of the postwar Austrian four-power occupation in general and to Soviet occupation studies in particular.

Notes

1. Günter Bischof, *Austria in the First Cold War, 1945-55: The Leverage of the Weak* (Basingstoke: Macmillan, 1999), 87; Hans Seidel, *Österreichs Wirtschaft und Wirtschaftspolitik nach dem Zweiten Weltkrieg* (Vienna: Manz, 2005), 467.

2. For the company's noteworthy development, see my article "OMV: A Case Study of an Austrian Global Player" in this volume.

Thomas Fischer, *Neutral Power in the CSCE: The N+N States and the Making of the Helsinki Accords 1975* (Baden-Baden: Nomos, 2009)

Michael Cotey Morgan

When one thinks of history's great diplomatic conferences, the names Osnabrück, Münster, Vienna, and Paris spring to mind. The negotiations in those cities ended great conflicts and set forth new principles to create a more peaceful international system, or so their drafters hoped. Helsinki, where the Final Act of the Conference on Security and Cooperation in Europe (CSCE) was signed in 1975, deserves a prominent place on the same list. Although historians have only recently begun to give it the attention that it deserves, the CSCE was a watershed in international affairs. By contrast with the Peace of Westphalia, the Congress of Vienna, and the Paris Peace Conference, the CSCE did not bring a bloody war to an end, nor did it yield a legally binding treaty. But the Final Act—which was signed by the United States, Canada, and nearly every country in Europe—did make a major contribution to overcoming the Cold War. It also helped to reshape the state system, particularly by establishing respect for human rights as a fundamental principle of international security.

Drawing on newly declassified archival documents, scholars are now piecing together the tortuous story of how the Final Act came into being. Thomas Fischer, a research fellow at the Graduate Institute of International and Development Studies in Geneva, is at the leading edge of this effort. But whereas much of the new CSCE scholarship focuses on the Soviets and Americans and their respective allies, Fischer is more interested in the countries that stood outside the two Cold War blocs. His impressive new book, *Neutral Power in the CSCE*, examines the role that the Swiss, Austrians, Swedes, and Finns—and, to a lesser extent, the Yugoslavs, Maltese, and Cypriots—played in the negotiations. He contends that the neutral states made vital contributions to the CSCE by straddling the East-West divide and negotiating compromises that the opposing camps might not have been able to reach on their own.

Much like the Western allies, the neutrals initially disagreed about the USSR's repeated proposals to hold a pan-European security conference. Their attitudes reflected both their divergent understandings of neutrality—a point that Fischer brings out in his first chapter—and the places that they occupied in the Cold War international system. The Austrians were eager for the conference because they concluded that it would "enhance [their] room for political maneuver as a neutral state in a delicate geo-strategic position" (p. 87). By contrast, the Swiss were skeptical of Moscow's grand scheme. Because the division of Europe into opposing blocs "served their national security interests quite well," they were unenthusiastic about any initiative that threatened to overturn the status quo (p. 358). They eventually agreed to participate in the CSCE, but only because they feared being left out of the negotiations. They and the other neutrals came to recognize that the CSCE afforded relatively minor powers a rare opportunity to influence the grand drama of the Cold War.

The neutrals therefore resolved to seize the moment. But what did they want the negotiations to achieve? Strengthening détente was one obvious goal. To this end, they embraced the idea of "active neutrality," which sounded attractive but was hard to pin down. Some of the neutrals put forward substantive, if excessively optimistic, proposals. Austrian Chancellor Bruno Kreisky's pet project, for example, was the Middle East, and he argued that the conference should discuss ways to stabilize the region. The idea went nowhere because it threatened to complicate the CSCE's already ambitious agenda (pp. 189-91). The Swiss called for a binding system to resolve international disputes, a proposal that attracted considerable opposition from East and West alike. British officials insisted that Swiss tenacity on this point was harming Western progress on the CSCE's most important issues, namely human rights and freer movement. The Soviets, for their part, refused to accept any system that made arbitration compulsory. So despite the Swiss delegation's stubbornness, the cause was hopeless. "This episode exemplifies the constraints faced by a neutral state in seeing its proposals succeed," Fischer writes. "Individual projects stood no chance of acceptance if they did not find a critical mass of support, a support that could be found only if it did not interfere with the key interests and conference tactics of potential allies" (p. 233). The CSCE gave the neutrals a chance to shape international affairs, but only within very narrow bounds.

The neutrals' most important contribution to the conference was, as Fischer demonstrates, procedural rather than substantive. On more than one occasion, the negotiations stalled because of irreconcilable Eastern and Western views on key questions, particularly the limits of state sovereignty and the tension between universal standards of human rights and the principle of non-interference in domestic affairs. The neutrals' efforts were essential in breaking these log jams. Presenting themselves as honest brokers, they assembled finely balanced compromises that satisfied each side with cleverly ambiguous language. But while the neutrals belonged to neither alliance, their societies, economies, and forms of government were essentially Western. As a result, they largely supported NATO's humanitarian goals at the conference. The compromises that they arranged—particularly the so-called "package deal" of mid-1974—reflected these sympathies, much to the Western allies' benefit.

Fischer's book will stand as the definitive account of the part that the neutrals played in the genesis of the Final Act. His abundant footnotes demonstrate how deeply he has mined the Swiss, Austrian, and British archives, and his detailed reconstruction of obscure debates is formidable. His extensive multilingual research sheds new light on some key episodes, including Finland's 1969 offer to host the negotiations (pp. 89ff.). But by confining himself largely to the narrative of the CSCE, Fischer stops short of addressing some of the more interesting conceptual questions that his story raises. Why was it, for instance, that the neutrals came to regard human rights as a major question of Cold War politics? Did any of the neutral countries pursue coherent strategies of détente? More broadly, what does the CSCE tell us about the role of the neutrals in the Cold War as a whole?

The neutrals were "middle powers at best with second-rank importance in international affairs," Fischer argues. "They had little to gain in big power conflicts but much to lose. They represented no threat to their neighbors, as they were mostly preoccupied with the safeguarding of their sovereignty against external interference of any kind" (p. 54). In this light, perhaps the most salient question is a counterfactual one: Would the CSCE have turned out any differently had the neutrals simply sat quietly on the margins? This might be the best way to measure their contribution, even if it is impossible to provide a definitive answer. Regardless, historians of the CSCE and of the neutrals' foreign relations should welcome Fischer's useful work.

David Tréfás and Jens Lucht, eds., *Europe on Trial: Shortcomings of the EU with Regard to Democracy, Public Sphere, and Identity* (Innsbruck: Studienverlag, 2010)

Gertraud Diendorfer and Heidemarie Uhl, eds., *Europäische Bilderwelten: Visuelle Darstellungen EU-Europas aus österreichischer Perspektive* (Innsbruck: Studienverlag, 2009)

Manfred Kohler

As the title suggests, the volume edited by David Tréfás and Jens Lucht examines the purported weaknesses of the European Union (EU) in terms of democracy, public sphere, and identity. The two authors argue that the embeddedness of the public sphere in the national polity constitutes the main reason for the EU's "shortcomings" in terms of the three aspects mentioned above. The three main contributions by Kurt Imhof, Jens Lucht, and David Tréfás content-analyze war and crisis communication as well as EU institutional events—such as, among others, the Hungarian Uprising of 1956, the Iraq War in 2003, or the signing of the Maastricht Treaty in 1992—in the multiple media outlets of France, Germany, Great Britain, Austria, Hungary, and Switzerland across a time span ranging from 1956 to 2003. Such communication events normally "trigger an echo in different public arenas at the same time if they are socially relevant," as it is explained by Jens Lucht (p. 34). The authors of the volume correctly maintain that the coverage of war and crisis events especially includes semantics of identity, thus offering insightful views on identity dispositions in the said European countries. Kurt Imhof, in his contribution, comes to the conclusion that, in terms of the existence of a European identity, it is not so much Europe but the concepts of the West and the nation state that constitute the main identity markers for West Europeans during the Cold War. Only afterwards does Europe or the EU become slightly more significant in terms of media coverage, with the concept of the West still remaining closely tied to that of Europe when it comes to terrorism and the rise of Russia, for instance. Imhof holds that the European identity concept is deplete with national identity dispositions upon conducting his long-term content analysis. David Tréfás comes to a similar conclusion in his contribution with regard to identity. Considering European identity just a complement to already existing national identities, he concludes in his long-term content analysis that European identity is indeed evolving in the form of EU-issue convergences in the various national media arenas. He holds that European identity thus creeps in from below, that is, the national media spheres.

In terms of the democracy deficit in the EU, Frank Nullmeier et al. provide a comparative analysis of legitimation discourses in the media outlets of four democracies in Western Europe. They maintain that the often-cited "permissive consensus" of the EU has reached a limit, while the nation state is still considered strongly legitimate.

The authors of the volume, overall, do not properly address the reasons why there are more, albeit not much more, European references made in the media after the Cold War. Clearly they fail to trace this trend back to the formation of the structures of a truly political union with the 1993 Maastricht Treaty, as social constructivists would argue. With regard to a European public sphere, however, Imhof correctly states that after the Cold War there is a transnationalization of the public sphere to be observed in the form of EU-issue-centered publics in the national communication arenas as a result of increased political integration of the EU. Jens Lucht, in his contribution, confirms this view in his findings on whether or not there is a European public sphere: there is no infrastructure yet for the formation of a genuine European public sphere. He also finds that there is an absence of EU-level speakers in the national communication arenas, thus further confirming the view that there is a lack of visibility of EU protagonists, as Gerhards claims already in 1993.[1] Lucht attributes this finding to the decreased political legitimacy of EU institutions as a result of the often-cited democracy deficit. However, all authors of the volume fail to provide a clear definition of what constitutes the lack of legitimacy linked to the purported democracy deficit of the EU. This is very unfortunate, since the findings overall are up-to-date with research on identity and public sphere, and the methodology applied is quite firm because it covers a comprehensive time frame.

When it comes to the lack of visibility of EU protagonists and European identity as a simple variety of national identity, the overall tenor of the second volume under review here is quite the same: The volume edited by Gertaud Diendorfer and Heidemarie Uhl and its corresponding contributions content-analyze visual representations of EU-Europe that mainly refer to pictures and images presented in Austria's various media formats, such as audiovisual and print media as well as school books, between 1994 (the year of Austria's referendum on EU accession) and 2004 (the enlargement of the EU to twenty-five member states). One of the contributions by Oliver Rathkolb even content-analyzes the website presences of various rotating Council Presidencies between 1998 and 2004, with the iconography of national symbolisms clearly prevailing over European Union emblems on the various websites. Vrääth Öhner's contribution shows that the Austrian Broadcasting Corporation (ORF) first presents itself as the guarantor of European identity on its website during the information campaign in the run-up to Austria's referendum on EU accession in 1994. Öhner is thus interested in whether there are differences in the ORF's conveyance of EU images and pictures when comparing the 1994 campaign with that of 2004 concerning EU enlargement. He concludes that, while in 1994 the EU is portrayed quite favorably, Union issues from then on are increasingly presented in light of Austrian interests or perspectives, with the EU level of policy-making strongly under-represented in relation to its strong factual impact on Austrian politics. It is thus Austrian rather than European identity that is fostered by ORF in the period under examination. Images of the nation state prevail over those of the EU. Upon analyzing four of Austria's major newspapers, Petra Dorfstätter's contribution holds that, with regard to EU-related reports and articles, there is an image or picture deficit to be observed, with national elites predominantly depicted in EU contexts. Gertraud Diendorfer provides a similar finding after analyzing Austrian school books. Vrääth Öhner, in his second contribution, examines the Austria Press Agency's (APA) image and photographic archive, which mainly consists of the faces of Austrian politicians when it comes to the EU image series. The function of these facial images, according to Öhner, is to give a face to what otherwise remains without a face, that is, the complicated decision-making structures of EU politics and the unportrayable commonalities of all Europeans. Against the background of Hungary's accession to the EU in 2004, Éva Kovacs finally takes a close look at the pictures depicted by Hungarian media. She finds that the news magazines do not depict a single picture of the EU, but rather portray Hungary's role and alterity in the EU.

When it comes to European identity, a European public sphere and the visualization of the EU in selected national media arenas, the two volumes reviewed here send a clear message: The European is constantly weighed against the national—that is to say that national dispositions are still predominant. The overall picture is that European commonalities are indeed emerging on the horizon since the end of the Cold War, but they can only evolve from the national contexts and are reinterpreted by the latter. The European Union is not a federal state, but continues to be a compound of nation states—for now, at least. While both volumes speak of and mention the possible existence of a European *demos* on quite a number of occasions, they do not provide a clear definition thereof. Along with many other publications on identity and public sphere, they fail to see that, ever since the 1993 Maastricht Treaty, there is indeed a European *demos* in the form of an official EU citizenry directly subject to the legal acts of the Union. The books reviewed here are nevertheless quite valuable contributions to research on identity dispositions in today's European Union.

Notes

1. Jürgen Gerhards, "Westeuropäische Integration und die Schwierigkeiten der Entstehung einer europäischen Öffentlichkeit," *Zeitschrift für Soziologie* 22 (1993): 96-110.

ANNUAL REVIEW

Austria 2010

Presidential Elections
Elections in Burgenland, Styria, and Vienna
A-Tec Insolvency
Johanna Dohnal (1939-2010)
Christoph Waltz and Michael Haneke
Economic and Statistical Data

Reinhold Gärtner

Presidential Elections

In April 2010, Heinz Fischer (SPÖ) was reelected for president. In Austria, a president can be reelected once after a six-year term. There were two competitors—Barbara Rosenkranz, a very right-wing FPÖ-MP, and Rudolf Gehring from an ultra-conservative, reactionary, very small political party called *Christliche Partei Österreichs* (Christian Party of Austria). There was no candidate from ÖVP or Grüne. Fischer got 79.3 percent, Rosenkranz 15.2, and Gehring 5.4.

Dr. Karl Renner	1945-1950
Dr. Theodor Körner	1951-1957
Dr. Adolf Schärf	1957-1965
Dr. h.c. Franz Jonas	1965-1974
Dr. Rudolf Kirchschläger	1974-1986
Dr. Kurt Waldheim	1986-1992
Dr. Thomas Klestil	1992-2004
Dr. Heinz Fischer	since 2004

The most controversial president was Kurt Waldheim; his election campaign in 1986 was overshadowed by a discussion about his Nazi past in which once again the Austrian anti-Semitism could be seen. Waldheim, UN general secretary from 1971-81, had published his memoirs "*Im Glaspalast der Weltpolitik*" in 1985, but in this book some parts of his life in the National Socialist Wehrmacht were missing. In 1987, Waldheim was put on the watch list by the U.S. State Department.

The president in Austria has merely representative tasks to fulfill. According to the Austrian constitution he (or she) could appoint a government but usually the president asks the chairman of the party which gets the majority of seats in State Diet Elections to present a government, which then is officially appointed by the president.

The Austrian president is elected directly by those entitled to vote. If no candidate gets an absolute majority in the first run, one of the two most successful competitors of the first run is elected in a second run two weeks later (absolute majority vote, comparable to the French presidential election). In 2010, there was a discussion about the reasonability of this form of election. Mainly because of the unclear position of ÖVP, some thought a future president should not be elected directly but in a different way, e.g. similar to Germany by the *Bundesversammlung*. Another suggestion was to lengthen the term (e.g. eight years) and to forbid a reelection.

Elections in Burgenland, Styria, and Vienna

In 2010, elections were held in these three Länder. All of them were governed by a SPÖ majority and SPÖ governors (Niessl in Burgenland, Voves in Styria, and Häupl in Vienna). ÖVP had some hope to get the majority in Styria, which seemed to be very unlikely in Burgenland and impossible in Vienna.

Elections in Burgenland, 30 May 2010

	2010 (in percent)	2005 (in percent)	Seats 2010	Seats 2005
SPÖ	48.3 (- 3.9)	52.2	18 (- 1)	19
ÖVP	34.6 (- 1.8)	36.4	13 (+/- 0)	13
FPÖ	9.0 (+ 3.3)	5.7	3 (+ 1)	2
Grüne	4.1 (- 1.1)	5.2	1 (- 1)	2
Liste Burgenland	4.0	--	1	--

In Burgenland, Hans Niessl and the SPÖ could manage to get the majority of seats again, though not the absolute majority as in 2005. An interesting result was the four percent of *Liste Burgenland* (which ran for election for the first time). In Austria, a party must get at least four percent of the votes cast to get seats in country parliaments (which is similar to the State Diet elections—but here a party can also get seats if it gets a seat [*Grundmandat*] in one of forty-three constituencies). There were 188,960 votes cast in Burgenland and 7,559 people voted for *Liste Burgenland*—or exactly 4.000317 percent. One vote less—7,558—would have been 3.999788 percent.

An—almost incredible—affair became public a few months after the election. In October 2010, the mayor of a small village called Unterrabnitz, Wolfgang Heissenberger (ÖVP), had to confess that he had committed an election fraud. He had filled in thirteen voting cards by himself.

Elections in Styria, 26 September 2010

	2010 (in percent)	2005 (in percent)	Seats 2010	Seats 2005
SPÖ	38.3 (- 3.4)	41.7	23 (-2)	25
ÖVP	37.2 (- 1.5)	38.7	22 (-2)	24
FPÖ	10.7 (+ 6.1)	4.6	6 (+6)	0
Grüne	5.5 (+ 0.8)	4.7	3 (+/- 0)	3
KPÖ	4.4 (-1.9)	6.3	2 (- 2)	4
BZÖ	3.0 (+ 1.3)	1.7	0	0

As in Burgenland, SPÖ and Governor Franz Voves could keep the majority in Styria as well. As in 2005, the ÖVP was runner-up and the FPÖ managed to return into the country parliament, the *Landtag* (after severe losses in 2005). In Styria, the KPÖ (Communist Party of Austria) still has seats in the *Landtag*. This is not so much because of their communist ideology but because of the very much respected former KPÖ Chairman Ernst Kaltenegger, former member of the city government of Graz and very much dedicated in social policy. Since 1998, Kaltenegger has been spending half of his income for social projects and once a year he presents the results of this initiative. Not surprisingly, the BZÖ missed its target again and did not get a seat in the *Landtag*.

The election campaign in Styria was overshadowed by a racist and xenophobic FPÖ computer game called "*Moschee baba*" ("Mosque bye bye").

The players could shoot at minarets and stop them. If they missed them, a muezzin appeared and one could stop him, too. The game was designed by the Swiss advertiser Alexander Segert, who has been managing the election campaigns of the right-wing SVP (Swiss People's Party) for more than ten years and of FPÖ Vorarlberg in the 2009 election campaign.

Elections in Vienna, 10 October 2010

	2010 (in percent)	2005 (in percent)	Seats 2010	Seats 2005
SPÖ	44.3 (- 4.8)	49.1	49 (- 6)	55
ÖVP	14.0 (- 4.8)	18.8	13 (- 5)	18
FPÖ	25.8 (+ 10.9)	14.9	27 (+ 14)	13
Grüne	12.6 (- 2.0)	14.6	11 (- 3)	14
BZÖ	1.3 (+ 0.2)	1.1	0	0

As was expected, the SPÖ again was the strongest party, but it lost the absolute majority. The FPÖ was the winner of these elections—they got a plus of almost eleven percent, and this was the second best result in the FPÖ's Vienna election history (best result in 1996: 27.9 percent). ÖVP in turn had its worst result ever in Vienna: In 1996, the ÖVP got 15.3 percent, in 2010 only 14 percent.

In the election campaign, the FPÖ again had its xenophobic elements. One electoral slogan was "*Mehr Mut für unser Wiener Blut—zuviel Fremdes tut nicht gut*" ("More courage for our Viennese blood—too many foreign elements can be dangerous"). "*Wiener Blut*" is a well-known musical comedy by Johann Strauss. What the FPÖ and chairman Strache meant was that there would be too many foreigners in Vienna and Austria, respectively.

Christine Marek, the ÖVP's number one in the election, was cause for concern the next day. In an advertisement published in newspapers, she said: "*Wien hat gewählt. Aber Wahlkarten können Sie auch heute noch abschicken. Ihre Christine Marek!*" ("Though the election is over, you can still send your voting cards today")—which is a clear call for fraud.

A-Tec Insolvency

"*Der geniale Herr Kovats ist pleite. Politikern erklärte Mirko Kovats gern, wie sie Österreich sanieren sollen. Nun braucht einer der schillerndsten Industriellen der Alpenrepublik selbst eine Menge Geld. Denn sein A-Tec Konzern ist pleite*" wrote *Financial Times Germany* in October 2010. ("The brilliant Mr. Kovats is bankrupt. Quite often, Mr. Kovats likes to explain how Austria should be put back on its feet. Now one of the dubious industrialists of the Alps republic himself needs a lot of money. His A-Tec company is bankrupt"). With liabilities of some 677 million euros, it was the third-largest bankruptcy since 1945.

Johanna Dohnal (1939-2010)

Johanna Dohnal died on 20 February 2010. She was the first minister for women (1990) and certainly one of the most important women in the fight for equal rights for women and in gender politics. Dohnal began her political career in the late 1960s in Vienna. In 1978, she was responsible for the first women's shelter in Vienna, and in 1979 she became state secretary for women's politics in the Kreisky government. Important laws like the punishment of violence in marriages or sexual harassment were passed because of Dohnal's persistence.

Christoph Waltz and Michael Haneke

In March 2010, Christoph Waltz won the Academy Award as best actor in a supporting role. Waltz was born in Vienna in 1956 and he played SS-*Standartenführer* Hans Landa in Quentin Tarantino's "Inglourious Basterds." Already in January 2010, Waltz had been awarded the Golden Globe of the Hollywood Foreign Press Association. Michael Haneke was awarded with a Golden Globe, too. Haneke was director of "*Das Weiße Band—Eine Deutsche Kindergeschichte*" ("The White Ribbon"), and Haneke was among the nominees for the Academy Award as well.

Economic and Statistical Data

Inflation was at 1.9 percent in 2010 (compared to 0.5 percent in 2009), and the Harmonized Index of Consumer Prices (HVPI) was at 1.7 percent (compared to 0.4 percent in 2009). The public deficit amounted to 3.5 percent in 2010 (3.4 percent in 2009), and public debts amounted to 67.5 percent in 2010 (66.5 percent in 2009).

In 2009, GDP was at 274 billion euros, a minus of 9 billion euros in comparison to 2008 (32,800 euros per capita in 2009, compared to 33,960 euros in 2008).

In 2009, imports amounted 97.574 billion euros (71.292 billion euros from the EU-27), and exports amounted 93.7393 billion euros (66.527 billion euros to the EU). Imports from NAFTA were 3.033 billion euros

(4.021 billion in 2008); exports to NAFTA were 4.929 billion euros (6.444 billion in 2008).

In the third quarter of 2010, 4,147,500 people in Austria were employed (according to the Labor Force Concept; on average 4,077,700 were employed in 2009). Among them were some 450,000 foreigners (425,200 in the fourth quarter of 2009); about one-third of them were EU-27 citizens. The rate of unemployment was at 4.4 percent in 2010 (204,400 people; on average 4.7 percent in 2009).

At the end of 2009, 8,363,260 people were living in Austria; among them were 881,800 foreigners (and of them, 343,397 were from the EU-27 plus EEA plus Switzerland). In 2009, 76,344 children were born alive in Austria, and 77,381 people died. Life expectancy is at 77.4 years (men) and 82.9 (women).

List of Authors

Steven Beller is an independent scholar in Washington, D.C.

Peter Berger is chairman and professor of economic and social history at the Vienna University of Economics and Business.

Günter Bischof is Marshall Plan Professor of History and the director of CenterAustria, University of New Orleans.

Emil Brix is the Austrian ambassador in the United Kingdom and deputy chairman of the Institute for the Danube Region and Central Europe in Vienna.

Gary B. Cohen is professor and chairman of the Department of History, University of Minnesota, and former director of the Minnesota Center for Austrian Studies.

Andreas Exenberger is an associate professor of economic and social history at the School of Economics and Statistics, University of Innsbruck.

Eric Frey is managing editor of the Vienna daily *Der Standard* and an adjunct professor of international relations at Webster University in Vienna.

Reinhold Gärtner is a professor at the Department of Political Science, University of Innsbruck.

Thomas R. Grischany is an independent historian in Vienna.

Ke-chin Hsia is a Ph.D. candidate in the Department of History at the University of Chicago.

Tim Kirk is a professor of European history at Newcastle University.

Hansjoerg Klausinger is a professor at the Department of Economics, Vienna University of Economics and Business.

Manfred Kohler is an independent scholar and holds a Ph.D. in political science from the University of Innsbruck.

Jacques Le Rider is a professor (*directeur d'études*) of German Studies at the Ecole pratique des Hautes Etudes (EPHE), Paris.

David S. Luft is the Horning Endowed Chair in science and humanities at Oregon State University and the president of the Modern Austrian Literature and Culture Association.

Michael Cotey Morgan is an assistant professor at the Department of Strategy and Policy, U.S. Naval War College.

Rainer Münz is senior researcher at Erste Group and senior fellow at the Hamburg Institute for International Economics (HWWI).

Atsushi Otsuru is a professor of history at the Faculty of Humanities, University of Kobe.

Anton Pelinka is a professor of political science and nationalism studies at the Central European University in Budapest.

Fritz Plasser is a professor of political science and dean of the Faculty of Political Science and Sociology, University of Innsbruck.

Peter Pulzer is Gladstone Professor Emeritus of Government and Emeritus Fellow of All Souls College, University of Oxford.

Sonja Puntscher Riekmann is professor of political science and director of the Salzburg Centre of European Union Studies/Jean Monnet Centre of Excellence, University of Salzburg.

Andreas Resch is a professor of economic and social history at the Vienna University of Economics and Business.

Gilg Seeber is a professor of statistics in the Department of Political Science, University of Innsbruck.

Alexander Smith is a doctoral candidate in economic history and political science at the University of Innsbruck. He is also the 2010-11 Ministry of Science Fellow at CenterAustria and an adjunct lecturer in the Department of History, University of New Orleans.

Dieter Stiefel is a professor at the Department of Economic History and the Department of Economics, University of Vienna.

Julie Thorpe is a research lecturer in history at the University of Western Sydney.

Fei-Hsien Wang is a Ph.D. candidate in the Department of History at the University of Chicago.

James J. Weingartner is Professor Emeritus of History at Southern Illinois University at Edwardsville.

Contemporary Austrian Studies

Günter Bischof and Fritz Plasser, Editors

Volume 1 (1992)
Austria in the New Europe

Volume 2 (1993)
The Kreisky Era in Austria
Oliver Rathkolb, Guest Editor

Volume 3 (1994)
Austria in the Nineteen Fifties
Rolf Steininger, Guest Editor

Volume 4 (1995)
Austro-Corporatism: Past—Present—Future

Volume 5 (1996)
Austrian Historical Memory & National Identity

Volume 6 (1997)
Women in Austria
Erika Thurner, Guest Editor

Volume 7 (1998)
The Vranitzky Era in Austria
Ferdinand Karlhofer, Guest Editor

Volume 8 (1999)
The Marshall Plan in Austria
Dieter Stiefel, Guest Editor

Volume 9 (2000)
Neutrality in Austria
Ruth Wodak, Guest Editor

Volume 10 (2001)
Austria and the EU
Michael Gehler, Guest Editor

Volume 11 (2002)
The Dollfuss/Schuschnigg Era in Austria: A Reassessment
Alexander Lassner, Guest Editor

Volume 12 (2003)
The Americanization/Westernization of Austria

Volume 13 (2004)
Religion in Austria
Hermann Denz, Guest Editor

Volume 14 (2005)
Austrian Foreign Policy in Historical Perspective
Michael Gehler, Guest Editor

Volume 15 (2006)
Sexuality in Austria
Dagmar Herzog, Guest Editor

Volume 16 (2007)
The Changing Austrian Voter

Volume 17 (2008)
New Perspectives on Austrians and World War II
Barbara Stelzl-Marx, Guest Editor

Volume 18 (2009)
The Schüssel Era in Austria

Volume 19 (2010)
From Empire to Republic: Post-World War I Austria
Peter Berger, Guest Editor

Also Available from UNO PRESS

General Titles

**Sometimes Courage Looks Like Crazy: A Journalist's Story* by Kim Bondy, 978-1-60801-058-5 (2011)

Post-Katrina Brazucas: Brazilian Immigrants in New Orleans by Annie Gibson, 978-1-60801-070-7 (2011)

The Saratoga Collection, edited by Terrence Sanders, 978-1-60801-061-5 (2011)

**The Garden Path: The Miseducation of a City,* by Andre Perry, 978-1-60801-048-6 (2011)

Before (During) After: Louisiana Photographers Visual Reactions to Hurricane Katrina, edited by Elizabeth Kleinveld, 978-1-60801-023-3 (2010)

**Beyond the Islands* by Alicia Yánez Cossío, translated by Amalia Gladhart, 978-1-60801-043-1 (2010)

**Writer in Residence: Memoir of a Literary Translator* by Mark Spitzer, 978-1-60801-020-2 (2010)

**The Fox's Window* by Naoko Awa, translated by Toshiya Kamei, 978-1-60801-006-6 (2010)

Black Santa by Jamie Bernstein, 978-1-60801-022-6 (2010)

Dream-crowned (Traumgekrönt) by Rainer Maria Rilke, translated by Lorne Mook, 978-1-60801-041-7 (2010)

**Voices Rising II: More Stories from the Katrina Narrative Project* edited by Rebeca Antoine, 978-0-9706190-8-2 (2010)

**Rowing to Sweden: Essays on Faith, Love, Politics, and Movies* by Fredrick Barton, 978-1-60801-001-1 (2010)

Dogs in My Life: The New Orleans Photographs of John Tibule Mendes, 978-1-60801-005-9 (2010)

New Orleans: The Underground Guide by Michael Patrick Welch & Alison Fensterstock, 978-1-60801-019-6 (2010)

Understanding the Music Business: A Comprehensive View edited by Harmon Greenblatt & Irwin Steinberg, 978-1-60801-004-2 (2010)

**The Gravedigger* by Rob Magnuson Smith, 978-1-60801-010-3 (2010)

Portraits: Photographs in New Orleans 1998-2009 by Jonathan Traviesa, 978-0-9706190-5-1 (2009)

**I hope it's not over, and good-by: Selected Poems of Everette Maddox* by Everette Maddox, 978-1-60801-000-4 (2009)

Theoretical Killings: Essays & Accidents by Steven Church, 978-0-9706190-6-8 (2009)

**Voices Rising: Stories from the Katrina Narrative Project* edited by Rebeca Antoine, 978-0-9728143-6-2 (2008)

On Higher Ground: The University of New Orleans at Fifty by Dr. Robert Dupont, 978-0-9728143-5-5 (2008)

The Change Cycle Handbook by Will Lannes, 978-0-9728143-9-3 (2008)

Us Four Plus Four: Eight Russian Poets Conversing translated by Don Mager, 978-0-9706190-4-4 (2008)

The El Cholo Feeling Passes by Fredrick Barton, 978-0-9728143-2-4 (2003)

A House Divided by Fredrick Barton, 978-0-9728143-1-7 (2003)

William Christenberry: Art & Family by J. Richard Gruber, 978-0-9706190-0-6 (2000)

The Neighborhood Story Project

New Orleans in 19 Movements by Thurgood Marshall Early College High School, 978-1-60801-069-1 (2011)

The Combination by Ashley Nelson, 978-1-60801-055-4 (2010)

The House of Dance and Feathers: A Museum by Ronald W. Lewis by Rachel Breunlin & Ronald W. Lewis, 978-0-9706190-7-5 (2009)

Beyond the Bricks by Daron Crawford & Pernell Russell, 978-1-60801-016-5 (2010)

Aunt Alice Vs. Bob Marley by Kareem Kennedy, 978-1-60801-013-4 (2010)

Signed, The President by Kenneth Phillips, 978-1-60801-015-8 (2010)

Houses of Beauty: From Englishtown to the Seventh Ward by Susan Henry, 978-1-60801-014-1 (2010)

Coming Out the Door for the Ninth Ward edited by Rachel Breunlin, 978-0-9706190-9-9 (2006)

Cornerstones: Celebrating the Everyday Monuments & Gathering Places of New Orleans edited by Rachel Breunlin, 978-0-9706190-3-7 (2008)

The Engaged Writes Series

Medea and Her War Machines by Ioan Flora, translated by Adam J. Sorkin, 978-1-60801-067-7 (2011)

Together by Julius Chingono and John Eppel, 978-1-60801-049-3 (2011)

Vegetal Sex (O Sexo Vegetal) by Sergio Medeiros, translated by Raymond L.Bianchi, 978-1-60801-046-2 (2010)

**Wounded Days (Los Días Heridos)* by Leticia Luna, translated by Toshiya Kamei, 978-1-60801-042-4 (2010)

When the Water Came: Evacuees of Hurricane Katrina by Cynthia Hogue & Rebecca Ross, 978-1-60801-012-7 (2010)

**A Passenger from the West* by Nabile Farès, translated by Peter Thompson, 978-1-60801-008-0 (2010)

**Everybody Knows What Time It Is* by Reginald Martin, 978-1-60801-011-0 (2010)

**Green Fields: Crime, Punishment, & a Boyhood Between* by Bob Cowser, Jr., 978-1-60801-018-9 (2010)

**Open Correspondence: An Epistolary Dialogue* by Abdelkébir Khatibi and Rita El Khayat, translated by Safoi Babana-Hampton, Valérie K. Orlando, Mary Vogl, 978-1-60801-021-9 (2010)

Gravestones (Lápidas) by Antonio Gamoneda, translated by Donald Wellman, 978-1-60801-002-8 (2009)

Hearing Your Story: Songs of History and Life for Sand Roses by Nabile Farès translated by Peter Thompson, 978-0-9728143-7-9 (2008)

The Katrina Papers: A Journal of Trauma and Recovery by Jerry W. Ward, Jr., 978-0-9728143-3-1 (2008)

Contemporary Poetry

California Redemption Values by Kevin Opstedal, 978-1-60801-066-0 (2011)

Atlanta Poets Group Anthology: The Lattice Inside by Atlanta Poets Group, 978-1-60801-064-6 (2011)

Makebelieve by Caitlin Scholl, 978-1-60801-056-1 (2011)

Dear Oxygen: New and Selected Poems by Lewis MacAdams, edited by Kevin Opstedal, 978-1-60801-059-2 (2011)

Only More So by Tony Lopez, 978-1-60801-057-8 (2011)

Enridged by Brian Richards, 978-1-60801-047-9 (2011)

A Gallery of Ghosts by John Gery, 978-0-9728143-4-8 (2008)

The Ezra Pound Center for Literature

The Poets of the Sala Capizucchi (I Poeti della Sala Capizucchi) edited by Caterina Ricciardi and John Gery, 978-1-60801-068-4 (2011)

Trespassing, by Patrizia de Rachewiltz, 978-1-60801-060-8 (2011)

**The Imagist Poem: Modern Poetry in Miniature* edited by William Pratt, 978-0-9728143-8-6 (2008)

Contemporary Austrian Studies

Global Austria: Austria's Place in Europe and the World, Günter Bischof, Fritz Plasser (Eds.), Alexander Smith, Guest Editor, 978-1-60801-062-2 (2011)

From Empire to Republic: Post-World-War-I Austria Volume 19 edited by Günter Bischof, Fritz Plasser and Peter Berger, 978-1-60801-025-7 (2010)

The Schüssel Era in Austria Volume 18 edited by Günter Bischof & Fritz Plasser, 978-1-60801-009-7 (2009)

*Also available as E-book